T0365679

LET
SCRIPTURE
SPEAK FOR ITSELF

*An easy-to-read guide organized
by topics with scripture
proof and Church history*

PAUL WILCHEK

WESTBOW
PRESS®
A DIVISION OF THOMAS NELSON
& ZONDERVAN

WestBow Press books may be ordered through booksellers or by contacting:

WestBow Press
A Division of Thomas Nelson & Zondervan
1663 Liberty Drive
Bloomington, IN 47403
www.westbowpress.com
844-714-3454

ISBN: 978-1-6642-8577-4 (sc)
ISBN: 978-1-6642-8579-8 (hc)
ISBN: 978-1-6642-8578-1 (e)

Library of Congress Control Number: 2022922509

Print information available on the last page.

WestBow Press rev. date: 01/11/2023

This photograph was taken at Holmes Beach, Florida. It represents the essence of this book by the many different people standing in amazement of the wonders of God and his angel watching over them as well as adoring the cross. Also, it represents the Father, the Son, and the Holy Spirit.

This is dedicated to:

- My departed wife of 37 years, Lois Baumgardner (1934–1997).
- My four boys: David, Michael, Gregory, and Steven, who are my ongoing life support and love for so many years.
- My grandchildren Ashley, Chelsea, Connor, and Regina whose love is so enduring.
- My departed brother Dorance (1929–2015) with his strong devotion to God.
- My departed sister Coletta (1931–2004) who had such a wonderful sense of humor, loved to read, and her love and devotion to Jesus as well as her wonderful prayers.
- My departed second wife of 11 years, Shirley Holmes (1934–2010) who showed me how to love again and to turn depression into the Love of Jesus Christ.
- My step–children: Jeffery, Terry, Debra, and Pam. My step–grandchildren: Sean, Brenna, Ashley, Alexandra, and Allex. My step–great–grandchildren: Wyatt, and Sadie, all of who became my second family to cherish and love.
- My dear church friend Kristin Trepanier–Henry that helped with a great deal of editing.
- My departed special priest friend, Father Carl Birarelli (1926-2021, 63 years as a priest). He and I frequently met to just talk in general or sometimes about this book. He had such a great sense of humor. I especially remember the precious times father said mass, only he and I, using his dining room table.
- Last but not least, my departed friend Ed Hagen (1947–2022) and his wife Anita who offered welcomed suggestions and book editing.

A few of the chapters of this book were first distributed as separate articles to respond to discussions that came up in various Bible study classes that started about the year 2000. One chapter is actually the brief summary of a complete bible study class.

The background for this started to be assembled in written form about 2011 for its final assembly in August of 2022.

CONTENTS

INTRODUCTION

Let Scripture Speak for Itself provides an easy-to-read explanation of certain scripture passages that are organized into various topics or in a few cases shows you where more information on that topic can be found in scripture.

Actual scripture passages are grouped by topics pointing out some of the hidden meanings, symbolisms, prophecies fulfilled, and pointing out scripture proofs. Actual scripture responses of typical questions are provided to assist in defending the Catholic faith. Also, scripture passages are organized by certain key words to provide a reference for a better understanding of scripture. It includes an explanation of the apostles, disciples, early church fathers, brief history of the Catholic Church, and a chronological list of popes that all contributed to the many proofs and growth of the Catholic Church through apostolic succession.

Scripture quotations herein are mostly from the New American Bible (NAB), unless otherwise noted, and they are ***bold and italicized*** so one can easily recognize the actual scripture quotation. Quotations other than from scripture may be just *italicized*. In some cases, some words or phrases may be <u>**underlined,**</u> as emphasis added, to show its importance or may be further explained elsewhere. Many scripture passages have more than one meaning; therefore, you will find some duplication of certain passages under different topic headings.

In the course of the research for the various subjects herein, through reading articles and commentaries of the bible, there was some difficulty understanding what the author was trying to convey, which lead to additional research. So, the difficulty of understanding some writings prompted me to write about certain scripture topics in everyday common layperson's language that I understood and hopefully you will also understand. In a few cases some theological words are used, which are immediately defined.

I am somewhat of an analytical type of personality and tend to write the facts and to write in bullet type of statements rather than flowery paragraphs with a lot of unnecessary words. This method may come across to some people as rather "curt", it is not intended that way, it is just intended to be factual and to the point.

There are over 170 different topics covered herein which are intended to provide information to assist anyone with doubts by providing multiple proofs within Scripture. It is hoped that this will be used as a reference guide.

DESCRIPTION OF EACH CHAPTER

1. **ANGELS:** Scripture passages that describe who Angels are and what they do, also a description of the hierarchy of Angels.

2. **COVENANTS:** A description of God's Covenants, what they represent to us, and what scripture tells us we must do to obtain salvation.

3. **EUCHARIST AND THE MASS:** The Eucharist is traced through scripture form the fall of mankind to John's "Vision of Heavenly Worship" in Revelation, including listings of the many Old Testament verses fulfilled in the New Testament. Also, History of the Mass and Mass scripture references.

4. **HOLY DAYS AND FEAST DAYS:** Holy Days of Obligation, Marion feast days, Christmas, and Ash Wednesday are explained including brief history.

5. **HOLY SPIRIT; SPIRIT, SOUL, AND BODY:** This provides scripture passages that describe the Holy Spirit, the unique trinity connection, and how scripture uses symbols for the Holy Spirit, including several scripture passages that explain the Spirit, Soul, and Body.

6. **PROPHECIES, PARALLELS, SYMBOLISM, MIRACLES:** A listing of the prophecies fulfilled by Jesus, the parallels between Jewish and Christian feast days, some of the symbolisms and parallels in scripture, and some of the miracles in scripture as well as other miracles. Including the Miraculous Conception, Mary born full of grace, and Mary the Ark of the Covenant passages.

7. **PROPHETS:** A listing of all the Old and New Testament prophets.

8. **PURGATORY:** Passages from scripture that imply Purgatory listed by category.

9. **SCRIPTURE RESPONSE:** A list of typical questions and the responses from scripture.

10. **SELECTED SUBJECTS:** A listing of words with the scripture passage(s) that contain those word(s).

11. **THE APOSTLES, DISCIPLES, CHURCH FATHERS:** A description of the twelve Apostles, the early disciples, authors of the New Testament, women disciples, and Fathers and Doctors of the early Church.

12. **THE THEMES THROUGH SCRIPTURE:** Scripture passages are provided that trace the themes of Bread and Redemption through scripture.

13. **THE BRIEF HISTORY OF THE CATHOLIC CHURCH:** The description of significant events in chronological order that contributed to the over 2000 years of the Catholic Church's history.

14. **THE POPES:** A chronological listing of all popes including references of civil leaders, dominate powers, and notes on events during the pope's time frame.

About the Author: A brief background of the author.

Religious Experiences: Several religious experiences of the author.

Topics listed by chapter and topics listed alphabetically for reference purposes.

Appendix: Supplementary information on a few topics.

CHAPTER 1

ANGELS

Let Scripture Speak for Itself on Angels:

The "Catechism of the Catholic Church" (CCC 330) tells us: "As purely spiritual creatures angels have intelligence and will: they are personal and immortal creatures, surpassing in perfection all visible creatures, as the splendor of their glory bears witness."

St. Augustine says: (CCC 329) "Angel is the name of their office, not of their nature. If you seek the name of their nature, it is 'spirit'; if you seek the name of their office, it is 'angel'. With their whole beings the angels are servants and messengers of God." Because they *"...always look upon the face of my heavenly Father"* (Mat 18:10) and they *"Bless the Lord, all you angels, mighty in strength and attentive, obedient to every command."* (Psalms 103:20).

Scripture Describes Angels

Angels are messengers.

Judges 6:11–12. ₁₁*Then the <u>messenger of the Lord</u> came...* ₁₂*the <u>messenger of the Lord</u> appeared to him...*

Angels can appear in body form and disappear.

Judges 13:3,6,20. *₃An **angel of the Lord appeared** to the women...₆ she had the appearance of an **angel of God**...₂₀ the **angel of the Lord ascended** in the flame of the altar.*

Angels can be in the wind and fire.

Hebrews 1:7. ***Of the angels he says: "He makes his angels winds and his ministers a fiery flame."***

Angels serve and minister to humans.

Hebrews 1:14. ***Are they [Angels] not all ministering spirits sent to serve, for the sake of those who are to inherit salvation?***

Guardian angels.

Exodus 23:20. ***See, I am sending an angel before you, to guard you on the way and bring you to the place I have prepared.***

Daniel 4:10. ***In the vision I saw while in bed, a holy watcher came down from heaven...***

Psalms 91:11. ***For his angels he has given command about you, that they guard you in all your ways.*** Note: to *"guard you in all your ways"* they have to be with us always.

Angels are immortal.

Luke 20:36. ***They can no longer die, for they are like angels;***

Angels are mighty and obedient to God.

Psalms 103:20. ***Bless the Lord, all you angels, mighty in strength and attentive, obedient to every command.***

Angels are created by God, they praise God, and their assignment never changes.

Psalms 148: 5,6. *₅Let them [Angels] all praise the Lord's name; for he commanded and they were created ₆Assigned them their stations forever, set an order that will never change.*

Humans will judge angels.

1 Corinthians 6: 3. ***Do you not know that we will judge angels?***

Angels are countless in numbers.
Daniel 7: 10. *...Thousands upon thousands were ministering to Him.*

Angels always look upon the face of God.
Matthew 18: 10. *...I [Jesus] say to you that their <u>angels</u> in heaven always look upon the face of my heavenly Father.*

Angels can be female.
Zechariah 5: 9 *Then I raised my eyes and saw <u>two women</u> coming forth with a wind ruffling their wings, for they had wings like the wings of a stork. As they lifted the bushel into the air, I said to the <u>angel</u> who spoke to me, "where are they taking the bushel?"*

Angels have emotions.
Luke 15: 10. *... I [Jesus] tell you, there will be <u>rejoicing</u> among <u>the angels of God</u> over one sinner who repents.*

It appears that the time prior to the great flood, God allowed Angels in body form and to take wives: Genesis 6:2. *the <u>sons of heaven</u> [angels] saw how beautiful the daughters of man were, and so they took for their wives as many of them as they chose.*

Notice that it's not clear if the "sons of heaven", are good angels or the fallen angels.

In either case, at some unknown time, God stopped angels from taking wives:
Jude 1:6. *The angels too, who did not keep to their own domain but deserted their proper dwelling, he has kept in eternal chains, in gloom, for the judgment of the great day.*

An angel of the Lord is assigned to each person.
Psalms 34: 8. *The <u>angel of the Lord</u> <u>encamps</u> around those who fear him, and delivers them.*

Considering the above (an Angel <u>encamps</u> near us) in combination with the passages under "Guardian Angels" (who are always with us) and the scripture under "Angels always look upon the face of God", one may conclude that if our guardian angel is <u>always</u> with us and at the same time our guardian angel **"<u>always</u> look upon the face of my heavenly Father"** (Mt 18:10), then, that may mean that God is very close to us in order for our Angel to guard us and simultaneously look upon the face of God.

Angels are organized into orders.
Colossians 1:16. *For in him were created all things in heaven and on earth, the visible and invisible, whether <u>thrones</u> or <u>dominions</u> or <u>principalities</u> or <u>powers</u>; all things were created through him and for him.*

Angels can appear in a dream.
Matthew 1: 20. *...behold, the angel of the Lord appeared to him in a <u>dream</u> and said, "Joseph, son of David, do not be afraid to take Mary your wife into your home. For it is through the holy Spirit that this child has been conceived in her.*

Angels make announcements to people and praise God.
Luke 2: 9–14 (Birth of Jesus). *The <u>angel</u> of the Lord appeared to them [shepherds) and the glory of the Lord shone around them, and they were struck with great fear. The <u>angel</u> said to them. "Do not be afraid; for behold, I proclaim to you good news of great joy that will be for all the people. ... And this will be <u>a sign for you</u>: you will find an infant wrapped in swaddling clothes and lying <u>in a manger</u>." And suddenly there was a multitude of the <u>heavenly host</u> with the <u>angel</u>, <u>praising God</u> and saying: "Glory to God in the highest and on earth peace to those on whom his favor rests."*
Note: *"<u>a sign for you</u>"* places the infant Jesus *"<u>in a manger</u>,"* which is a feeding trough, which symbolizes that Jesus will become food for our salvation!

Angels assisted Jesus.
Matthew 4:11 [Jesus tempted in the desert] *Then the devil left Him and, behold, <u>angels</u> came and ministered to Him [Jesus].*
Luke 22: 43 [Agony in the Garden] *And to strengthen Him [Jesus] an <u>angel</u> appeared to Him.*

Angels can physically do things.

Matthew 28: 2 *And behold, there was a great earthquake; for an <u>angel</u> of the Lord descended from heaven, approached, <u>rolled back the stone</u>, and sat upon it. His appearance was like lightning and his clothing was white as snow. ... Then the <u>angel</u> said to the women [Mary Magdalene and the other Mary] in reply, "Do not be afraid I know that you are seeking Jesus the crucified. He is not here, for He has been raised just as He said. ..."*

Angels can appear to clarify a situation.

Acts 1: 10–11 [The Ascension of Jesus] *While they were looking intently at the sky as He [Jesus] was going, suddenly two men <u>dressed in white garments</u> stood beside them. They said, "Men of Galilee, why are you standing there looking at the sky? This Jesus who has been taken up from you into heaven will return in the same way as you have seen Him going to heaven."*

White garments were not common at the time of Jesus, they signify angels.

Angels can ascend and descend from heaven.

John 1: 51. *And He [Jesus] said to him, "Amen, amen, I say to you, you will see the sky opened and the angels of God <u>ascending and descending</u> on the Son of Man."*

The Seraphim and Cherubim don't seem to function as God's messengers to humans, possibly because of their bizarre appearance that could frighten humans. Some science fiction programs sometimes quote scripture (out of context) Claiming Scripture description is of a space vehicle (maybe due to **"<u>like</u> four wheels"**), but, as we read further from Ezekiel 10: 12–14, **"they were indeed the <u>living creatures</u>."**

Christian Angelic Hierarchy [B]

There have been many different hierarchies proposed (see reference B), however, the following appears to be the most popular: According to medieval Christian theologians, Angels are organized into 9 orders called "Angelic Choirs". In the 4th or 5th century a book called "On the Celestial Hierarchy", by Pseudo–Dionysius and Thomas Aquinas' book "Summa

Theologica", both authors drew from Scripture to develop three Spheres with each containing three Orders or Choirs. In spite of the fact that both authors drew from scripture, the Biblical Canon is silent on the subject. Therefore, consider the hierarchy used here only as a means to list each office so that they can be identified and to "Let Scripture Speak for Itself" about them.

First Sphere – Angels that serve as heavenly counselors:

Seraphim, meaning "burning ones" is mentioned in Isaiah 6:1–7. *...I saw the Lord seated on the high and lofty throne, ...Seraphim were stationed above; each of them had six wings: with two they covered their faces, with two they covered their feet, and with two they hovered.*

Cherubim, as described in Ezekiel 10: 12–14. *Their entire bodies—backs, hands, and wings—and wheels were covered with eyes all around like the four wheels. I heard the wheels called "wheelwork." Each living creature had four faces: the first a cherub, the second a human being, the third a lion, the fourth an eagle. When the <u>Cherubim</u> rose up, they were indeed the <u>living creatures</u> I had seen by the river Chebar.*

The Cherubim guard the way to the tree of life in the Garden of Eden (Genesis 3:24) and the throne of God (Ezekiel 28: 14–16), as well as adorn the cover of The Ark of the Covenant (Exodus 25:17–21).

Thrones or Ophanim are closely connected with the Cherubim, living symbols of God's justice and authority, and have as one of their symbols the throne, they appear as beryl–colored wheel–within–a–wheel, their rims covered with hundreds of eyes. Thrones as mentioned in Colossians 1:16 as well as Daniel 7: 9–10.

Second Sphere – Angels that work as heavenly governors:

Dominions or Lordships regulate the duties of lower Angels. It is only with extreme rarity that the angelic lords make themselves physically known to humans. They are also the Angels who preside over nations. The Dominions are believed to look like divinely beautiful humans with a pair of feathered wings they may be wielding orbs of light fastened to the heads of their scepters or on the knob of their swords.

Virtues or Strongholds, their primary duty is to supervise the movements of the heavenly bodies in order to ensure that the cosmos remain in order. It is not clear because some theological conceptions of the Virtues appear to describe the same order called Thrones, in which case the Ophanim order may not be the same thing as the Thrones as listed above.

Powers or Authorities appear to collaborate, in power and authority, with the Principalities or Rulers. The Powers are bearers of conscience and keepers of history. They are also warrior Angels created to be completely loyal to God. Some believe that no Power has ever fallen from grace, but other theories state that Satan was the Chief of the Powers before he fell. Their duty is to oversee the distribution of power among humankind, hence the name.

Third Sphere – Angels who function as heavenly messengers and soldiers:

Principalities or Rulers are said to carry out the orders given by the Dominions and provide blessings to the material world. They oversee groups of people and are educators as well as guardians of the realm of earth. They may inspire living things such as art or science. The Principalities are shown wearing a crown and carrying a scepter.

Archangels, which means first in rank of Angels (which means messenger). The word Archangel is only used twice in the New Testament: 1 Thessalonians 4:16. *For the Lord himself, with a word of command, with the voice of an archangel and with the trumpet of God will come down from haven*, Jude 1:9. *Yet the archangel Michael, when he argued with the devil in a dispute over the body of Moses, did not venture to pronounce a reviling judgment upon him but said, "may the Lord rebuke you!"* Michael (Hebrew, who is like God) is named four times in Old and New Testament: Daniel10:13;12:1; Jude 1:9 (above); Revelation 12:7. Michael the archangel appears as the patron and protector of the nation of Israel and looks after Gentile nations along with other angelic princes. Michael, called Prince of Light, leads the angelic hosts into battle against the spirits of darkness as found in nonbiblical texts among the "Dead Sea Scrolls." The veneration of Michael dates to very early in

Christian history with many interventions. One was where he appeared to Emperor Constantine (AD 337) in Rome during the plague, after which the plague stopped, establishing Michael's roll as an Angel of healing. In 1950 Pope Pius XII named Michael as patron of policemen.

Gabriel (Hebrew, God is my Warrior) is considered an Archangel by most Christian traditions, however there is no direct statement in scripture to support this.

Daniel 8: 15,16. *I [Daniel] had seen, one who looked like a man stood before me, and on the U'lai I heard a human voice that cried out, Gabriel, explain the vision to this man.*

Luke 1:11,19. *"The angel of the Lord appeared to him [Zechariah]...., 19 And the angel said to him in reply, "I am Gabriel, who stand before God.*

Luke 1: 26,27. *...the angel Gabriel was sent from God to a town of Galilee called Nazareth, to a virgin [Mary].* Gabriel is also called "Angel of the Annunciation."

Raphael (Hebrew: God heals) only appears in the book of Tobit, a book not in all Bibles, see Note (1).

Tobit 12: 15. *I am Raphael, one of the seven angels who stand and serve before the Glory of the Lord.* Not all of the seven Archangels are named in Scripture*, however, they are said to be the guardian of nations and countries, concerned with issues of: politics, military matters, commerce and trade. Raphael does not appear in the New Testament but is in Jewish theological writings (outside of the Bible) as healer and victor over demons. Raphael is venerated in the Church, especially as an Angel of healing as well as the Angel of knowledge, and science.

*One of the "Dead Sea Scrolls" (non–biblical) names all seven Archangels: Michael, Gabriel, Raphael, Remiel (Jeremine), Raguel, Sariel, and Uriel.

Angels, the messengers to mankind, the lowest order of Angels, the most recognized, concerned with the affairs of living things.

SUMMARY–ANGELS:

WHO ARE THE ANGELS?
- Created by God and immortal (Lk 20:36)
- Purely spiritual creatures (CCC 350)
- Have high intelligence and will (CCC350)
- They are personal (CCC 330)
- They have emotions (Lk 15:10)
- They are countless in number (Dn 7:10)
- Can appear like lightning
- They may have clothing as white as snow

WHAT DO ANGELS DO?
- They are mighty and obedient to God (Ps 103:20)
- Assigned to stations that never change (Ps 148:5–6)
- Messengers of God to humans (Jgs 6:11–12)
- Minister to humans (Heb 1:14)
- Guardians for humans (Ex 23:20; Dn 4:10)
- Can appear in body form and can disappear (Jgs 13:3,6,20)
- Can be in the wind and fire and be invisible (Heb 1:7)
- Assigned to each person (Ps 34:8) while simultaneously looking upon the face of God (Mt 18:10)
- Make announcements to people
- They praise God
- They can do physical things on earth (Mt 28:2)
- They only do what is directed by God
- They can ascend and descend from Heaven (Jn 1:51)
- Can strengthen and minister
- Angels can appear in dreams (Mt 1:20)
- Angels announced Jesus' birth (Lk 2:9–14), ministered to Jesus, strengthened Jesus, rolled the grave stone, and clarified the ascension of Jesus Christ (Acts 1:10–11).

HIERARCHY OF ANGELS:
Heavenly Counselors: Seraphim, Cherubim, Thrones (Col 1:16)
- They guard the Tree of Life in the Garden of Eden (Gn 3:24)
- The Cherubin adorns the Ark of the Covenant (Ex 37:7–9)
- God's Justice and Authority

Heavenly Governors: Dominions, Virtues, Powers
- Preside over Nations
- Supervise Movements of the Cosmos
- Bearers of Conscience and Keepers of History
- They are also Warrior Angels

Heavenly Messengers and Soldiers: Principalities, Archangels, Angels
- Provide blessings to the material world
- Oversee groups of People
- Are educators as well as guardians of the realm of earth
- Inspire Art and Science
- Guardian of Nations and Countries
- Battle against Spirits of Darkness
- Concerned with politics, military matters, commerce and trade
- Messengers to Mankind

Notes:

1. The Book of Tobit is considered Deuterocanonical (belonging to the Cannon) by Roman Catholics (both Eastern and Western Rites), Eastern Orthodox Christians, and Anglicans. The Book of Tobit is also read by Lutherans, but not normally by other Protestant denominations including Reformed Christians and Baptist.
2. The words "Angel" and "Angel of God" appear in Scripture over 85 times, plus there are many references in Scripture about Angels without actually using the "Angel" word, making the appearance in Scripture much higher than 85.
3. In Scripture, there may be a distinction between the use of archangel (lower–case "a") and Archangel (upper–case "A"). The lower–case "a" may be just above the angels only. The upper–case "A" may be those above all angels. However, Seraphim and Michael appear to be the highest of all Angels.
4. ANGELS: Compiled by Paul Wilchek, edited by Kristin Trepanier–Henry. 24JAN20

References:

(A) Scripture quotations herein are ***italicized and bold*** from the "New American Bible" (NAB), Catholic Book Publishing Co. Certain words may be <u>underlined</u> for emphasis added.

(B) The reference under the title of "Christian Angelic Hierarchy" is Wikipedia, the free encyclopedia as of 3/17/2015, in some cases paraphrased herein and some scripture passages that were just referenced, are herein written out from (NAB).

(C) There are 10 different schemes of the Hierarchy developed, ranging from the 1st century through to the 14th century as follows: 8 schemes having 9 choirs, 1 scheme having 7 choirs, and 1 scheme having 11 choirs. Therefore, this write–up used the 9 choirs' scheme as being the most popular.

(D) The "Catholic Dictionary" General Editor, Scott Hahn, by Doubleday. The Oxford Companion to The Bible, edited by Bruce M Metzger, Michael D Coogan, Oxford University Press 1993.

CHAPTER 2

COVENANTS

The following are a few re-phased excerpts from The Catholic Bible Dictionary:

The definition of "covenant" has been widely debated by biblical scholars. "Covenants" frequently contain "laws" or "obligation." However, research has established a general consensus among Protestant, Catholic, and Jewish scholars that a "covenant" is, in its essence, a legal means to establish kinship between two previously unrelated parties.

A covenant is also the master-theme of the Bible, which records the various ways throughout history that God has drawn humanity into a relationship with himself through divine oaths. A covenant is not a contract. Generally, a contract involves the exchange of goods, whereas a covenant involves the exchange of persons. In almost every case the central act of covenant-making was the swearing of an oath by one or both parties to the covenant (Gn 21:31–32, 22:16, 26:28; Jos 9:15; Ez 16:59, 17:13–19). Covenants often have a penalty should one party fail to keep the obligations of the covenant. The ritual of using the blood of animals was to signify what could happen if violated. Occasionally the covenant-making parties shared a common meal to confirm their covenant relationship (end of The Catholic Bible Dictionary excerpts).

Theologians have different opinions as to how many major <u>covenants</u> exist between God and humanity primarily due to the many different types of <u>covenants</u>. There are cases in scripture of reparation, or punishment for the violation of a <u>covenant</u>; however, in all of scripture, God has never rescinded or has taken back any of His promises. The bible also contains <u>covenants</u> between two persons (usually kings), this write–up only covers those <u>covenants</u> between God and humanity. The Agape Bible Study has a publication, which is used as reference herein, titled: "YAHWEH'S EIGHT COVENANTS": (1) Adam, (2) Noah and the earth, (3) Abraham, Isaac, Jacob and descendants, (4) Moses and Israel, (5) Aaron and Sons – priesthood of the Levites, (6) Phinehas – perpetual priesthood, (7) David and descendants, (8) Jesus – New Covenant Forever.

Some people have felt, after reading the Old Testament, that God is a "mean" God. However, after looking at the real circumstances, one would have to recognize that it is the people that were "mean." In every case in scripture, it was the people (or the nation) that violated the agreed upon conditions of the <u>covenant</u>, and for the violation, God could have shed their blood. But God is a righteous, just, and merciful God where He may remove His protection, allowing hardships to occur for the <u>covenant</u> violation. Hardships such as natural disasters, loss of their nation, exile, or slavery of the people rather than shedding their blood. Blood sealed most covenants for the following reason: Leviticus 17:11 ***Since the life of a living body is in its blood, I have made you put it on the altar, so that atonement may thereby be made for your own lives, because it is the blood, as the seat of life, that makes atonement.***

The following is an example of a command that was violated and the chastisement that followed: Leviticus 25:3–4 ***For six years you may sow your field, and for six years prune your vineyard, gathering in their produce. But during the seventh year the land shall have a complete rest, a sabbath for the Lord, when you may neither sow your field nor prune your vineyard.*** The Israelites violated this for 490 years along with other <u>covenant</u> violations. 490 divided by 7 equals 70 years. The Israelites were in exile, away from their land, for 70 years as just punishment.

There are three different categories of covenants: (1) <u>Conditional covenants</u> based on certain obligations and/or prerequisites where if the obligations are not fulfilled, the covenant is broken. (2) <u>Unconditional covenants</u> are where the conditions will be kept regardless of either party. (3) <u>General covenants</u> are not specific to one group of people and may involve a wide range of people.

To summarize: a <u>covenant</u> is an agreement between a more powerful one and a lower powerful one, where the more powerful one gives the conditions of the <u>covenant</u> and the lower powerful one either accepts or rejects the <u>covenant</u>. If the lower one accepts the <u>covenant,</u> then violates it, they may lose God's protection and be punished according to any conditions of the <u>covenant</u>. If the lower one rejects the <u>covenant,</u> then they are not under the protection of God. In contrast, a contract is between two parties of about equal status where one has the material or service and the other has the funds to acquire it and they then negotiate the terms and conditions. If one party violates a contract, usually it becomes null and void, or canceled. A <u>covenant</u> is not negotiated. A <u>covenant</u> cannot be canceled but could be modified by the more powerful one.

Covenant with Adam
Also called Creation Covenant.

Time Frame	Type	Category	Sign(s)
Creation	Everlasting	General	The tree of life, dominion over earth

On the fifth day of creation, God created male and female in his image then in Genesis 1:28 ***God blessed them, saying: Be fertile and multiply; fill the earth and subdue it. Have dominion over the fish of the sea, the birds of the air, and all the living things that move on earth.*** This passage continues through verse 30 where God, in addition to all living things, God gives mankind all plants, seed–bearing fruit and green plants for food. God gives mankind the mandate to procreate and God gave mankind dominion over the earth and all the animals (some called this the <u>Creation Covenant</u>).

Genesis 2:16–17 ...***You are free to eat from any of the trees of the garden except the tree of knowledge of good and bad. From that tree you shall*** *not eat; the moment you eat from it you are surely doomed to die.* The original <u>covenant</u> with Adam and Eve was a conditional <u>covenant</u>; then after the fall, it became an unconditional <u>covenant</u> with certain hardships instituted. Genesis 3: ₁₆ *To the woman He said: "I will intensify the pangs of your childbearing; in pain shall you bring forth children. Yet your urge shall be for your husband, and he shall be your master."* And also, ₁₉ *By the sweat of your face shall you get bread to eat, …* The <u>covenant</u> established with Adam was then continued on with Noah. Also see: Genesis 6:18, Hosea 6:7. God gives mankind the mandate to procreate and God gives mankind dominion over the earth and all the plants and animals.

What does the Adam Covenant Represent for Us?
We are all represented by Adam and Eve because we came from them and are under the same <u>covenant</u> and guilty of failing. Romans 5:12 *Therefore, just as through one–person sin entered the world, and through sin, death, and thus death came to all. Inasmuch as all sinned…* 1 Corinthians 15:20 *But now Christ has been raised from the dead, the first fruits of those who have fallen asleep. For since death came through a human being, the resurrection of the dead came through a human being.* Even though the <u>covenant</u> was broken, God still keeps his promise to *Have dominion over the fish of the sea, the birds of the air, and all the living things that move on earth* (Gn 1:26).

Covenant with Noah and the Earth

<u>Time Frame</u>	<u>Type</u>	<u>Category</u>	<u>Sign(s)</u>
2348 BC	Everlasting	General	Rainbow, water as a sign of salvation

The <u>covenant</u> with Noah applies to all of humanity and all other living creatures. God promises never again to destroy all life on earth by a flood; water will become a sign of salvation. The sign of Noah's <u>covenant</u> is the rainbow. In exchange, Noah and following generations were required never to shed blood, nor to consume blood.

Genesis 9:9–13 ₉…*I am now establishing my <u>covenant</u> with you* [Noah] *and your descendants after you* ₁₀ *and with every living creature that was with you…* ₁₁ …*never again shall all bodily creatures be destroyed* *by the waters of a flood;...* ₁₂ *This is the sign that I am giving for all ages to come, of the* <u>*covenant*</u> *between me and you and every living creature with you;* ₁₃ *I set my* <u>*bow in the clouds*</u> *to serve as a sign of the* <u>*covenant*</u> *between me and the earth.* After the flood, the wording in Genesis 9:1–17 indicates that the original "creation <u>covenant</u>" is renewed with Noah, although with modifications due to the original sin of Adam and Eve. Also see: Genesis 6:18, 9:15–17, Sirach 44:17–18, Isaiah 24:5.

What does the Noah Covenant Represent for Us?
God continues to give us the <u>sign of the rainbow</u> as a reminder that he will never again destroy the entire earth by "*the waters of a flood.*"

Covenant with Abraham, Isaac, Jacob, and Descendants

<u>Time Frame</u>	<u>Type</u>	<u>Category</u>	<u>Sign(s)</u>
1913 BC	Everlasting	Unconditional	Worldwide blessing, circumcision

Genesis 12:2–3 ₂ *I will make of you* [Abraham] *a great nation, and I will bless you; I will make your name great, so that you will be a blessing.* ₃ *I will bless those who bless you and curse those who curse you. All communities of the earth shall find blessing in you.* Genesis 17:2,7 ₂ *Between you [Abraham] and me I will establish my* <u>*covenant,*</u> *and I will multiply you exceedingly.* ₇ *I will maintain my* <u>*covenant*</u> *with you and your descendants after you throughout the ages as an everlasting pact, to be your God and the God of your descendants after you.* God does not put any requirements for Abraham; the <u>covenant</u> is unconditional; however, later on there is a sign of the <u>covenant</u>: Genesis 17:10 *This is my* <u>*covenant*</u> *with you and your descendants after you that you must keep; every male among you shall be circumcised.* The removal of the foreskin symbolically represents a sealing (or blood) of the <u>covenant</u>. Therefore, this <u>covenant</u> is: 1. To make Abraham a great nation and bless Abraham and make his name great so that he will be a blessing, to bless those who bless him and curse him who curses him and all peoples on earth would be blessed through Abraham. 2. To give Abraham's descendants all the land from the river of Egypt to the Euphrates (Genesis 15:18–21). 3. To make Abraham the father of many nations and of many descendants and give the whole land of Canaan to his descendants (Genesis 17:2–9). 4. The sign of Circumcision is to be the <u>covenant</u> with Abraham and his descendants. The animals that are slaughtered

in the <u>covenant</u> are considered a sacrificial offering. Scripture states: "***God of Abraham, the God of Isaac, the God of Jacob***" (Exodus 3:15) because the <u>covenant</u> of Abraham was continued on by his descendants as predicted. Also see: Genesis 15:18: 17:13,14,19,21; Exodus 2:24; 6:2–5; Leviticus 26:42–45; 2 Kings 13:23; 17:15,35,38; 18:12; 23:2,3,21; 1 Chronicles 16:15–17; Sirach 44:19–20; Psalms 105:9; Acts 3:25; 7:8.

What does thew Abraham Covenant Represent for Us?
Psalms 105:8–10 ***He [God] remembers forever His <u>covenant,</u> the pact imposed for a thousand generations, which was made with Abraham, confirmed by oath to Isaac, and ratified as binding for Jacob, an <u>everlasting covenant</u> for Israel.***
Galatians 3:29 ***And if you belong to Christ Jesus, then you are Abraham's descendant, heirs according to the promise.*** By receiving Jesus Christ as your savior, we are heirs of Abraham thus sharing in all his blessings, ***I will bless those who bless you and curse those who curse you*** (Genesis 12:3).

Covenant with Moses and Israel
Also Called Old Covenant and Sinai Covenant.

Time Frame	Type	Category	Sign(s)
1491 BC	Temporary	Conditional	Ten Commandments, signs and Wonders, Ark of the Covenant

Three months after the Israelites departed Egypt, they arrived at Mount Sinai, for the <u>covenant</u> at Mount Sinai, the ten Commandments and other commands. Exodus 19:5 ***Therefore, if you harken to my voice and keep my <u>covenant,</u> you shall be my special possession, dearer to me than all other people, through all the earth is mine.*** Exodus 20:1 ***Then God delivered all these commandments:*** ... After this passage, Scripture lists the ten commandments from God plus later on Moses gives the Israelites 613 specific commands from God.

Ratification of the <u>Moses Covenant</u>: Exodus 24:7–9 ***Taking the book of the <u>covenant,</u> he read it aloud to the people, who answered, "All that the Lord has said, we will heed and do." Then he took the blood [the sacrifice of young bulls] and sprinkled it on the people, saying, "This is the blood of the <u>covenant</u> which the Lord has made with you in*** *accordance with all these words of his.*" Notice that all the people agreed to all the conditions of the <u>covenant.</u> Exodus 24:9–11 *Moses then went up with Aron, Nadab, Abihu, and seventy elders of Israel, and they beheld God of Israel. Under his feet there appeared to be sapphire tilework, as clear as the sky itself. Yet he did not smite these chosen Israelites. After gazing on God, they could still eat and drink.*

Exodus 34:10 *here, then, said the Lord, is the <u>covenant</u> I will make. Before the eyes of all your people I will work such marvels as have never been wrought in any nation anywhere on earth, ...* God promises to make the Israelites a holy nation if they followed God's commandments of this <u>conditional covenant.</u> The blood of a sacrificial oxen is then sprinkled on the altar and on the people to seal the <u>covenant.</u> The Lord said to Moses: Exodus 31: ₁₃... *Take care to keep my sabbaths, for that is to be the token between you and me throughout the generations, to show that it is I, the Lord, who make you holy.* ₁₆ *So shall the Israelites observe the sabbath, keeping it throughout their generations as a perpetual <u>covenant</u>.* A full account of this <u>Covenant</u> with Moses is in the book of Deuteronomy.

What does the Moses Covenant Represent for Us?
In the Old Testament there are 613 laws commanded by God through Moses (The Laws of Moses). These strict laws demonstrated to Israel (and us) that it is impossible to keep these laws perfectly, showing the need for help through a savior. In the New Testament there are 1050 commands by Jesus Christ such as, Honor God's law, follow Christ, work toward perfection, seek God's Kingdom, judge not, ask/seek/and knock, forgive others, love the Lord, keep my commandments, confess our sins, take/eat/ and drink, and many more, all of which are doable. However, in the event we violate them, Christ assures us if we ask for forgiveness (mercy), we will be forgiven; plus, He gave us the Holy Spirit to assist us. Notice that the <u>Moses Covenant</u> was ratified by the sacrifice of blood followed by a meal with God to prefigure the Catholic sacrifice of the mass and the Eucharist.

Covenant with Aaron and sons – Priest of the Levites
Sign: priesthood, salt.
Exodus 40:15 *As you have anointed their father, anoint them also as my priests. Thus, by being anointed, they shall receive a perpetual*

priesthood throughout all future generations. Leviticus 2:13 *However, every cereal offering of first fruits to the Lord shall be seasoned with salt. Do not let the salt of the <u>covenant</u> of our God be lacking from your cereal offering. On every offering you shall offer salt.*

Covenant with Phinehas – Perpetual Priesthood
Sign: priesthood forever, prefigures Christ.
Numbers 25:11–13 *₁₁ Phinehas, son of Eleazar, son of Aron the priest, ... ₁₂ Announce, therefore that I hereby give him my pledge of friendship, ₁₃ which shall be for him and for his descendants after him the pledge of an everlasting priesthood,*
Sirach 45:24 *Therefore on him* [Phinehas] *again God conferred the right, in a <u>covenant</u> of friendship, to provide for the sanctuary, so that he and his descendants should possess the high priesthood forever.*

The Aaron and sons <u>covenant</u> and the Phinehas <u>covenant</u> are considered to be the "Everlasting Priesthood <u>Covenant</u>."

What does the Everlasting Priesthood Covenant Represent for Us?
Jesus Christ became the everlasting priest for our salvation.

Covenant with David and Descendants
<u>Time Frame</u>   <u>Type</u>   <u>Category</u>   <u>Sign(s)</u>
1042 BC   Everlasting   Unconditional   Throne forever
The Lord's promise to David, 2 Samuel 7:16 *Your house and your kingdom shall endure forever before me; your <u>throne</u> will stand firm forever.*
Sirach 46:25 *For even his <u>covenant</u> with David, the son of Jesse of the tribe of Judah, was an individual heritage through one son alone; but the heritage of Aron is for all his descendants.* The son of David, Solomon ruled over Israel and he failed to keep God's commands. It wasn't until the descendant of David, Jesus Christ, who became the true and faithful son that fulfilled the everlasting promised Kingdom forever. Jesus obeyed God in all things (the only obedient King), even giving His own life for the world to earn the right to rule in glory forever, securing eternal life for all who believe in Him.

What does the Covenant with David Represent for Us?

Through this unconditional <u>covenant</u>, God made a promise that he would raise up David's offspring and establish the throne of his kingdom forever. This was fulfilled by Jesus Christ giving us the comfort in knowing that through the cross and resurrection Christ is the one truly righteous King who in addition to securing eternal life for us, in the future (the end of earth time) promises that all injustice and evil will end. Revelation 21:4 *He will wipe every tear from their eyes, and there shall be no more death or mourning, wailing or pain, for the old order has passed away.*

The New Covenant Forever – Jesus
The New Covenant of Eternal Salvation.

<u>Time Frame</u>	<u>Type</u>	<u>Category</u>	<u>Sign(s)</u>
33 AD	Everlasting	Unconditional	The Cross, the true tree of life, And the gift of salvation

The prophet Jeremiah predicted the New <u>Covenant</u>, Jeremiah 31:31 *The days are coming, says the Lord, when I will make a <u>New Covenant</u> with the house of Israel and the house of Judah.* This prophecy was fulfilled, Luke 22:20 [Jesus talking] *This cup is the <u>New Covenant</u> in my blood, which will be shed for you.* Also St. Paul in 1 Corinthians 11:25 *This cup is the <u>New Covenant</u> in my blood, do this, as often as you drink it, in remembrance of me.* At "The Last Supper", the sharing of a meal between the Apostles and the Son of God is a parallel to Moses and the elders sharing a meal with God on Mount Sini. Hebrews 9:22 *According to the law almost everything is purified by blood, and without the shedding of blood there is no forgiveness.*

What does the New Covenant Represent for Us?
This <u>covenant</u> is unconditional however it does require that we have faith in Jesus. Ephesians 2:8 *For by grace you have been saved through faith…* John 1:12 *But to those who did accept him he gave power to become children of God, to those who believe in his name…* We can now be joyful that we have peace with God. Romans 5:1 *Therefore, since we have been justified by faith, we have <u>peace</u> with God through our Lord Jesus Christ, through whom we have gained access [by faith] to this grace in which we stand…* This peace leads us to the promise of eternal life. Romans 6:23 *For the wages of sin is death, but the gift of God is eternal life in Christ Jesus our*

Lord. To assist us in our journey through life we are given the Holy Spirit. 1 Corinthians 3:16 ***Do you not know that you are a temple of God, and that the Spirit of God dwells in you?*** Through our journey, before eternity, in the event we should fail, we have the promise of forgiveness if we confess our sins. 1 John 1:9 ***If we confess our sins, he is faithful and just and will forgive our sins and cleanse us from every wrongdoing.***

The word "covenant" appears in the Old Testament 282 times and in the New Testament 34 times, which tells us of its significance as the master–theme of the Bible. Covenants are used by God to establish a relationship with humanity; to lead humanity to salvation. The Old Testament covenants with Adam, Noah, Abraham, Priesthood, and David are all everlasting. The covenant with Moses was temporary and conditional; therefore, we are not bound by the 613 commands, only by the ten commandments which are mentioned by Christ. The New Covenant of Eternal Salvation, established by Jesus Christ, is everlasting and unconditional; however, we have our free will to reject or to accept certain things in order to obtain salvation. The New Covenant puts an end to the temporary Covenant: Hebrews 10:8–10 ***"Sacrifices and offerings, holocaust and sin offerings, you neither desired nor delighted in." These are offered according to the law. Then he says, "Behold, I come to do your will." He takes away the first to establish the second. By this "will," we have been consecrated through the offering of the body of Jesus Christ once for all.***

The Jerusalem Temple was the only place where the Covenant people (the Israelites) could offer the blood of animal sacrifice for the atonement of their sins. After the destruction of the Temple (AD70), atonement for sins, for Christians, was replaced with the forgiveness of sins through the blood of Jesus Christ, the Lamb of God in the Eucharist.

Old Covenants Fulfilled:

OLD TESTAMENT COVENANTS	FULFILLED BY JESUS CHRIST
Covenant with Adam and Eve: Gn 1:28 ***God blessed them, saying: Be fertile and multiply; fill the earth and subdue it.*** Adam and Eve violated their covenant with God. Gn 3:11 *... **You have eaten, then, from the tree of which I had forbidden you to eat!***	(CCC 416) *By his sin Adam as the first man, lost the original holiness and justice he had received from God, not only for himself but for all human beings.* Jesus, the "new Adam" atoned for the "original sin" of the first Adam. Rom 5:19 ***For just as through the disobedience of one person the many were sinners, so through the obedience of one the many will be made righteous.***
Covenant with Noah: Gn 9:9 *...**I am now establishing my covenant with you [Noah] and your descendants after you...*** Noah was saved through water.	John 3:5 ... ***I** [Jesus] **say to you, no one can enter the kingdom of God without being born of water and Spirit.*** Jesus' gift of the Sacrament of Baptism restored man through water and the Spirit, to a renewed life.
Covenant with Abraham: Abraham's covenant had three blessings: ***1.Make of you a great nation.*** ***2.Multiply you exceedingly.*** ***3.Bless those who bless you.*** (Gn 12:2–3, 17:2)	Jesus fulfilled Abraham's promises: Mt 4:17 [Jesus] ***Repent, for the kingdom of heaven is at hand.*** 1.Jesus established the Kingdom of Heaven on earth, His Church. Gal 3:29 ***And if you belong to Christ, then you are Abraham's descendant, heirs according to the promise.*** 2.Accepting Christ makes us spiritual children of Abraham. Gal 3:8 ***Scripture, which saw in advance that God would justify the Gentiles by faith, foretold the good news to Abraham saying, "Through you shall all the nations be blessed."*** 3.The New Covenant of Jesus brought a worldwide blessing to all.

OLD TESTAMENT COVENANTS	FULFILLED BY JESUS CHRIST
Covenant with Moses (Sinai Covenant): Ex 24:7–9 *Taking the book of the covenant, he read it aloud to the people … Then he took the blood [the sacrifice of young bulls] and sprinkled it on the people, saying, "This is the blood of the covenant which the Lord has made with you …"*	By Jesus' one perfect bloody sacrifice on the altar of the cross, He fulfilled all the blood rituals and purification rituals of the old Law. Heb 9:15 *For this reason he is mediator of a New Covenant; since death has taken place for deliverance from transgression under the first covenant, those who are called may receive the promised eternal inheritance.*
Covenant with Aaron and Sons: Priests of the Levites handed down to generations. Exodus 40:15 *As you have anointed their father, anoint also as my priests. Thus, by being anointed, they shall receive a perpetual priesthood throughout all future generations.*	Matthew 28:19–20 *[Jesus] Go therefore, and make disciples of all nations, baptizing them in the name of the Father, and of the Son, and of the holy Spirit, teaching them to observe all that I have commanded you…* The New Covenant priesthood is a universal priesthood based on the holy Spirit and not on heredity.
Covenant with Phinehas (Perpetual Priesthood): The covenant of ministerial priesthood. Numbers 25:11–13 *Phinehas; son of Eleazar, son of Aron the priest, … I hereby give him my pledge of friendship, which shall be for him and for his descendants after him the pledge of an everlasting priesthood, …*	Hebrews 4:14 *Therefore, since we have a great high priest who has passed through the heavens, Jesus, the Son of God, let us hold fast to our confession.* Jesus Christ is the eternal High Priest of the New and Everlasting Covenant.
Covenant with David: The Lord's promise to David: 2 Samuel 7:16 *Your house and your kingdom shall endure forever before me; your throne will stand forever.*	Jesus is the heir of David and the King of the Universal Kingdom; thus, fulfilling God's promise to David that his throne would endure forever. Luke 1:32 *He [Jesus] will be great and will be called Son of the Most High, and the Lord God will give him the throne of David his father, …*

References: (CCC) The Catechism of the Catholic Church.
Internet: agapebiblestudy.com/Sunday Readings, Michal E. Hunt.

Old Testament Prophesy Fulfilled in the New Covenant:

OLD TESTAMENT PROPHESY	FULFILLED BY JESUS
Jeremiah 31:31 *The days are coming, says the Lord, when I will make a __new covenant__ with the house of Israel and the house of Juda.*	Luke 22:19–20 [Jesus speaking] *This is my body, which will be given for you; __do this in memory of me__, … This cup is the __new covenant__ in my blood, which will be shed for you.*

Jesus, at the "Last Supper" established the final everlasting covenant with all of humanity through the Eucharist, commanding us to: *"__do this in memory of me__"* (Lk 22:19) which is a direct order from Jesus that is to be honored.

What must we do to Obtain Salvation?
Be Baptized:
  + Mark 16:16 *Whoever __believes__ and is __baptized__ will be saved; whoever does not believe will be condemned.* Also, Titus 3:4, 1 Peter 3:20–21.
Believe in Jesus:
  + Acts 16:31 *__Believe__ in the Lord Jesus and you and your household will be saved.*
Endure to the End:
  + Matthew 10:22 *You will be hated by all because of my name, but whoever __endures__ to the end will be saved.* Also, Matthew 24:13, Mark 13:13.
Accept Your Cross (suffering):
  + Matthew 10:38 *and whoever does not __take up his cross__ and __follow after me__ is not worthy of me.* Also, Matthew 16:24–25, Mark 8:34, Luke 9:23, Luke 14:27.
Keep God's Commandments:
  + Matthew 5:19 *… But whoever __obeys__ and teaches these __commandments__ will be called greatest in the kingdom of heaven.* Also, Matthew 7:21.
Participate in God's True Church:
  + Acts 2:47 *__praising God__ and enjoying favor with all the people.*

Follow the Words of St. Peter and His Successors (popes):

+ Acts 15:7 *...Peter got up and said to them, "my brothers, you are well aware that from early days God made his choice among you that <u>through my mouth</u> the Gentiles would hear the word of the gospel and believe..."*

Confess Our Sins:

+ 1 John 1:9 *If we <u>acknowledge our sins,</u> he is faithful and just and will forgive our sins and cleanse us from every wrongdoing.* Also, James 5:16.

Believe in and Often Receive the Eucharist:

+ John 6:53–54 *Jesus said to them, "Amen, amen, I say to you, unless you <u>eat the flesh of the Son of Man and drink his blood,</u> you do not have life within you. Whoever eats my flesh and drinks my blood has eternal life, and I will raise him on the last day..."* 1 Corinthians 11:25 *For as <u>often</u> as you eat this bread and drink the cup, you proclaim the death of the Lord until He comes.* Also, 1 Corinthians 10:16, 1 Corinthians 11:23–29.

Have Faith and Accept the Grace of Justification:

+ Romans 5:17 *...how much more will those who receive the abundance of <u>grace</u> and the gift of <u>justification</u> come to reign in life through the one person Jesus Christ.*

Beatitudes of Jesus Christ – the New Covenant
Moses gave us the 10 commandments that might be considered somewhat negative.

Jesus Christ gave us 10 Beatitudes that are of love and are the foundation of the <u>New</u> Everlasting Covenant of Salvation.

Based on Matthew 5:3–12. The first 8 Beatitudes have two parts, a <u>blessing</u>, and a *<u>promise</u>* as listed below:

First blessing: *Blessed are the poor in spirit* (verse 3).
Blessing in Hebrew means happy. *Poor in spirit* means spiritual poverty or little spirit and one must depend on God. In this blessing Jesus is teaching that the first step on the pathway to Heaven is to admit that you

cannot make it on your own in this life or on your own to victory in the next life.

> First promise: *for theirs is the kingdom of heaven.* (2nd part of verse 3).
> We understand that our inheritance of **the Kingdom of Heaven** is first dependent upon our response to God's grace through faith.

Second blessing: ***Blessed are they who mourn*** (verse 4).
Mourn in Hebrew means the pain of a loss, grieving, spiritual suffering. The result is, becoming aware of our moral failures, we mourn our sins.

> Second promise: ***for they will be comforted*** (2nd part of verse 4).
> It is God who will comfort those who mourn. God's grace will come to those who mourn the suffering of sin. We have the promise that when we mourn our sins and turn to Christ that He will give us the strength and the courage to overcome our weaknesses and inadequacies so that we can take up our crosses and follow Him as He commanded.

Third blessing: ***Blessed are the meek*** (verse 5).
"meek" in Hebrew means gentle, patient, it does not mean weak or submissive. It means thinking of yourself less, not less of yourself. For the Christian, submission to God's control results in strength; it is the strength that is not our own but which comes from God's will working though our lives.

> Third promise: ***for they will inherit the land*** (2nd part of verse 5).
> God willed creation as a gift addressed to mankind, an inheritance destined for and entrusted to all of mankind.

Fourth blessing: ***Blessed are they who hunger and thirst for righteousness*** (verse 6). ***Righteousness*** in Hebrew means one to be ready for salvation, right with God. The fourth beatitude is a pivotal step in our spiritual

journey. It is where we move from what we need to give to God; to the miracle of what God plans to give us. In the New Covenant, we must actively, diligently, and relentlessly seek righteousness as though our very lives depended upon it, for it does.

> Fourth promise: *for they will be satisfied* (2nd part of verse 6).
> This verse is the turning point in the Beatitudes. Up to this point, the focus has been on the most basic aspects of our relationship with God. Until this point, the focus has been our need: our need for God throughout the world, our need for repentance, and our need for humility, thirsting for salvation. But now the focus changes to our need for union with the fullness of God. Jesus gives Himself to us entirely in His Body, Blood, Soul, and Divinity in His gift of the Holy Eucharist.

Fifth blessing: *Blessed are the merciful* (verse 7).
Merciful in Hebrew is forgiveness and compassion. Also, it is to forgive others even if they do not deserve it. The "*merciful*" are those who are not passive in showing love and compassion but who take an active role in bringing aid to those who are in need.

> Fifth promise: *for they will be shown mercy* (2nd part of verse 7).
> Love is stronger than sin. The sin of failing to forgive binds and wounds the soul so much more deeply than the barbs of your enemy. Forgive your enemy, set your soul free, and feel the power of God's grace working in you.

Sixth blessing: *Blessed are the clean of heart* (verse 8).
Clean of heart means free of sin. Sacred scripture recognizes that the heart represents the hidden depths of one's moral and spiritual being and regards the heart as the focus of divine influence from which a man or woman could be purified by God from the inside out. It is that whatever you do, or say, or see, which reflects the image of God.

Sixth promise: *for they will see God* (2nd part of verse 8). Filling our hearts with Christ produces a purity of spirit that creates a peace in our hearts which overflows and touches each person we meet. A right relationship with God leads to the desire for a right relationship with others.

Seventh blessing: ***Blessed are the peacemakers*** (verse 9).
Peacemakers are people that seek and pursue peace for themselves and between others. Verse 9 is the seventh step on the pathway to salvation. With our hearts purified by Christ living in us, we actively seek to extend His peace to others.

Seventh promise: ***for they will be called children of God*** (2nd part of verse 9).
Empowered by the Holy Spirit as God's children, He commands us to bear much "fruit" by Christ who has grafted us onto Himself as the "true vine". The "fruit" or works we bear is an outpouring of the gifts the Holy Spirit imparts to us.

Eighth blessing: ***Blessed are they who are persecuted for the sake of righteousness. Persecuted*** for the sake of God has been going on since the early Church where many were put to death. Persecution is still with us today, where in this country it may be harassment of some type. However, there are still parts of the world where persecution by death is still occurring.

Eighth promise: ***for theirs is the kingdom of heaven*** (verse 10).
Verse 10 above parallels verse 5: ***for they will inherit the land***, where it is assumed that they both mean heaven. Also, the blessings are not earthly blessings but heavenly blessings.

Ninth statement: ***Blessed are you when they insult you and persecute you and utter_every kind of evil against you falsely because of me.*** (Verse 11).

Notice that Jesus changes the "*they*" identity to "*you.*" This is most lightly directed to the destiny of the Apostles who are to suffer as successors to the holy prophets.

Tenth statement: *Rejoice and be glad, for your reward will be great in heaven.* (Verse 12). The Beatitudes are an invitation to put these spiritual precepts of the New Covenant law into practice as conditions for Christians to gain entrance into the Kingdom of Heaven. Heaven is stated in the first statement and also in the last statement that further indicates that the promises are not earthly but heavenly.

Deuteronomy 27:1–14, Moses lists all the blessings the Israelites will receive if they keep the commandments of the Lord. Then verse 15 through 37 Moses lists all the curses to come upon the Israelites if they do not follow the law. As you may know, later in scripture, the Israelites did not keep the commandments and suffered the curses, including 70 years of exile.

SUMMARY–COVENANTS:
+ A covenant is a kinship with God that may be unconditional or conditional.
+ The original covenant with Adam was a conditional covenant; after the fall it became an unconditional covenant. Adam failed, but God kept His promise: "*Have dominion over the fish of the sea, the birds of the air, and all the living things that move on earth.*" (Gn 1:28)
+ The Covenant with Noah is an everlasting covenant. (Gn 9:9–13) The sign of Noah's covenant is the rainbow giving us a reminder that God will never again destroy the entire earth by the waters of a flood.
+ The Covenant with Abraham is an unconditional covenant that is everlasting. By receiving Jesus Christ as our savior, we are heirs of Abraham, thus sharing in his blessing: "*I will bless those who bless you and curse those who curse you.*" (Gn 12:2–3)

+ The <u>Covenant</u> with Moses was a <u>conditional covenant</u> with temporary laws that were difficult to keep showing the need for a savior. Moses' <u>covenant</u> was ratified by a bloody sacrifice followed by a meal with God that prefigured the Catholic Mass (un–bloody) sacrifice through the Eucharist.

+ The unconditional <u>covenant</u> with David tells us: ***"Your house and your kingdom shall endure forever before me; your throne will stand firm forever."*** (2 Sm 7:16) This was fulfilled by Jesus Christ through the cross and resurrection giving us the truly righteous King Jesus to secure eternal life for us.

+ The unconditional <u>covenants</u> with Aaron and sons (Ex 40:15) as well as with Phinehas (Nm 25:11–136) were the <u>covenants</u> of the everlasting priesthood, prefigured and fulfilled by Jesus Christ.

+ The New <u>Covenant</u> of Eternal Salvation is unconditional but does require one to accept Jesus Christ by faith to obtain eternal salvation. (Lk 22:20)

+ To obtain eternal salvation, according to scripture, we must: Be baptized, believe in Jesus, endure to the end, accept our cross, keep God's commandments, participate in God's true Church, follow the words of Peter's successors (popes), confess our sins, believe in and often receive the Eucharist, and have faith by accepting the grace given to us.

+ The Beatitudes of Jesus Christ is the foundation of the New Everlasting Covenant of Salvation.

SUMMARY – SALVATION:
+ Be Baptized (Mk 16:16)
+ Believe in Jesus (Acts 16:31)
+ Endure to the end (Mt 10:22)
+ Accept your cross (Mt 10:38)
+ Keep God's commandments (Mt 5:19)
+ Participate in God's true Church (Acts 2:47)
+ Follow the words of St. Peter and his successors (Acts 15:7)
+ Confess our sins (1 Jn 1:9)
+ Believe in and often receive the Eucharist (Jn 6:53–54; 1 Cor 11:25)
+ Have faith and accept the grace of justification (Rom 5:17)

SUMMARY – BEATITUDES:

+ Blessed are the Poor in Spirit – theirs is the Kingdom of Heaven (Mt 5:3)
+ Blessed are they who morn – they will be comforted (Mt 5:4)
+ Blessed are the meek – they will inherit the land (Mt 5:5)
+ Blessed are they who hunger – they will be satisfied (Mt 5:6)
+ Blessed are the merciful – they will be shown mercy (Mt 5:7)
+ Blessed are the clean of heart – they will see God (Mt 5:8)
+ Blessed are the peacemakers – they will be called children of God (Mt 5:9)
+ Blessed are they who are persecuted – theirs is the kingdom of heaven (Mt 5:10)
+ Blessed are you they insult/persecute/utter evil against you (Mt 5:11)
+ Rejoice and be glad – your reward will be great in heaven (Mt 5:12)

References:
Scripture quotations are ***italicized and bold*** from The New American Bible (NAB) Certain words may be <u>underlined</u> for emphasis added.

Covenant References:
Agape Bible Study – YAHWEH'S EIGHT COVENANTS, GotQuestions.org – What are the Covenants in the Bible? Wikipedia.org/wiki/Covenant_(biblical) COVENANT Assembled by Paul Wilchek 11JAN21.

Beatitudes Reference: This, in part, is a reference from the "Agape Bible Study" – Sunday commentary by Michal E. Hunt – revised 2018. Based on The Gospel of Matthew 5:1–12,
BEATITUDES: Assembled by Paul Wilchek 20FEB20.

CHAPTER 3

EUCHARIST AND THE MASS

The Eucharist name does not appear in scripture, however, "Thanksgiving" does appear in reference to the Last Supper and the Greek word for thanksgiving is *eucharistesas,* where the Eucharist name derived from. Eucharist, dictionary definition: the sacrament of Holy Communion; the sacrifice of the Mass; the Lord's Supper; the consecrated elements of Holy Communion, the giving of thanks; thanksgiving.

This has extensive comparisons between the Old and New Testament showing predictions, foretelling, symbolisms and fulfillments. As proof, therefore, it is important to understand that more than 500 Old Testament documents were archaeologically discovered between 1946 and 1956 (called the Dead Sea Scrolls). These were scientifically tested to date them more than a century prior to New Testament times. This confirms God's inspired words in the Old Testament, predictions, were written long before New Testament times, when they were fulfilled.

Certain words or statements herein may be <u>underlined</u> for emphasis added to show their importance or the <u>underlined</u> word(s) may be explained later. ***Quotations from scripture herein are bold and italicized like this.***

1.   **A few of the names for the Eucharist that appear in scripture:**
Luke 22: 19 *the bread. This is my body.* Luke 22: 20 *the cup This cup my blood.* 1 Cor 11:*20 Lord's Supper.* Acts 2:42 *breaking of the bread.* 1 Cor 10:16 *The cup of blessing that we bless, is it not a participation in the blood of Christ? The bread that we break, is it not a participation in the body of Christ?*

Scripture quotes Jesus as saying: John 6:35 *I am the bread of life,* John 6:41 *I am the bread that came down from heaven,*
John 6:48 *I am the bread of life,* John 6:51 *I am the living bread…, the bread that I will give is my flesh for the life of the world,* John 6:54 *Whoever eats my flesh and drinks my blood has eternal life,* John 6:55 *For my flesh is true food, and* **my blood is true drink.**

In John chapter 6 verses 22 through 71, Jesus references 15 times that He is the Bread.
Christ was born in Bethlehem, which means "House of Bread."

2.   **The fall of mankind:**
The fall of mankind was in the act of eating what was forbidden from the tree of life as described in Genesis 3:1–24. The fall of mankind could have been any number of sins but scripture has it as the act of eating. As a result of this sin there were ramifications for Adam and Eve. One of which is: Gn 3:19 *By the sweat of your face shall you get bread to eat….* This is the first mention of bread in scripture, which prefigures bread & eating throughout scripture.

3.   **The first sacrifice in scripture:**
Gn 4:4 *while Abel, for his part, brought one of the best firstlings of his flock. The Lord looked with favor on Abel and his offering,*
Ex 34:19 *To me belongs every first–born male that opens the womb among your livestock…*
Heb 11:4 *by faith Abel offered to God a sacrifice.*

4.   **Prefigured sacrifice of the Mass:**
Gn14:18 *Melchizedek, king of Salem, brought out bread and wine, and being a priest of God Most High, he blessed Abram with these*

words: *"Blessed be Abram by God Most High, the creator of heaven and earth; and blessed be God Most High, who delivered your foes into your hands." Then Abram gave him a tenth of everything.*
The blessing given to Abram (later called Abraham) with the bread and wine must have been highly valued for Abram to give Melchizedek one tenth of everything. King of Salem is interpreted as King of Peace (shalom) in the following:

Hebrews 7:1–3 *This Melchizedek, king of Salem and priest of God Most High, "met Abraham as he returned from his defeat of the kings" and "blessed him." And Abraham apportioned to him a tenth of everything." His name first means righteous king, and he was also "King of Salem," that is, king of peace. Without father, mother, or ancestry, without beginning of days or end of life, thus made to resemble the Son of God, he remains a priest forever.*

Melchizedek, king of rightness, foreshadows Jesus, the eternal high priest's offering of bread and wine in thanksgiving to the Father. Melchizedek's offering of bread and wine looks forward to both the Last Supper and the Mass, where not only bread and wine are offered, but they are now changed into the Body and Blood of Jesus. In the New Testament where Jesus is talking about the law: Matthew 5:17: *I have come not to abolish but to fulfill.* The New Testament (Hebrews) tells us that Jesus is: Heb 5:14 *...a great high priest...*

Thus, Jesus fulfilled the prefigured Old Testament statement of:
"Priest of God Most High" (Heb 7:1) as well as fulfilling the "blessing" and distribution of bread performed at the Last Supper.

5. Pre–Configuration of Calvary when Abraham offered Isaac:

Old Testament:	New Testament – Fulfilled:
Gn 22:2 *your <u>only son</u>* (Isaac)	Jn 1:18 *The <u>only Son</u>, God, who is at the Father's side, has revealed Him.*
Abraham and Isaac traveled to: Gn 22:2 *land of <u>Moriah</u>"* Where is Moriah? 2 Chr 2:1 *build the house of the Lord in Jerusalem on Mt. Moriah*	Jesus was sacrificed in Jerusalem on Mt. <u>Moriah</u>

Old Testament:	New Testament – Fulfilled:
Gn 22:4 *on the third day*	Luke 18:33 *...on the third day He will rise.*
Gn 22:6 *Abraham took the wood... and laid it on his son Isaac's shoulders:*	Jesus carried the cross (wood) on His shoulders.
Gn 22:7 *Isaac spoke to his Father, Abraham: "father! he said.*	Luke 23:34 *(Jesus said) Father, forgive them, they know not what they do.*
Gn 22:8 *God himself will provide the sheep [lamb].*	John 1:29 *behold the Lamb of God.* God provided the Lamb of God (Jesus).
Gn 22:9 Isaac was a young man and did not object to the sacrifice, he willingly offered Himself.	Jesus offered himself willingly. Luke 22:42 *...not my will but yours be done.* John 6:42 *...I came down from heaven not to do my own will but the will of the one who sent me.*
Passover:	
Ex 12:5 *The lamb must be a year old male and without blemish.*	Heb 4:15 *[Jesus] ...yet without sin.* Jesus also without blemish (sin)
In the Jewish tradition the lamb was sacrificed by the father of the household.	Christ's sacrifice was willed by His Father according to Luke 22:42 above.
Ex 12:22 *Take a bunch of hyssop and dipping it in the blood* [of the lamb] *... sprinkle the lintel and two doorposts with this blood.*	Jn 19:29 *...so they put a sponge soaked in wine on a sprig of hyssop and put it up to His mouth.*

Notice the use of hyssop in the Old and New Testament. Also notice the physical action of putting blood on the lintel first, then on the two doorposts; this action generates the sign of the cross. These similarities are meant to prefigure Calvary.

Ex 12:8 *...eat its roasted flesh with unleavened bread...* Ex 12:17 *keep, then, this custom of the unleavened bread.*	The Jews were directed to eat the flesh with bread in order to complete the requirements of sacrifice.

Ex 12:14 ***This day shall be a <u>memorial feast</u> for you, which all your generations shall celebrate with pilgrimage to the Lord, as a <u>perpetual institution.</u>***	The Eucharist is the <u>memorial</u> of Christ's Passover made present to us the same as the Jews made Passover present to them.

The "burnt offering" of the Jews was a total sacrifice in which the sacrifice was entirely consumed by fire. However, at the Passover they were instructed to eat the lamb with unleavened bread, then anything leftover was to be burnt. The eating of the flesh and bread pre–figures the Mass.

6. Miracle of manna (heavenly bread):

Old Testament:	New Testament – Fulfilled:
Ex 16:4 ***Then the Lord said to Moses, "I will now rain down <u>bread from heaven</u> for you."***	Jn 6:41 ***The Jews murmured about Him because He said, "I am the bread that came down <u>from heaven</u>,"***
Ex 16:8 ***...the Lord gives you <u>flesh</u> to eat in the evening...and in the morning your fill of <u>bread</u>...***	Jn 6:51" ***...the <u>bread</u> that I will give is my <u>flesh</u> for the life of the world."***
Ex 16:31 ***The Israelites called this food manna. ...it tasted like <u>wafers</u> made with honey.***	The Eucharist also looks like a <u>wafer</u>.
Ex 16:35 ***The Israelites ate this manna for forty years.***	Jn 6:34 ***So they said to Him [Jesus], "Sir, give us this bread <u>always</u>."***

The bread and flesh in the Old Testament foreshadow the Eucharist including its appearance as a <u>wafer</u>. The Jews in the New Testament asked Jesus for "***this bread <u>always</u>***" because they knew that their ancestors received bread from heaven that ended after forty years.

The Lord instructed Moses in Ex 17:6 to: ***...strike the <u>rock</u> and the water will flow from it for the people to drink.*** Then the New Testament tells us about the Jewish ancestors in 1 Cor 10:3 ***All ate the same spiritual food, and all drank the same spiritual drink, for they drank from a spiritual <u>rock</u> that followed them, and the rock was the Christ.*** These two statements from the Old and New Testament in relation to the rock verify that they were very much aware of the symbolism used in the Old Testament to foreshadow New Testament times. Christ tells us in Jn 4:14 "***...whoever drinks the water I shall give will never thirst.***"

7. **Mysteries of the Tabernacle:**

Notice the [**numbers 1,3,12**] that are prefigured in the Old Testament and the New:

Old Testament:	New Testament – Fulfilled:
Ex 24: 2 *...Moses <u>alone</u> is to come close to the Lord...*	[1] Mt 26:13 [Jesus] *Sit here while I go over there and pray.* [alone]
Ex 24:1 *Moses himself was told, "Come up to the Lord You, Aaron with Nadab, ..."*	[3] Mk 14:33 *He* [Jesus] *took with Him Peter, James and John.*
Ex 24: 4 *...<u>twelve</u> pillars for the twelve tribes of Israel.*	[12] Mk 6:7 *He summoned the <u>twelve</u>* (apostles).

God's instructions for worship (Ex 24 below) are repeated, using the same words, only one other time at the Last Supper (Mt 26) to establish the format of the Liturgy:

Ex 24:8 (Moses said)	Mt 26:28 (Jesus said)
This is the <u>blood of the covenant</u> which the Lord has made with you in accordance with all these words of his.	*For this is my <u>blood of the covenant</u>, which will be shed on behalf of many for the forgiveness of sins.*

Ex 24:9 *Moses then went up* [to Mount Sinai] *with Aaron, Nadab, Abihu, and seventy elders of Israel, and they <u>beheld the God of Israel</u>.* Ex 24:11 *...after gazing on God, they could still eat and drink.*

The Jews believed that to see God one would die, yet in the above passage they all *"<u>beheld the God of Israel</u>"* and lived. There is nothing mentioned that Moses and the others were instructed to take food and drink with them; therefore, God must have provided what they ate and drank at this heavenly sacrificial meal on Mount Sinai which prefigures the Holy Mass.

God provided very detailed instructions on how to assemble the Tabernacle of Moses (which later was replicated as the Temple). The following is a summary of those instructions in Ex 25 thru 30:

The Tabernacle of Moses is divided into three main courts:

(1) Outer Court of Sacrifice – containing a Bronze Altar of Sacrifice and a Bronze Laver of Water.

(2) The Holy Place – (also called Inner Court) where a Veil separated the Outer Court from the Holy Place, a Golden Altar of Incense, a Golden Lampstand (Menorah), a Golden Table of the *"Bread of the Presence"* (Ex 26:30) (showbread, bread and drink offerings). Entering this area, one moved from bronze/blood sacrifice to gold and unbloody sacrifice.

(3) Holy of Holies – had a veil separating it from the Holy Place that contained the Ark of the Covenant including the Ten Commandments, jar of manna, and rod of Aaron. This place could only be entered by the high priest, representing the crossing over from earth to heaven and represents the heavenly sacrifice on Mount Sinai.

This Tabernacle represents a portable Mount Sinai with the Outer Court as being the base of the mountain. The Bronze Altar recalls the altar Moses built for the bloody sacrifice that took place at the base of Mt. Sinai. The Bronze Laver recalls that the people and priest were instructed to wash with water before entering God's presence. Ex 30:20 *when they are about to enter the meeting tent, they must wash with water, lest they die.* Just as the priest today washes with water at Mass.

The Holy Place recalls the middle of the mountain which sets up the liturgical and symbolic progression of the journey to the top of Mount Sinai. The Golden Altar of Incense and Lampstand represents the smoke and fire in which God descended upon the mountain. The Table of the *"Bread of the Presence"* (Ex 26:30) (also called "Bread of the Face") with bread and wine recall the heavenly banquet that Moses and the others had with God. This prefigures the Real Presence in the Eucharist and the Mass resembles the sacrifice on Mount Sinai with God.

The Holy of Holies represents the throne of God at the top of the mountain.

The Trinity of the Tabernacle:
Holy of Holies represents God the Father.
Holy Place with "Bread of the Presence" represents The Son of God.
Holy Place with incense and Lampstand represents The Holy Spirit.

The first–century Jewish priest had a custom during the Passover of taking the *"Bread of the Presence"* (Ex 26:30) out of the Holy Place and lifting it up to the pilgrims saying "Behold God's love for you". The priest today holds up the Eucharist saying "Behold the lamb of God". The Eucharist is the fulfillment of the Old Testament "Bread of the Presence."

8. Miracles of Jesus:

Old Testament:	New Testament – Fulfilled:
Dt 18:18 *I will raise up for them a Prophet like you* [Moses] *from among their kinsmen, and will put my words into his mouth; ...*	Jn 6:14 *when the people saw the sign, He* [Jesus] *had done, they said, "This is the Prophet, the one who is to come into the world.*

The prediction in Dt 18:18 of *"a Prophet"* is fulfilled in Jn 6:14, the Jews knew of this prediction and referred to Jesus as *"the Prophet."*

Notice the significance of the first miracle of Jesus that was performed on the third day: Jn 2:1 *On the third day there was a wedding in Cana...* Moses' first sign was to turn the water of the Nile into blood, which prefigured the first miracle of Jesus where Jesus turned water into wine at Cana. This action demonstrated that Jesus has the power over physical things, turning 6 jars (180 gallons) of water into fine wine. Then again at the Last Supper Jesus uses his power to turn bread and wine into His body and blood, the Eucharist miracle.

Lk 2:7 *...she wrapped Him [Jesus] in swaddling clothes and laid Him in a manger.*

A manger is a feeding trough, symbolizing that Jesus will become food for our salvation.

The miracle of the multiplication of loaves and feeding of 5,000 can be found in Mathew, Mark, Luke, and John. The scripture words of "given thanks" before the distribution of the bread is "eucherestein" (euxapiotia) in Greek, where the word Eucharist derived from.

Mk 8:6 *...Then, taking the seven loaves He [Jesus] gave thanks, broke them, and gave them to His disciples to distribute, ...*

Mk 8:8 *They ate and were satisfied. They picked up the fragments left over – seven baskets. There were about four thousand people.*

Mk 8:18–21 [Jesus speaking] *Do you have eyes and not see, ears and not hear? And do you not remember, when I broke five loaves for the five thousand, how many wicker baskets full of fragments you picked up?*

They answered him, "Twelve." When I broke the seven loaves for the four thousand, how many full baskets of fragments did you pick up? They answered him, "Seven." He said to them, "Do you still not understand?"
In the above, Jesus is pointing out to His disciples (and us) that scripture is full of signs and prefigured messages that we need to understand. The feeding of the five thousand was in Israel territory, and the twelve baskets represents the twelve tribes of Israel. The feeding of the four thousand was in Gentile territory, and the seven baskets represents the seven Gentile nations in that area. Acts 13:19 *When he* [Moses] *had destroyed seven nations in the land of Canaan.*

The act of: blessing, breaking, and distribution of bread prefigures Holy Communion by using similar terminology:
Lk 22:19 *Then He took the bread, said the blessing, broke it, and gave it to them, saying, "This is my body, which will be given for you; do this in memory of me."*
In a similar manor, the priest at Mass blesses, breaks and distributes the Eucharist.
The five thousand and four thousand, and the 180 gallons of wine at Cana, all signify an abundance that is foretold in the Old Testament. It also prefigures the abundance of Holy Communion to be distributed up to today and the future.

Ex 24:3 *When Moses came to the people and related all the words and ordinances of the Lord, they all answered with one voice.*
The Catholic Mass follows the same format of: "*they all answered with one voice*", when the people respond to the priest with one voice.
Ex 23:33 *Hang the veil from clasps. The ark of the commandments you shall bring inside, behind this veil which divides the Holy Place from the Holy of Holies.*
Mk 15:38 *The veil of the sanctuary was torn in two from top to bottom.*
The action of the torn veil (after the crucifixion of Jesus), represents (or symbolizes) that the Holy of Holies is now open and accessible to everyone.

9. The Bread of Life Discourse:
Now let's turn to the New Testament. "The Bread of Life Discourse" that is in John chapter 6 can be divided into two main parts. Ironically both

parts, (1) Jn 6:35 and (2) Jn 6:48, both start with the exact same statement: *I am the bread.*

Part (1) Jn 6: 35 – 42. In this first part, Jesus compares Himself to the Old Testament manna (which the Jews listening understood) that came down from heaven.

Jn 6: 41 *I am the bread that came down from heaven.*

Therefore, Jesus wants us to believe and have faith in His divinity that He is the Holy One of God. So, in part one we need to believe and have faith that Jesus came down from heaven in order to understand part (2).

Part (2) Jn 6: 48 – 58. The second part of this discourse is about eating and the spiritually of Jesus.

Jn 6: 51. *I am the living bread that came down from heaven; whoever **eats** this bread will live forever; and the bread that I will give is my flesh for the life of the world.*

Jn 6: 55 – 56. *For my flesh is true **food**, and my blood is true **drink**, whoever **eats** my flesh and **drinks** my blood remains in me and I in him.*

Some of Jesus' disciples did not have the faith (that Jesus explained in part 1), because they misunderstood eating His flesh:

Jn 6: 60. *Then many of His disciples who were listening said, "This saying is hard; who can accept it?"* By this statement, they had to have been thinking of cannibalism, which verifies that they understood that Jesus was talking about <u>real</u> flesh and <u>real</u> blood.

John chapter 6: [61] *Since Jesus knew that His disciples were murmuring about this, He said to them, "Does this shock you?* [62] *What if you were to see the Son of Man **ascending** to where He was before?* [63] *It is the **spirit that gives life**, while **the flesh** is of no avail. The words I have spoken to you are **spirit and life**. But there are some of you who do not believe."*

Notice in the above that Jesus states *"**the flesh**,"* this most lightly refers to Jn 8: 15 *You judge by appearances, ...* Of which, the literal translation of *"by appearances"* is "according to the flesh". In other words, they see and judge His earthly body (flesh) and do not see or understand His spirit.

It is important to put the above scripture statement: *"it is the spirit that gives life, while the flesh is of no avail."* Into its proper context within this entire discourse:

1. Jn 6:41 *...I am the bread that came down from heaven.* Note here that only the spirit can come down from heaven.
2. Jn 6:51 *...the bread that I will give...* Notice here that Jesus states *"that I will give"* (future tense), not his current earthly body, which was misunderstood by the disciples until after Jesus' Resurrection.
3. In Jn 6:62 above, *"...see the Son of Man ascending..."*, this sets the spiritual framework for *"the flesh is of no avail"* (judging by appearance).

Therefore, the bread and wine of the Eucharist is the resurrected, glorified living body and blood, as well as the divinity of Jesus Christ: Jn 6: 51 *I am the living bead that came down from heaven; ...* Jn 6:48 *I am the bread of life.* Jn 6: 63 *It is the spirit that gives life.* When one combines the meaning of the two parts of the "Bread of Life Discourse:" (1) faith and believing in the divinity of Christ, (2) the eating of bread and the spirituality of Jesus, one can now conclude:

Faith in Christ's divinity is foundational to the faith in His real presence in the Eucharist.

Jn 6: ₆₈ *Simon Peter answered Him, "Master, to whom shall we go? You have the words of eternal life.* ₆₉ *We have come to believe and are convinced that you are the Holy One of God."* This occurred in scripture right after Jesus stated: *"my flesh is true food and my blood is true drink"* (Jn 6:55) By saying *"we"*, Simon Peter must be talking for all the apostles, they may not have understood, but they did believe Jesus is *"the living bread that came down from heaven"* (Jn 6:51) of which they are to eat so that they *"may have eternal life"* (Jn 6:64), and where Jesus *"remains in me and I in him."* (Jn 6:56) The real presence.

10. **The Last Supper and the Cross** (The Passover of Christ):
Luke 22: ₇ *when the day of the Feast of Unleavened Bread arrived, the day for sacrificing the Passover lamb,* ₈ *He [Jesus] sent out Peter and John, instructing them, "Go and make preparations for us to eat the Passover."*

There were many Jewish requirements for the Passover preparations, just a few of them are: (1) Secure a lamb without blemish. (2) Take the lamb to the Temple in Jerusalem to be slaughtered where a priest caught the blood that was poured on the altar *, while they sang praise psalms (called Hallel – Psalms 113 – 118). (3) The lamb was then skinned and put on a spit that was in the shape of <u>a cross</u>. (4) The lamb was roasted, using the <u>cross</u> shaped spit as support. (5) The lamb was to be eaten with unleavened bread along with four wine offerings in order to complete the Passover requirements.

Note above * The blood of the lamb that was poured on the altar then drained to <u>the side</u> of the Temple where it mixed with <u>water</u> from a stream, creating a visible flow of <u>blood and water</u> from the <u>side</u> of the Temple. Thus, prefigured Christ's <u>side</u> pierced where <u>blood and water</u> flowed, and Jesus being the new Temple.

Luke 22: ₁₉ **Then He took <u>the bread</u>, said the blessing, broke it, and gave it to them, saying, "<u>This is my body</u>, which will be given for you; do this in <u>memory</u> of me."**

₂₀ **And likewise <u>the cup</u> after they had eaten, saying, "<u>This cup</u> is the new covenant in <u>my blood</u>, which will be shed for you."**

Notice in the above that there is no mention of lamb or flesh. Lamb is not mentioned because the true Lamb, Jesus, sat at the head of the table, the ultimate fulfillment in the sacrifice of the spotless (un–blemished) Lamb of God. Flesh is not mentioned, as stated earlier: *"the flesh is of no avail"* (Jn 6:63).

The emphasis in this Last Supper discourse is on bread and wine as being: *"This is my body"* (Lk 22:19) and we are to eat and drink it in *"memory"* of Him. The *"memory"* (or memorial) is the fulfilment of Ex 12:14 *"...a memorial feast for you..."*, *"as a perpetual institution."* (Ex 12:14). The act of taking the <u>bread</u>, <u>blessing it</u>, and <u>distributing it</u>, is performed by a priest at every Catholic Mass in the world to fulfill the command of Jesus to: *"do this in memory of me."* (Lk 22:19) And (from the Old Testament) *"as a perpetual institution."* (Ex 12:14).

11. The Road to Emmaus:

The New Testament account of the Road to Emmaus is a very interesting story, part of which is as follows:

Lk 24: ₁₃ *Now that very day* [the 1ˢᵗ Easter Sunday] *two of them* [disciples – one named Cleopas] *were going to a village seven miles from Jerusalem called Emmaus,* ₁₄ *and they were conversing about all the things that had occurred...* ₁₅ *Jesus himself drew near and walked with them but their eyes were prevented from recognizing him. He asked them, "what are you discussing as you walk along?"*

Notice that they were prevented from recognizing Jesus. Then after His question, the disciples proceeded to explain about the Jesus of Nazarene: Lk 24 ₂₀ ... *how our chief priests and rulers both handed him over to a sentence of death and crucified him...* ₂₁ *But we were hoping that he would be the one to redeem Israel; and besides all this, it is now* <u>*the third day*</u> *since this took place.* ₂₂ *Some women from our group, however, have astounded us: they were at the tomb early in the morning* ₂₃ *and did not find his body; they came back and reported that they had indeed seen a vision of angels who announced that he was alive.* ₂₅ *And He [Jesus] said to them, "Oh, how foolish you are! How slow of heart to* <u>*believe all that the prophets spoke!*</u> ₂₆ *Was it not necessary that the Messiah should suffer these things and enter into his glory?"* ₂₇ *Then beginning with Moses and all the prophets, He interpreted to them what referred to Him in all the scriptures.*

Notice the above Bible quotation "*believe all that the prophets spoke*", is another reference pointing to the fulfillment of things in the Old Testament. Two of the many prophecies in the Old Testament fulfilled in the New Testament by Jesus:

Old Testament:	New Testament – Fulfilled:
Ps 110:4 *You are a* <u>*priest*</u> *forever, According to the order of* <u>*Melchizedek.*</u>	Heb 5:5–6 *In the same way, it was not Christ who glorified himself in becoming high* <u>*priest*</u>*, but rather the one who said to him: ... "You are a priest forever according to the order of* <u>*Melchizedek.*</u>*"*
Is 53: 1 *Who would* <u>*believe*</u> *what we have heard? To whom has the arm of the Lord been revealed.*	Jn 12:37 *Although he had performed so many signs in their presence they did not* <u>*believe*</u> *him, in order that the word which Isaiah the prophet spoke might be fulfilled: "to whom has the might of the Lord been revealed?"*

Continuing on; when the disciples arrived in Emmaus:

Lk 24: ₃₀*And it happened that, while He* [Jesus] *was with them at table, He took bread, said the blessing, broke it, and gave it to them.* ₃₁ *With that their eyes were opened and they recognized Him, but He vanished from their sight.*

Notice the same words as the Last Supper of taking the bread, blessing it, breaking it, and giving it. This was the very first Mass performed by Jesus Himself (after His Resurrection). One might question; why did Jesus vanish after giving them the bread? The only logical answer is that Jesus was showing us that His glorified, resurrected body is in the bread (real presence in the Holy Communion, Eucharist).

Lk 24: 35 *Then the two recounted what had taken place on the way and He was made known to them in the breaking of the bread.*

St. Paul established a Christian community in Corinth about the year 51AD, where they continued the perpetual institution of bread and wine. There apparently was some misunderstanding in Corinth regarding the Lords Supper for St. Paul to write the following:

1 Cor 11: ₂₇ *Therefore whoever eats the bread or drinks the cup of the Lord unworthily will have to answer for the body and blood of the Lord.* ₂₈ *A person should examine himself, and so eat the bread and drink the cup.* ₂₉ *For anyone who eats and drinks without discerning the body, eats and drinks judgement on himself.*

Two important elements in the above: (1) "*the cup of the Lord*" tells us that the Lord is present in the cup. (2) It is very clear here that these early Christians believed in the Real Presence in the bread and wine, otherwise, why such a stern warning of "*judgment*" if eaten "*without discerning?*" St. Paul is establishing himself as having the authority and also pointing out the proper way to celebrate the Eucharist according to the instructions from Jesus:

1 Cor 11 ₂₃ *For I* [St. Paul] *received from the Lord what I also handed on to you, that the Lord Jesus, on the night he was handed over, took bread,* ₂₄ *and, after he had given thanks, broke it and said, "This is my body that is for you. Do this in remembrance of me."* ₂₅ *In the same way also the cup, after supper, saying, "This cup is the new covenant in my blood. Do this, as often as you drink it, in remembrance of me."* ₂₆ *For as often as you eat this bread and drink the cup, you proclaim the death of the Lord until he comes.*

The Hebrew definition of *"remembrance"* or *"memory"* is to re–live. We may interpret memory to just recall to mind, but the meaning here is to re–live. We are told here to do (re–live) this **often,** just as in the prayer Jesus gave us: *"give us this day our daily bread"*. To "proclaim" is to announce officially as being true. Therefore, at every Catholic Mass when we eat His Bread and/or drink the **Cup of the Lord** we publicly announce (proclaim) that Christ is really present.

The Jewish tradition is to fast prior to the Passover, just as Catholics fast (one hour) prior to Mass. Also, similar to above, the people at Mass are led by the priest to a prayer of forgiveness (discerning) prior to the Eucharist.

12. **Vision of Heavenly Worship** (The title of Revelation chapter 4):
The Catholic Mass is modeled after St. John's *"Vision of Heavenly Worship"* in the book of Revelation chapters 4 and 5. In addition to many of the words in the Catholic Mass prayers being from scripture, the Mass structure and form itself is modeled according to Scripture (Rev 4 & 5). However, the most important point is that the Mass follows the command of Jesus, as Scripture states, *"do this in memory of me"* (Luke 22:19). Also, one can conclude that attending a Catholic Mass is as close to *"Heavenly Worship"* (as described in scripture) here on earth that one can possible experience.

The following chart lists the passages in scripture of St. John's *"Vision of Heavenly Worship"* that relates to our earthly worship in the Catholic Mass.

SCRIPTURE QUOTATIONS FROM Revelation CHAPTER 4 AND 5	HOW SCRIPTURE RELATES TO THE CATHOLIC MASS
(4:2) *"A throne was there in heaven"* {1}	just as there is a special chair for the priest at Mass to represent the throne.
(4:4) *"twenty–four elders"* {2}	meaning the 12 tribes of Israel and the 12 Apostles (as described in Rev 21:12–14), represents the priest(s) at Mass.
(4:4) *"white garments"*	or vestments similar to those used by a priest at mass.

SCRIPTURE QUOTATIONS FROM Revelation CHAPTER 4 AND 5	HOW SCRIPTURE RELATES TO THE CATHOLIC MASS
(4:5) *"Seven flaming torches"* {3}	means the Menorah's 7 candles which are represented by the candles at every Catholic Mass.
(4:8) *"four living creatures"* {4} *"exclaiming: Holy, holy, holy is the Lord God almighty"* {5}	similar to Holy, holy, holy sung at Mass (the Sanctus).
(4:10) *"elders fall down before the one who sits on the throne and worship him, who lives forever and ever."* {6}	Just as the people kneel, stand and sit to honor certain parts of the Mass and the intention of Mass is to *"worship him"*
(4:11) *Glory and honor and power* {7}	Said at Mass following the "Our Father"
(5:1) *"I saw a scroll in the right hand of the one who sat on the throne"* {8}	Just as there are scripture readings at Mass from the sacred book (scroll).
(5:3) *"open the scroll with its seven seals"* {9}	Representing the New Covenant of the Lamb who is honored at every Mass.
5:6) *"a Lamb that seemed to have been slain"* {10}	Representing the risen Christ and the display of the Cross with Christ's body in every Catholic Church. (*)
(5:8) *"a harp"* {11}	Representing the music at most Masses.
(5:9) *"they sang a new hymn"* {12}	At every Mass, psalms of praise are usually sung.
(5:11) *"I looked again and heard the voices of angels who surrounded the throne and the living creatures and the elders. They were countless in number, and they cried out in a loud voice: "Worthy is the Lamb that was slain…"*	Tradition tells us that there are many angels present at every mass. *"Worthy is the Lamb…"* is paralleled in the prayers at the Communion Rite.
(5:14) *"The four living creatures answered, "Amen"*	just as at Mass the people respond "Amen"

(*) Note: A lamb slain is recognized by the Jews because the slain lamb is fastened to a spit that is in the shape of a cross, one of the reasons the Catholic Church displays the body of Christ on the crucifix.

The bracketed numbers {} noted in the above chart are further explained with the following excerpt quotes from the footnotes of the "Didache Bible":

{1} The vision of the <u>throne</u> recalls the prophecies of Isaiah (chapter 6) and (Ez 1:26–28)

{2} The <u>twenty–four elders</u> probably represent the Twelve Tribes of Israel and the Twelve Apostles, the Israel of old and the New Israel.

{3} <u>seven torches</u>: these symbolize the Holy Spirit and his seven gifts; it also recalls the Spirit who maintained the seven flames of a lampstand (Zec 4:1–6, CCC 1831)

{4} The early Church Fathers associated the <u>four living creatures</u> with the four Gospel writers. The singing of the <u>living creatures</u> represents the worship of the Pilgrim Church on earth, which is united to the worship of the <u>elders</u>, representing the just souls in the Church in Heaven. The celebration of the Eucharist, though celebrated here on earth, includes the saints in Heaven where Christ reigns with the Father (CCC 293, 662, 2642)

{5} <u>Holy, holy, holy</u>: The threefold repetition indicates unsurpassed holiness. This phrase, derived from Isaiah 6:3, is repeated at every Mass in the Sanctus at the beginning of the Eucharist Prayer. The triple repetition of the word "Holy" also points to the Trinity: one God in three persons. (CCC 559)

{6} Regarding the <u>elders,</u> see {4} above.

{7} <u>Glory and honor and power</u>: This recalls the doxology following the Lord's prayer at Mass.

{8} and {9} The sacred <u>scroll</u> contains the details of God's plan. Only Christ – described here as the Lion of Judah and the Root of David – is worthy to open and reveal its contents. For this reason, the <u>scroll</u> may be a type, or figure, of Scripture. (CCC 663)

{10} Christ is the <u>Lamb</u> of the New Passover who has been sacrificed but is alive again, risen from the dead to ransom all people through his Blood.

{11} The <u>harp</u> represents liturgical song, and the bowls of incense represent the prayers of the saints and martyrs, who intercede for the faithful on earth (Ps 142:2; Rev 8:3–4)

{12} The <u>hymn</u> of all creatures that follows praises both Christ and God the Father ("him who sits upon the throne") in similar terms that affirm the co–equality of the First and Second Persons of the Trinity. (CCC 328–336, 449,2642,2855) (end of the Bible footnote quotations)

Continuing on in scripture, at the end of time, St. John in Revelation 19:7 tells us:

For the wedding day of the Lamb has come, his bride has made herself ready.

Experts tell us that the "bride" represents the church and all its saints. Then in Rev 22:2 ***"...On either side of the river grew the <u>tree of life</u>...*** Which brings us full circle, pointing back ***to <u>the tree of life</u>*** in Genesis chapter 3.

There are many additional places in scripture that point toward the Sacrifice of the Mass and the Eucharist than those mentioned herein. Therefore, just considering the few numbers of prophecies and foreshadowing (pointed out herein), that have been fulfilled, certainly could not have been by accident but only by the design by God Himself.

"Let Scripture Speaks for itself on the Eucharist" tells us that "***The Bread***", "***My Body***," "***My Blood***" <u>is</u> the resurrected, glorified Living Body, and divinity of Jesus Christ.

Jesus Himself is quoted in scripture as saying:
John 6:35 ***I am <u>the bread</u> of life***
John 6:41 ***I am <u>the bread</u> that came down from heaven***
John 6:48 ***I am <u>the bread</u> of life***
John 6:51 ***I am <u>the living bread</u>…, <u>the bread</u> that I will give is <u>my flesh</u> for the life of the world.***
John 6:54 ***Whoever eats <u>my flesh</u> and drinks <u>my blood</u> has eternal life***
John 6:55 ***For <u>my flesh</u> is true food, and <u>my blood</u> is true drink.***

Therefore, one has to conclude that Jesus Christ's institution of the Eucharist is where He offered His Body and His Blood as food for our salvation which is under the appearance of bread and wine (Holy Communion).

Saint Justin Martyr (100–165) wrote:
We call this food Eucharist. For not as common bread nor common drink do we receive these. The food which has been made into the Eucharist by the Eucharistic prayer set down by Him…is both the flesh and the blood of that incarnate Jesus.

SUMMARY – EUCHARIST:
1. Eucharist Names: The Bread, the Cup, Last Supper, my Flesh, Living Bread, and my Body, used in scripture. (Lk 21:19,20; 1 Cor 11:20; 10:19)
2. The Fall of Mankind: the first sin was eating from the forbidden "Tree of Life" and is the first mention of bread to signify its importance. (Gn 3:19)

3. The First Sacrifice: Genesis has the first mention of sacrifice in scripture where Abel offered the firstborn male from his flock that was looked upon by God as favorable, to prefigure the Sacrifice of Jesus. (Gn 4:4; Ex 34:19)

4. The Prefigured Sacrifice of the Mass: Melchizedek "*priest of God Most High*" (Heb 7:1) foreshadowed Jesus by offering bread and wine to prefigure the Sacrifice of the Mass. (Gn 14:18)

5. The Prefiguration of Calvary: Isaac, Abraham's first son, willingly offered himself for sacrifice that foreshadowed God's only son, Christ's willing sacrifice on Calvary. (Gn 22:9; Lk 22:42)

6. The Miracle of Manna: The bread from heaven that the Jews ate, foreshadows Jesus from heaven and the Eucharist for us to eat. There are many elements of the Jewish Passover that prefigure Christ: without sin, willed by the Father, blood of the Lamb, use of hyssop, bread, a memorial, and a perpetual institution that were all fulfilled by Christ. (Ex 16:4; JN 6:41)

7. The Mysteries of the Tabernacle: The Tabernacle of Moses was designed to reflect the sacrifice that occurred on Mount Sinai where Moses and the elders experienced it with God. The Tabernacle of Moses is where the "Holy of Holies" represents God the Father, the "Bread of the Presence" represents the Son of God (bread from heaven), and the "Holy Place" (lampstand) represents the holy Spirit, all of course representing the Trinity. (Ex 24:8; MT36:28)

8. The Miracles of Jesus: Prefigured by Moses, water to wine at Cana, multiplication of bread for 5000, and for 4000, prove that Jesus has the power over all things including his spiritual body and divinity present in the Eucharist. (Dt 18:18; Jn 6:14)

9. The Bread of Life Discourse: This tells us that we need to first of all have faith in the divinity of Christ in order to accept His instructions to eat His resurrected Body (Eucharist) and to understand His spirituality. (Jn 6:22–59)

10. The Last Supper: That was performed by Jesus fulfills the Jewish Passover: blood of the Lamb, the bread, in memory, and perpetual institution. Also, the statements in scripture (pointed out) prove the early Christians believed in Christ's Real Presence in the Breaking of Bread (Eucharist). (Lk 22:7–8,19–20)

11. The Road to Emmaus: This is the scripture story where the resurrected Jesus performed the first Holy Mass. Also, the many statements in scripture, pointed out herein, that prove scripture has signs, symbols, and prophesies that were fulfilled in Jesus.
12. Heavenly Worship: The Catholic Mass worshiping parallels the Heavenly Worship as described in the book of Revelation. Also, the Catholic Church design elements resembles the Heavenly Worship design, Tabernacle of Moses, as described in scripture. (Rev 4 & 5)

Regarding the Eucharist, also see: Chapter 6, "Miracles of the word of Jesus"; and Chapter 9, "How can the body and blood of Christ be in communion?"

References:
The **bold and italicized** Bible quotes are from The New American Bible, St. Joseph Edition.
Certain words may be <u>underlined</u> for emphasis added.
Some statements herein may be similar to short excerpts from the Augustine Institute publication called "Eucharist", South Syracuse Way, Suite 310, Greenwood Village, CO 8011 and Brant Pitre's video titled "Eucharist" available on Formed.org.
A copy of the EUCHARIST section was submitted to Augustine Institute 7 April 2017.

Additional supporting resources on the Eucharist:
1. "Road to Emmaus" by Dr. Brant Pitre – Study Program – https://store.catholicproductions.com.
2. "Jews & Jewish Roots of the Eucharist" by Dr. Brant Pitre – www.BrantPitre.com.
3. "A Father Who Keeps His Promises" by Dr. Scott Hahn – available through Dynamic Catholic https://cart.dynamiccatholic.com.

EUCHARIST: Compiled by Paul Wilchek, edited by Kristin Trepanier–Henry, and reviewed by Father Carl Birarelli, 2017.

THE HOLY MASS

This has two parts:
History of the Roman Catholic Mass, providing a brief background of the development of the Catholic Mass to what it is today.

The Holy Mass in Scripture, which is a listing of most of the prayers said at the Catholic Mass showing which words are from scripture.

History of the Roman Catholic Mass
The year 33 AD:
The First Mass was instituted by Jesus Christ at the Last Supper, on the first Holy Thursday. The unbloody sacrifice of the Last Supper is a memorial of Christ's bloody sacrifice on the cross and the fulfillment of the sacrifices of the Old Testament. In the year 33AD Jesus stated in Luke 22:19–20 *Then He took the bread, said the blessing, broke it, and gave it to them, saying, "This is my body, which will be given for you; do this in memory of me." And likewise the cup after they had eaten saying, "This cup is the new covenant in my blood, which will be shed for you."* The act of taking the bread, blessing it, breaking it, and distributing it, is performed by a priest at every Catholic Mass in the world to fulfill the command of Jesus to: ***"do this in memory of me"*** and as prophesied in the Old Testament ***"as a perpetual institution."*** (Ex 12:14)

Jesus also said Mass after His resurrection with two disciples in Emmaus: Luke 24: 30–31 *And it happened that, while He* [Jesus] *was with them at table, He took bread, said the blessing, broke it, and gave it to them. With that their eyes were opened and they recognized Him, but He vanished from their sight.* Christ vanished from their sight to signify and verify that he was now present within the Eucharist.

The year 51 AD:
About the year 51AD, St. Paul established a Christian community in Corinth where they continued the ***"perpetual institution"*** (Ex 12:14) of bread and wine. This is the earliest written account of the Christian Eucharist. St. Paul writes to the Corinthians, 1 Cor 11: 27–29 *Therefore whoever eats the bread or drinks the cup of the Lord unworthily will*

have to answer for the body and blood of the Lord. A person should examine himself, and so eat the bread and drink the cup. For anyone who eats and drinks without discerning the body, eats and drinks judgment on himself. There are two important elements in this passage: (1) *"the cup of the Lord"* tells us that the Lord is present in the bread and the cup. (2) It is very clear here that these early Christians believed in the real presence in the Eucharist, otherwise, why such a stern warning of *"judgement"* if the Eucharist is taken *"without discerning the body"* ahead of time?

The year 62 TO 63 AD:
The book of Acts was written between the year 62 to 63 AD, Acts 2: 42, tells us, *They devoted themselves to the teaching of the apostles and to the communal life, to the <u>breaking of the bread</u> and to the prayers.* Then verse 46 states: *Every day they devoted themselves to meeting together in the temple area and to <u>breaking bread</u> in their homes.* The early Christians met in the Temple for the Old Testament readings, after which they went to homes to share in the Eucharist. In A.D. 70, after the destruction of the Temple, the Christians did their own Scripture readings along with the Eucharist and as they expanded, they started having services in small churches.

The year 80 AD:
In 1983 an original copy of a document called "The Didache", also known as "The Teaching of the Twelve Apostles" was discovered in an accent Constantinople Monastery of which scholars verified its organ to be the year 80 AD (according to some theologians it may have been completed in A.D 50 to 110). In the year 80 AD, St. John the Apostle was still alive, he died in 103 AD at the age of 97. "The Didache" document instructs early converts on the ethics and practices on how to be a Christian. "The Didache" includes descriptions of the rituals of Baptism (including using the Sign of The Cross on a candidate's forehead), fasting, and a description of the Eucharist Ritual (being the very first known text using the term Eucharist). This verifies (in writing) that the early Christians believed in the real presence in the Eucharist, which was during the time when the Apostle John was still live, with him being a firsthand witness of the true intentions of Jesus Christ.

The year 110 AD:

One of the early Fathers of the Church, St. Ignatius of Antioch (at the age of 75, died 110 AD), was a disciple of St. John the Apostle. St. Ignatius wrote about Mary as the mother of God and is the first written recorded use of the term "Catholic." In his letter to the Romans he stated, "I have no taste for the food that parishes...I want the Bread of God which is the flesh of Christ... and for drink I desire His blood, which is love that cannot be destroyed." He also referred to the Holy Eucharist as "medicine of immortality."

Justin Martyr (100–165) wrote one of the oldest descriptions of the Rite of the Mass which is very similar to today's Mass. When describing the Eucharist, Justin refers to "bread and wine and water" and emphasizes that when blessed, it becomes the body and blood of Christ: a quote from Justin, *"For not as common bread and common drink do we receive these; but in like manner as Jesus Christ our Savior, having been made flesh by the Word of God, had both flesh and blood for our salvation, so likewise we have been taught that the food which is blessed by the prayer of His word, and from which out blood and flesh by transmutation are nourished, is the flesh and blood of that Jesus who was made flesh."*

Note: "transmutation" is the action of changing or the state of being changed into another form.

In the first century, the Christians shared a full meal including the breaking of the bread as part of Christian Communities. Then in the second and third centuries through the influence of Ignatius of Antioch, Justin Martyr, and others, the Mass developed to reding scripture and the use of bread and wine that was no longer associated with a full meal. By the fourth century Christianity was granted the status of legal religion and viewed with favor by the Roman Emperors. At that point in time, the Mass took on a more formal appearance with the use of vestments, candles, incense, and formal prayers.

The Early Mass:
+ Christians gathered to celebrate the Eucharist on Sunday
+ They did readings from the Old and New Testaments, had a homely, and said prayers of the faithful

+ There was a procession with bread and wine, the Eucharist Prayer was said, and they distributed communion (*)
+ A collection was taken for the poor
+ The elements of our modern mass not included in the Early Mass: Our Father, Entrance Rite, Penitential Rite, and the Creed

(*) Note: Initially in the early Church, the Bishops were the only ones that could concentrate the Bread and Wine. Therefore, they had "runners" that took the Eucharist to other churches. Eventually this became impractical, so the bishops ordained (passed on this rite) so the Priests could concentrate the Bread and Wine.

The year 590:
The 64th Pope St. Gregory the Great (590–604) established the cannon of the Mass that has remained unchanged for over 1,000 years.

The year 597:
Augustine of Canterbury a monk who became Archbishop of Canterbury in 597 introduced the Roman Mass to Germany, England, and was accepted in Ireland.

The year 800:
Charlemagne (Charles the Great) Emperor of the Romans from 800 to 814, encouraged the use of the Roman Rite Mass throughout his empire.

The year 1545 to 1572:
The 19th Ecumenical Council of the Catholic Church (1545–1563) confirmed the seven sacraments of the Church and established the "Tridentine Mass", which is the Latin form of the Mass, that remained in effect for over 395 years. This council also first used the term "transubstantiation." The Roman Missel was published first in 1570 through to 1962. Over time, a few popes made minor changes to the Missel.

Note: "transubstantiation" is the conversion of the substance of the Eucharist elements into the body and blood of Jesus Christ, only the appearances of bread and wine remain.

The 225th Pope Pius V (1566–1572) enforced the use of the Tridentine (Latin) Mass.

The 261ˢᵗ Pope John XXIII (1958–1963) added the Blessed Virgin Mary and St. Joseph to the Eucharistic Prayer. Other than minor changes, the Eucharistic Prayer has remined about the same for well over 1,000 years.

The year 1962:
The Second Vatican Council (1962–1965) and by the 262ⁿᵈ Pope Paul VI (1963–1978) replaced the Tridentine (Latin) Mass of 1570 with the local vernacular language Mass, the priest to face the people, and women no longer had to cover their hair.

The year 2002:
In the year 2002, the 264ᵗʰ Pope John Paul II (1978–2005) made some revisions to the Mass of Pope Paul VI, which is the Mass of today.

The Holy Mass in Scripture
Some people may have wondered where all the prayers at mass came from. As you will see, a large amount came directly from scripture. In the following actual Mass prayers, the ***bold and italicized words*** are the words from scripture followed by the (scripture chapter & verse where they can be found). In some cases, due to various translations, the actual scripture passage may be worded slightly different, however, the meaning is the same.

THE INTRODUCTORY RITES

GREETING OF THE ASSEMBLED PEOPLE:
In the name of the Father, and the Son, and the Holy Spirit (Mt 28:19).
<u>Response</u>: ***Amen*** (1Chr 16:36).

<u>Form A</u>: ***The grace of our Lord Jesus Christ, and the love of God, and the communion of the Holy Spirit be with you all*** (2 Cor 13:13).

<u>Form B</u>: ***Grace to you and peace from God our Father and the Lord Jesus Christ*** (Rom 1:7; 1 Cor1:3; Gal 1:3; Col 1:2; 1 Thes 1:1; Rev 1:4).

<u>Form C</u>: ***The Lord be with you*** (Ruth 2:4; Jgs 6:12; Chr 15:2; Lk 1:28).
<u>Response</u>: ***And with your spirit*** (2 Tm 4:22).

On certain Sundays especially during Easter season, instead of the Penitential Act, a blessing and sprinkling of holy water may take place.

THE PENITENTIAL ACT:
Brethren, let us **acknowledge our sins** (1 John 1:9), and so prepare ourselves to celebrate the sacred mysteries.

Response:
Form A: *I confess to almighty God and to you, my brothers and sisters, that **I have greatly sinned** (1 Chr 21:8), **in my thoughts** (2 Chr 10:5; Mt 5:28; Phil 4:8) and **in my words** (Jas 3:5), in what I have done and in what I have **failed to do** (Jas 4:17; Lk 10:30–32), [striking one's breast] (Lk 18:13) through my fault, through my fault, through my most grievous fault; therefore I ask blessed Mary ever–Virgin, all the Angels and Saints, and you, my **brothers and sisters**, to **pray for me** (1 Thes 5:25) to the Lord our God.*

Form B: **Have mercy on us, O Lord. For we have sinned against you** (1 Jn 1:9). Show us, O Lord, your mercy. And grant us your salvation.

Form C: **Lord, have mercy. Christ, have mercy. Lord, have mercy** (Tb 8:4; 1 Tm 1:2).
Or: Kyrie, eleison. Christie, eleison. Kyrie, eleison.

GLORIA:
The Gloria is omitted during Advent, Lent, and most weekdays
Glory to God in the highest, and on earth peace to people of good will (Lk 2:14). We praise you; **we bless you**; we adore you; **we glorify you** (Rev 7:12); **we give you thanks** (Eph 5:20) for your great glory, Lord God heavenly King, **O God almighty Father** (Rev 19:6). Lord **Jesus Christ, only Begotten Son** (2 Jn 3), Lord God, **Lamb of God, Son of the Father, you take away the sins of the world** (Jn 1:29), have mercy on us; you take away the sins of the world, receive our prayer; you are seated **at the right hand of the Father** (Rom 8:34), have mercy on us. **For you alone are the Holy One** (Rev 15:4), **you alone are the Lord, you alone are the Most High** (Ps 83:19), Jesus Christ, with **the Holy Spirit** (Jn 14:26), in the glory of God the Father. **Amen.**

COLLECT

FIRST READING
(After the reading) Reader: *The word of the Lord* (1 Pt 1:25).

Response: *Thanks be to God* (Rom 7:25).

RESPONSORIAL PSALM (may be sung)

SECOND READING
(After the reading) Reader: *The word of the Lord* (1 Pt 1:25).
Response: *Thanks to be God* (Rom 7:25).

GOSPEL READING
Before the Gospel:
Acclamation is sung (Cantor then all): **Alleluia, alleluia, alleluia.**
    During Lent (Cantor then all); Praise and honor to you, O Lord
    Jesus Christ.
Deacon or priest: *The Lord be with you* (2 Thes 3:16). Response: *And*
with your spirit (Gal 6:18)
Deacon or priest: A reading from the holy Gospel according to _____
    Response: Praise to you, Lord Jesus Christ.

HOMILY

PROFESSION OF FAITH:
I believe in one God, the Father almighty, maker of heaven and earth, of
all things visible and invisible (Col 1:16).

I believe in one Lord Jesus Christ, the *Only Begotten Son* (Jn 1:18) of
God, born of the Father before all ages. God from God, Light from Light,
true God from true God, begotten, not made, consubstantial with the
Father; *through him all things were made* (Jn 1:3). For us men and for
salvation *he came down from heaven* (Jn 3:13).
(All bow at the following words up to: and became man.)
And by *the Holy Spirit was incarnate of the Virgin Mary* (Lk 1:35).
And became man (Jn 1:14).

For our sake he was *crucified under Pontius Pilate* (Jn 19:16), *he suffered death and was buried and rose again on the third day I accordance with Scripture* (1 Cor 15:3–4). *He ascended into heaven* (Lk 25:51) and is *seated at the right hand of the Father* (Col 3:1). *He will come again in glory* (2 Thes 21:1) to *judge the living and the dead* (2 Tm 4:1; Acts10:42) and *his kingdom will have no end* (Lk 1:33).

I believe *in the Holy Spirit* (2 Cor 3:17), the Lord, *the giver of life* (2 Cor 3:6), who *proceeds from the Father* (Jn 15:26) and the Son who with the Father and the Son is adored and glorified, *who has spoken through the prophets* (2 Pt 1:21; 1 Pt 1:10–11).

I believe in one, holy, *catholic and apostolic Church* (1 Tm 3:15; Mt 28:18–20). I confess *one Baptism* (Eph 4:4–6) *for the forgiveness of sins* (Acts 2:38) and I look forward to the *resurrection of the dead and the life of the world to come* (Rom 6:5). *Amen.*

PRAYER OF THE FAITHFUL

The people respond to each petition as follows:
Deacon or cantor: Let us pray to the Lord.
<u>Response</u>: Lord, here our prayer. Or: Lord, have mercy.

LITURGY OF THE EUCHARIST

PRESENTATION AND PREPARATION OF THE GIFTS:
Priest: *Blessed are you, Lord God* (1 Chr 29:10; Ps 89:52; Rom 9:5) of all creation, for through your goodness we have received the bread we offer you: *fruit of the earth* (Jas 5:7) and work of human hands, it will become for us *the bread of life* (Jn 6:48).

People: Blessed be God forever.

Blessed are you, Lord God of all creation, for through your goodness we have received the wine we offer you: *fruit of the vine* (Mt 26:29; Lk 22:18) and work of human hands, it will become our *spiritual drink* (1 Cor 10:4).

People: Blessed be God forever.

Private Prayer of the Priest: ***With humble spirit and contrite heart may we be accepted by you*** (Dn 3:39), O Lord, and may our sacrifice in your sight this day be pleasing to you, Lord God. ***Wash me, O Lord from my iniquity and cleanse me from my sin*** (Ps 51:4).

Priest: Pray, brethren (brothers and sisters), that my sacrifice and yours may ***be acceptable to God, the almighty Father*** (Heb 12:28).

People rise and reply: May the Lord accept the sacrifice at your hands for the praise and glory of his name, for our good and the good of all his holy Church.

Priest says the prayer over the offerings and all respond: ***Amen.***

PRAYER OVER THE OFFERINGS – THE EUCHARISTIC PRAYER:

Priest: The Lord be with you.　　　People: And with your spirit.

Priest: ***Lift up your hearts*** (Lam 3:41).　People: We lift them up to the Lord.

Priest: ***Let us give thanks to the Lord our God*** (Col 3:17).　People: It is right and just.

EUCHARIST PRAYER I: (or see EUCHARIST PRAYER II)

To you, therefore, most merciful Father, we make humble prayer and petition through Jesus Christ, your Son, and Lord: that you accept and bless these gifts, these offerings, these holy and unblemished sacrifices, which we offer you firstly for your holy catholic church. Be pleased to grant her peace, to guard, unite and govern her throughout the whole world, together with our servant _____ our Pope and _____ our Bishop, and all those who, holding to the truth, hand on the catholic and apostolic faith.

Remember, Lord, your servants (Ps 106:4) _____ and _____, and all gathered here, whose faith and devotion are known to you. For them, ***we offer you this sacrifice of praise*** (Heb 13:15) or they offer it for themselves and all who are dear to them: for the redemption of their souls, in hope of health and well–being, and praying their homage *to you, the eternal God* (Jer 10:10), living and true.

In communion with those whose memory we venerate, especially the glorious ever–Virgin Mary *Mother of our God and Lord, Jesus Christ* (Lk 1:43) and blessed Joseph, her Spouse, your blessed Apostles and Martyrs, *Peter and Paul, Andrew, (James, John, Thomas, James, Philip, Bartholomew, Matthew, Simon and Jude; Linus, Cletus, Clement, Sixtus, Cornelius, Cyprian, Lawrence, Chrysogonus, John and Paul, Cosmas and Damian)* (Lk 6:13–16; Mt 10:2–4; Mk 3:14–19) and all your Saints; we ask that through their merits and prayers, in all things we may be defended by your protecting help.

Therefore, Lord, we pray: graciously accept this oblation of our service, that of your whole family; order our days in your peace, and command that we be delivered from eternal damnation and *counted among the flock* (Jn 10: 14,16) of those you have chosen.

Be pleased, O God, we pray, to bless, acknowledge, and approve this offering in every respect; make it *spiritual and acceptable* (Rom 12:1), so that it may become for us the Body and Blood of your most beloved Son, our Lord Jesus Christ.

On the day before he was to suffer, he took bread in his holy and venerable hands, and with *eyes raised to heaven to you, O God* (Mt 14:19; Mk 6:41; Lk 9:16), his almighty Father, giving you thanks, *he said the blessing, broke the bread and gave it to his disciples* (Lk 22:19), saying:
TAKE THIS, ALL OF YOU, *AND EAT OF IT* (Mk 26:26; Mk 14:22), *FOR THIS IS MY BODY, WHICH WILL BE GIVEN UP FOR YOU* (Lk 22:19).

In a similar way when supper was ended (Lk 22:20), he took this precious chalice in his holy and venerable hands, and once more giving you thanks, he said the blessing and gave the chalice to his disciples, saying:

TAKE THIS, ALL OF YOU, AND DRINK FROM IT, FOR THIS IS THE CHALICE OF MY BLOOD, THE BLOOD OF THE NEW

AND ETERNAL COVENANT (Mt 26:27–28; Heb 13:20), ***WHICH WILL BE POURED OUT FOR YOU AND FOR MANY FOR THE FORGIVENESS OF SIN*** (Mt 26:28). ***DO THIS IN MEMORY OF ME*** (1 Cor 11:25; Lk 22:16).

Therefore, O Lord, as we celebrate the memorial of the blessed Passion, the Resurrection from the dead, and the glorious Ascension into heaven of Christ, your Son, our Lord, we, your servants and your holy people, offer to your glorious majesty from the gifts that you have given us, this ***pure victim, this holy victim, this spotless victim*** (1 Pet 1:18–19; Heb 9:13), the holy Bread of eternal life and ***the Chalice of everlasting salvation*** (Ps 116:12).

Be pleased to look upon these offerings with a serene and kindly countenance, and to accept them, as once you were pleased to accept ***the gifts of your servant Abel*** (Heb 11:4; Gn 4:4) and just, ***the sacrifice of Abraham*** (Gn 22:1–14), our father in faith. And the offering of your high priest ***Melchizedek, a holy sacrifice, a spotless victim*** Gn 14:18; Heb 5:10). In humble prayer we ask you, almighty God: command that these gifts be borne by the hands of your ***holy Angel to your altar on high in the sight of your divine majesty*** (Rev 8:3–4), so that all of us, who through this ***participation at the altar*** (1 Cor 10:18) receive the most holy Body and Blood of your Son, may be filled with ***every grace and heavenly blessing*** (Eph 1:3).

Remember also, Lord, your servants _____ and _____, who have gone before us with the sign of faith and rest in the sleep of peace.

Grant them, O Lord, we pray, and ***all who sleep in Christ*** (1 Thes 4:14), a place of refreshment, light and peace.

To us, also, your servants, who, through sinners, hope in your abundant mercies, graciously grant some share and fellowship with your holy Apostles and Martyrs: with John the Baptist, Stephen, Matthias, Barnabas, (Ignatius, Alexander, Marcellinus, Peter, Felicity. Perpetua, Agatha, Lucy, Agnes, Cecilia, Anastasia) and all your Saints; admit us, we beseech you, into their company, not weighing our merits, but grant us your pardon, through Christ our Lord.

Through whom you continue *to make all these good things* (Ps 65:4), O Lord; you sanctify them, fill them with life, bless them, and bestow them upon us.

PREFACE FOR EUCHARIST PRAYER II:
It is truly right and just, our duty and salvation, always and everywhere to give you thanks, Father most holy, through your *beloved Son* (Col 1:13), Jesus Christ, your Word *through whom you made all things* (Jn 1:3), whom you sent as our Savor and Redeemer, incarnate by the Holy Spirit and *born of the Virgin* (Gal 4:4; Mt 1:18; Lk 1:26–35).

Fulfilling your will and gaining for you *a holy people* (1 Pt 2:9), *he stretched out is hands* (Is 65:2; Rom 10:21) as he endured his Passion, so as to *break the bonds of death and manifest the resurrection* (2 Tm 1:10).

And so, with the Angels and all the Saints we declare your glory, as with one voice we acclaim:

SANCTUS (Sing):
Holy, Holy, Holy Lord God of host (Rev 4:8). *Heaven and earth are full of your glory Hosanna in the highest* (Is 6:3). *Blessed is he who comes in the name of the Lord. Hosanna in the highest* (Mt 21:9; Mk 11:9-10).

Form A:
We proclaim your Death. O Lord, and profess your Resurrection until you come again

Form B:
When we eat this Bread and drink this Cup, we proclaim your Death, O Lord, until you come again.

Form C:
Save us, Savior of the world, for by your Cross and Resurrection you have set us free.

EUCHARIST PRAYER II: Thanksgiving & Epiclesis
You are indeed Holy, O Lord, the fount of all holiness (2 Mc 14:36).

Make holy, therefore, these gifts, we pray, by sending down your Spirit upon them *like the dewfall* (Nm 11:9; Ex 16:13), so that they may become for us *the Body and Blood of our Lord Jesus Christ* (Jn 6:49–51).

At the time *he was betrayed* (Mt 26:21) and *entered willingly into his Passion* (Jn 10:17–18), *he took bread and, giving thanks, broke it, and gave it to his disciples*, saying:

TAKE THIS, ALL OF YOU, *AND EAT OF IT* (Mk 26:26; Mk 14:22), *FOR THIS IS MY BODY, WHICH WILL BE GIVEN UP FOR YOU* (Lk 22:19).

In a similar way, when supper was ended, *he took the chalice* (Lk 22:20) and, once more giving thanks, he gave it to his disciples, saying:

TAKE THIS, ALL OF YOU, AND DRINK FROM IT, FOR THIS IS THE CHALICE OF MY BLOOD, THE BLOOD OF THE NEW AND ETERNAL COVENANT (Mt 26:27–28; Heb 13:20), *WHICH WILL BE POURED OUT FOR YOU AND FOR MANY FOR THE FORGIVENESS OF SIN* (Mt 26:28). *DO THIS IN MEMORY OF ME* (1 Cor 11:25; Lk 22:19).

The mystery of faith (1 Tm 3:16).
We proclaim your Death, O Lord, and profess your Resurrection until you come again.

When we eat this Bread and drink the Cup, we proclaim your Death, O Lord, until you come again (Rom 10:9).

Save us, *Savior of the world* (Jn 4:42), for by your Cross and Resurrection you have set us free.

Therefore, as we celebrate the memorial of his Death and Resurrection, we offer you, Lord, *the Bread of life* (Jn 6:35,48) and the *Chalice of salvation, giving thanks that you have held us worthy to be in your presence and minister to you* (Ps 116:12; Dt 10:8; Dt 18:5,7).

Humbly we pray that, partaking of the Body and Blood of Christ, we may be *gathered into one by the Holy Spirit* (Jn 11:51–52).

Remember, Lord, your Church, spread throughout the world, and bring her to the fullness of charity, together with _____ our Pope and _____ our Bishop and all the clergy.

Remember also our brothers and sisters *who have fallen asleep in the hope of the resurrection* (1Thes 4:14), and all who have died in your mercy, welcome them *into the light of your face* (Ps 89:16).

Have mercy on us all, we pray, that with the Blessed Virgin Mary, Mother of God *with the blessed Apostles and all the Saints who have pleased you throughout the ages* (Rom 8:15–17), we may merit to be coheirs to eternal life, and may praise and glorify you through your Son, Jesus Christ.

Concluding Doxology
Through him, and with him, and in him (Rom 11:36), O God, almighty Father in *the unity of the Holy Spirit* (Eph 4:3), all *glory and honor* (Rev 4:11; Eph 3:20–21) is yours, for ever and ever.
People: *Amen* (Neh 8:6; Ps 41:13; Rom 16:27; Heb 13:20–21; Rev 7:12)

COMMUNION RITE

All join in the Lord's Prayer:
Our Father, who art in heaven, hallowed be thy name; thy kingdom come, thy will be done on earth as it is in heaven. Give us this day our daily bread, and forgive us our trespasses, as we forgive those who trespasses against us; and lead us not into temptation, but deliver us from evil (Mt 6:9–13; Lk 11:2–4).

Priest: Deliver us, Lord, we pray, *from every evil* (2 Thes 3:2–3), graciously grant peace in our days, that, by the help of your mercy, we may be always *free from sin* (Rev 1:5–6) and safe from all distress *as we await the blessed hope and coming of our Savior, Jesus Christ* (Titus 2:13).

People: For the *kingdom, the power and the glory are yours now and for ever* (Jude 1:25); (Rev 4:11)

THE RITE OF PEACE:
Priest: Lord Jesus Christ, who said to your Apostles: *Peace I leave you, my peace I give you* (Jn 14:27); look not on our sins, but on the faith of your Church, and graciously grant her peace and unity in accordance with your will. Who live and reign for ever and ever.

People: *Amen.*

Priest: The *peace of the Lord be with you* (Jn 20:21) always.

People: *And with your spirit.*

Priest or Deacon: Let us *offer each other the sign of peace* (Rom 16:16; 1 Cor 16:20; 2 Cor 13:12; 1 Thes 5:26; 1 Pt 5:14).

THE FRACTION OF THE BREAD:
Cantor and People:
Lamb of God, you take away the sins of the world (Jn 1:29), have mercy on us. *Lamb of God, you take away the sins of the world* (Jn 1:29), have mercy on us. *Lamb of God, you take away the sins of the word* (Jn 1:29), grant us peace.
Reference: Rev 5:12 *"Worthy is the Lamb who was slain."*

COMMINGLING:
Priest: May this mingling of the Body and Blood of our Lord Jesus Christ bring eternal life to us who receive it.
Private prayer of the Priest: Lord Jesus Christ, Son of the living God, who, by the will of the Father and the work of the Holy Spirit, through your Death gave life to the world, free me by this, your most holy Bread and Body, from all my sins and from every evil; keep me always faithful to your commandments, and never let me be parted from you.

Or: May the receiving of your Body and Blood, Lord Jesus, not bring me to judgement and condemnation, but through your loving mercy be for me protection in mind and body and a healing remedy.
References: John 6:54 *Whoever eats my flesh and drinks my blood has eternal life, and I will raise him on the last*

day. John 6:51 *whoever eats this bread will live forever; and the bread that I will give is my flesh for the life of the world.* 1 Cor 11:28–29 *A person should examine himself, and so eat the bread and drink the cup. For anyone who eats and drinks without discerning the body, eats and drinks judgement on himself.*

COMMUNION:

Priest: *Behold the lamb of God, behold him who takes away the sins of the world* (Jn 1:29). *Blessed are those called to the supper of the lamb* (Rev 19:9).

People: Lord, *I am not worthy that you should enter under my roof, but only say the word and my soul shall be healed* (Lk 7:6–7; Mt 8:8).

Minister of communion: The Body (Blood) of Christ.

Communicant: *Amen.*

CONCLUDING RITES

GREETING AND FINAL BLESSING:

Priest: *The Lord be with you.*

People: *And with our spirit.*

DISMISSAL:

Form A: Go forth, the Mass is ended.

> Reference: Jn 20:21 *As the Father has sent me, so I am sending you.*

Form B: Go and announce the Gospel of the Lord.

> Reference: Mk 16:15 *Go into the world and preach the gospel to the whole creation.*

Form C: Go in peace, glorifying the Lord by your life.

> Reference: 1 Cor 10:31 *...do all to the glory of God.*

People: *Thanks be to God* (2 Cor 9:15). (End of Mass prayers)

SUMMARY – THE HOLY MASS:

+ The Mass was prophesied in the Old Testament as a pure offering
+ 33 AD – The First Mass was institute by Jesus at the Last Supper (Lk 22:19–20)
+ 33 AD – The second Mass was performed by Jesus in Emmaus with two disciples (Lk 24:30–31)
+ 51 AD – St. Paul established Christian Communities where they Broke Bread together (Eucharist) (1 Cor 11:27–29)
+ 62–63 AD – In the Acts of the Apostles, it tells us about Communal Life of the Christians that Broke Bread together (Acts 2:42)
+ 80 AD – The "Didache" document was written that instructs and explains Baptism and the Eucharist Rite, the first time the term Eucharist was used
+ 110 AD – St. Ignatius and Justin Martyr wrote documents about the early Church and the real presence of Jesus in the Eucharist
+ The Early Mass was celebrated on Sunday and they performed readings, had a homily, prayed, professed with bread and wine, said the Eucharist Prayer, and distributed the Eucharist
+ 590 AD – Pope St. Gregory established the Cannon of the Mass
+ 800 AD – Charles the Great encouraged the use of the Roman Rite Mass
+ 1545 – The 10th Ecumenical Council confirmed the Seven Sacraments of the Church and the "Tridentine Mass" (Latin Mass)
+ 1962–1965 – The Second Vatican Council changed the "Tridentine Mass" to Local Vernacular Language Mass
+ The prayers of the Holy Mass today contain more than 33% of its words directly from scripture

Note:
The words in all the prayers at Mass, excluding the words of the headings and explanations, contain more than 33% that are related to Scripture, this percent does not include the four Scripture reading at Mass.

References:
The **bold and italicized** Bible quotations are from The New American Bible, revised edition, World Publishing. Certain words may be underlined for emphasis added.

Paul Wilchek

WORSHIP, Fourth Edition GIA Publications, Inc., Chicago (the chapter on the Mass 202–222), (the book used by Our Lady of the Angels Church, Lakewood Ranch, Florida).
Wikipedia/wiki/Mass_in_the_Catholic_Church.
Catholic–pages.com/mass/history.asp.
The Mass in Scripture (internet).
THE MASS: Assembled by Paul Wilchek, 10JUN21

## CHAPTER 4

HOLY DAYS AND FEAST DAYS

Holy Days of Obligation (In the USA)

+ January 1, **The Solemnity of Mary, the Holy Mother of God** is in honor of the Blessed Virgin Mary as being the mother of Jesus Christ, the Mother of God.

+ 40 days after Easter, **The Ascension of the Lord** also called **Ascension Thursday** commemorates the bodily ascension of Jesus into heaven after He spent 40 days teaching on earth, and after His death and resurrection.

+ August 15, **The Assumption of The Blessed Virgin Mary.** Mary's assumption into heavenly glory, body and soul was dogmatically defined by Pope Pius XII in the year 1950. The remains (bones) of all the Apostles are accounted for. The early Church was very meticulous in recording where the bones of the Apostles (even including Judas) are buried and there is no record of any relics or bones of Mary. This fact must have been very instrumental for the 260th Pope Pius XII to make his decision in 1950. According to records, Mary lived 11 years after the death of her son Jesus.

+ November 1, **All Saints Day** also called **All Hallows' Day** or **Hallowmas Day** commemorates all the saints of the Church, both known and unknown, who have attained heaven. Also, it commemorates all the martyrs who died due to persecution for their faith. The word Halloween comes from Hallows and means hallowed evening, hundreds of years ago, people dressed up as saints and went door to door, which is the origin of Halloween costumes.

+ December 8, **The Immaculate Conception of the Blessed Virgin Mary** honors the conception of Mary in her mother's (St. Anne) womb without original sin. By her Immaculate Conception she was conceived in the fullness of grace, in the state of closest possible union with God in view of her future role as Mother of God. Pope Pius IX in 1854 first proclaimed the dogma of the Immaculate Conception.

December 25, **The Nativity of the Lord – Christmas**.

The Brief History of Christmas and Advent:

In the year of 200 it is recorded that Clement of Alexandra wrote:

"There are those who have determined not only the year of our Lord's birth, but also the day; and they say it took place in the 28ᵗʰ year of Augustus, and the 25ᵗʰ day of (the Egyptian month) Pachon."

Various factors contributed to the selection of December 25ᵗʰ as a date of Christ's birth. It was the date of the Winter Solstice on the Roman Calendar and it was 9 months after the Vernal Equinox (March 25) – the date linked to the conception of Jesus (now Annunciation). Also, during the time of Jesus, the shepherds would normally herd their sheep, in the evening, into a central sheep pen with other sheep for the night. In the morning the shepherd would call his sheep, they knew his voice, and only the shepherd's sheep would follow him for their day time pastoring. Jesus referred to this Jewish tradition in John 10:27, He said: *"My sheep here my voice and I know them, and they follow me."*

Luke 2:8, tells us that at the time of Jesus's birth the shepherds were: *"keeping the night watch over their flock."* There is only one time of the year that the shepherds watch their sheep at night and that is during the time when the lambs are being born, which occurs during the Winter Solstice. Ironically, the lambs were being born the same time the Lamb of God was born, similar to the parallel where during Jesus' crucifixion, a lamb was being sacrificed in the temple.

Luke 2:7 *...She wrapped Him [Jesus] in swaddling clothes and laid Him in a manger.* Only one other place in scripture a king to be is wrapped in swaddling clothes, thus pointing to Jesus as king. A manger is a feeding trough, symbolizing that Jesus will become food for our salvation.

Records dated the year of 354 states that Christ's birth celebration mass took place in Rome in the year of 336 (during the Roman Emperor Constantine).

Therefore, the first recorded Christ's birth celebration was in the year of 336 under the 34th Pope Marcus, then in the year 337, under the 35th Pope St. Julius I. December 25th was declared the date of Christ's birth. First it was called "Christ's Mass". Then called "Christianmas," then eventually called "Christmas."

Based on the written records of the year 200, it is very possible, and very logical that the early Christians celebrated the birth of Christ from the very beginning but the first written or "recorded" celebration was in the year 336.

The 49th Pope St. Gelasius I (492–496) was the first recorded mention of Advent in France. The 64th Pope St. Gregory I (590–604) established the liturgies for Advent. The 157th Pope Gregory VII (1073–1085) established the four Sundays of Advent prior to Christmas, as we celebrate today.

Easter Sunday, ranked as one of the highest holy days is not listed above because it always falls on a Sunday, which is always a day of obligation. Originally **Easter** was linked to the Jewish Passover. The First Council of Nicaea (325) established an independent computation by Christians to determine the date of **Easter**. Sometime after Nicaea, the date of **Easter** was determined to be the full moon after the Spring Equinox that occurs on or soon after the 21st of March.

Additional Holy Day (celebrated in most of Europe).

The Catholic Cannon Law lists a total of nine holy days other than Sunday, however, the local conference of bishops may suppress some of them or transfer them to a Sunday, which is the case in the USA for the following:

+ January 6, **The Solemnity of the Epiphany of the Lord** (USA celebrates on Sunday) is the celebration of the visit of the Maji (Matthew 2:1–12) to the Christ child, also called "**Three Kings Day**" meaning the manifestation or showing faith by the gentiles as represented by the magi. Also, the manifestation of the divine nature of Jesus Christ. Epiphany was established by Pope Pius V (1566–1572).

+ March 19, **The Solemnity of St. Joseph, Spouse of the Blessed Virgin Mary**, legal father of Jesus Christ is observed, in addition to the Catholic Church, by the Lutherans, and Anglican Church. New Orleans, USA typically celebrates St. Joseph day as well as the Italian and Polish communities.

+ June 29, **Solemnity of Saints Peter and Paul, Apostles** is in honor of the martyrdom, in Rome, of the Apostles Peter and Paul. This has ancient Christian origins and in addition to the Catholic Church, is celebrated by the Eastern Orthodox Church, Lutherans, Oriental Orthodoxy, and Malta.

Marion Feast Days in the Catholic Calendar.
The following are six Marion Fast days in the Catholic calendar:

+ December 12, **Our Lady of Guadalupe**. In December of 1531 St. Juan Diego, Mexico, had five Marian apparitions, one of which, the image of the Blessed Virgin Mary was miraculously imprinted on Juan's cloak, an image that is still venerated today. In modern times it was discovered that, after electronic enlargement of Mary's eyes, Juan Diego image is within Mary's eyes.

+ February 11, **Our Lady of Lourdes**. In February of 1858, 14-year-old St. Bernadette Soubirous had 18 occasions in a grotto, in France where the Blessed Virgin Mary appeared. Mary identified herself as "Immaculate Conception" and generated a spring of water that is the sight of many miracles.

+ May 13, **Our Lady of Fatima**. May through October of 1917 three Portugal children, Lucia Santos, Francisco Marto, and Jacinta Marto has six apparitions with the Blessed Virgin Mary. The three main items of the apparitions are: (1) Their vivid vision of souls in hell. (2) The prediction that WWI would end and the start of WWII, including the request to consecrate Russia to the immaculate Heart of Mary. (3) The vision of the Pope, bishops, priests, religious, and lay people being killed by soldiers. Mary requested everyone to pray the rosery. To prove her apparitions, over 100,000 people witnessed the "miracle of the Sun."

+ May 31, **Visitation of the Blessed Virgin Mary.** The visitation as described in Luke 1:39–56, is where the Virgin Mary, pregnant with Jesus, visits her pregnant cousin Elizabeth to help her. John the Baptist in Elizabeth's womb jumps for joy, which signified that he had become blessed and sanctified. Then Mary recited the Magnificat. (Luke 1:46-55)

+ Saturday after "Sacred Heart of Jesus" is the **Immaculate Heart of Mary** to honor Mary as our mother and her pierced heart as described in Luke 2:25 by Simeon. Also, St. John's Gospel tells us the fulfillment of Simeon's prediction of Mary's pierced heart of sorrow at the foot of the cross of Jesus' crucifixion. St. John Eudes started the devotion in honor of the Heart of Mary in 1648, however, it wasn't until Pope Pius VII, in 1805 allowed the feast. Then Pope Pius XII in 1944 instituted the **Immaculate Heart of Mary** after which Pope Paul VI in 1969 established the celebration to be the Saturday after the "Sacred Heart of Jesus."

+ September 8, **Nativity of the Blessed Virgin Mary.** The Church has celebrated Mary's birth since at least the sixth century. According to written records (not scripture) Mary's parents, St. Ann and St. Joachim, were infertile but prayed for a child. They receive a promise of a child who will advance God's plan of salvation for the world. This Nativity was established by Pope Innocent IV in 1243.

Ash Wednesday

The blessing of using the thumb to put a cross on one's forehead is documented to have been the custom back in the 2nd century (*), as well as Christians sprinkling ashes on themselves during lent to publicly express their mortality and the need for repentance of sins, then later recorded by the 64th Pope Gregory the Great (590–604). Church records show that the first official universal Ash Wednesday was declared by the 159th Pope

Urban II at the Council of Benevento in the year 1091. The use of ashes on Ash Wednesday, the first day of lent season, has deep roots in Jewish scripture and tradition.

In Genesis 3:19, Adam was told by the Lord: *By the sweat of your face shall you get bread to eat, until you return to the ground, from which you were taken; For you are dirt, and to dirt you shall return.* Some scripture versions use ash or dust in place of dirt, now expressed as: "Ashes to ashes, dust to dust.", or, "you are dust, and to dust you shall return." Job 42:6, *... repent in dust and ashes.*

Daniel 9:3, *I [Daniel] turned to the Lord God, pleading in earnest prayer, with fasting, sackcloth, and ashes.*

The scripture passages of: Leviticus 23:26–32 established the holiest day of the year in Judaism later called "Yom Kippur", which is a day of atonement and repentance for sins with 25 hours of intense prayer, and fasting that is to be celebrated each year.

1 Maccabees 3:47, *That day they fasted and wore sackcloth; they sprinkled ashes on their heads...*

Esther 4:1, *put on sackcloth and ashes, and walk through the city.*

Ezekiel 9:4, [Ezekiel] *saying to him: Pass through the city [through Jerusalem] and mark an X on the foreheads of those who moan and groan over all the abominations that are practiced within it.*

Notice in the above passages, they put *"ashes on their heads"* and were instructed to publicly *"walk through the city"* and display their repentance for themselves as well as reminding others to do the same. The Old Testament symbolism of ashes is: mortality, humility, sorrow, and repentance for sins.

The first reading on Ash Wednesday is Joel 2:12–18. The following are just a few selected verses, not the complete reading: $_{12}$ *Yet even now, says the Lord, return to me with your whole heart, with fasting, and weeping, and mourning;* $_{13}$ *Rend your hearts, not your garments, and return to the Lord, your God.* $_{15}$ *Blow the trumpet Zion! Proclaim a fast, call an assembly.*
Notice that we are told to proclaim a public fast (assembly) for everyone together so that through fasting we are not distracted by food or drink and that our fasting is to remind us that we are to repent and *"return to the Lord"* and the Lord wants *"your hearts, not your garments."*

The second reading on Ash Wednesday is 2 Corinthians 5:20– 6:2. The following are just a few selected verses, not the complete reading: *5:20·...We implore you on behalf of Christ, be reconciled to God. 6:2 ...Behold, now is a very acceptable time; behold, now is the day of salvation.* Notice that we should not wait, now is the time to "*be reconciled to God.*"

The Gospel reading on Ash Wednesday is Matthew 6:1–6, 16–18. The following are just a few selected verses, not the complete reading: *3 But when you give <u>alms</u>, do not let your left hand know what your right is doing, 4so that your <u>almsgiving</u> may be secret. And your father who sees in secret will repay you. 6But when you <u>pray</u>, go to your inner room, close the door, and <u>pray</u> to your Father in secret, and your Father who sees in secret will repay you. 17But when you <u>fast</u>, anoint your head and wash your face, 18so that you may not appear to be <u>fasting</u>, except to our Father who is hidden. And our Father who sees what is hidden will repay you.*
Notice the three elements of Ash Wednesday and during all of lent are: <u>almsgiving</u>, <u>prayer</u>, and <u>fasting</u>.

The Old Testament tells us that for one day to publicly display the" ashes" on us as a reminder, and to others, the need for change (repentance). The ashes on our forehead on Ash Wednesday is the physical sign for us and others that symbolizes:
- Our mortality "you are dust, and to dust you shall return"
- We are announcing publicly to everyone the universal day of fast and repentance for sins, the first day of lent
- We are announcing that we belong to Jesus Christ
- We are announcing the start of lent where we are to then start our *"secret"* almsgiving, prayer, and fasting as told to us in Matthew chapter 6 (above).

The Didache:
(*) The 2nd century (AD101–200), the Apostle St. John was still alive, he died in the year 103 at the age of 97. "The Didache" (AD80) is a document written by the early Christians known as, "The Teaching of the Twelve Apostles." All the books of the New Testament were written by the year

AD80 except for 1,2,3 John and Revelation. In 1983 an original copy of "The Didache" was discovered in an accent Constantinople Monastery that scholars verified its organ to the year AD80. The document instructs early converts on the ethics and practices on how to be Christians and it includes descriptions of the rituals of Baptism, fasting, and the Eucharist Ritual (being the first known text using the term "Eucharist"). Along with other early documents such as the writings of the Fathers of the Church such as: St. Ignatius of Antioch (AD110), that verify the Apostles and early Christians believed in Christ's Real Presence in the Eucharist, which has been handed down to the present day. "The Didache" includes a description of using the sign of the cross on a candidate's forehead for Baptism, which was then adopted for applying ashes on Ash Wednesday. Luke 11:1–4 Gives us the short version of the "Our Father." Matthew 6:9–13 Gives us a longer version to the "Our Father." However, "The Didache" document added a doxology at the end of the "Our Father" prayer of which Catholics and Protestants adopted until today, *"For Thine is the power and the glory for evermore."*

SUMMARY – HOLY DAYS
+ January 1 – Solemnity of Mary
+ 40 days after Easter – Ascension of the Lord
+ August 15 – Assumption of the Blessed Virgin Mary
+ November 1 – All Saints Day
+ December 8 – The Immaculate Conception of the Blessed Virgin Mary
+ December 25 – The Nativity of the Lord – Christmas

USA HOLY DAYS CELEBRATED ON SUNDAY
+ The full moon after Spring Equinox after 21st March – Easter Sunday
+ January – Solemnity of the Epiphany of the Lord
+ March – Solemnity of St. Joseph, Spouse of the Blessed Virgin Mary
+ June – Solemnity of Saints Peter and Paul, Apostles

MARION FEAST DAYS

+ December 12 – Our Lady Guadalupe
+ February 11 – Our Lady of Lourdes
+ May 13 – Our Lady of Fatima
+ May 31 – Visitation of the Blessed Virgin Mary
+ Sunday after the "Sacred Heart of Jesus" – Immaculate Heart of Mary
+ September 8 – Nativity of the Blessed Virgin Mary

ASH WEDNESDAY

+ The first day of lent season

The **bold and italicized** Bible quotations are from the New American Bible (NAB). Certain words may be underlined for emphasis added.
HOLY DAYS AND FEAST DAYS: Assembled by Paul Wilchek 17SEP20.

CHAPTER 5

HOLY SPIRIT; SPIRIT, SOUL, AND BODY

This is intended to summarize what scripture tells us about the holy Spirit, and to better understand the third person of the trinity. Also, how God the father, God the son, and the holy Spirit of God relate to each other and how they relate to us. This is not in any way meant to distract from the worship, adoration and deity of our dearly beloved Jesus Christ.

1. **The "Holy Spirit" is in Scripture from Genesis through Revelation:**
    Creation:
    Genesis 1:2 (NAS) (Old Testament*). And the earth was formless and void, and darkness was over the surface of the deep; and the <u>Spirit of God</u> was moving over the surface of the waters.*
    Conception:
    Matthew 1:20. *For it is through the <u>Holy Spirit</u> that this child has been conceived in her.*
    Resurrection:
    Romans 8:11. *... the <u>Spirit</u> of the one who raised Jesus from the dead...*

Ascension:

Acts 1:9. *He [Jesus] was lifted up, and a cloud took Him from sight.*
   (A cloud is one of the symbols of the Holy Spirit)

End times:

Revelation 22:17. *The Spirit and the bride [Jesus] say, come.*

2. **The Persons of the Trinity are Uniquely Unified:**

The Holy Spirit teaches, reminds, and speaks to us from the Father and
the Son:

> John 14:26. *The Advocate, the Holy Spirit that the Father will send in my name… He will teach you everything and remind you of all that [I] told you.*

3. **Each Person of the Trinity Serves the Others:**

   (1) The Son only states what He hears from the Father:

   John 12:49–50. *Because I did not speak on my own, but the Father who sent me commanded me what to say and speak. And I know that His commandment is eternal life. So what I say, I say as the Father told me.*

   (2) The Father glorifies the Son:

   John 8:54. *Jesus answered, If I glorify myself, my glory is worth nothing; but it is my Father who glorifies me, of whom you say, He is our God.*

   The Father and the Son honor the Holy Spirit by commissioning the
   Spirit to speak in their name:

   John 14:16. **And I will ask the Father, and He will give you another Advocate to be with you always, the Spirit of Truth, which the world cannot accept, because it neither sees nor knows it. But you know it, because it remains with you, and will be in you.** One
   might question, with Jesus Christ being fully God and fully man, why
   did Jesus have to pray, speak, or ask the Father? Consider the following
   Scripture passage:

   Philippians 2:7. *He [Jesus] emptied Himself, taking the form of a slave, coming in human likeness; …*

Scripture implies and Jewish tradition believed that if a human saw the face of God (meaning to be in God's full presence), it would be so overwhelming, one would die. Therefore, Jesus *"emptied Himself"* of those aspects of divinity, thus allowing Him to associate with humans without overwhelming them with God's full power.

This may be one of the purposes of the Trinity. Jesus asks the Father and the Father directs the <u>Holy Spirit,</u> delivering the request, all without overwhelming humans with God's omnipotent presence.

(3) The <u>Holy Spirit</u> is the Third Person of the Trinity. The "Trinity" concept is difficult for us to comprehend. We can somewhat understand the relationship between God the Father and God the Son based on our worldly experience. However, we have no earthly reference to compare to the relationship of God the Father and/or God the Son to the <u>Holy Spirit</u> of God. The only reference we have is Holy Scripture. So, Let Scripture Speak for Itself on the <u>Holy Spirit.</u>

4. **Titles of the Holy Spirit in Scripture:**
   Paraclete, means he who is called to one's side.
   Advocate means helper and counselor. Other titles are: The Spirit of Truth, Spirit of Promise, Spirit of Adoption, Spirit of Christ, Spirit of the Lord, Spirit of God, Spirit of Glory.

5. **Symbols of the Holy Spirit in Scripture:**
   Water.
   John 4:14. *... the <u>water</u> I [Jesus] shall give will become in him a spring of <u>water</u> welling up to eternal life.*
   1 Corinthians 12:13. *For in one <u>Spirit</u> we were all baptized into one body, whether Jews or Greeks, slaves or free persons, and we were all given to drink of one <u>Spirit</u>.* (CCC 694) The symbolism of water signifies the Holy Spirit's action in Baptism...the water of Baptism signifies that our birth into the divine life is given to us in the Holy Spirit.
   Anointing.
   1 John 2:20. *... you have the anointing that comes from the <u>holy one,</u> and you all have knowledge.* (CCC 695) The symbolism of anointing

with oil signifies the Holy Spirit. In Christian initiation, anointing is the sacramental sign of Confirmation.

Fire.

Luke 3:16. *... He will baptize you with the <u>Holy Spirit</u> and <u>fire</u>.* (CCC 696) Fire symbolizes the transforming energy of the Holy Spirit's actions. Spiritual tradition has retained the tongues "as of fire" that were cast on the disciples at Pentecost which filled them with the Holy Spirit, as being one of the most expressive images of the Holy Spirit's actions.

Cloud and light.

Luke 1:35. *... And the angel said to her [Mary] in reply, "The <u>Holy Spirit</u> will come upon you, and the power of the Most High will <u>overshadow</u> you, ..."*

Acts 1:9. *.... as they were looking on, He [Jesus] was lifted up, and a <u>cloud</u> took Him from their sight.* (CCC 697) Cloud and Light occur together as manifestations of the Holy Spirit. In the Old Testament, the cloud veiled God's Glory with Moses on Mount Sinai, at the tent of meeting, during the wondering, and with Solomon at the dedication of the Temple. The Spirit comes upon the Virgin Mary and "overshadows" her. The cloud came at the Transfiguration of Jesus, and finally, the cloud took Jesus up from the disciples at His ascension.

Seal.

2 Corinthians 1:22. *He has also put His <u>seal</u> upon us and given the <u>Spirit</u> in our hearts as a first installment.* (CCC 698) The seal is a symbol close to that of anointing. The Father has set this "seal "on Christ and also seals us in Him. Because this seal indicates the indelible effect of the anointing with the Holy Spirit in the sacraments.

Hand.

Mark 16: 18. *... They will lay <u>hands</u> on the sick, and they will recover.* (CCC 699) Jesus heals the sick and blesses little children by laying hands on them. It is by the Apostles' imposition of hands that the Holy Spirit is given. The Church has kept this sign of the all–powerful outpouring of the Holy Spirit.

Finger.

Luke 11: 20. *But if it is <u>by the finger of God</u> that [I] [Jesus] drive out demons, then the kingdom of God has come upon you.* (CCC 700) God's law was written on tablets of stone "*<u>by the finger of God</u>.*"

Dove.

Matthew 3:16. *After Jesus was baptized, He came up from the water and behold, the heavens were opened and he saw the <u>Spirit</u> of God descending like a <u>dove</u> coming upon Him.*

Luke 3:22. *And the <u>Holy Spirit</u> descended upon Him [Jesus] in bodily form like a <u>dove.</u>* (CCC 701) When Christ comes up from the water of His baptism, the Holy Spirit, in the form of a dove, comes down upon Him and remains with Him. The Spirit comes down and remains in the purified hearts of the baptized.

6. **The Coming of the Holy Spirit was Prophesied:**
    Joel 3:1 (NAS) (Old Testament). *And it will come about after this that I will pour out <u>My Spirit</u> on all mankind; ...*

7. **The Holy Spirit is the Power that Brings Christians to Faith:**
    And gives us life as well as understanding.
    Acts 1:8. *But you will receive power when the <u>Holy Spirit</u> comes upon you,*
    John 3:5–7. *[Jesus] I say to you, no one can enter the Kingdom of God without being born of water and <u>Spirit</u>. What is born of flesh is flesh and what is born of spirit is spirit. Do not be amazed that I told you 'You must be born from above.'*
    John 6:63. *It is the <u>Spirit</u> that gives life, while the flesh is of no avail. The words I have spoken to you are spirit and life.*
    Notice in the above passage occurs shortly after Jesus said: "**Whoever eats my flesh and drinks my blood has eternal life.**" (Jn 6:54) After which many disciples said: *"This saying is hard; who can accept it?"* (Jn 6:60: Therefore, it appears that Jesus is clarifying that He was talking about His spiritual flesh and His spiritual blood, of which the disciples did not understand until after the resurrection of Jesus.
    John 15:26. *When the <u>Advocate</u> comes whom I will send you from the Father, the <u>Spirit of the Truth</u> that proceeds from the Father, he will testify to me.*

8. **The Spirit of God has the Power to Drive out Demons:**
    Matthew 12:28–29. *[Jesus] But if it is by the <u>Spirit of God</u> that I drive out demons, then the kingdom of God has come upon you.*

9. **The Holy Spirit Baptizes and Pours out Gifts:**

Acts 1:5. *For John baptized with water, but in a few days, you will be baptized with the <u>Holy Spirit</u>.*

The seven gifts of the Holy Spirit are given at baptism and reminded at confirmation. Isaiah 11:2 *The spirit of the Lord shall rest upon him: a spirit of <u>wisdom</u> and of <u>understanding</u>, a spirit of <u>counsel</u> and <u>strength</u> [fortitude], a spirit of <u>knowledge</u> and of <u>fear of the Lord</u> [piety], and his delight shall be <u>the fear of the Lord</u>.* Notice regarding Isaiah 11:2, the translators of the Septuagint (the earliest Greek Old Testament translation from Hebrew), included the gift of *piety*. Therefore, all seven gifts are listed in The Catechism of the Catholic Church (1831).

Charisms may be given to specific individuals as the Holy Spirit chooses that are for the service of others and the building up of the Church. 1 Corinthians 12: 8–11 *To one is given through the Spirit the expression of <u>wisdom</u>; to another the expression of <u>knowledge</u> according to the same Spirit; to another <u>faith</u> by the same Spirit; to another gifts of <u>healing</u> by the one Sprit; to another <u>mighty deeds</u>; to another <u>prophecy</u>; to another <u>discernment</u> of spirits; to another <u>varieties of tongues</u>; to another <u>interpretation of tongues</u>. But one and the same Spirit produces all of these, distributing them individually to each person as he wishes.*

A person full of the Spirit can be recognized: Galatians 5: 22–23 *…the fruit of the Spirit is <u>love</u>, <u>joy</u>, <u>peace</u>, <u>patience</u>, <u>kindness</u>, <u>generosity</u>, <u>faithfulness</u>, <u>gentleness</u>, <u>self–control</u>.*

Luke 11:13. *If you then, who are wicked, know how to give gifts to your children, how much more will the Father in heaven give the <u>Holy Spirit</u> to those who ask Him?*

10. **Saint Paul Tells us what the Holy Spirit does for us:**

It is by the <u>Holy Spirit</u> that one confesses that Jesus Christ is Lord.

1 Corinthians 12:3. *… And no one can say, "Jesus is Lord," except by the <u>Holy Spirit</u>.*

Gifts are given by the <u>Holy Spirit</u>.

1 Corinthians 12:4 & 7. *₄There are different kinds of spiritual gifts but the same Spirit; ₇To each individual the manifestation of the <u>Spirit</u> is given for some benefit.*

The <u>Holy Spirit</u> is the way to Jesus Christ and the Father.

Romans 8:14–15. ***For those who are led by the <u>Spirit of God</u> are children of God. For you did not receive a spirit of slavery to fall back into fear, but you received a <u>Spirit of Adoption</u>, through which we cry, "Abba, Father!"***

The <u>Holy Spirit</u> intercedes for us.

Romans 8:26,27. ***26... the <u>Spirit</u> too comes to the aid of our weakness; for we do not know how to pray as we ought, but the <u>Spirit</u> itself intercedes with inexpressible groanings. 27And the one who searches hearts knows what is the intention of the Spirit, because it intercedes for the holy ones according to God's will.***

The <u>Holy Spirit</u> reveals the things of God and scrutinizes everything.

1 Corinthians 2:10. ***This God has revealed to us through the <u>Spirit</u>. For the <u>Spirit</u> scrutinizes everything, even the depths of God.***

The <u>Holy Spirit</u>, with God the Father and God the Son has put His seal upon us.

2 Corinthians 1:21,22. ***21... the one who gives us security with you in Christ and who anointed us in God; 22he has also put His seal upon us and given the <u>Spirit</u> in our hearts as a first installment.***

The <u>Holy Spirit</u> fills us with joy, peace, hope, and believing.

Romans 15:13. ***May the God of hope fill you with all <u>joy</u> and <u>peace</u> in <u>believing</u>, so that you may abound <u>in hope</u> by the power of the <u>Holy Spirit</u>.***

St. Paul tells us how to recognize the fruit of the <u>Spirit.</u>

Galatians 5:22–23. ***...The fruit of the Spirit is love, joy, peace, patience, kindness, generosity, faithfulness, gentleness, self–control. Against such there is no law.*** Notice regarding Galatians 5:22–23, The Catechism of the Catholic Church (1832) refers to the Latin Vulgate Bible which was translated from Hebrew and Aramaic by St. Jerome (382 to 405) that lists ***charity*** in place of love and includes: ***goodness, modesty,*** and ***Chasity.***

At every mass, the priest calls upon the <u>Holy Spirit</u> to ascend upon the bread & wine like the "dew–fall."

11. **Never Misrepresent the Work of the Spirit:**

Matthew 12:31. ***...I say to you, every sin and blasphemy will be forgiven people, but blasphemy against the <u>Spirit</u> will not be forgiven.***

Bible Footnote: "Blasphemy against the Spirit: The sin attributing to Satin what is the work of the <u>Spirit of God</u>". Blasphemy means the act or offense of speaking sacrilegiously about God or sacred things, profane talk.

Ephesians 4:30. *And do not grieve the <u>Holy Spirit of God</u>, with which you were sealed for the day of redemption.*

12. **Jesus was Full of the Power of the <u>Spirit</u>:**

Luke 4:1. *Jesus returned to Galilee in the power of the <u>Spirit</u> and news of Him spread.*

Luke 4:17. [*Jesus*] *unrolled the scroll and found the passage where it is written:* [Isaiah 61:1–2] *The <u>Spirit</u> of the Lord God is upon me,* ...

Note: At Jesus' first public appearance, He reads Isaiah about the <u>Holy Spirit</u> and then states: *"Today this scripture passage is fulfilled in your hearing."*

Acts 10:38. ... *God anointed Jesus of Nazareth with the <u>Holy Spirit</u> and power.*

13. **The Holy Spirit Teaches Us What to Say and to Pray:**

Luke 12:12. *For the <u>Holy Spirit</u> will teach you at that moment what you should say.*

Ephesians 6:18. *With all prayer and supplication, pray at every opportunity in the <u>Spirit</u>.*

Supplication means asking or begging earnestly or humbly.

14. **The Leaders of the Church were given the Power to Forgive or Retain Sin:**

John 20:22. ... *He [Jesus] breathed on them and said to them, receive the <u>Holy Spirit</u>, whose sins you forgive are forgiven them, and whose sins you retain are retained.*

15. **The Holy Spirit Speaks through Prophets:**

Acts 28:25. Did the <u>Holy Spirit</u> speak to our ancestors through the prophet Isaiah,

16. **Your Body is a Temple of the Holy Spirit:**
    1 Corinthians 6:19,20. *Do you not know that your body is a temple of the Holy Spirit within you, whom you have from God, and that you are not your own? For you have been purchased at a price. Therefore glorify God in your body.*

17. **The Same Spirit that Raised Christ from the Dead Dwells in Us:**
    Romans 8:10,11. *But if Christ is in you, although the body is dead because of sin, the Spirit is alive because of righteousness. If the Spirit of the one who raised Jesus from the dead dwells in you, the one who raised Christ from the dead will give life to your mortal bodies also, through His Spirit that dwells in you.*
    Notice what a very profound quotation! What a wonderful God we have to give us the same Spirit that raised Christ from the dead, to dwell within us and gives life to our mortal bodies! Mortal means a living body, therefore, *"give life to your mortal bodies"* must mean to give us eternal life.
    Romans 8:16. *The Spirit itself bears witness with our spirit that we are children of God, ...*

This is not, by far, all the quotations in scripture about the Holy Spirit. Herein, there are about 45 quotations out of over 110 Scriptural quotations about the Holy Spirit and Spirit.

SUMMARY – HOLY SPIRIT:
So, what is this Scriptural information telling us about the Holy Spirit?
1. The Holy spirit is in scripture from Genesis right through to Revelation.
2. God the Father, God the Son, and the Holy Spirit of God are uniquely unified as one Triune God that individually serves each other and each of us. (Jn 14:26)
3. *"Jesus emptied Himself, coming in human likeness"* (Phil 2:7) so that the full power of God would not overwhelm humans. Therefore, Jesus prays and asks the Father and the Father sends the Holy Spirit to perform God's desire.

4. The <u>Holy Spirit</u> has many titles in scripture: Paraclete, Advocate, Spirit of Truth, Spirit of Promise, Spirit of Adoption, Spirit of God, Spirit of Christ, Spirit of the Lord, Spirit of Glory.

5. Symbols of the <u>Holy Spirit</u> include: Water (baptism), Anointing, Baptize with Fire, Cloud and Light, His seal upon us, Hands that can heal, Finger of God, and He can be in bodily form *"like a dove."* (Mt 3:16)

6. The Old Testament predicted: *"I will pour out My Spirit."* (Joel 3:11)

7. *"You will receive power when the <u>Holy Spirit</u> comes upon you."* (Acts 1:8)

8. God's Spirit can *"drive out demons."* (Mt 12:28–29)

9. *"In one <u>Spirit</u> we were all baptized"* (Acts 1:5) and the <u>Holy Spirit</u> pours out gifts, *"distributing them individually to each as He wishes."* (1 Cor 12:11)

10. The <u>Holy Spirit</u> does many things for us: *"no one can say, Jesus is Lord, except by the <u>Holy Spirit</u>."* (1 Cor 12:3) He gives us different spiritual gifts; He bears witness with our spirit; He aids us in our weakness; He intercedes for us; He scrutinizes everything; He places His seal upon us; He anoints us; He fills us with joy, peace and hope. *"The fruit of the <u>Holy Spirit</u> is love, joy, peace, patience, kindness, generosity, faithfulness, gentleness, self-control."* (Gal 5:22–23)
The Holy Spirit ascends upon the bread & wine at Mass, like the "dew–fall."

11. Scripture tells us: *"do not grieve the <u>Holy Spirit of God</u>."* (Eph 4:30)

12. Jesus is the ultimate example of being full of the power of the <u>Spirit</u>.

13. *"… the <u>Holy Spirit</u> will teach you at that moment what you should say."* (Lk 12:12)

14. The <u>Holy Spirit</u> gave the Church leaders the power to forgive/ retain sin. (Jn 20:22)

15. The <u>Holy Spirit</u> speaks through prophets (Acts 28:25).

16. *"Do you not know that your body is a temple of the <u>Holy Spirit</u>."* (1 Cor 6:19)

17. *"The <u>Spirit</u> of the one who raised Jesus from the dead dwells in you,"* (Rom 8:10–11)

Our *"Father in heaven [will] give the <u>Holy Spirit</u> to those who ask Him."* (Lk 11:13)

Scripture promises us that the <u>Holy Spirit</u>: *"to be with you always"*, *"it remains with you, ... and will be in you"* (Jn 14:16–17), and the <u>Holy Spirit</u> works with our spirit to make us children of God. We may not understand the enormity of the "free will" that God has given us. However, Scripture is telling us that we need to take the first step to "ask" God: "ask" for our sins to be forgiven; "ask" Him to give us the <u>Holy Spirit</u>; and "ask" for our prayers to be answered, earnestly, with humility and with love. Because, *"the one who searches hearts knows what is the intention..."* (Rom 8:27)

References:
Bible quotations are: *italicized and bold.* Certain words may be <u>underlined</u> for emphasis added.
Quotations marked (NAS) are from: New American Standard Bible, Thomas Nelson Publishers. All other quotations are from The New American Bible, St. Joseph Edition, Catholic Book Publishing Co.
Doctrinal Bible Index of The New American Bible. Footnotes of The New American Bible.

The word(s) in [brackets] indicate word(s) added for clarity, usually as in scripture. Statements preceding or ending with ... indicates word(s) not included.

(CCC) = Catechism of the Catholic Church. Published by Doubleday.
Concordance and Biblical Cyclopedic Index of The New American Standard Bible. The Cyclopedic Index of The New American Standard Bible lists the "<u>Holy Spirit</u>" as appearing in the Old Testament 10 times and in the New Testament 86 times.
The Latin Vulgate Bible referred to herein was translated from Hebrew and Aramaic by St. Jerome about 382 to 405 it was the standard bible used by the Catholic Church for over one and a half millennia.
The word "<u>Spirit</u>" only appears 9 times in the Old Testament and 7 times in the New Testament.
Compact Bible Dictionary, Thomas Nelson Publishers.

HOLY SPIRIT – Compiled by Paul Wilchek, edited by Kristin Trepanier–Henry 10DEC19 Revised 27FEB21.

SPIRIT, SOUL, AND BODY

According to Scripture, humans were created in the image of God making them the only triune beings consisting of ***entirely, spirit, soul, and body*** (1 Thes 5:23):

1 Thessalonians 5:23 ***May the God of peace himself make you perfectly holy and may you entirely, spirit, soul, and body, be preserved blameless for the coming of our Lord Jesus Christ.***

The spirit, soul, and body in scripture indicates that they are different from each other; however, they are somehow inter-connected to make up one human being entirely.

The New American Bible (NAB) distinguishes between the holy Spirit and other spirits by only capitalizing "Spirit" when it references the holy Spirit. The New American Bible Concordance lists spirit(s), with a small "s", as being in Scripture 95 times. The NAB lists capitalized "Spirit" (Holy Spirit of God) in Scripture 77 times. This same capitalization procedure will be used here in.

Let Scripture Speak for Itself on the Spirit

The Glossary of "The Didache Bible" tells us:

SPIRIT: *That which is immaterial, having no dependence on matter for its existence or activities.*

The spirit and soul are different:

Genesis 49: 6 ***Let not my soul enter their council, or my spirit be joined with their company.***

Hebrews 4:12 ***Indeed, the word of God is living and effective, sharper than any two–edged sword, penetrating even between soul and spirit.***

Luke 1:46–47 ***My soul proclaims the greatness of the Lord; My spirit rejoices in God my savior.***

1 Peter 3:18–19 ***For Christ also suffered for sins once, the righteous for the sake of the unrighteous, that he might lead you to God. Put to death in the flesh, he was brought to life in the spirit. In it he went to preach to the spirits in prison.***

The spirit (breath) is from God and gives understanding:

Job 32:8 *But it is a spirit in man, the breath of the Almighty, that gives him understanding.*

Job 34:14–15 *If he [God] were to take back his spirit to himself, withdraw to himself his breath, all flesh would perish together, and man would return to the dust.*

Psalms 31:6 *Into your hands I commend my spirit.* Note: His spirit within us.

1 Corinthians 2:12–13 *We have not received the spirit of the world but the Spirit that is from God, so that we may understand the things freely given us by God. And we speak about them not with words taught by human wisdom, but with words taught by the Spirit, describing spiritual realities in spiritual terms.*

Humans cannot live without God:

Romans 8:4 *... live not according to the flesh but according to the spirit.*

The spirit returns to God upon the death of the body:

Ecclesiastes 12:7 *And the dust returns to the earth as it once was, and the life breath [spirit] returns to God who gave it.*

Matthew 5:3 *Blessed are the poor in spirit, for theirs is the kingdom of heaven.*

The spirit is willing:

Matthew 26:41 *Watch and pray that you may not undergo the test. The spirit is willing, but the flesh is weak.*

The spirit can have wisdom, knowledge, power, love, and self-control:

Ephesians 1:17 *that the God of our Lord Jesus Christ, the Father of glory, may give you a spirit of wisdom and revelation resulting in knowledge of him.*

2 Timothy 1:7 *For God did not give us a spirit of cowardice but rather of power and love and self-control.*

The spirit frees one from earthly death:
Romans 8:2 *For the law of the spirit of life in Christ Jesus has freed you from the law of sin and death.*

The spirit, within humans, can make a choice:
Revelation 22:17 *The Spirit and the bride say, "Come" … Let the one who thirst come forward, and the one who wants it receive the gift of life–giving water.*
Ezekiel 36:27 *I will put my spirit within you…*

The holy Spirit and our spirit communicate:
Romans 8:16 *The Spirit itself bears witness with our spirit that we are children of God.*
1 Corinthians 2:10 *this God has revealed to us through the Spirit. For the Spirit scrutinizes everything, even the depths of God. Among human beings, who knows what pertains to a person except the spirit of the person that is within.*

The last line verifies that humans have a spirit within.
According to the internet on this subject, most theologians tell us that when Adam and Eve fell, their spirit separated from God. Also, if a person does not accept God or rejects God, their spirit separates from God, loosing God's protection. One's spirit has the ability for an intimate relationship with God through the grace of baptism.

Let Scripture Speak for Itself on the Sole
The Glossary of "The Didache Bible" tells us:
SOUL: *Immaterial and immortal principle of the human person, endowed with reason and intellect. Along with the body, constitutes the substantial unity of the human person.*

The Catechism of the Catholic Church (CCC 363): "*In Sacred Scripture the term "soul" often refers to human life or the entire person. But "soul" also refers to the innermost aspect of man, that which is of greatest value in him, that by which he is most especially in God's image: "soul" signifies the spiritual principle of man.*"

The soul is not well described in Scripture, but It does tell us the soul came from God:

Genesis 2:7 *The Lord God formed man out of the clay of the ground and blew into his nostrils <u>the breath of life</u>, and man became a living being.*

The soul can love:

Matthew 22:37 [Jesus said] *You shall love the Lord, your God, with all your <u>heart</u>, with all your <u>soul</u>, and with all your mind.*

The soul has emotions:

Matthew 26:38 [Jesus said] *My <u>soul</u> is sorrowful even to death,*
Lamentations 3:20 *Remembering it over and over leaves my <u>soul</u> downcast within me.*

Accept suffering of the soul:

1 Peter 4:19 *...those who suffer in accord with God's will hand their <u>souls</u> over to a faithful creator as they do good.*

The soul can have wisdom, knowledge, and understanding:

Proverbs 2: 10–11 *For <u>wisdom</u> will enter your <u>heart</u>, <u>knowledge</u> will enter your <u>soul</u>, discretion will watch over you, <u>understanding</u> will guard you.*

No wisdom dwells in the soul of an evil <u>body/heart</u>:

Wisdom 1:4 *Because into a <u>soul</u> that plots evil wisdom enters not, nor dwells she in a <u>body</u> under debt of sin.* Wis 9:15 *For the corruptible <u>body</u> burdens the <u>soul</u> and the earthen shelter weighs down the mind that has many concerns.*

Matthew 10:28 *And do not be afraid of those who kill the <u>body</u> but cannot kill the <u>soul</u>; rather, be afraid of the one who can destroy both <u>soul and body</u>.*

Hebrews 3:12 *take care brothers, that none of you may have an evil and unfaithful <u>heart</u>, so as to forsake the living God.*

The soul is the seat of the will and it does not get converted but needs to be renewed daily through prayer and reading the Bible. After death of the body, the soul can go to heaven, purgatory or hell.

(CCC 366) *"The Church teaches that every spiritual <u>soul</u> is created immediately by God – it is not "produced" by the parents – and also that it is immortal. ... It will be reunited with the body at the final resurrection."*

(CCC 367) *"Sometimes the <u>soul</u> is distinguished from the <u>spirit</u> (1 Thes 5:23): The Church teaches that this distinction does not introduce a duality into the <u>soul</u>. "<u>Spirit</u>" signifies that from creation man is ordered to a supernatural end and that his <u>soul</u> can gratuitously* [without good reason, unjustifiably, free of charge] *be raised beyond all it deserves in communion with God."*

(CCC 368) *"The spiritual tradition of the Church also emphasizes the <u>heart</u>, in biblical sense of the depths of one's being, where the person decides for or against God."*

The <u>soul</u> is associated with the <u>heart</u>:
Matthew 22:37 **He [Jesus] said to him, "you shall love the Lord, your God, with all your <u>heart</u>, with all your <u>soul</u>, and with all your mind..."**

The <u>heart</u> is the first organ to appear during embryonic development and since Aristotle the <u>soul</u> is traditionally considered to be within the <u>heart</u>. In 1991, Doctor J. Andrew Armor, discovered that the <u>heart</u> has an area containing neurons that are the same type of neurons in the brain, which allows the <u>heart</u> to communicate with the brain. After which some referred to the <u>heart</u> as the "little brain."

According to Father Robert Spitzer, the absolute best proof of the existence of the human <u>soul</u> is all the many documented near death (out of body) experiences. There are hundreds of documented reports where many <u>souls</u> were able to observe and remember situations that ordinarily could not have possibly been known or observed while the person's brain was "clinically dead."

Let Scripture Speak for Itself on the Body
(CCC 364) *"The <u>human body</u> shares in the dignity of "the image of God": it is a <u>human body</u> precisely because it is animated by a spiritual <u>soul</u>, and it is the whole <u>human person</u> that is intended to become, in the <u>body</u> of Christ, a temple of the <u>Spirit</u>."*

1 Corinthians 6: 19 ***Do you not know that your <u>body</u> is a temple of the <u>holy Spirit</u> within you, whom you have from God, and that you are not your own?***

The <u>body</u> is created by God and is found very good:
Genesis 1:27,31 ₂₇***God created man in his image; in the divine image he created him; male and female he created them.*** ₃₁***God looked at everything he made, and he found it very good.***

The <u>body</u> (flesh) is weak:
Matthew 26:41 ***Watch and pray that you may not undergo the test. The <u>spirit</u> is willing, but <u>the flesh is weak</u>.***

An immoral sin is against the <u>body</u>:
1 Corinthians 6:18 ***Avoid immorality. Every other sin a person commits is outside the <u>body</u>, but the immoral person sins against his own <u>body</u>.***
Romans 8:13 ***For if you live according to the <u>flesh</u>, you will die, but if by the <u>spirit</u>, you put to death the deeds of the <u>body</u>, you will live.***

Our <u>body</u> can be a living sacrifice:
Romans 12:1 ***I urge you therefore, brothers, by the mercies of God, to offer your <u>bodies</u> as a living sacrifice, holy and pleasing to God, your spiritual worship.***

Our <u>body</u> is one in Christ and of one another:
Romans 12:4–5 ***For as in one <u>body</u> we have many parts, and all parts do not have the same function, so we, though many, are one <u>body in Christ</u> and individually parts of <u>one another</u>.***

(CCC 365) *"The unity of <u>soul</u> and <u>body</u> is so profound that one has to consider the <u>soul</u> to be the "form" of the <u>body</u>: It is because of its spiritual <u>soul</u> that the <u>body</u> made of matter becomes a living, <u>human body</u>; <u>spirit</u> and matter, in man, are not two natures united, but rather their union forms a single nature."*

According to Scripture:

SPIRIT	SOUL	BODY
The breath of the Almighty	The breath of life	Created by God as good
From God	Immaterial/immortal part of humans, reason, intellect	The image of God
The spirit and soul are closely related	Innermost aspect, spiritual principle of humans, will	A temple of the holy Spirit
Is willing	Has emotions	Body (flesh) is weak
Wisdom, knowledge, power, love, and self–control	Love the Lord with all your soul. The soul can love and has emotions	Immoral sin is against the body
Frees one from the law of sin and earthly death	Accept suffering of the soul. Sin and corruption blocks wisdom	The body can be a living sacrifice
Can make a choice. Communicates with the holy Spirit, intimate with God, Baptism renews the spirit from original sin.	The center of human personality, wisdom, Knowledge, discretion, and understanding, associated with the heart	One in Christ and one another, body and soul a single nature
Upon death the spirit returns to God	Upon death can go to Heaven, purgatory, or hell	At the final resurrection, the body and soul reunite.

According to Common Use:

SPIRIT	SOUL	BODY
Spiritual	Psychological	Physiological
Awareness	Unique to each person	Has natural instincts
Sensitivity, impersonal or universal	Insight, understanding, and reasoning powers	Reacts to immediate surroundings: sight, taste,
Understanding	Heart, and Mind	hearing, touch, smell
Motivation	Will (free will)	
Conscience	The seat of emotion	
Intuition	Intellect	
Meaning, purpose, and love	Fears, passions, and creativity	
God–consciousness	Self–consciousness	World–consciousness

According to Most Theologians:

SPIRIT	SOUL	BODY
The spirit communicates with God through the holy Spirit, then with the soul	The soul communicates with one's spirit and then with the body	The body communicates with the soul
The human spirit translates the things of the holy Spirit for one's consideration	The soul has the free will to accept or reject that of the spirit	The desires of the body are communicated to the soul for a decision
Can be transformed	Needs ongoing prayer	Can resist wrong–doing

The holy Spirit of God dwells within our spirit:

Romans 8:27 ***And the one who searches hearts knows what is the intention of the Spirit, because it [the Spirit] intercedes for the holy ones according to God's will.***

John 14:26 ***The Advocate, the holy Spirit that the Father will send in my name – he will teach you everything and remind you of all that [I] told you.***

SUMMARY – SPIRIT, SOUL, AND BODY
SPIRIT:

+ God and the angels are pure spirit
+ The spirit is the innermost part of the human being, giving spirituality
+ The spirit within Christians freely communicates with God according to God's will (ROM 8:27). The only way to experience God is through the spirit (Rom 8:4)
+ The spirit is always pointed toward and exists exclusively for God
+ Believers worship through and with the aid of the spirit
+ Our spirit is from God and after death it returns to God who gave it (Eccl 12:7)

SOUL:

+ The <u>soul</u> is that which gives life, free will, and is who we are (CA)
+ All living <u>bodies</u> have a <u>soul</u>. If they did not have <u>souls</u>, they would not be alive. While plants, animals, and anything living contains a <u>soul</u>, the human <u>soul</u> is very unique (CA)
+ The human <u>soul</u> has sensitive powers and rational powers that separates humans from other beings, animals are not spiritual (CA)
+ Only humans have both a <u>soul and spirit</u>... having a <u>spiritual soul</u> (CCC 363–364)
+ The <u>soul</u>, unique to each person, can be self–centered and accept or reject God
+ After death, the <u>soul </u>may end up in heaven, temporally in purgatory, or hell

BODY:

+ The <u>body</u> created by God and declared as good (Gn 1:31)
+ Due to the fall of Adam and Eve, the <u>body</u> lost its spiritual communication with God and became corrupt
+ Baptism restored the spiritual communications with God and allowed the dwelling of the holy Spirit within (1 Cor 6:19)
+ After death the <u>body </u>returns to dust, then at the final resurrection, the <u>body</u> and <u>soul</u> reunite

Our <u>spirit</u> communicates with our <u>soul</u>, and our <u>soul </u>and our <u>body</u> communicate using the free will God gave us to make a final decision. The final conclusion can be stated as:
YOUR SOUL IS YOURS, YOUR SPIRIT IS GOD'S

(CA) is "Catholic Answers" on the internet, (CCC) is Catechism of the Catholic Church.
References: The New American Bible (NAB), World press, Translated from the Original Languages
The New American Bible Concordance, J.R. Kohelenberger III editor, Oxford University Press
The Didache Bible, Ignatius Bible Edition, Compact Bible Dictionary, R.F. Youngblood, F.F. Bruce & R.K. Harrison, Thomas Nelson press. SPIRIT, SOUL AND BODY: Assembled by Paul Wilchek 21MAY21.

CHAPTER 6

PROPHECIES, PARALLELS, SYMBOLISMS, MIRACLES

There are many prophecies, symbolisms, hidden messages, and parallels in scripture as well as many miracles within scripture. There are also miracles that occurred that are not in scripture.

Luke 24:27. ***Then beginning with Moses and all the prophets, He [Jesus] interpreted to them what referred to Him in all the scriptures.***

St. Augustine stated: "The Old Testament is the New Testament concealed. The New Testament is the Old Testament revealed."

Prophecies of the Messiah Fulfilled in Jesus Christ: (partial list)

Prophetic Scripture:	Subject:	Fulfilled:
Gn 3:15	Seed of a Woman	Gal 4:4
Gn 12:3	Descendant of Abraham	Mt 1:1
Gn 17:19	Descendant of Isaac	Luke 3:34
Nm 24:17	Descendant of Jacob	Mt 1:2
Gn 49:10	From the tribe of Judah	Luke 3:33
Is 9:7	Heir to the throne of David	Luke 1:32–33
Ps 45:6	Anointed and eternal	Heb 1:8–12

Prophetic Scripture:	Subject:	Fulfilled:
Mi 5:1 *But you, <u>Bethlehem</u>–Ephrathah least among the clans of <u>Judah,</u> from you shall come forth for me one who is to be ruler of Israel; Whose origin is from old, from ancient times.*	Born in Bethlehem	Luke 2:4–5 *And Joseph too went up from Galilee from the town of Nazareth to <u>Judea,</u> to the city of David that is called <u>Bethlehem,</u> because he was of the house and family of David, to be enrolled with Mary, his betrothed, who was with child.*
Dn 9:25	Time for His birth	Luke 2:1,2
Is 7:14	To be born of a Virgin	Luke 1:26–27,30–31
Jer 31:15	Slaughter of children	Mt 2:16–18
Hos 11:1 *When Israel was a <u>child</u>, I loved him, out of <u>Egypt</u> I called my son.*	Flight to Egypt	Mt 2:14–15 *Joseph rose and took the <u>child</u> and his mother by night and departed for <u>Egypt</u>. He stayed there until the death of Herod, that what the Lord had said through the prophet might be fulfilled, "Out of <u>Egypt</u> I called my son."*
Is 40:3–5	The way prepared	Luke 3:3–6
Mal 3:1	Preceded by a forerunner	Luke 7:24
Mal 4:5–6	Preceded by Elijah	Mt 11:13–14

Prophetic Scripture:	Subject:	Fulfilled:
Ps 2:7 *I will proclaim the decree of the Lord, he said to me, "You are my son; today I have begotten you.*	Declared the Son of God	Mt 3:17 *And a voice came from the heavens saying, "This is my beloved Son, with whom I am well pleased."*
Is 9:1–2	Galilean ministry	Mt 4:13–16
Mal 3:1 *And the Lord whom you seek will come suddenly to his <u>temple</u>*	Appearance at the temple	Mark 11:15 *They came to Jerusalem, and on entering the <u>temple</u> area he began to drive out those selling and buying there.*
Ps 78:2–4 *I will open my mouth in a <u>parable</u>, unfold the puzzling events of the past. What we have heard and know; things our ancestors have recounted to us. We do not keep them from our children; we recount them to the next generation, The praiseworthy deeds of the Lord and his strength, the wonders that he performed.*	Speaks in parables	Mt 13:34–35 *All these things Jesus spoke to the crowds in <u>parables</u>. He spoke to them only in parables, to fulfill what had been said through the prophet: "I will open my mouth in <u>parables</u>, I will announce what has lain hidden from the foundation [of the world]."*
Dt 18:15	A prophet	Acts 3:20,22
Is 61:1–2	To bind up the brokenhearted	Luke 4:18–19
Is 53:3	Rejected by His own people, the Jews	John 1:11 Luke 23:18
Ps 110:4	Priest after order of Melchizedek	Heb 5:5–6

Prophetic Scripture:	Subject:	Fulfilled:
Zec 9:9	Triumphal entry	Mark 11:7,9,11
Ps 8:2	Adored by Infants	Mt 21:15–16
Is 53:1	Not believed	John 12:37–38
Ps 41:9	Betrayed by a close friend	Luke 22:47–48
Zec 11:12 *Then I said to them, "If it seems good to you, give me my wages; but if not, withhold them." And they counted out my wages, thirty pieces of silver.*	Betrayed for 30 pieces of silver	Mt 26:14–15 *Then one of the Twelve, who was called Judas Iscariot, went to the chief priests and said, "What are you willing to give me if I hand him over to you?" They paid him thirty pieces of silver, ...*
Ps 35:11	Accused by false witnesses	Mark 14:57–58
Is 53:7	Silent to accusations	Mark 15:4,5
Is 50:6	Spat on and struck	Mark 26:67
Ps 35:19	Hated without reason	John 15:24–25
Is 53:5	Vicarious sacrifice	Rom 5:6,8
Is 53:12	Crucified with malefactors	Mark 15:27–28
Zec 12:10	Pierced through hands and feet	John 20:27
Ps 22:7–8	Sneered and mocked	Luke 23:35
Ps 69:9	Was reproached	Rom 15:3
Ps 109:4	Prayer for His enemies	Luke 23:34
Ps 22:18–19 *I can count all my bones. ... they divide my garments among them; for my clothing they cast lots.*	Soldiers gambled for His clothing	Mt 27:35 *After they had crucified him, they divided his garments by casting lots;*
Ps 22:1	Forsaken by God	Mt 27:46
Ps 34:20	No bones broken	John 19:32–33,36

Prophetic Scripture:	Subject:	Fulfilled:
Zec 12:10	His side pierced	John 19:34
Is 53:9	Buried with the rich	Mt 27:57–60
Ps 16:10 & Ps 49:15	To be resurrected	Mark 16:6–7
Ps 68:19 *You went up to its lofty height; you took captives, received slaves as tribute, even rebels, for the Lord God to dwell.*	His ascension to God's right hand	Mark 16:19 *So then the Lord Jesus, after he spoke to them, was taken up into heaven and took his seat at the right hand of God.* 1 Cor 15:4 *...he was buried; ...he was raised on the third day in accordance with the scriptures;* Eph 4:8 *Therefore, it says: "He ascended on high and took prisoners captive; he gave gifts to men."*
Zec 12:10 *I will pour out on the house of David and on the inhabitants of Jerusalem a spirit of mercy and supplication, so that when they look on him whom they have thrust through, they will mourn for him as one mourns for an only child, and they will grieve for him as one grieves over a firstborn.*	Jesus' body is pierced Jesus, both God and man Jesus not accepted	John 19:34 *...But one soldier thrust his lance into his side...* John 10:30 [Jesus] *The Father and I are one.* John 1:11 *He came to what was his own, but his own people did not accept him.*

In addition to the above 46 out of 351 prophecies fulfilled, see the section titled: "Let Scripture Speak for Itself on the Eucharist" for 23 additional prophecies that are only specific to the Eucharist.

Reference: www.newtestamentchristians.com/bible–study–resources/351–old–testament–prophecies–fulfilled–in–jesus–christ/ Twenty pages long.

The use of fulfilled prophecies for proof of the divine nature of Jesus Christ is not a new concept. It has been used since the time of the early Christians, where Justin Martyr, a Christian apologist from the second century, wrote a letter to the Roman Emperor 150 years after Jesus' birth stating, "We will now offer proof, not trusting mere assertations, but being of necessity persuaded by those who prophesied [of Him] before these things came to pass...and this will, we think appear even to you the strongest and trusted evidence." (Apparently this was followed by some of the prophecies fulfilled as listed above.)

Jesus Himself attested to the prophecies in Scripture, when on the road to Emmaus, Jesus said to two disciples: ***"Then beginning with Moses and all the prophets, he interpreted to them what referred to Him in all the scriptures."*** (Luke 24:27).

Prophecies Jesus made that have been Fulfilled:

Prophecy by Jesus:	Subject:	Fulfilled:
Mt 24:35	His words would be everlasting	The words of Jesus are still with us today.
Mt 26:11–13	Mary of Bethany anointed Jesus in anticipation of His death	Jesus predicted His death and that the gospel was to be preached in the whole world
Mt 26:21–22	Betrayal by one of His disciples	Luke 22:47–48
Mt 26:31–32	Jesus' disciples would scatter from Him	Mt 26:56
Mt 26:33–34	Peter would deny Him three times	Mt 26:74–75
Mt 16:21	Jesus to suffer under religious rulers	Luke 22:63–65
Mt 16:21	Jesus would die in Jerusalem	Mark 15:40–41
Mt 26:2	Jesus would die by crucifixion	Mark 15:26–27
Mt 26:2	Jesus to die during Passover	John 19:14–16

Prophecy by Jesus:	Subject:	Fulfilled:
John 2:18–22 Mt 16:21	Jesus' resurrection on the third day	Mt 27:62–63 Mt 28:6
John 14:26	The coming of the Holy Spirit	Acts 2:1–4
Luke 19:43–44 Luke 21:20	Jesus predicted Jerusalem's destruction	Jerusalem was destroyed in the year 70
Mt 24:1–2 Mt 24:34	Jesus predicted the destruction of the Temple within a generation	Titus the Roman destroyed the temple 40 years after Jesus' prediction
Luke 21:24	People would be scattered	When Jerusalem was destroyed, its people scattered. Those left not killed were sold into slavery.
Luke 21:24	Holy Land ruled by Gentiles	Except for a few years, the Holy Land was under Gentile domination for two thousand years until 1967.
Luke 23:28–30	The Jewish people would be persecuted as Jesus predicted	History records show that the Jews have been persecuted more than any other people in history – from the ghettos of the Middle Ages to the Holocaust of WW II
Luke 21:24	The Jewish nation will survive	Once the period of Gentile rule was over, the Jews again have self–rule

The information listed above proves to us that Jesus was a true prophet. There are at least seventeen specific predictions He made, each miraculously fulfilled exactly as He gave them. The scientific probability that any one person could fulfill just eight prophecies is calculated to 1 in 10 to the 17th power that's: (1 in 100,000,000,000,000,000).

Parallels Between the Jewish Passover and The Passion of Christ:

JEWISH PASSOVER & OLD TESTAMENT	PASSION OF JESUS CHRIST PARALLELS
Genesis 3 Adam was <u>tested</u> in the garden of Eden.	Luke 22:39–46 Jesus was <u>tested</u> in the Garden of Gethsemane.
Genesis 3:19 Adam was told: *"by the <u>sweat</u> of your brow shall you eat bread, until you return to the <u>ground</u>,"*	Luke 22:44 Jesus: *"...His <u>sweat</u> became like drops of blood falling on the <u>ground</u>."*
Genesis 22:2 Abraham and Isaac traveled to the *"land of <u>Moriah</u>"* 2 Chronicles 3:1 *"build the house of the Lord in Jerusalem on <u>Mt. Moriah</u>"*	Jesus was crucified just outside the Jerusalem wall on <u>Mt. Moriah</u>.
Genesis 22:6 *"Abraham took <u>the wood</u>...and laid it on his son Isaac's shoulders."*	John 19:17 *"So they took Jesus, and carrying the cross himself..."* Jesus carried the cross, *<u>the wood</u>,* on His shoulder.
Genesis 22:8. *"God himself will provide the sheep [<u>lamb</u>]"*	John 1:29 *"Behold the lamb of God."* God provided the *"<u>Lamb</u> of God"* (Jesus).
In Genesis 22:9 Isaac was a young man and did not object to the sacrifice. He was <u>willing</u> to allow it.	Jesus offered himself <u>willingly</u>. Luke 22:42 *"...not my will but yours be done."* John 6:42 *"...I came down from heaven not to do my own will but the will of the one who sent me."*
The Jewish Passover tradition was to take the sacrificial lamb to the Temple to be slaughtered. There, its blood would drain out from the <u>side</u> of the Temple, mixing with water in the Kidron Brook. Thus, <u>blood and water flowed out</u> from the <u>side</u> of the <u>Temple</u>.	John 19:34 *"...one soldier thrust his lance into His <u>side</u>, and immediately <u>blood and water flowed out</u>."* Jesus is the new *<u>Temple</u>,* and His *<u>blood and water flowed out</u>* of His side.

JEWISH PASSOVER & OLD TESTAMENT	PASSION OF JESUS CHRIST PARALLELS
Jewish Passover lamb regulation: Exodus 12:46 *"...You shall not break any of its bones."* Psalms 35:21. *"not a one [bone] shall be broken."*	John 19:36 *"For this happened so that the scripture passage might be fulfilled: 'not a bone will be broken.'"* Note (4)
The skinned lamb was fastened to a spit for it to be carried home for preparation.	Skinning the lamb parallels Jesus clothing being removed. The spit that held the lamb was in the shape of a cross.
Exodus 12:5 *"the lamb must be a year-old male and without blemish."*	Hebrews 4: 15 *"[Jesus] yet without sin."* Jesus also the lamb *"without blemish"* [sin].
Exodus 12; 8 *"...they shall eat its roasted flesh with unleavened bread and bitter herbs."* Note (1)	John 6:51 *"I am the living bread that came down from heaven; whoever eats this bread will live forever; and the bread I will give is my flesh for the life of the world."*
Exodus 12:14 *"This day shall be a memorial feast for you, which all your generations shall celebrate with pilgrimage to the Lord, as a perpetual institution."*	At the last supper, Jesus established the Eucharist as a *"memorial"* Luke 22:19 *"[Jesus] do this in memory of me."* Thus, setting up the Eucharist as *"a perpetual institution."* "memory" Note (3)
Exodus 12:22 *"Take a bunch of hyssop and dipping it in the blood of the lamb ... sprinkle the lintel and two doorposts with this blood."*	John 19:29 *"... they put a sponge soaked in wine on a sprig of hyssop and put it up to His [Jesus] mouth."* The physical action of putting blood on the lintel and two doorposts generates the sign of the cross.
Exodus 16:4 *"Then the Lord said to Moses, 'I will now rain down bread from heaven for you.'"*	John 6:41 *"The Jews murmured about Him [Jesus] because He said, 'I am the bread that came down from heaven,'"*
Exodus 16:31 *"The Israelites called this food manna. ...it tasted like wafers made with honey."*	The Eucharist also resembles a *"wafer."*

Paul Wilchek

JEWISH PASSOVER & OLD TESTAMENT	PASSION OF JESUS CHRIST PARALLELS
Exodus 24:8 Moses said: *"This is the blood of the covenant which the Lord has made with you..."*	Matthew 36:28 Jesus said: *"For this is my blood of the covenant, which will be shed on behalf of many for the forgiveness of sins."*
The Jewish Passover tradition: the lamb was to be sacrificed by the *father* of the household.	Luke 22:42 *"...not my will but yours be done."* Jesus' sacrifice was willed by His *Father.*
2 Samuel 15:12 David was betrayed by his counselor Ahithophel. 2 SAMUEL 31. *"...Ahithophel was among the conspirators..."*	Luke 22:48 *"Judas are you betraying the Son of Man with a kiss?"* Parallel to King David: Jesus was betrayed by His apostle Judas.
2 Samuel 17:23 David's counselor – *"[Ahithophel]...he hanged himself."*	Matthew 27:5 An apostle of Jesus – *"[Judas]...he departed and went off and hanged himself."*
2 Samuel 15:23 *"...the king [David] crossed the Kidron Valley..."*.	John 18:1 *"Jesus went out with his disciples across the Kidron Valley..."*
2 Samuel 15:30 *"...David went up the Mount of Olives,"*	Luke 19:29 *"[Jesus]...at the place called the Mount of Olives..."*
Deuteronomy 18:18 *"I will raise up for them a prophet like you [Moses] from among their kinsmen, and will put my words into his mouth;"*	John 6:14 *"when the people saw the sign He [Jesus] had done, they said, 'This is the prophet, the one who is to come into the world.'"*
Wisdom 7:4 *"[Solomon] In swaddling clothes and with constant care I was nurtured."* Note (2)	Luke 2:7 *"...She wrapped Him in swaddling clothes and laid Him in a manger, ... Parallel:* King Solomon and The King Jesus both wrapped *in swaddling clothes*. Also, a *"manger"* is a feeding trough, which symbolizes Jesus as our food for salvation.

Note (1): Bitter herbs, usually vinegar or sometimes salted water. On certain occasions, a dipping bowl may contain a chopped fruit mixture. Note (2): Swaddling clothes, a strip of linen or cotton 5 to 6 feet long by 4 to 6 inches wide, wrapped around a newborn for warmth and restriction. Note (3): "Memory" in Hebrew means to re–live. Note (4): Jewish regulations site punishment if a lamb bone was broken in preparation of the Passover, and if broken it rendered the sacrifice invalid.

Parallels between Jewish Feast Days and Christian Holy Days:

As part of the Sinai Covenant, also called the Mosaic Covenant with Moses, God told the Israelites in Leviticus 23:1 ***The Lord said to Moses, "Speak to the Israelites and tell them: The following are the festivals of the Lord, my feast days, which you shall celebrate with a sacred assembly..."*** Chapter 23 of Leviticus goes on to describe the details of the seven sacred annual feasts of which the Israelites are told to relive the themes of mercy and redemption and commemorate the Israelite's Exodus liberation. Some of the feasts have more than one name, and they are: The Passover, Feast of Unleavened Bread, Feast of Firstfruits, Feast of Pentecost (Feast of Weeks) (Feast of the Harvest), New Year's Day, The Day of Atonement (Trumpets), Feast of Booths (Booth of Tabernacles). Three of the feasts, Passover, Pentecost, and Tabernacles require every Israelite of the Covenant to come before Yahweh's holy altar of sacrifice.

Scripture describes that the day after The Sabbath of the holy week of the Feast of Unleavened Bread is to be the Feast of Firstfruits. Scripture then states, ***"The day after seven weeks, the fiftieth day"*** (Lev 23:16) they are to celebrate the Feast of Pentecost. At that time, they counted with no zero–place value. Therefore, the Jewish Feast of Pentecost (50 days after the Feast of Firstfruits) always falls on what is now our Sunday. In AD 33, Jesus arose from the dead on the Jewish Feast of Firstfruits, which is Christian Easter Sunday. Fifty days later was the first Christian Pentecost, where the Holy Spirit fell upon the 120 Apostles, disciples, and Mary the mother of Jesus (Acts 2:2,3,4). After Jesus' Resurrection, He taught the Apostles and disciples for 40 days until His Ascension. Jesus instructed them to wait in Jerusalem for the coming of the Holy Spirit, Pentecost, which turned out to be 10 days. Therefore, Easter Sunday and the Feast of Firstfruits are both 50 days to the Jewish Pentecost and Christian Pentecost. The New Testament of Jesus Christ parallels the Old Testament feast requirements as ordered by God. An additional parallel is the Jewish Pentecost was the birth of the Jewish nation while the Christian Pentecost was the birth of the Catholic Church.

Old Covenant Feasts – Fulfilled by Christ:

OLD COVENENT ANNUAL FEASTS (Hebrew name)	FULFILLED BY CHRIST
PASSOVER: (Pesach) (*) Lv 24:5 *The Passover of the Lord falls on the fourteenth day of the first month, at the evening twilight.* Passover is a meal commemorating the sacrificed lamb's blood that saved the Israelites.	The Passover and Good Friday typically fall on the same day. The presence of the lamb's blood that was shed saved the Israelites. Christ was crucified for the salvation of many. The Passover prefigured Christ as mankind's Passover sacrifice for salvation.
UNLEAVENED BREAD:(Hagha–matzoth) Lv 23:6 *The fifteenth day of this month is the Lord's feast of Unleavened Bread. For seven days you shall eat unleavened bread.* Celebrates the journey of the Israelites through the wilderness following Passover and the Exodus. Celebrated for seven days and eight nights to commemorate the liberation from 400 years of slavery in Egypt Ex 12:14 *This day shall be a memorial feast for you, which all your generations shall celebrate...as a perpetual institution.*	Jesus' crucifixion and death occurred on the Fest of Unleavened Bread. The Israelites believed that the yeast in bread symbolized sin. Therefore, unleavened bread is unblemished, symbolizing Jesus, the unblemished Lamb of God who at the Last Supper instituted the Eucharist, the bread containing His unblemished body, blood, soul, and divinity.
FIRST FRUITS: (Shavuot) Lv 23:10 *When you come into the land which I am giving you, and reap your harvest, you shall bring a sheaf of the first fruits...* Celebration of the harvest of the first fruits in the promised land.	The Resurrection of Jesus occurred on the Feast of First Fruits, Easter Sunday, the day after the Old Covenant Saturday Sabbath.

OLD COVENENT ANNUAL FEASTS (Hebrew name)	FULFILLED BY CHRIST
PENTECOST: (Shavuot) (*) Also called: Feast of Weeks, Feast of Harvest. Celebrated 50 days from the First Fruits is the remembrance of the Law given by God to Moses on Mount Sini, the birth of the Jewish nation.	The descent of the Holy Spirit occurred on the Feast of Pentecost, 50 days after His Resurrection, the birth of the Catholic Church, Christ's Kingdom on earth, the New Covenant.

Old Covenant Feasts – To Be Fulfilled:

OLD COVENENT ANNUAL FEASTS	TO BE FULFILLED AT END TIMES
TRUMPETS: (Rosh Hashanah) Lv 23:24 *...with a sacred assembly and with the trumpet blast as a reminder; you shall then do no sort of work, and you shall offer an oblation to the Lord.* Celebration of the Jewish New Year.	The trumpet blast will announce the return of Jesus Christ in glory. Mt 24:30–31 *...the Son of Man coming upon the clouds of heaven with power and great glory. And he will send out his angels with a trumpet blast.*
ATONEMENT: (Yom Kippur) Lv 23 28 **On this day you shall not do any work, because it is the Day of Atonement, when atonement is made for you before the Lord, your God.** The holiest day of the year in Judaism for atonement and repentance.	Parallels the final judgement at end times. 2 Cor 5:10 *For we must appear before the judgement seat of Christ, so that each one may receive recompense, according to what he did in body, whether good or evil.*
TABERNACLES: (Sukkot) (*) Lv 24: 43 *that your descendants may realize that, when I led the Israelites out of the land of Egypt, I made them dwell in booths.*	Feast of Tabernacles parallels or is symbolic of Christ's second coming and the creation of the new Heaven on earth.

Also called: Feast of Booths, Festival of Shelters, or Feast of Ingathering. A festival requiring the Israelites pilgrimage to the Temple for a sacred assembly, bringing their tithes and offerings.	Rev 21:1 *Then I saw a new heaven and a new earth.*

(*) Passover, Pentecost, and Tabernacles require that every Israelite of the Covenant to personally appear before Yahweh's holy altar of sacrifice in the Temple.

Parallel Between God the Father and Jesus' Commanding Nature:

OLD TESTAMENT:	NEW TESTAMENT:
GOD SAVES SAILORS IN A STORM AT SEA Psalms 107: (LORD/Yahweh)	JESUS SAVES THE DISCIPLES IN A STORM AT SEA Matthew 8: Mark 4: and Luke 8:
SAILORS IN SHIPS: Ps 107:23 *Some went off to sea in ships, plied their trade on the deep waters.*	DISCIPLES IN A BOAT: Mt 8:23 *He [Jesus] got into a boat and his disciples followed him.* Also, Mk 4:36, Lk 8:22
WAVES THREATENS SHIPS: Ps 107:25 *He spoke and roused a storm wind; it tossed the waves high.*	WAVES THREATENS THE BOAT: Mt 8:24 *Suddenly a violent storm came up on the sea, so that the boat was being swamped by waves.* Also, Mk 4:37, Lk 8:23
SAILORS WERE FRIGHTENED: Ps 107:26 *their hearts trembled at the danger.*	DISCIPLES BECAME FRIGHTNED: Mt 8:25 *They came and woke him [Jesus], saying, "Lord save us! We are perishing!"* Also, Mk 4:37, Lk 8:23
SAILORS CRY OUT TO THE LORD: Ps 107 28 *In their distress they cried to the LORD.*	DISCIPLES CRY OUT TO JESUS: Mt 8:25 ... *"Lord save us! We are perishing!"* Also, Mk 4:39, Lk 8:23

OLD TESTAMENT:	NEW TESTAMENT:
THE LORD STOPS THE STORM: Ps 107:29 *...the LORD ... Hushed the storm to a murmur; the waves of the sea were stilled.*	JESUS STOPS THE STORM: Mt 8:26 *...He [Jesus] got up, rebuked the winds and the sea,* Also, Mk 4:39, Lk 8:24
THE LORD CALMS THE SEA: Ps 107:30 *They rejoiced that the sea grew calm.*	JESUS CALMS THE SEA: Mt 8:26 *... and there was great calm.* Also, Mk 4:39, Lk 8:24

GOD (LORD/Yahweh) commands nature in the Old Testament just as the Son of God commands nature in the New Testament to convince the disciples that Jesus is GOD. The disciples also witness Jesus walking on the sea and calming a storm in John 6:16–21. The book of JOB tells us that only GOD can walk, treads upon, the sea: Job 9:8 *He alone stretches out the heavens, and treads upon the crest of the sea.* If GOD can control the wind and sea (nature), GOD can also save those who have faith and trust in Him when there are storms in human lives. He will never abandon us if we only have faith. Also, if GOD can control the wind and sea (nature), He most certainly can have Jesus Christ's body, soul, and divinity present within the Eucharist.

Notice in Job 9:8 above that GOD *"stretches out the heavens."* It has only been in modern times, through the Hubble telescope, that science has determined that the universe is expanding (*stretches out*).

Reference:
agapebiblestudy.com, The Feast of Pentecost
The New American Bible, World press.
agapebiblestudy.com, Michael E. Hunt, 12th Sunday in Ordinary Time (B).

Parallels of Feeding the 5 thousand to the Last Supper:

FEEDING OF THE 5 THOUSAND	THE LAST SUPPER PARALLEL
Matthew 14:15 **When it was evening...** The feeding of the 5 thousand took pace in the <u>evening</u>.	The Last supper took place in the <u>evening</u>
The Passover (Unleavened Bread) began after sundown. Exodus 12:6,8 ₆**...it will be slaughtered during the evening twilight.** ₈**They will consume its meat that same <u>night</u>.**	The Last supper took place in the <u>evening</u> The Last Supper took place on the Jewish Passover.
Matthew 14:19 **and he ordered the crowds to <u>sit down</u> on the grass.** They <u>reclined</u> to eat.	Matthew 26:20 **When it was <u>evening</u>, he [Jesus] <u>reclined</u> at table with the Twelve.** They <u>reclined</u> to eat.
Matthew 14:19 **...Taking the five <u>loaves</u> and the two fish, and looked up to heaven, he said the <u>blessing</u> ...** Jesus <u>blessed</u> the <u>bread</u>.	Matthew 26:26 **...Jesus took <u>bread</u>, said the <u>blessing</u>...** Jesus <u>blessed</u> the <u>bread</u>.
Matthew 14:19 **...[Jesus] <u>broke</u> the loaves, and <u>gave</u> them to the disciples...** Jesus <u>broke</u> the bread and <u>gave</u> it.	Matthew 26:26 **[Jesus] <u>broke</u> it [the bread] and <u>giving</u> it to his disciples...** Jesus <u>broke</u> the bread and <u>gave</u> it.
Matthew 14:20 **They all <u>ate</u> and were satisfied.** They <u>ate</u> the bread that Jesus blessed.	Matthew 26:26 **...Take and <u>eat</u>; this is my body.** They <u>ate</u> the bread that Jesus blessed.

+ The Jewish feast of Passover, also called Unleavened Bread, begins after sundown just as the Last Supper began at sundown.
+ Our communion hoist is unleavened bread just as the unleavened bread that was eaten at Passover.
+ The feeding of the 5 thousand and the Last Supper have <u>seven</u> parallels: they both took place in the (1) <u>evening</u>, they (2) <u>reclined</u> to eat, (3)Jesus <u>blessed</u> the (4) <u>bread</u>, Jesus (5) <u>broke</u> the bread, Jesus (6) <u>gave</u> the bread, and they (7) <u>ate</u> the bread that Jesus blessed.

+ There are also some dis–similar items: The 5 thousand had barley bread not unleavened bread, they ate fish not roasted lamb.

+ The multiplication of bread miracle of the 5 thousand, prefigured the miracle at the Last Supper where Jesus stated, *"this **is** my body"* (Mt 26:26), the miracle that would become available for the many according to the command of Jesus, *"do this in memory me."* (Lk 22:19)

Reference: The above chart is similar, not a copy, of Agape Bible Study, Michael E. Hunt 2013.

Parallels of the Trinity of God to Human Creation:

Image of the Trinity of God

Genesis 1:27 *God created man **in his image**; in **divine image** he created him; male and female he created them.* Genesis 2:7 *... the Lord God ... blew onto his nostrils the **breath** of life, and so man became a living being.* The **breath** in Scripture is a representation of the **spirit**. Adam and Eve were perfect humans and their **spirits** had intimate communications with God. After the fall, they were dead to the **spirit**, and it wasn't until baptism where the **spirit** was re–introduced. Humans are the only creatures created that parallel the trinity of God's nature. Scripture tells us we are **in his image** (**divine image**) and **you entirely** are **spirit**, **soul**, and **body**. Notice that the **spirit**, the **soul**, and the **body** are three separate entities **entirely** within humans:

Image of the Trinity of Humans

1 Thessalonians 5:23 *May the God of peace himself make you perfectly holy and may* <u>*you entirely, spirit, soul,*</u> *and* <u>*body,*</u> *be preserved blameless for the coming of our Lord Jesus Christ.*

John 3:5 [Jesus stated]: *Amen, amen, I say to you no one can enter the kingdom of God without being born of water and* <u>*spirit.*</u> The <u>*spirit*</u> within us, freely has two–way communications with God. Romans 8:27 *...because it [the spirit] intercedes for the holy ones according to God's will.* Our <u>*spirit*</u> then communicates with our <u>*soul*</u> then our <u>*soul*</u> and <u>*body*</u> have two–way communications using the free will that was given to us, leading us to a final decision. One can be influenced by an outside spirit as 1 John 4 states: ₁*...test the* <u>*spirits*</u> *to see whether they belong to God...* ₂*...every spirit that acknowledges Jesus Christ...belongs to God.* Galatians 4:22 *... the fruit of the* <u>*spirit*</u> *is love, joy, peace, patience, kindness, generosity, faithfulness, gentleness, self–control.*

One has to observe that the books of Scripture were written by different people and had to be inspired by God in order for so many parallels to be coordinated like above.

Hidden Prophecy: (one example)
Gabriel came to Daniel with a vision and (in part) stated the following: Daniel 9:25 *"Know and understand this: From the utterance of the word that Jerusalem was to be rebuilt until* <u>*one who is anointed*</u> *and a leader, there shall be seven weeks. During sixty–two weeks it shall be rebuilt, With streets and trenches, in time of* <u>*affliction.*</u>*"* The *"*<u>*one who is anointed*</u>*"* is a reference the Son of Man (Jesus).

Also, it was determined that the 7 weeks and 62 weeks were written in such a way that it was coded and referred to Ezekiel. Ezekiel 4:6 *"...one day for each year I have allotted you."* During a time of affliction, in the year 457 BC, the King of Persia issued a decree to rebuild Jerusalem. 7 weeks plus 62 weeks is 69 weeks. 69 weeks times 7 days/week is 483 days. 483 days means 483 years (per Ezekiel). Therefore, 483 years forward from the decree year of 457 BC is the year 27 AD, the year that Jesus started his ministry, (this takes into account that there is no registered year of zero).

Theologians calculated that in the year 27 AD, Jesus unrolled the scroll and read: *"The Spirit of the Lord is upon me. To bring glad tidings to the poor. He has sent me to proclaim liberty to captives and recovery of sight to the blind, to let the oppressed go free, and to proclaim a year acceptable to the Lord."* This is a quotation from Luke 4:18, of which Luke in quoting Isaiah 61:1–2.

Hidden Message in Scripture: (one example)
Genesis 5: Titled: "Generations: Adam to Noah." (In order as they appear):

Descendants' names:	Hebrew meaning:
Adam	man
Seth	appointed
Enoch	mortal
Kenan	sorrow
Mahalalel	the blessed God
Jared	shall come down
Enoch	teaching
Methuselah	his death shall bring
Lamech	the despairing
Noah	comfort, rest

Now if you read the Hebrew meaning of the 10 names as if it were a sentence, it tells us:

Man *[is]* appointed *[as]* mortal *[and lives in]* sorrow, the blessed God shall come down, teaching *[and]* his death shall bring the despairing comfort *[and]* rest. The odds of all 10 of the above being in this order are astronomical.

Paul Wilchek

Hidden Symbolism in Scripture: (one example)
Luke 2:7 ...*she gave birth to her firstborn son. She wrapped him in swaddling clothes and laid him in a manger, because there was no room for them in the inn.*

Have you ever wondered why we are given the detail of Jesus being *"wrapped in swaddling clothes and laid him in a manger"* as stated above? *"Swaddling clothes"* are narrow bands of cloth wrapped around an infant to restrain the child and keep it warm, it was a practice commonly used in that time period. Solomon, a great king and the son of David, according to scripture, was also wrapped in swaddling clothes. So, this may symbolize the kingship of Jesus. But then why *"laid in a manger?"* Possibly two reasons: First, the shepherds were told by an angel: *"this will be a sign for you: you will find an infant wrapped in swaddling clothes and lying in a manger."* Being in a manger is rather unique, so it must have been to aid them in finding Jesus. Second, a manger is a feeding trough which most lightly is meant to symbolize that Jesus was to become our food for salvation.

Hidden Numbers in the Bible:
John 21:10–11 *Jesus said to them, "bring some of the fish you just caught." So Simon Peter went over and dragged the net ashore full of <u>one hundred fifty-three</u> large fish.*
Have you ever wondered why scripture gives us this kind of detail, <u>153</u> large fish?
Researching Scripture, found the following:
In the book of Matthew, Jesus blessed a total of 47 people. Some of those to whom God's grace was bestowed include a leper (Matthew 8:2), a non–Israelite woman and her daughter (Matthew 15:22), Mary Magdalene (Matthew 27:56), and Joseph of Arimathea (Matthew 27:57).
The book of Mark recorded Jesus, on a total of 3 occasions, personally blessing 3 people. These events were the healing of a man with an unclean spirit (Mark 1:23), healing a man who was deaf (Mark 7:32), and making whole another who was blind (Mark 8:22).
Luke wrote that on 14 occasions 94 people were blessed. They include the 70 disciples sent out to preach and heal (Luke 10:1), ten lepers cleansed at the same time (Luke 17:1), and Zacchaeus (Luke 19:2).

— 120 —

The book of John records 8 incidents where 9 people were helped by Jesus. Some are: Nicodemus (John 3:1), the woman accused of adultery (John 8:11), and the raising of Lazarus (John 11).

Therefore, Jesus directly blessed a total of <u>153</u> people, explaining the scripture statement of: ***"...one hundred fifty-three large fish"*** (Jn 21:11) The Footnote of the Didache Bible states: St, Jerome claimed that the Greeks of that time had catalogued 153 different species of fish. The symbolism expressed in John 21:1–15, therefore, the number would indicate the Apostles were going to win converts to the Church from people of every nation on earth.

The Number Seven in Scripture:
The number <u>seven</u> is considered the "perfect" number in Scared Scripture, reflecting fullness and perfection, especially spiritual perfection. From the very start of Scripture, after creation, God rested on the <u>seven</u>th day, followed by the many times <u>seven</u> is used, in addition to the use of the actual word seven, there are many insaneness where a particular occurrence happens <u>seven</u> times.

Seven in the Old Testament.

Genesis 2:2 ***Since on the <u>seventh</u> day God was finished with the work he had been doing, he rested on the <u>seventh</u> day ...***

<u>Seven</u> times God mentioned the word "good" and "created" in Genesis 1.

The Lord said to Noah: Genesis 7:2 ***Of every clean animal, take with you <u>seven</u> pairs, ...***

After Noah entered the Ark: Genesis 7:10 ***As soon as <u>seven</u> days were over, the waters of the flood came upon earth.***

Noah entered the Ark with <u>seven</u> family members (Gn 7:13); Noah was the eighth. The number eight represents rebirth and a new beginning.

Genesis 8:4 *...On the <u>seventeenth</u> day of the month, the ark came to rest ...*

Genesis 8:10 *He [Noah] waited <u>seven</u> days more and again sent the dove out from the ark.*

Genesis 8:12 *He waited still another <u>seven</u> days and then released the dove once more; ...*

Genesis 9:13 *I set my <u>bow in the clouds</u> to serve as a sign of the <u>covenant</u> between me and the earth.* The rainbow has <u>seven</u> colors, red, orange, yellow, green, blue, indigo, and violet.

The Old Testament has <u>seven</u> <u>covenants</u>: Adam, Noah, Abraham, Moses, Aaron, Phinehas, and David. The eighth <u>covenant</u> being The <u>New Covenant</u> (eight meaning rebirth, new beginning) was established by Jesus.

There are <u>seven</u> sacred Jewish feasts: (1) <u>The Sabbath</u>, (2) <u>The Passover</u>, (3) <u>Feast of Unleavened Bread</u>, (4) <u>Feast of Firstfruits</u>, (5) <u>Feast of Pentecost</u> – (Feast of Weeks)– (Feast of the Harvest), (6) <u>The Day of Atonement</u>– (Trumpets), (7) <u>Feast of Tabernacles</u>– (Booth of Tabernacles).

Genesis 22:28 *Abraham also set apart <u>seven</u> ewe lambs of the flock.*

Genesis 29:18 *I [Jacob] will serve you <u>seven</u> years for your younger daughter Rachel.*

Genesis 41:1–7 *Pharaoh had a dream where he saw <u>seven</u> items a total of <u>seven</u> times.*

Exodus 2:16 *<u>Seven</u> daughters of a priest of Midian came to draw water...*

Exodus 12 15 *For <u>seven</u> days you must eat unleavened bread.* (Passover memorial fest)

Exodus 23:11 *But the <u>seventh</u> year you shall let the land lie untilled and unharvested.*

Exodus 25:37 *You shall then make <u>seven</u> lamps...*

Exodus 29:35 *<u>Seven</u> days you shall spend in ordaining them...* (The Jewish Ordination Sacrifices)

Numbers 23: 1 (after Balaam saw an angel) *... Build me <u>seven</u> alters, and prepare <u>seven</u> bullocks and <u>seven</u> rams for me here.*

Deuteronomy 7: 1 (to Abraham) *... <u>seven</u> nations more numerous and powerful than you – ...God, delivers them up to you and you defeat them, ...*

Joshua 6:4 (the fall of Jericho) *with <u>seven</u> priests carrying ram's horns ahead of the ark. On the <u>seventh</u> day march around the city <u>seven</u> times, and have the priest blow the horns.*

Judges 16:13 (Samson mocking Delilah as to where his strength comes from) *If you weave my <u>seven</u> locks of hair into the web and fasten them with the pin, I shall be as weak as any other man.*

2 Kings 5:10 *The prophet [Elisha] sent him the message: Go and wash <u>seven</u> times in the Jordan, and your flesh will heal, and you will be clean.*

Psalms 19:8–10, attributed to King David, describes the Law of Yahweh using <u>seven</u> synonyms: Perfect, Trustworthy, Right, Clear, Pure, True, and Just.

Psalms 119:164 *<u>Seven</u> times a day I praise you because your edicts are just.*

Seven in the New Testament.
Jesus replied to Peters question that one must forgive, Matthew 18:22 *I say to you, not <u>seven</u> times but <u>seventy–seven</u> times.*

The Seven Times Jesus Said "I Am" in the Gospel of John
John 6:35 *"I am the bread..."*
John 8:12 *'I am the light of the world..."*
John 10:9 *"I am the gate..."*
John 10:11,14 *"I am the good shepherd..."*
John 11:25 *"I am the resurrection..."*
John 14:6 *"I am the way and the truth and the life."*
John 15: 1,5 *"I am the true vine..."*
The original Hebrew word in scripture for God ment "I am that I am that" then it became Yahweh which generally means "he brings into existence whatever exists" or "He who makes that which has been made."

The Seven Sacraments in Scripture (**bold** passages are the words of Jesus).
Anointing of Sick: Mk 6:13, Jas 5:14
Baptism: **Jn 3:5, Mt 28:19, Mk 16:16**, Acts 2:38/19:5
Confirmation: Acts 19 5,6, Heb 6:2, 2 Cor 1:21–22, Eph 1:13
Eucharist: **Mt 26:26–28, Mk 14:22–24, Lk 22:19–20**
Holy Orders: **Jn 20:21–23, Lk 22: 28–30**
Matrimony: **Mt 19:4–6**, Eph 5:25–31, **Mk 10:7**
Penance: **Mt 18:18/16:19**, Mk 1:4, **Jn 20:21–23**, 2 Cor 5:18–20
Note: For more details on the Sacraments see Chapter 9

Seven Miracles that Occurred at the Crucifixion of Christ:
Each of: Matthew 27 starting at verse 45, Mark 15 starting at verse 33. Luke 23 starting at verse 44, and John 19 starting at verse 17, all tell us the details of Christ's crucifixion and the miracles that occurred.

1. *"From noon onward, darkness came over the whole land until three in the afternoon."* (Mt 27:45, Mk 14:33, Lk 23:44) (a)
2. One of the criminals next to Jesus recognized and defended Jesus. The condemned criminal admitted that his punishment was just and asked Jesus to: *"remember me."* (Lk 23:43). Jesus told the criminal, *"Amen, I say to you, today you will be with me in Paradise."* (Lk 23:43).
3. *"Jesus cried out in a loud voice, 'Father, into your hands I commend my spirit'"* (Lk 23:46). Jesus willingly died fulfilling His mission to bring salvation to humankind, which included taking upon Himself all the sins of the world. After which, Jesus descended into "hell" (some

passages called it *"prison"**) where He may have deposited those sins, and preached to the dead.

"Prison" reference: 1 Peter 3:18–19, *"For Christ also suffered for sins once. the righteous for the sake of the unrighteous, that He might lead you to God. Put to death in the flesh, He was brought to life in the spirit. In it He also went to preach to the spirits in prison,"* Then in 1 Peter 4:6 it states: *"For this is why the gospel was preached even to the dead…"* The people in *"prison"* since the time of Noah were given the opportunity to accept Jesus and enter the now opened heaven.

4. *"And behold, the veil of the sanctuary was torn in two from top to bottom."* (Mt 27:51, Mk 15:38, Lk 23:45). It is told that the *"veil"* was as thick as a person's hand.
5. *"The earth quaked, rocks were split."* (Mt 27:52) (a)
6. *"…tombs were opened, and the bodies of many saints who had fallen asleep were raised… they entered the holy city and appeared to many."* (Mt 27:51–52) (a)
7. A centurion (possibility other soldiers) was converted and said: *"Truly this man was the Son of God."* (Mt 27:54, Mk 15:39, Lk 23:47)

(a) Secular public Roman records verified three of these events. Pontius Pilate wrote: *"at the time he was crucified there was darkness over all the world."* Pontius Pilate also wrote: *"people were terrified seeing dead men walking and that there was an earthquake at that time."*

A 2nd century Christian Historian, Julius Africanus, (born 160–died 240) wrote about the three hours of darkness. He explained that the darkness may have been *"like an eclipse."* However, it could not have been an eclipse of the sun because the time period was the Jewish Passover, which always occurs at a full moon, making an eclipse impossible. In addition, an eclipse does not last three hours in one location. He further explains that the three hours of darkness had to be by divine intervention.

The Seven Statements of Jesus on the Cross.
Jesus spoke seven statements from the cross.

Luke 23:34 *"Father, forgive them, they know what they do."* In Acts 8:60, Stephen made a similar statement at his death.

Luke 23:43 *"Amen, I say to you, today you will be with me in paradise."*

John 19:26–27 *"Woman behold, your son." "Behold your mother."*

Matthew 27:46 *"My God, my God, why have you forsaken me?"* also Mark 15:34 and Psalms 22:1.

John 19:28 *"I thirst."*

John 19:30 *"It is finished."*

Luke 23:46 *"Father, into your hands I commend my spirit"* also Psalms 31:6 then in Acts 7:59, Stephen made a similar statement at his death.

Seven Gifts of the Holy Spirit.
The seven gifts of the Holy Spirit are given at baptism and reminded at confirmation. Isaiah 11:2 *The spirit of the Lord shall rest upon him: a spirit of <u>wisdom</u> and of <u>understanding</u>, a spirit of <u>counsel</u> and <u>strength</u> [fortitude], a spirit of <u>knowledge</u> and of <u>fear of the Lord</u> [piety], and his delight shall be <u>the fear of the Lord</u>.*

There are 17 first appearances of <u>seven</u> in Revelation: <u>seven</u> churches, <u>seven</u> spirits, <u>seven</u> gold lampstands, <u>seven</u> stars, <u>seven</u> flaming torches, <u>seven</u> seals, <u>seven</u> horns, <u>seven</u> eyes, <u>seven</u> angels, <u>seven</u> trumpets, <u>seven</u> thunders, <u>seven</u> diadems, <u>seven</u> heads, <u>seven</u> plagues, <u>seven</u> gold bowls, <u>seven</u> hills, and <u>seven</u> kings.

This is not a complete list, <u>seven</u> is in Scripture over 700 times.

Reference:
The New American Bible (NAB), World Press.
The New American Bible Concordance, Oxford University Press.

Miracles at the Temple:

The "Talmud" is the written record of Jewish rabbis discussing or debating what things mean, including scripture commentary and religious history. One is known as the "Jerusalem Talmud" and another as the "Babylonian Talmud."

The following is a quotation from each of these Jewish civil records: Jerusalem Talmud: "Forty years before the destruction of the Temple, the western light went out, the crimson thread remained crimson, and the lot for the Lord always came up in the left hand. They would close the gates of the Temple by night and get up in the morning and find them wide open" [the Temple was destroyed in the year 70].

Babylonian Talmud: "Our rabbis taught: During the last forty years before the destruction of the Temple the lot ['For the Lord'] did not come up in the right hand; nor did the crimson–colored strap become white; nor did the western most light shine; and the doors of the Hekel [Temple] would open by themselves."

The "Talmud" in Jerusalem and the "Talmud" in Babylon both recount the same basic information that indicates these events (miracles) were accepted by the widespread Jewish community. To understand this, we need to look at Jewish tradition regarding "Lot," "Crimson strap," "Temple doors," and "Temple Menorah."

Miracle of the "Lot:" The "Lot" is the Jewish procedure of random selection which was cast on the Day of Atonement (Yom Kippur) to determine which of two goats would be "For the Lord" (sacrificed) and which goat would be the "Azazel" (scapegoat). For two hundred years prior to the year 30, the High Priest randomly selected a white stone as often as a black stone. However, for forty years in a row, beginning in the year 30, the High Priest always randomly picked the black stone! The odds against this occurring are astronomical! The random selection of a black stone came up 40 times in a row from the year 30 to the destruction year of 70. This was considered a dire event because something changed in the Jewish Yom Kippur ritual.

Miracle of the "Crimson Strap:" A crimson strap, strip, thread, or cloth was tied to the Azazel goat (scapegoat) which was let free and a separate portion of the crimson strap was tied to the Temple door. Prior to the year 30, the crimson strap on the Temple door usually turned white to signify atonement and that another Yom Kippur was acceptable to the Lord. However, for forty years in a row, from the year 30 to the destruction year of 70, the strap, strip, thread, or cloth remained crimson. This traditional practice caused consternation among the Jews because sin was represented by the red color (crimson, the color of blood) and Israel's sins were not being pardoned or "made white." Isaiah 1:18, *Come let us reason together, saith the Lord: though your sins be as scarlet [crimson], they shall be white as snow; though they be red like crimson, they shall be as [white] wool.*

The Miracle of the "Temple Doors:" For forty years, beginning in the year 30, the Temple doors *"would open by themselves"* every night. The leading Jewish authority at that time, Yohanan ben Zakkai, declared that this was a sign of impending doom, that the Temple itself would be destroyed. Might the doors to the Temple have opened to signify that all now have access to the Lord's house of worship? This would be similar to the meaning of: *"the veil of the sanctuary was torn in two from top to bottom."* (Mt 27:51).

The Miracle of the "Temple Menorah": According to Jewish tradition, the 'western lamp' (menorah) was to be kept lit at all times. To assure this, the priest kept extra reservoirs of olive oil and other implements in ready supply to keep the 'western lamp' lit. However, for forty years, beginning at year 30, the 'western lamp' would go out each night, in spite of the fact that each evening the priests prepared a special way for the 'western lamp' to remain burning all night. The odds of this lamp going out over 12,500 nights in a row are astronomical. Plus, there were actually a total of four menorah lights, and the only lamp that was reported as going out each night for forty years was the 'western lamp.' The menorahs that lit the Temple were very large; the priest had to use a ladder to light them.

There is no natural way to explain all four of these documented signs that transpired for forty years. One can only conclude that these were the supernatural events (miracles) that occurred during the time Jesus was on earth and after His resurrection (until the destruction of the Temple), which Jesus foretold.

The "Miracles at the Temple" is a partial excerpt and paraphrased from: "Talmudic Evidence for the Messiah at 30 C.E." by Federoff & T. Peterson – provided by Howard Glickman.

Eucharist Miracle:
There have been many Eucharistic miracles in the world, however, one of the best documented miracles occurred in Buenos Aires, Argentina. The details can be found in a book called "The Eucharistic Miracles of the World" as well as in a discussion by Father Mark Goring on "YouTube" called "The World's 2nd Most Impressive Eucharist Miracle." The following from the above book is condensed and paraphrased:

August 15, 1996, during the normal distribution of the Eucharist at Mass, a host accidently fell to the ground. According to Catholic procedure, the host was put in water to dissolve with the intention to later pour it into the ground, also standard procedure.

On August 26, 1996, the tabernacle was opened. Inside it was found that the host was not dissolved and it now contained within it many red streaks. The priest contacted the Archbishop of Buenos Aires (who is now Pope Francis). The consecrated host was photographed and documented and taken to Doctor Gomez* to examine. He determined that the tissue was from an inflamed heart and from a person who suffered.

March 2, 2004, the tissue was taken to Doctor Fredrick Thomas Zugibe at Columbia University, the greatest doctor known worldwide who could examine heart tissue and determine how the person died. Dr. Zugibe was not told it was from a consecrated host.

Doctor Zugibe's findings: "The tissue is myocardium" (muscular tissue of the heart's left ventricle that pumps purified blood), "the patient suffered greatly," "at a point in time patient could not breathe – oxygen did not enter," "the tissue upon arrival contained white blood cells and was pulsating." (White blood cells (WBC) rush to an area under stress as part of the body's natural immune system.)

NOTE: (*) *Gomez, may not be correct spelling, here it is spelled as it sounded on "YouTube"

SUMMARY – MIRACLES:
+ There was darkness for three hours.
+ A criminal next to Jesus confessed and was promised heaven.
+ The death of Jesus brought about salvation to humankind.
+ Upon Jesus' death the Temple sanctuary veil, which was as thick as a person's hand, tore in two.
+ Upon Jesus' death the earth quaked.
+ Upon Jesus' death tombs opened and the dead walked the city.
+ After Jesus' death a Roman centurion (possibly others) was converted.
+ For 40 years the Temple door's crimson strip did not turn white.
+ For 40 years the Temple doors opened by themselves every night.
+ For 40 years the Temple's western menorah lamp went out every night (12,500 times in a row).
+ There have been many recorded Eucharist Miracles.

The Miraculous Conception, Mary Born Full of Grace, Mary the Ark of the New Covenant
The Miraculous Conception: (one of the greatest miracles in Scripture) Luke 1: 31, is where the angel Gabriel said to Mary, ***"Behold, you will conceive in your womb, and bear a son, and you shall name him Jesus."*** This is very unique in scripture! All other passages in Scripture using the word "conceive" are all connected to a physical relationship. The following Scripture references give examples:
Genesis 4:17, ***"Cain knew his wife and she conceived."***

Genesis 30:5, *"... Jacob had intercourse with her. [She] conceived."* 1 Chronicles 7:23, *"[Ephraim] he had relations with his wife, who conceived."* Isaiah 8:3, *"Then I went to the prophetess and she conceived and bore a son."*

Therefore, Luke's unique passage of *"you will conceive in your womb"* describes the miraculous conception that occurred without any physical contact *"in your womb"*, thus maintaining the virginity of Mary.

Luke 1:35, Gabriel said to Mary, *"...the power of the Most High will overshadow you."* The word "overshadow" is another uniquely used term, because the only two other places in Scripture where "overshadow" or "cloud" indicating "overshadow" are used. One is during the Transfiguration. It is described in Matthew 17:5, Mark 9:7, and Luke 9:34, where God "overshadows" three Apostles and speaks to them. Matthew then tells us that *"they fell prostate."*

Exodus 40:34–35 *Then the cloud covered* [overshadowed] *the meeting tent, and the glory of the lord filed the Dwelling. Moses could not enter the meeting tent, because the cloud settled down upon it and the glory of the Lord filled the Dwelling.* God's Spirit "overshadowed" the tent in the desert which held the Ark of the Covenant. The Fathers of the Church wrote about the connection between the Virgin Mary and the Ark of the Covenant.

Our Savior's miraculous conception is unique in all of Scripture where the seed of Jesus is placed into the Virgin Mary's womb without any physical contact in order to fulfill the prophesy of Isaiah 7:14, *"the virgin shall be with child, and bear a son, and shall name him Immanuel."*

The Catechism of the Catholic Church (CCC 510) tells us the following: Mary "remained a virgin in conceiving her son, a virgin in giving birth to Him, a virgin in carrying Him, a virgin in nursing Him, always a virgin" (St. Augustine). It also states in (CCC 499): The Church celebrates Mary as ever–virgin.

Mary Born Full of Grace:
Luke 1:28 *And coming to her, he said "Hail, full of grace! The Lord is with you."* This is according to Jerome's Latin Vulgate translation, however,

the Greek words for "Full of grace" is interpreted as "has been graced" indicating the past, which is Mary's unique conception without original sin. This verifies that Mary possesses and always possessed divine grace. The Fathers and Doctors of the Church taught what the 255th Pope Pius IX (1846–1878) stated in his encyclical: "this singular, solemn and unheard–of greeting showed that all the divine graces reposed in the Mother of God and that she was adorned with all the gifts of the Hoy Spirit. This singular condition meant that Mary was never subject to the curse of original sin and that she was preserved from all sin. The theological explosive words of the Archangel Gabriel constitute one of the important text sources which reveal the dogma of Mary's Immaculate Conception."

Mary the Ark of the New Covenant:
The Ark of the Covenant with its sacred lid was last seen just before Jerusalem's destruction in 587 to 586 BC. The prophet Jeremiah took the Ark out of the Temple and hid it in a cave on Mt. Nebo. 2 Maccabees 2:5–7 *Jeremiah…found a room in a cave in which he put the tent, the Ark, and the altar of incense; then he blocked up the entrance. Some of those who followed him came up intending to mark the path, but they could not find it. When Jeremiah heard of this, he reproved them; "The place is to remain unknown until God gathers his people together again and shows them mercy…"*

St. Augustine tells us: "The Old Testament is the New Testament concealed." He is Telling us the New Testament in only completely understood in light of the Old Testament – part of which is revealed in the following:

THE OLD TESTAMENT	CONFIRMED IN THE NEW TESTAMENT
Exodus 40:34–35 *Then the cloud covered the meeting tent, and the glory of the Lord filled the Dwelling.* God the Holy Spirit overshadowed the tent where the Ark contained the dwelling place of the Lord.	Luke 1:35 *And the angel said to her in reply, "The holy spirit will come upon you, and the power of the Most High will overshadow you.* God the Holy Spirit overshadowed Mary to place within her womb the dwelling place of Jesus.
The Word of God in the Ark (10 Commandments)	The Word of God in Mary's Womb (Jesus)

THE OLD TESTAMENT	CONFIRMED IN THE NEW TESTAMENT
Exodus 25:16 *In the <u>ark</u> you are to put the <u>commandments</u> which I will give you.* The ark contained the <u>word of God</u>.	Luke 1:35 (above) The womb of the virgin Mary contained Jesus, the <u>word of God</u>.
2 Samuel 6:2 *Then David and all the people who were with him <u>set out</u> for Baala of <u>Judah</u> to bring up from there the <u>ark of God</u>.*	Luke 1:39 *Mary <u>set out</u> and traveled to the hill country in haste to a town of <u>Judah</u>.*
2 Samuel 6:16–17 *King David <u>leaping</u> and dancing before the Lord ... The ark of the Lord.* King David danced and <u>leaped</u> with the presence of the Lord within the ark.	Luke 1:41 *When Elizabeth heard Mary's greeting, the infant <u>leaped</u> in her womb.* John the Baptist <u>leaped</u> in the womb (ark of Mary) in the presence of the Lord, Jesus.
2 Samuel 6:15 *[David] he and all the Israelites were bringing up the <u>ark of the Lord</u> with <u>shouts</u> of joy...*	Luke 1:41–42 *Elizabeth, filled with the holy Spirit, cried out in a <u>loud voice</u> ...* (shout of joy)
2 Samuel 6:9 *David feared the Lord that day and said: "How can the <u>ark of the Lord</u> come to me?"*	Luke 1:43 *[Elizabeth] And how does this happen to me. That the mother of my Lord should <u>come to me</u>?*
2 Samuel 6:11 *The ark of the Lord remained in the house of Obededom the Gittite for <u>three months</u>...*	Luke 1:56 *Mary remained with her about <u>three months</u>...*
2 Samuel 6:11 *...the Lord <u>blessed</u> Obededom and his whole house.*	The word *<u>blessed</u>* is used three times in Luke 1:39–45 in reference to Mary at Elizabeth's house.
1 Kings 8:6 *The priests brought the <u>ark of the covenant</u> of the Lord to its place beneath the wing of the cherubim in the sanctuary, the holy of holies of the <u>temple</u>.* The ark resided in the new temple in <u>Jerusalem</u>.	Luke 2:22 *When the days were completed for their purification according to the law of Moses, they [Joseph & Mary] took him [Jesus] up to <u>Jerusalem</u> to present him to the Lord.*
The staff of Aaron was kept in the <u>ark</u> and at some point, it <u>sprouted</u> and returned to life. The staff returning to life symbolizes the death of Jesus and him returning to life, the resurrection.	Hebrews 9:4 *... the ark of the covenant entirely covered with gold. In it were the gold jar containing the manna, the <u>staff of Aaron</u> that had <u>sprouted</u>, and the tablets of the covenant.*

THE OLD TESTAMENT	CONFIRMED IN THE NEW TESTAMENT
Aaron's Staff Sprouted in the Ark (<u>Returned to life</u>)	Jesus, the One Who Died and <u>Returned to Life.</u>
The Ark of the Covenant and the Virgin Mary were visualized by St. John in the book of Revelation.	Revelation 12:1 *A great sign appeared in the sky, a woman clothed with the sun, with the moon under her feet, and on her head a crown of twelve stars.* The confirmation of this vision is the occurrence of Juan Diego when the Virgin Mary appeared to him in Mexico in 1531. The image Mary imprinted on Juan's cloak is the same as the vision St. John describes in the book of Revelation. (See note below)
The Bread from Heaven in the Ark (Manna)	Jesus, is the Living Bread from Heaven

Reference: Agape Bible Study – Solemnity of the Assumption of the Virgin Mary, Michael E. Hunt.
The New American Bible, World Press.

The scripture verse just prior to Revelation 12:1 above is: Revelation 11:19 **Then God's temple in heaven was opened, and the <u>ark of his covenant</u> could be seen in the temple.** This ties Mary to the Ark of the Covenant along with Juan Diego's cloak image of Mary that duplicated St. Johns vision and Juan telling us that she identified herself as the Virgin Mary, all of which confirms that the Virgin Mary is the New Ark of the Covenant.

The power of the Holy Spirit made Mary the Ark of the New Covenant as she bore the presence of God in her womb: "The Word of God," "The Living Bread from Heaven," and the one who "Came Back to Life," our beloved Jesus.

Assumption of Mary:

The Old Testament tells us of two that were taken body and soul:

Genesis 5:23–24 *The whole lifetime of Enoch was three hundred and sixty-five years. Then Enoch walked with God, and was no longer here, for God took him.*

2 Kings 2:11 *As they walked on conversing, a flaming chariot and flaming horses came between them, and Elijah went up to heaven in a whirlwind.*

The Jewish tradition, believed by most Jews, was that after death they would go to Sheol, a place of waiting, where a person's soul could either be purified and sent to Gan Eden (Hebrew for Paradise), or sent for punishment in Gahanna. It is believed that Sheol (Hebrew), and Hades (Greek) in the Old Testament are referenced in the New Testament as the "*bosom of Abraham*" (Luke 16:22) and in 1 Peter 3:19 as "*prison*." Because all of mankind inherited original sin, Enoch and Elijah had to be purified of original sin before entering haven. That was accomplished in Sheol then their entrance into heaven may have occurred after the resurrection of Jesus, 1 Peter 3:18 *[Jesus Christ] Put to death in the flesh, he was brought to life in the spirit. In it he went to preach to the spirits in prison, ...* Therefore, when Enoch and Elijah, as well as the other spirits in "*prison*," accepted the word of Jesus, they were taken into the newly opened heaven, which Jesus opened up by his resurrection. Also, in the Apostles Creed we acknowledge this fact by stating, "He descended into hell," of which "hell" could have been stated as the "bosom of Abraham", "prison", or even "Sheol."

If God can take up body and soul of two prophets, Enoch and Elijah, He most certainly can take up body and soul the beloved mother of his Son, Jesus Christ.

Luke 1:26,27,28 26*...the angel Gabriel was sent from God ...* 27 *to a virgin...Mary...*28 *And coming to her, he said, "Hail, <u>favored one</u>! The <u>Lord is with you</u>."* Luke 1:42 [Elizabeth cried out to Mary] *"<u>Most blessed</u> are you among women, and blessed is the fruit of your womb..."* God cannot have anything to do with sin, therefore, in order for Mary to become the mother of God she had to be full of grace and born without the stain of original sin. Mary is the ark of the New Covenant because she carried (contained) the word of Jesus just as the ark contained the word of God.

Written civil tradition (not scripture) tells us: Three days after the Virgin Mary died, the Apostle Thomas arrived and requested to see Mary. When they opened her burial place, her body was not there. Also, records were very well kept as to where the bones of all the Apostles are kept (known to today), even the bones of Judas. There is absolutely no known record of any bones of the Virgin Mary. Therefore, Mary was assumed directly into heaven body and soul because she was full of grace and without the stain of original sin.

Records indicate that the Feast of the Assumption of Mary was celebrated by the Catholic Church very early on, however, after much prayer and discussion by the Church, in 1950 Pope Pius XII issued the dogma of the Assumption of Mary, making it a Holy Day of Obligation. Therefore, Mary is the only one to go <u>directly</u> to heaven body and soul.

References:
The New American Bible (NAB).
Certain words may be <u>underlined</u> for emphasis added.
Catholic Answers.com, and Scott Hahn's talk on Assumption.
Partial reference from a write-up by Gordie Ormerod
Assembled by Paul Wilchek 27AUG21.

Miracles of the Word of Jesus:
John 1: $_1$ "...the <u>word</u> *was with God, and the <u>word</u> was God.*" $_{14}$ "*And the <u>word</u> became flesh...*"
Matthew 8:23–27: The <u>word</u> of Jesus calmed the sea.
John 9:1–7: The <u>word</u> of Jesus healed a blind man from birth.
Luke 17:11–19: The <u>word</u> of Jesus healed 10 lepers.
John 11:1–45: The <u>word</u> of Jesus raised Lazarus from the dead.

Therefore, since the <u>word</u> of Jesus can: Calm the sea, heal the blind, cure lepers, raise Lazarus from the dead, then surely the <u>word</u> of Jesus actually changes bread and wine into His Body and Blood as: Matthew 26:26, *"…Jesus took bread, said the blessing, broke it, and giving it to His disciples said, 'take and eat; this is my body.'"*

The Catechism of the Catholic Church (CCC 1548) tells us that by virtue of our priest's sacrament of Holy Orders, the priest's role at Mass is to act in the person of Jesus Christ himself, who is present to his Church "In the person of Christ the Head" *(in persona Christi Capitis).*

At mass, when the priest recites the scriptural <u>words</u> of Jesus, *"this is my body," "this is my blood,"* (Mt 26:26,28) it is the same as Jesus himself being present and speaking. Therefore, at every Mass, Jesus is re–living His miraculous <u>words</u> that transform bread and wine into the living Body and Blood of Jesus Christ, (transubstantiation).

Jesus himself in Matthew 10:33, stated, *"But whoever denies me before others, I will deny before my heavenly father."* Then in Mark 8:38, Jesus stated, *"Whoever is <u>ashamed</u> of me and of my <u>words</u> … the Son of Man will be <u>ashamed</u> of when he comes in his Father's glory…"* It can be understandable that a person may have some difficulty believing in His real presence in the Eucharist, that person needs to work on their faith. On the other hand, any person that *denies* or is *ashamed* of His <u>*words*</u> and denies His actual living presence in the Eucharist has a problem because scripture states: *"But whoever denies me before others, I will deny before my heavenly father."* Scripture confirms His real presence in John 6:51, *"I am the living bread… the bread that I will give is my flesh…"* and in John 6:55, *"For my flesh is true food, and my blood is true drink."* Therefore, the Eucharist truly is the resurrected, spiritual, glorified living body, blood, and divinity of Jesus Christ. Of which we cannot earthly see, in the same way we cannot see Christ or the Holy Spirit even though Christ himself told us: Matthew 28:20 *"I am with you always…"*

Genesis 1:3 *"Then God said…"* Therefore, God created everything by His spoken word – not by the written word. During Jesus time on earth, he never told his disciples to write anything (*). He instructed them to: *"follow after me"* (Mt 10:38), *"whoever loves me will keep my word."* (Jn 14:23), and, *"do this in memory of me."* (Lk 22:19). The development of Christianity was accomplished in scripture by: the spoken word, actions, way of thinking, which is the tradition handed down generation to generation before the written word was ever fully established. God reveals Himself through tradition.

Jesus told His disciples in John 14:26: *"The Advocate, the holy Spirit that the Father will send in my name – he will teach you everything and remind you of all that I told you."* This statement continued the tradition of actions and way of thinking that developed Christianity through the direction of the holy Spirit after Christ ascended.

The earliest written word of the New Testament is Matthew in the year 50. By the year 50 the Catholic Church was established through tradition with its many churches, hierarchy of bishops and priests, as well as practicing many of the sacraments, including: baptism, anointing, and the braking of bread (The Eucharist). The actual written words (Scripture) tells us about the traditions already established. So, tradition far proceeded the written word.

(*) After the ascension, Jesus instruct John in Rev 1:19 and Rev 19:5 to "write down" and "write these words.'" Jesus did not give similar instructions during his time here on earth. Instructions to Moses in the Old Testament: *"write this down"* (Ex 17:14), *"write down these words."* (Ex 34;27). Tradition, definition, "hand down of legends, customs, etc. was a long–established way of thinking or acting."

Miracles in Chronological Order:

MIRACLES OF JESUS CHRIST	Matthew	Mark	Luke	John
Water into Wine at Cana				2:1–11
Healing of Nobleman's son				4:46–54
The Catch of Fish			5:1–11	
The Man with an Unclean Demon		1:23–26	4:33–35	
Cure of Peter's Mother–in–law	8:14–15	1:30,31	4:38–39	
Healing a Leper	8:2–4	1:40–45	5:12–14	
Healing the Paralytic	9:2–8	2:1–12	5:17–26	
The Ill Man				5:1–16
The Withered Hand	12:9–14	3:1–6	6:6–11	

MIRACLES OF JESUS CHRIST	Matthew	Mark	Luke	John
The Centurion's Servant	8:5–13		7:1–10	
The Widow's Son at Nain			7:11–17	
The Man Mute and Blind	12:22			
Calming the Storm	8:23–27	4:35–41	8:22–25	
The Gadarene Demoniac	8:28–30	5:1–20	8:26–39	
The Daughter of Jairus	9:28–26	5:21–43	8:40–56	
The Afflicted Woman	9:20–22	5:25–34	8:43–48	
Two Blind Men, Dumb Demoniac	9:27–34			
Feeding the Five Thousand	14:13–23	6:30–46	9:10–17	6:1–15
Jesus Walking on the Water	14:24–36	6:47–56		6:16–21
Canaanite Woman's Daughter	15:21–28	7:24–30		
Deaf and Mute Man	15:29–30	7:31–37		
Feeding the Four Thousand	15:32–38	8:1–9		
The Blind Man Near Bethsaida		8:22–26		
The Demoniac Boy	17:14–20	9:14–29	9:37–43	
The Temple–tax	17:24–27	9:33		
The Man Born Blind				9:1–41
The Mute Demoniac			11:14	
The Crippled Woman			13:10–21	
The Man Having Dropsy			14:1–6	
The Rising of Lazarus				11:1–46
The Ten Lepers			17:11–19	
The Blind Man Near Jericho	20:29–34	1046–52	18:35–43	
The Withered Fig Tree	21:20–22	11:20–25		
Healing the Ear of Priest's Servant	26:50–51	14:47	22:49–51	
The Catch of Fish				21:6–11
(* end of the NAB Bible chart)				
THE MIRACLE OF THE EUCHARIST:				
Last Supper (Jesus establishes the Mass)	26:26–30	14:22–26	22:14–20	14:1–31
THE CRUCIFIXION:				
Darkness over the Land at the Crucifixion	27:45	14:33	23:44	
Criminal to be in Paradise at the Crucifixion			23:43	
I Commend my Spirit at the Crucifixion			23:46	

MIRACLES OF JESUS CHRIST	Matthew	Mark	Luke	John
The Veil Torn in Two after Crucifixion	27:51	15:38	23:45	
The Earth Quaked after Crucifixion	27:52			
Tombs Opened, Bodies appeared after Crucifixion	27:51–52			
Soldiers converted after Crucifixion	27:54	15:39	23:47	
THE RESURRECTION:				
The Resurrection of Jesus	28:1–10	16:1–8	24:1–12	20:1–9
APPEARANCE AFTER THE RESURRECTION:				
Appearance of Jesus after His Resurrection, Commissioning of Disciples, Start of the Church.	28:16–20	16:9–18	24:13–49	20:11–30, 21:1–23
The Road to Emmaus (Mass by Jesus)			24:13–35	
THE ASCENSION:				
The Ascension of Jesus		16:19–20	24:50–53	

Reference:

The New American Bible (NAB), World Press, "Miracles in Chronological Order" through to "The Catch of Fish" as noted.

* The Last Supper, Crucifixion, Resurrection, Appearance, and Ascension Miracles were added to the (NAB) Bible chart.

SUMMARY – PROPHECIES:

+ There are over 351 prophecies in the Old Testament that have been fulfilled by Jesus Christ.

+ Jesus Himself made over 17 prophesies that have all been fulfilled.

+ There are parallels of Jesus' passion, hidden prophecies, messages, and numbers in Scripture that are still being deciphered today.

+ Scripture contains a multitude of parallels: God the Father/Jesus, feeding 5 thousand/Last Supper, Trinity of God/human creation. As the Dead Sea Scrolls are being analyzed, new symbolisms may be discovered.

+ Scripture tells us of the 7 miracles that occurred at the crucifixion of Christ and public documents tell us of the 4, forty–year miracles that occurred at the Temple.

+ There are still miracles occurring today to testify to the presence of Jesus Christ. These include the many medical miracles and the documented Eucharist miracles.

+ The wording in Scripture verifies that Mary's miraculous conception, *"in your womb..."* (Lk 1:31) occurred such that Mary remained a virgin.

+ Mary is the ark of the new covenant.

+ The assumption of Mary body and soul.

+ Scripture verifies that the "word of Jesus" is accurate and reliable, so when Jesus told us, *"... take and eat; this is my body"* (Mt 26:26), Jesus meant exactly what He said – the Eucharist is His body, blood, and divinity, even though we cannot physically see Him.

Transubstantiation: The transformation of the bread and wine into the Body and Blood of Jesus Christ through the grace of the Holy Spirit at the Consecration during the Mass. Only the appearance of bread and wine remain, but the elements are substantially changed into the Body, Blood, Soul, and Divinity of Christ.

References:

The **bold and italicized** Bible quotations are from The New American Bible, Fireside Catholic Press.

Certain words may be underlined for emphasis added.

The "Word of Jesus" portion is referenced from: "The Mass" by Bishop R. Barron.

"Parallels of Jesus" is partially referenced from: "No Greater Love" by Dr. Edward Sri, Ascension Press, West Chester, PA.

PROPHECIES, PARALLELS, SYMBOLISM, MIRACLES: Assembled by Paul Wilchek, edited by Kristin Trepanier–Henry. 2JUN20. Revised 10JAN22 & 17JUN22.

## CHAPTER 7

PROPHETS

A prophet in scripture is a person who revealed a message from God. Some of the prophets heard directly from God and passed it on. Some prophets interpreted dreams or visions. Through scripture, the prophecies passed on a message which was relevant for that time period, or warnings for others and nations, or even future predictions. In the following, those considered by some theologians to be the four major prophets are **highlighted** and **underlined**, and the twelve minor prophets are only **highlighted**. The major and minor refers to the size of each book, not their significance.

OLD TESTAMENT PROPHETS	FIRST APPEARANCE AND OTHER SCRIPTURE PASSAGE(S)	NOTES
Aron	Exodus 7:1–7	The spokesperson for Moses, rebuking and giving warnings to others.
Abel	Luke 11:50–51	Abel, the second son of Adam offered an acceptable sacrifice Gn 4:4.
Abraham	Genesis 20:3–4,6–7	God spoke to Abraham several times giving glimpses of the future.

OLD TESTAMENT PROPHETS	FIRST APPEARANCE AND OTHER SCRIPTURE PASSAGE(S)	NOTES
Agur	Proverbs 30:1	The son of Jakeh, author of Proverbs 30
Ahijah	1 Kings 11:29	Solomon did not always listen to Ahijah's wisdom and future predations. Ahijah predicted that Jeroboam would take command of 10 of the tribes of Israel after Solomon died.
Amos	Amos 7: 14–15 2 Kings 14:23–15;7	Amos (760–753 BC) a Judean shepherd prophesied against Israel, his warnings were ignored, Israel taken captive by Assyria.
Asaph	2 Chronicles 29:30	A worship leader appointed by David, Asaph was a Levite and a prolific writer.
Azariah	2 Kings 15 2 Chronicles 15:1–8	Gave warnings to King Asa to rid Judah of idols.
Daniel	The Book of Daniel Matthew 24:15	Daniel (605–535 BC) revealed more about end times than any other book besides Revelation. Daniel was the first Jew into Babylon exile where he interpreted dreams of Nebuchadnezzar.
David	Psalms 21,22,23 Psalms 8: 22; 110 Hebrews 11:32 Daniel, 2 Kings 23:34 to 25:30, 2 Chronicles 36:4–23	Many of David's Psalms prophesy the coming of Jesus, such as Psalms 8:22, 110. God appeared to speak to David mostly through prophets.
Deborah	Judges 4:4	Deborah, the only recorded female judge of Israel, scripture indicates she was a prophetess passing on God's message to military commander Barak, prophesying future events.

OLD TESTAMENT PROPHETS	FIRST APPEARANCE AND OTHER SCRIPTURE PASSAGE(S)	NOTES
Eldad	Numbers 11:26	One of the seventy elders of Moses that stayed in his tent and prophesied for a short period of time.
Eliezer	2 Chronicles 20:37	Prophesied against Jehoshaphat – you allied with Ahaziah; the Lord destroyed your works.
Elijah	1 Kings 18;36 2 Kings 2:11–12 Malachi 4:5–6	One of the most significant prophets that did not author a book. Elijah proclaimed God's word in the northern kingdom of Israel. A chariot of fire took him to heaven, Elisha was his successor.
Elisha	2 Kings 2:9. 9:1	Elisha was the successor of Elijah after seven years as an apprentice. Elisha helped to wipe out Ball worship, brought a widow's son back to life, and cured leprosy. His power was so great, when a dead man was thrown into Elisha's grave, the man sprang back to life.
Enoch	Jude 1:14–15 Genesis 4:17–18, Genesis 5:18–24, Hebrews 11:15	A prophet, Son of Cain, said to have walked with God. Taken up by God.
Ezekiel	Ezekiel 1:3, 48:30–35 The book of Obadiah, 2 Kings 24:8–25, 24:30, 2 Chronicles 36:9–21	Ezekiel (590–571 BC) was a priest exiled to Babylon, his book of prophecy has some strange visions. Ez 48:30–35 he prophesied about the coming of Jesus.

OLD TESTAMENT PROPHETS	FIRST APPEARANCE AND OTHER SCRIPTURE PASSAGE(S)	NOTES
Gad	1 Samuel 22:5	Gad the prophet sent words from God to David as to what David was to do when he met up with Saul.
Habakkuk	Habakkuk 1:1 2 Kings 23:31 to 24:7, 2 Chronicles 36:1–8	Habakkuk (610–605) prophesied Assyria's fall, Babylonian exile, and future victory of the Persians. His prophecies were in the form of a conversation with God, he asked questions, and God responded.
Haggai	Haggai 1:1 Ezra 5:1 to 6:15	Haggai (520 BC) through Zechariah and Zerubbabel, Haggai called the Jews to seriously consider their priorities and rebuild the temple after their exile.
Hanani	2 Chronicles 16:7	Hanani the seer – said to Asa king of Judah, you have not relied on the Lord your God.
Hosea	Hosea 1:1 2 Kings 14:23, 18:12	Hosea (750–715 BC) prophesied: Called out of Egypt – fulfilled Mat 2:13-15. He prophesied Gentiles would one day follow God.
Huldah	2 Kings 22:8–20	One of the few women prophetesses in scripture. She affirmed that Judah's rejection of God meant the nation would be destroyed, but not in his time due to his penitence.
Iddo	2 Chronicles 9:29, 12:15, and 13:27.	The prophet Iddo is mentioned several times in scripture, he predicted the rise of Jeroboam and wrote a record of Rehoboam and Abijah.

OLD TESTAMENT PROPHETS	FIRST APPEARANCE AND OTHER SCRIPTURE PASSAGE(S)	NOTES
Isaiah	2 Kings 15:1 to 20:21 Isaiah 1:1>, 2 Chronicles 25:16 to 32:33	Isaiah (740–680 BC) prophesied: (partial list) Born of a virgin – fulfilled Mt 1:20–23 Line of David – fulfilled Lk 1:32–33 Called Emmanuel – fulfilled Mt 1:23 To be rejected – fulfilled Mt 26:3–4 Sacrifice for sin – fulfilled Jn 1:29 Speak in parables –fulfilled Mt 13:10–15 Lamb to slaughter –fulfilled Acts 8:32 Buried in rich man's grave – fulfilled Mt 27:57–60
Jacob	Genesis 28:11–16	Jacob had a dream of the stairway to heaven and accurate prophecy of the future of his sons' descendants.
Jahaziel	2 Chronicles 20:14	Listen King Jehoshaphat and all of Judah – do not fear for the battle is not yours, but God's.
Jehu	1 Kings 16:7	The word of the Lord spoke through the prophet Jehu.
Jeremiah	Jeremiah 20:2 2 Kings 22:3–25 to 25:30, 2 Chronicles 34 to 36 Author of Lamentations	Jeremiah (625–580 BC) was the last prophet of the Kingdom of Judah and observed the Babylonians would take the nation apart. He gave Israel a word of hope that they would return from captivity in 70 years.
Joel	Acts 2:16–21, Joel 3:1-5 2 Kings 17–22, 2 Chronicles 29–32	Joel (722–701 BC) compared a locust devastation to what God would do if people did not return to Him. He predicted the outpouring of the Holy Spirit at Pentecost.

OLD TESTAMENT PROPHETS	FIRST APPEARANCE AND OTHER SCRIPTURE PASSAGE(S)	NOTES
Jonah	2 Kings 14:23–27 Book of Jonah	Known for his reluctance to go to Nineveh, served as prophet in Israel. He was sent to Jeroboam II and lead him to restore a border against their enemies.
Joseph	Genesis 37:5–11	Joseph dreamt that he would one day rule over his brothers which came true, then interpreted Pharaoh's dreams that lead him to a high political position.
Joshua	Joshua 1:1	After the death of Moses Joshua took command of the Israelites' campaign into the Promised Land. God gave Joshua encouragement and a warning to obey the law God gave to Moses.
King Nebuchadnezzar of Babylon	Daniel 2:1	Nebuchadnezzar was troubled with dreams that his staff could not interpret. Finally, David interpreted his dreams.
King Saul	1 Samuel 10:10	King Saul followed the directions given to him from the prophet Samuel, then King Saul prophesied with him.
King Solomon	1 Kings 3:5 1 Kings 11:29–30	In a dream, God asked Solomon if he wanted anything from God, Solomon chose wisdom. Later on, Solomon married too many women and through them was drawn to worshiping their false gods.
Malachi	Malachi 1:1> Nehemiah 13:1–31	Malachi (432–424 BC) prophesied: Way prepared by messenger – fulfilled Luke 3:3–6 Proceeded by Elijah – fulfilled Matthew 11:13–14

OLD TESTAMENT PROPHETS	FIRST APPEARANCE AND OTHER SCRIPTURE PASSAGE(S)	NOTES
Medad	Numbers 11:26	One of Moses' seventy elders that stayed in his tent and prophesied for a short period of time.
Micah	Micah 1:1 2 Kings 15:32 to 19:37 2 Chronicles 27:1 to 32:23	Micah (735–700 BC) prophesied: born in Bethlehem – fulfilled in Matthew 2:1, Luke 2:4–6
Micaiah	1 Kings 22:9	Micaiah told the king of Juda and Israel to go up and succeed, the Lord will give it into the hand of the king.
Miriam	Exodus 15:20 Numbers 12	The sister of Moses is identified as a prophet.
Moses	Deuteronomy 34:10, 18:15,18:18–20 Exodus, Leviticus, Numbers.	Prophesied there would be a prophet like Moses, fulfilled in Acts 3:20–23, John 7:40–42. Most of Exodus, Leviticus, Numbers, and Deuteronomy have messages to and through Moses. God spoke more to Moses than anyone else in scripture.
Nahum	Nahum 1:1>	Nahum promised that Assyria's days were numbered and that Judah would be delivered from their threat.
Nathan	2 Samuel 7:2 & 12:1–5 Nahum, 2 Kings 21:1–18, 2 Chronicles 33:1–20	Nathan (664–654 BC) told David that Solomon would build the temple. Nathan rebuked David for committing adultery and killing her husband.
Noah	Genesis 7:1	Noah a prophet because God spoke to him about the future.
Obadiah	Obadiah 1:1	Obadiah (586 BC) the prophet had a message for a nation other than Israel, he prophesied against Edom and Esau, descendants of Jacob's brother.

OLD TESTAMENT PROPHETS	FIRST APPEARANCE AND OTHER SCRIPTURE PASSAGE(S)	NOTES
Oded	2 Chronicles 28:1–15	The Syrians invaded and killed 120,000 and took captive 200,000 Israelites in Judah. Oded, the prophet, on God's orders stopped the Syrians and had them return the captives and spoils.
Samuel	1 Samuel 3:20; 8:6; & 9	Samuel spent his life as God's messenger. He anointed Saul and David to be king.
Shemaiah	1 Kings 12:22	The word of God came to Shemaiah – thus says the Lord, you must not fight against your relatives, the sons of Israel.
The Seventy Elders of Israel	Numbers 11:25	Moses ordered the seventy elders to a tent meeting; the Holy Spirit temporarily endowed them the ability to prophesy.
Uriah	Jeremiah 26:20–23	Uriah prophesied against evil in Judah, he was hunted down and killed by King Jehoiakim.
Zechariah, son of Berechiah	Zechariah 1:1> Ezra 5:1 to 6:15	Zechariah (520–480 BC) prophesied: A King would enter Jerusalem on a donkey – fulfilled Mt 21:8–11 Betrayed for 30 pieces of silver – fulfilled Mt 26:14–16 Hands/feet pierced – fulfilled John 20:25–27 Side pierced – fulfilled John 19:34
Zechariah, son of Jehoiada	2 Chronicles 24:20	Thus, God has said, why do you transgress the commandments of the Lord and do not prosper? Because you have forsaken the Lord, He has forsaken you. King Joash had him stoned to death.

OLD TESTAMENT PROPHETS	FIRST APPEARANCE AND OTHER SCRIPTURE PASSAGE(S)	NOTES
Zephaniah	Zephaniah 1:1	Zephaniah warned Judah about their impending doom and promised that a remnant would return.

NEW TESTAMENT PROPHETS	FIRST APPEARANCE AND OTHER SCRIPTURE PASSAGE(S)	NOTES
Anna	Luke 2:36–38	Anna an elderly prophetess that spent her days worshiping at the temple, she recognized baby Jesus as the long–awaited Messiah.
Agabus	Acts 21:10	By the spirit, Agabus predicted a severe famine that occurred under Claudius.
Barnabas	Acts 13:1	Identified as a prophet in Acts
Elizabeth, mother of John the Baptist	Luke 1:41–45	Elizabeth, cousin of Mary, while she was pregnant with John the Baptist, was visited by Mary. When they met, Elizabeth was filled with the Holy Spirit and proclaimed Mary's child was the Messiah.
Jesus	Luke 24:19 Matthew 24 & 25	Jesus described as teacher and prophet, even though He is the Son of God. In Matthew Jesus clearly prophesied about end times.
John the Apostle	Revelation 1:1>	Perhaps the most famous prophet for his book Revelation filled with chastisements to the churches and prophecies of the end times.
Joel	Joel 2:28–29	Joel prophesied about the day when God would pour out His Spirit upon all flesh and they would speak prophecies, have dreams, and visions.

NEW TESTAMENT PROPHETS	FIRST APPEARANCE AND OTHER SCRIPTURE PASSAGE(S)	NOTES
John the Baptist	Luke 7:28, John 1:19–28	John the Baptist and prophet, the last prophet of the Old Testament, speaking in New Testament times. John spent his life telling people to confess their sins, turn to God, and to follow Jesus.
Joseph, foster father of Jesus	Matthew 1:20	Joseph received a message from an angel that Mary was to give birth to the Messiah.
Judas Barsabbas	Acts 15:32	Identified as a prophet in Acts.
Manaen	Acts 13:1	Manaen was identified as prophet and teacher.
Lucius of Cyrene	Acts 13:1	Identified as a prophet in Acts.
Mary, mother of Jesus	Luke 1:26–28, 46–51	Mary, engaged to Joseph was told by the angel Gabriel that she would give birth to the Messiah.
Paul the Apostle	Acts 9:20 1 Thessalonians 4:13–18 2 Thessalonians 1:5–12, 2:1–11	Paul a prophet and prophetic writer of several New Testament books in which he prophesied of the end times and the Antichrist.
Peter	Acts 12:6–12, 2Peter 3:1>	Peter the apostle and prophet heard from heaven after the ascension of Jesus. An angel came to Peter when he was in prison and helped him escape.
Philip the Evangelist	Acts 8:26–40	Philip the evangelist was told by an angel to go into the desert where he evangelized an Ethiopian official and baptized him.
Silas	Acts 15:32	Identified as a prophet in Acts.
Simeon Niger	Acts 13:1	Identified as a prophet in Acts.

NEW TESTAMENT PROPHETS	FIRST APPEARANCE AND OTHER SCRIPTURE PASSAGE(S)	NOTES
Simeon of Jerusalem	Luke 2:22–35	Simeon a righteous old man was promised by God he would see the Messiah before he died. When Joseph and Mary took baby Jesus to the temple, Simeon knew who Jesus was.
The four daughters of Philip the Evangelist	Acts 21:7–9	These women are identified as prophets in Acts.
Two Witnesses	Revelation 11:3–12	Two Witnesses are the last prophets in Revelation who are to appear performing signs and prophesy in Jerusalem, be assassinated, then return to life.
Zechariah	Luke 1:8–23, 67–79	Zechariah was a priest chosen to burn incense in the temple where an angel appeared and told him his elderly wife would have a son and to name him John. He prophesied after John's birth

In addition to the above prophets there are false prophets mentioned in scripture.

FALSE PROPHETS	FIRST APPEARANCE AND OTHER SCRIPTURE PASSAGE(S)	NOTES
Ahab	JEREMIAH 29:15–23	Jeremiah rebuked Ahab who falsely prophesied in God's name.
Hananiah	Jeremiah 28:5	Hananiah publicly contradicted Jeremiah's prophecies.

FALSE PROPHETS	FIRST APPEARANCE AND OTHER SCRIPTURE PASSAGE(S)	NOTES
Noadiah	Nehemiah 6: 14	Noadiah the prophetess and the rest of the prophets were trying to frighten the people.
Zedekiah	Jeremiah 29:21 2 Chronicles 36:12 1 Kings 22:24	Zedekiah did evil in the sight of the Lord his God; he did not humble himself before Jeremiah the prophet.
Elymas (Bar–Jesus)	Acts 12:4–12	Elymas, a Jewish magician and false prophet, opposed Paul and Barnabas's message.
Jezebel (not same Jezebel as Old Testament	Revelation 2:20–23	Jesus condemned the church in Thyatira for accepting the woman Jezebel for leading God's people into sexual immorality and idolatry.
Simon the magician	Acts 8:9–24	Simon made a profession of accepting Christ and wanted to pay for the power of the Apostles. He was rebuked by Peter.
The false prophet of the Book of Revelation	Revelation 13:11–15; 16:13; 19:20: 20:10	The Antichrist in end times will have a false prophet who will encourage the world to worship the Antichrist by performing miracles.
The fortune–telling girl	Acts 16:16–24	Paul grew weary of the fortune–telling girl's unwanted prophecies and finally told the spirit to leave her, which it did. The girl's owners had Paul and Silas put into prison for ruining their fortune–telling business.

There are many other prophets in scripture that are not listed by name, as an example:

- 1 Samuel 10:10 after Saul was anointed king, *"a band of prophets met him, ..."*
- 1 Chronicles 25:1–7 tells us about several Tabernacle musicians that David commissioned to perform before the tabernacle and were identified as prophets.
- 1 Kings 20:22–42 an unnamed prophet assured King Ahab that Israel would triumph. Which it did. Maybe the same or another prophet disguised himself as a wounded soldier and prophesied against the king.
- 2 Kings 2:3,5,7 there was a school of prophets, ₃ *"...the guild prophets, ..."* during the time of Elijah that are not named. ₇ *"fifty of the guild prophets followed, ..."*

SUMMARY – PROPHETS:
- + The Old Testament lists 54 prophets by name
- + The New Testament lists 22 prophets by name
- + The Old Testament lists 4 false prophets by name
- + The New Testament lists 5 false prophets by name
- + Scripture lists many other prophets that are unnamed

References:
Biblical Cyclopedic Index of The New American Standard bible, Thomas Nelson Publishers–1977.
The New American Concise Concordance – Oxford University press.
Azbible.com, gotquestions.org. The New American Bible – World press.
PROPHETS: Assembled by Paul Wilchek 12MAY20.

CHAPTER 8

PURGATORY

According to the "Catechism of the Catholic Church" (CCC 1030), under the title of: "The Final Purification, or Purgatory", it states: "All who die in God's grace and friendship, but still imperfectly purified, are indeed assured of their eternal salvation; but after death they undergo purification, so as to achieve the holiness necessary to enter the joy of heaven." (Also see CCC 1031–1032)

Let Scripture Speak for Itself on Purgatory:

Purification:
1 Corinthians 3:15. But *if someone's work is burned up, that one will suffer loss; the person will be saved, but only as through fire.*
To *"suffer loss"* cannot refer to consignment to hell, since no one is saved there. It cannot mean heaven since there is no suffering there. Purgatory can be the only logical place where *"the person will be saved, but only as through fire."*

Revelation 21:27. *... but nothing unclean will enter it [heaven].*
The above supports the need for <u>purification</u> (Purgatory) to enter heaven.

Cleansing by Fire:
1 Peter 1:7. *...so that the genuineness of your faith, more precious than gold that is perishable even though tested by fire, may prove to be for praise, glory, and honor at the revelation of Jesus Christ.*
(CCC 696) "The tradition of the Church, by reference to certain texts of Scripture, speaks of a cleansing fire."

In the Age to Come:
Matthew 12:32. *And whoever speaks a word against the Son of Man will be forgiven; but whoever speaks against the Holy Spirit will not be forgiven, either in <u>this age</u> or <u>in the age to come</u>.*
The above indicates that certain offenses can be forgiven in "***<u>this age</u>***," certain others can be forgiven "***<u>in the age to come</u>***." Logically, a person with sin(s) cannot enter heaven, but if certain sin(s) can be forgiven "***<u>in the age to come</u>***," then that place can only be Purgatory, it certainly cannot occur in heaven.
According to Karl Keating's book "Catholicism and Fundamentalism," the above scripture passage: "***<u>in the age to come</u>***" implies expiation can occur after death.
Expiation means to make amends or reparation for wrongdoing, atonement.

Theologians tell us that most of the New Testament writings were about controversial subjects during the time of the early Christians. There is no scriptural controversy about praying for the dead, because it was common practice (tradition) at that time. This may be why there is very little about praying for the dead in the New Testament. St. Paul stated the following, praying for a recently deceased friend: 2 Timothy 1:8, *May the Lord grant him to find mercy from the Lord on that day."* St. Paul prayed for a dead friend, one of the few references in scripture.

Historically, the Catacombs of the early Christians contain written records of prayers for the dead. Also, non–inspired Christian writings of the second century, such as "Acts of Paul & Thecla," refer to the Christian custom (tradition) of praying for the dead.
One would not pray for the dead unless they believed in Purgatory. The problem is the Greeks had two words for "dead" where we only have one.

Catholics do not pray for the "dead" (corpse); they pray for the person's spiritual, immortal, living spirit (soul).

Praying for the Dead:

2 Maccabees 12:46 (Old Testament*). **Thus he [Judas Maccabeus] made atonement for the dead that they might be absolved from their sin.*** The historical book of Maccabees tells us that praying for the dead to *"be absolved from their sin"* was a tradition in Old Testament times.

Spirits in Prison:

1 Peter 3:18,19,20. *For Christ also suffered for sins once, the righteous for the sake of the unrighteous, that He might lead you to God. Put to death in the flesh, He was brought to life in the spirit. In it He also went to <u>preach to the spirits in prison</u>, who had once been disobedient while God patiently waited in the days of Noah ...*

John 5:25. Amen*, **amen I [Jesus Christ] say to you, the hour is coming and is now here when the dead will hear the voice of the Son of God, and <u>those who hear will live</u>.***

Ephesians 4:8,9,10. *He [Jesus] ascended on high and took prisoners captive; He gave gifts to men." What does "He ascended" mean except that He also descended into the lower [regions] of the earth? The one who descended is also the one who ascended far above all heavens, that He might fill all things.*

1 Peter 4:6. *For this is why the gospel was preached <u>even to the dead</u> that, though condemned in the flesh in human estimation, they might live in the spirit in the estimation of God.*

The four readings above tell us that Jesus descended to a place called *"Prison"* where He preached *"<u>even to the dead</u>"* giving them the opportunity to accept Him. There is nothing in scripture saying that this place, **"Prison"** (Purgatory) was ever abolished. We pray this in The Apostles' Creed: "...He descended into hell; on the third day He rose again from the dead;" According to the above four Scripture quotations, Jesus Christ, after His resurrection, *"<u>preached to the spirits in prison</u>"* (1Pet 3:19) and it further states: *"<u>those who hear will live</u>."* (1Pet 3:6).

Scripture does not tell us that Christ's preaching "*__even to the dead__*" was a "one time" occurrence. Therefore, one could conclude that Jesus Christ may still preach "*__even to the dead__*" so that "*__those who hear will live.__*" Very interesting, re–read 1 Peter 4:6 above!

Matthew 18: 30,34–35. *₃₀ ... he had him put in __prison__ __until__ he paid back the debt. ₃₄ Then in anger his master handed him over to the __torturers__ __until__ he should pay back the whole debt. ₃₅ So will my heavenly Father do to you, unless each of you forgives his brother from his heart.* Notice the use of "*until*" meaning it is temporary.

The prison/torturers that the servant was handed over to, verse 30 and 34, cannot be Hell/Gehenna. Prison is a temporary place where Hell/Gehenna is forever. In Scriptural times, prison was temporary confinement for someone who broke the law or debtors that were confined until the dept was "*paid in full.*" In other scriptural passages, Jesus is very straightforward when He referred to eternal punishment. He either referred directly to Gehenna (Mt 5:29,30) or indirectly to Gehenna as the place of "*wailing and grinding of teeth*" (Mt 13:42,50), or "*thrown into the fire*" (Mt 7:19). Verses 30 and 34 use none of those descriptions. Therefore, the above indicates that after the debt is paid, the servant can be released. There is no release from Hell, but there is release from Hades (abode of the dead in Greek and Sheol in Hebrew), what we now call Purgatory, where once one has become purified, they are released. Matthew 5:25–26 *__Settle with your opponent__ quickly while on the way to court with him. Otherwise, your opponent will hand you over to the judge, and the judge will hand you over to the guard, and you will be thrown into __prison__. Amen, I say to you, you will not be released until you have __paid the last penny__.*

In the above, Jesus uses "*__prison__*" and "*__Settle with your opponent__*", referring to Hades/Sheol in this teaching because "*__prison__*" is not final, there is a release.

Atonement:

Atonement is the reparation or expiation, pay the penalty, for a wrong or injury.

Hebrews 9:27. *Just as it is appointed that human beings die once, and after this the judgment, ...*

Judgment is immediate, however between the individual judgment and general judgment a soul may be purified in Purgatory for a period of time. Luke 12:59. *I say to you, you will not be released until you have paid the last penny* (reparation).

St Augustine said in his book "City of God," "Temporary punishments are suffered by some in this life only, by others after death, by others both now and then; but all of them before that last and strictest judgment." Therefore *"the person will be saved, but only through fire,"* (1Cor 3:15) saved after a person: *"paid the last penny,"* (Mt 5:26) which is the expiation (atonement) for sin(s).

2 Samuel 12:14 *But since you [David] have utterly spurned the Lord by this deed, the child born to you will surely die.*

Even after David was forgiven, he had to undergo expiation (atonement), pay the penalty for his sin. Can we expect anything less? Having one's sins forgiven is not the same as having the punishment (atonement) for those sins wiped out. There is no contradiction between the redemption of Jesus Christ to take away sins and our suffering for the expiation of our sin(s), whether that suffering is in this life or the next. St. Paul tells us: Colossians 1:24. *Now I rejoice in my sufferings for your sake, ...*

Christ's sufferings, although fully satisfactory on behalf of our sins, leaves us with the debt to pay for our sins as a matter of justice. Scripture tells us we have a "just" God.

Sin:

1 John 5:17. **All wrongdoing is sin, but there is sin that is not deadly.**

This indicates that not all sin is a capital offense. Deadly (Mortal sin) must meet 3 conditions: (1) A Grave Matter, (2) Full knowledge, (3) Deliberate (complete) consent.

Tradition:

Catholics: They believe and put their faith in the Bible, and they use the traditions handed down as a means to worship and praise the Lord as instructed in Scripture:

2 Thessalonians 2:15. ***Therefore, brothers, stand firm and hold fast to the <u>traditions</u> that you were taught, either by oral statement or by letter of ours.***

Praying for the living souls in Purgatory is a Tradition in the Catholic Church.

Judaism: They believe "Sheol" (in Hebrew, Hades in Greek) is an abode of the dead, a place of purification. Zechariah 13:9. *I will refine them as one refines silver...*

Islam: They believe one is punished according to their deeds, and released after their habits are purified. (Similar to Purgatory).

SUMMARY – PURGATORY:

+ PURIFICATION: Purgatory is a place of purification. Scripture tells us: ***"the person will be saved, but only through fire."*** (1Cor 3:15) ***"nothing unclean will enter it [heaven]."*** (Rev 21:27)

+ CLEANSING BY FIRE: Cleansing by fire can only occur in a place other than heaven or hell.

+ IN THE AGE TO COME: Some sins can be forgiven ***"in the age to come"*** (Mt 12:32)

+ PRAYING FOR THE DEAD: In Old Testament times they prayed for the dead to: ***"be absolved from their sin."*** (2 Mc 12:46) The early Christians prayed for the dead persons living soul as historically recorded in the catacombs. Catholics do not pray for the dead; they pray for the living soul of the person whose body has died. Most Christians pray to aid a living person. Catholics do also but they continue to pray for that person's living soul after their body dies.

+ SPIRITS IN PRISON: After Christ's crucifixion, He descended to a place called ***"Prison"*** (1 Pt 3:18) where He preached to the dead. Theologians point to ***"<u>prison</u>"*** (1 Pt 3:18) in reference to Sheol/Hades in the Old Testament.

+ ATONEMENT: Scripture tells us: "***the person will be saved, but only through fire,***" (1 Cor 3:15) saved after a person has: "***paid the last penny.***" (Mt 5:26)

+ SIN: Scripture tells us: ***"All wrongdoing is sin, but there is sin that is not deadly."*** (1Jn 5:17)
+ TRADITION: Catholic traditions are according to scripture: "*...* ***hold fast to the tradition that you were taught..."*** (2 Thes 2:15).

Scripture quotations are ***italicized and bold.,*** <u>underlining</u> is for emphasis added
References: The New American Bible, Catechism of the Catholic Church, St, Augustine's book "City of God," and Karl Keating's book "Catholicism and Fundamentalism."
PURGATORY: Compiled by Paul Wilchek, edited by Kristin Trepanier–Henry, 1JAN18.
Revised 12SEP20.

CHAPTER 9

SCRIPTURE RESPONSE

QUESTION: Have you been born again? Have you been saved?
You need to confess your sins and invite Jesus into your heart in order to be born again. Is this according to Scripture?

RESPONSE: Part of the above is scriptural. Being born again is in Scripture. John 3:3 [Jesus said]: *"Amen, amen, I say to you no one can see the kingdom of God without being born from above."* However, Scripture does not state that we need to invite Jesus into our hearts in order to be born again. Inviting Jesus into our hearts is a good practice (one should do that every day) but not a condition to being born again (nor is it scriptural). One needs to read on a bit further to John 3:4 [Nicodemus said to Jesus]: *"...Surely. He cannot reenter his mother's womb and be <u>born again,</u> can he?"* Then in John 3:5 [Jesus answered]: *"Amen, amen, I say to you no one can enter the kingdom of God without being born of <u>water and spirit.</u>"* Here Jesus explains that "*<u>being born again</u>*" requires "*<u>water and spirit.</u>*" This takes place with the sacrament of baptism and then again in Conformation. Therefore, the answer to, "Have you been born again?" would be: "Yes, I have been born again, but according to Scripture, with **"water and *spirit.*""** Another scriptural reference is found in Titus 3:5,6: *"...because of His mercy, He saved us through the bath of rebirth and renewal by the Holy Spirit, whom He richly poured out on us through Jesus Christ our savior."* Also see 1 Peter 1:23.

QUESTION: Why do Catholics pray for the dead?
RESPONSE: Catholics only pray for the living soul of a person whose body has died. 2 Timothy 1:16,18: ₁₆*"May the Lord grant mercy to the family of Onesiphorus because he often gave new heart and was not ashamed of my chains.* ₁₈ *May the Lord grant him to find mercy from the Lord..."*. Note: *"Onesiphorus"* apparently died prior to St. Paul writing this letter, also, note that the above quotes use the words, *"gave"* and *"was,"* indicating past tense, therefore, St. Paul is praying for the dead. 1 Corinthians 15:29. *"...what will people accomplish by having themselves baptized for the dead?"* This practice (baptized for the dead) is not explained any further. However, in this section of Scripture, St. Paul is talking about Christian practices that would be meaningless if the resurrection were not a fact. Also note the response on "Purgatory" below.

QUESTION: Why do Catholics believe in Purgatory?
RESPONSE: If a person prays for the living soul of a person whose body has died, they must believe that a person's soul can be helped by prayer. Revelation 21:27: *"...but nothing unclean will enter it [heaven]."* 2 Maccabees 12:46: *"Thus [Judas Maccabeus] made atonement for the dead that they might be absolved from their sin."* 1 Peter 3:18. *"[Christ]...went to preach to the spirits in <u>prison</u>, who had once been disobedient while God patiently waited in the days of Noah..."* This clearly speaks of a place called *"<u>prison</u>"* (not heaven or hell) where Christ went after His death where the just who died before Christ's Redemption were waiting for heaven to be opened for them. Therefore, the Bible confirms that a temporary place exists other than heaven or hell. Nothing in Scripture tells us that this place, *"<u>prison</u>,"* was ever abolished.

John 5:25: *"Amen, amen I [Jesus Christ] say to you, the hour is coming and is now here when the dead will hear the voice of the Son of God, and those who hear will live."* 1 Corinthians 3:5: *"But if someone's work is burned up, that one will suffer loss; the person will be saved, but only as through fire."* To *"suffer loss"* and *"be saved"* cannot refer to consignment to hell, since no one is saved there. It cannot mean heaven since there is no suffering there. Purgatory can be the only logical place where *"the person will be saved, but only through fire."*

QUESTION: Why do Catholics baptize infants?

RESPONSE: First of all, The Catholic Church (first called the "Catholic Church" in the year 107) has baptized infants as a consistent practice from the beginning and it is supported by Scripture. Acts 16:15, Acts 16:33, and Acts 18:8 describe the apostles baptizing adults along with their entire household (which had to include small children). Second, one needs to understand the real objective of baptism. The effects of baptism are not dependent on faith or understanding. Scripture tells us it is for the *"forgiveness of your sins."* Acts 2:38: *"...be baptized, every one of you, in the name of Jesus Christ for the forgiveness of your sins..."* Note, it states *"every one of you,"* with no limitations, which would include infants. Baptism washes away both Original Sin and actual sins from one's soul and provides a number of God's divine graces. St. Irenaeus (125–203) was a bishop and the second generation from the apostles. He was trained by St. Polycarp, who himself was taught by St. John the Apostle. He wrote that Christ came to save those who are *"born again in God"* through baptism, including "infants and children." Colossians 2: 11–12: 11 *"In him you were also circumcised..."* 12 *"You were buried with him in baptism, in which you were also raised with him through faith in the power of God..."* The tradition of baptism replaced Jewish circumcision, which the Jews performed on infants on their eighth day of life.

QUESTION: Why do Catholics call Reverend (Priest) "Father"?

Matthew 23: 8–10: [Jesus speaking] 8 *As for you, do not be called 'Rabbi.' You have but one teacher, and you are all brothers.* 9 *Call no one on earth father; you have but one Father in heaven.* 10 *Do not be called 'Master'; you have but one master, the Messiah.* Note: When Jesus says, *"As for you,"* He is speaking directly to the Pharisees.

RESPONSE: In Matthew 23: 2–7, the passage just prior to the above, Jesus is rebuking the Pharisees for their spiritual pride. He reminds them that God alone (God the Father) is ultimately the source of all authority. The *"father"* example that Jesus uses certainty is not intended for us to never speak of the Church fathers, founding fathers, or even our biological fathers. This cannot be Jesus' intent because in several places in Scripture, Jesus Himself uses the term *"father"* (Mt 15:4–6, 19:5, 19:19, 19:29, 21:31, and Jn 8:56). Jesus has the rich man (in the parable of the rich man and Lazarus) use the title *"Father*

Abraham" three times (Lk 16:24,27,30). There is more evidence of this in the following passages: 1 Corinthians 4:15: [St. Paul speaking] *"Even if you should have countless guides to Christ, yet you do not have many fathers, for I became your father in Christ Jesus through the gospel."* Philippians 2:22: [St. Paul speaking] *"but you know his [Timothy] worth, how as a child with a father he served along with me in the cause of the gospel."* In the above Scripture passages, St. Paul certainly has no qualms about using the term, "*father*", even calling himself "*your father.*" Isaiah 22:21, Isaiah is speaking about Eliakim son of Hilkiah where he states: *He shall be a father to the inhabitants of Jerusalem and the house of Judah.* Any Bible concordance will list many other occurrences of the words: "father," "fathers," "teacher(s)," "Master," or "Rabbi" all throughout Scripture.

QUESTION: Why do Catholics confess their sins to a priest?
RESPONSE: The tradition of confessing sins to a priest started in Old Testament times. For example, when the Jews were in exile in Babylon, they confessed their sins to God and to the priests in Jerusalem. Baruch 1:13: *"Pray for us to the Lord, our God, for we have sinned against the Lord, our God..."* They were asking the priests in Jerusalem to intercede for them for forgiveness. Leviticus 5: 5–6: *When someone is guilty ... that person shall confess the wrong committed, and make reparation to the Lord for the wrong committed; Thus, the priest shall make atonement of the individual's behalf for the wrong.* Leviticus 19: 21–22: *"The man shall bring to the entrance of the tent of meeting as his reparation to the Lord a ram as a reparation offering. With the ram of reparation offering the priest shall make atonement before the Lord for the wrong the man has committed, so that he will be forgiven for the wrong he has committed."* This shows that there was an ancient practice of the Jews where the authority of the priest, who represented God, was sought for a person's forgiveness. Later on, the Jews, in order to maintain confidentiality, would bend over the ram and quietly confess their sin(s); then the ram had to die to atone for their sin(s), this sounds kind of familiar. Therefore, the practice of confessing sins to God as represented by a priest and having the priest respond with prayer for divine mercy has ancient precedent. The Catholic practice also includes the priest (in confidentiality) not only praying for the penitent,

but also imposing penance (satisfaction) and speaking on God's behalf the words of forgiveness (absolution). The Catholic priest's authority was given directly by Jesus to St. Peter and the other Apostles, and by extension, to all the successive priests they ordained. As Jesus said to the Apostles in John 20:23 ***"Whose sins you forgive are forgiven them, whose sins you retain are retained."*** In the early Church, confession of grave sin was often made to the entire Christian assembly as well as to the priests. James 5:16: ***"Therefore, confess your sins to one another and pray for one another..."*** As the Church progressed, to maintain confidentiality, confession (as today) was done privately to a priest.

QUESTION: Why do Catholics make the sign of the cross?
RESPONSE: Ezekiel 9:4: ***"...the Lord said to him*** [Ezekiel] ***Pass through the city, through the midst of Jerusalem, and mark an X on the foreheads of those who grieve and lament..."*** In the Greek language of Ezekiel's vision above, the ***"X"*** mark is actually the Greek letter *tau*, which was written more like an upright cross.
Revelation 7:3: [St. John's vision] ***"Do not damage the land or the sea or the trees until we put the seal on the foreheads of the servants of our God."*** Also,
14:1: ***"...who had His [Christ's] name and his Father's name written on their foreheads."*** Early Christian teachers saw in Ezekiel's vision and St. John's vision the Christian baptismal ceremony of that day in which the Sign of the Cross was used along with saying, "In the name of the Father, and of the Son, and of the Holy Spirit." As early as the 2nd century, making the Sign of the Cross was a common well–established custom. Also, the early Christians used the Sign of the Cross at other times as well, including the beginning and end of prayers. It is rumored that during the persecution of Christians (prior to AD 400) that they were identified by the Sign of the Cross, so, they started using the sign of a fish which was not recognized by their persecutors. Today, when entering church, Catholics apply holy water to themselves with the Sign of the Cross to recall their baptism. Tertullian, Christian apologist author (155–240), wrote: "we mark our foreheads with the sign of the cross."

QUESTION: Where do all the 7 sacraments of the Catholic Church come from?

RESPONSE: All of the 7 SACRAMENTS can be found in Scripture:

1. ANOINTING OF SICK: Mark 6:13: *... anointed with oil many that were sick and healed them.* James 5:14: *Is any among you sick? ... let them pray over him, anointing him with oil in the name of the Lord.* Lk 13:13, Acts 9:17–18, Jas 5:14

2. BAPTISM: (Commanded by Christ) John 3:5: *Jesus answered, "Truly, truly, I say to you, unless one is born of water and the Spirit, he cannot enter the kingdom of God.* (Also, Mt 28:19 & Mk 16:16, words of Jesus.), Acts 2;38; 16:15, 33; 18:8

   ~ Baptized and received the Holy Spirit: Acts 2:38 & 19:5

   ~ Taught and administered by the Apostles: Acts 2:4, Acts 8:12 & 8:38, Acts 10:48

   ~ St. Paul baptized: Acts 9:18

   ~ To take away sins: Mk 1:4 & 16:16, Jn 3:5, Acts 2:38 & 8:12, Rom 6:3–6, Gal 3:27, 1 Cor 6:11, Eph 5:26, Col 2:12–14, Lk 3:3, Heb 10: 22

   ~ Administered to entire households, which had to include children: Acts 16:15 & 16:33, Acts 2:38–39

   ~ Jesus blesses children: Mt 18:14 & 19:13, Mk 10:13–16, 1 Cor 1:16 ~Infants: Lk 18: 15–17

3. CONFIRMATION: Acts 19: 5,6 *₅ ... they were baptized in the name of the Lord Jesus. ₆And when Paul had laid his hands on them, the Holy Spirit came upon them;* (Also see Heb 6:2, 2 Cor 1:21, Eph 1:13)

4. EUCHARIST: (Instituted by Jesus) Matthew 26:26–28 *₂₆Now as they were eating, Jesus took bread, and blessed, and broke it, and gave it to the disciples and said, "Take, eat; this is my body." ₂₇And he took a chalice, and when he had given thanks he gave it to them, saying, "Drink of it, all of you; ₂₈for this is my blood of the covenant, which is poured out for many for the forgiveness of sins..."* (Prophesied): Mal 1:11. (Prefigured): Ex 16:15. (Promised): Jn 6:32–60. (Instituted): Mt 26:26–28, Mk 14:22–24, Lk 22:19.20, 1 Cor 11:23–27 & 10:16 & 11:27,29. (Receive frequently): Acts 2:42 & 20:7, Ps 78:24, Prv 9:2, Wis

16:20. (Eucharist under one kind): Lk 24:30, Jn 6:59. (Also see): Jn 6:33,38,51,52,58; Acts 2:42 & 20:7 & 1 Cor 11:27.

5. HOLY ORDERS: (Instituted by Christ) John 20:21,22,23. *₂₁ Jesus said to them again, "Peace be with you. As the Father has sent me, even so I send you." ₂₂And when he had said this, he breathed on them, and said to them, "Receive the Holy Spirit. ₂₃If you forgive the sins of any, they are forgiven; if you retain the sins of any, they are retained."* (Also see Luke 22:28–30)

6. MATRIMONY: Matthew 19:4,5,6. (Jesus): *₄ He answered, "Have you not read that he who made them from the beginning made them male and female, ₅and said, 'For this reason a man shall leave his father and mother and be joined to his wife, and the two shall become one?' ₆ So they are no longer two but one. What therefore God has joined together, let no man put asunder."* Also see: Eph 5:25–31, Mk 10:7–9.

7. PENANCE: 2 Cor 5:18. *All this is from God, who through Christ reconciled us to himself and gave us the ministry of reconciliation; ...* Also see: Mt 18:18 & 16:19, Mk 1:4, Jn 20:21–23, 2 Cor 5:20.

QUESTION: How can Catholics believe in the Bible and Traditions?
RESPONSE: St. Paul in Scripture itself really answers this question: 2 Thessalonians 2:15. *"Therefore, brothers, stand firm and hold fast to the traditions that you were taught, either by oral statement or by letter of ours."* Catholics put their faith in the Bible and they use traditions handed down as a means to worship and praise the Lord as instructed in Scripture. The early Christians understood that the oral teachings of the apostles (what Catholics call Tradition) endorsed the Bible, not contradicted it. Without the tradition of bishops and councils over a period of 180 years, we would not have the New Testament.

QUESTION: Why are there more books in the Catholic Bible than in the Protestant Bible?
RESPONSE: The short answer is: certain books were removed.
Records show that in the year 367, St. Athanasius listed 27 books that are currently the same as the Catholic New Testament. At several councils of

the Catholic Church (years: 387, 392, 393, 397, and 419), they discussed and listed the books to be in the Bible, then finally at the Council of Trent (1546) the list was finalized. Originally, the book of James was not in the Protestant New Testament, however, in modern times it was added back into their Bible. Today, the following 7 books are not in the Protestant Bible: Baruch, Tobit, Judith, 1 & 2 Maccabees, Wisdom (Wisdom of Solomon), Sirach (or Ecclesiasticus). These books are called Deuterocanonical texts. The Protestants required these books to have been written in Hebrew. The findings of the "Dead Sea Scrolls" have located most of these in Hebrew. The Old Testament has 46 books and the New Testament has 27 books (total:73) in the Catholic Bible, long before the Protestant Reformation.

QUESTION: Is "Rapture" in Scripture?

Rapture teachers typically cite St. Paul's words: 1 Thessalonians 4:16,17. [16] *"For the Lord himself, with a word of command, with the voice of an archangel and with the trumpet of God, will come down from heaven, and the dead in Christ will rise first. [17] Then we who are alive, who are left, will be caught up together with them in the clouds to meet the Lord in the air."* Rapture teachers claim that Christians will be *"caught up"* (snatched) from the world because God promised them an escape from the "great tribulation" on the last days.

RESPONSE: To put this in proper perspective, several points need to be clarified.

First, around the year 1830, John Nelson Darby invented what was called "Pre-tribulation Secret Rapture" doctrine. At that time, most Christians classified Darby's "rapture" doctrine as false. The idea of "rapture" was never used or heard of in the first eighteen centuries after Christ, including Christian teachers of every sort: Catholic, Orthodox, and Protestant. Prior to the 1830's, there is no known record of any church teaching, creed, catechism, or statement of faith recorded regarding "rapture." Even today, the majority of Christians worldwide, including Protestants, do not accept "rapture."

Second, regarding verse 16 above, by the use of: ***"word of command,"*** ***"voice of an archangel,"*** **and** ***"the trumpet,"*** St. Paul is clearly talking about the second coming of Christ with obvious parallels to other biblical text (see Matthew 24:31 below). Certainly, there are no indications in Scripture or any references to a separate secret invisible coming of Christ just for the "rapture." Christ's second coming will be universally visible and undeniable: Matthew 24:27. ***"For just as lightning comes from the east and is seen as far as the west, so will the coming of the Son of Man be."***

Third, Matthew 24:37. ***"For as it was *in the days of Noah,* so it will be at the coming of the Son of Man."*** Scripture tells us that ***"In the days of Noah,"*** the flood destroyed the wicked and the righteous were saved (just the reverse of the "rapture" theory). Also consider: Matthew 24:13. ***"...the one who perseveres to the end will be saved."*** Overall, the "rapture" concept is not supported by Scripture. Jesus Christ's life, death, resurrection, and ascension is just a part of the gospel, it is not yet complete. Christ came the first time as our suffering redeemer, now he must return as our Holy Judge to set the world aright, and the evil one will be powerless to those who love God. Matthew 6:10." ***... on earth as it is in heaven."***

Fourth, Matthew 24:29–31. ₂₉ ***"Immediately *after the tribulation* of those days...*** ₃₀ ***...they will see the Son of Man coming upon the clouds of heaven with power and great glory.*** ₃₁ ***And He will send out His angels with a trumpet blast..."*** This Scripture passage tells us that Christ will return, in glory, after the tribulation. There is nothing in Scripture to indicate that anything like the "rapture" will occur prior to the tribulation. So, ***"caught up together"*** only occurs ***"after the tribulation,"*** then, ***"they will see the Son of Man coming."*** Therefore, ***"caught up together"*** only occurs ***"after the tribulation,"*** the one and only second coming of Jesus in scripture.

QUESTION: How can the body and blood of Christ be in Holy Communion?

RESPONSE: From the Catholic point of view, this question is a bit backwards. After one studies the 6th chapter of John (and other Scripture passages), Holy Communion (Eucharist) is in fact the body and blood of

Jesus Christ in the form of bread and wine. John 6:55. [Jesus speaking] *"For my flesh is true food, and my blood is true drink."* 1 Corinthians 11:27–29. *"Therefore whoever eats the bread or drinks <u>the cup of the Lord</u> unworthily will have to answer for the body and blood of the Lord. A person should examine himself, and so eat the bread and drink the cup. For anyone who eats and drinks <u>without discerning</u> the body, eats and drinks <u>judgment</u> on himself."* This Scripture passage is very clear that the early Christians believed in the Real Presence in the Eucharist. Otherwise, why would St. Paul issue such a stern warning of *"<u>judgment</u>"* if eaten *"<u>without discerning?</u>"* Also, note that *"<u>the cup of the Lord</u>"* tells us that the Lord is present in the cup even if it appears still to be wine. Prior to this passage, St, Paul establishes himself as having the authority and is pointing out the proper way to celebrate the Eucharist according to the instructions from Jesus: 1 Corinthians 11:23 *"For I* [St. Paul] <u>*received from the Lord*</u> *what I also handed on to you,"*

Here is something puzzling. Worldwide, Christians believe and accept the miracles of Jesus. Turning water into wine, the multiplication of loves that feed the 4000 and the 5000, healing the sick, and raising Lazarus from the dead are all examples of accepted miracles. Seventeen of these miracles are only mentioned <u>one time</u> in Scripture. Also, Christians have no idea how the miracle and supernatural mystery of the incarnation of Jesus occurred, or how the Trinity is possible, or how the supernatural mystery of the Resurrection and Ascension occurred, but by faith they believe in them. Yet, the greatest miracle of all that is prefigured/predicted in the Old Testament and mentioned all through the New Testament, including all the gospels and even mentioned 15 times alone by Jesus himself, speaking in the Gospel of John chapter 6: 41 *"I am the bread that came down from heaven."* 48 *"I am the bread of life."* 51 *"I am the living bread…, the bread that I will give is my flesh for the life of the world."* 53 *"…unless you eat the flesh of the son of man and drink His blood, you do not have life within you."* 54 *"Whoever eats my flesh and drinks my blood has eternal life."* The Eucharist is the most mentioned supernatural mystery and the longest lasting miracle in all of Scripture (perpetual institution), yet why is it that so many Christians have difficulty accepting it? Maybe Scripture can answer part of this. In Scripture, right after the above passage from John, many disciples responded: John 6:60. ***"Then many of His disciples who were listening said, "this saying is hard, who can accept it?"*** The disciples at that time did not know about Holy Communion (Eucharist), therefore they understandably and mistakenly thought Jesus was talking about His human, physical flesh and human, physical blood. After the Resurrection, the early Christians knew that Jesus was referring to the Eucharist that actually is the resurrected, glorified, living body, blood, soul, and divinity of Jesus Christ under the signs of bread and wine. Catholics believe in the real presence in the Eucharist because Christ Himself told us so in Scripture.

QUESTION: Why does the priest break the host at Mass?
RESPONSE: The short answer is the <u>breaking</u> of bread is tradition, following Christ's example, and symbolism.

Traditionally the Jewish people have a long–standing ritual of <u>breaking</u> bread along with a blessing to start each meal. Jesus <u>broke</u> bread on several occasions. Some examples include the multiplication of loaves (two times), when Jesus <u>broke</u> bread at the last supper, when Jesus said the first Mass (<u>broke</u> bread) with two disciples in Emmaus (Luke 24:30–31), and when Jesus <u>broke</u> bread with St. Peter and the other Apostles on various occasions. It is interesting to note that at most of these occasions, Scripture tells us that Jesus ***"Took the bread, said a blessing, <u>broke</u> it, and gave it to them,"*** just as what is done at every Mass to follow Christ's commands.

Finally, the <u>breaking</u> of bread symbolizes the separation of Christ's body and blood in His death on the cross, so the priest places a portion of the Eucharist into His blood (under the appearance of wine) to show Christ's Real Presence at Mass.

QUESTION: Was the creation of the universe (cosmos) random?
RESPONSE: There are two scientific facts that the universal scientific community agree upon:
(1) One cannot obtain anything from nothing. Something can generate other things, but nothing cannot generate anything.
(2) The universe has at least 20 *precise constants*, such as: the speed of light (186,000 miles per second); gravitation; electromagnetism; and there

are 6 to the 23rd power number of atoms in 12 grams of carbon, etc. All of these, as well as the remaining constants, have precise mathematical numbers that science communities all over the world agree upon.

Considering the above, a researcher asked the scientific community, "What would happen to our universe if any one of the 20 precise constants varied?" The response was that if any one of the *20 precise constants* varied by a factor of 10 to the minus 10th power (which is 0.000,000,000,1, or one billionth), the universe would not be what it is today, it would be chaotic. For example, if the 12 grams of carbon had more or less than 6 to the 23rd power number of atoms, it would not be carbon, thus no life. In other words, there cannot be any variance of any one of the *precise constants.* They have to be exact to maintain our stable universe.

The second question asked was, "What are the odds of a <u>random</u> occurrence to generate 20 precise constants in our universe?" The response to this question was that the odds would be 10 to 10th with 123rd power to one. In other words, the odds would be 10 billion to the 123rd power $(10,000,000,000^{123})$. This has more zeroes than what can be displayed here. Or, it is virtually impossible for 20 precise constants to have occurred randomly, they had to be guided by intelligence.

The Big Bang Theory (not initially called that) was originally proposed by Monsignor Georges Lemaitre, a Belgian Catholic priest/astronomer. Later, the science community jokingly named it the Big Bang Theory. The name stuck and is still used today.

The Hubble telescope confirmed the Big Bang Theory by showing that the universe is expanding (stretching out). Isaiah 42:5. *"Thus says God, the Lord, who created the heavens and <u>stretched them out</u>,"*

If the Big Bang occurred randomly, then where did the material come from to originate the Big Bang? Remember, you cannot obtain anything from nothing/void (Genesis 1:2 calls it *"the abyss"*). A scientist recently admitted that each element of the Big Bang had to be precisely programed by some intelligence in order to generate 20 precise constants that keep our universe stable. Genesis was not written as a science text. However, it is interesting to note that certain elements of scripture are very similar to what science states. Genesis 1:3. [the 1st day] *". God said: Let there be light,"* Science agrees that a tremendous light had to occur, this light was not the sun which was created 3 days later: Genesis 1:14. [the 4th day] *"Then God said: Let there be lights in the dome of the sky. To separate day from night."* Many times, in Scripture certain things have double meanings. Some theologians state that the first day of "light" may be the creation of angels. Or, that first "light" that God created could also be the "light" of the Big Bang that created all the elements!

QUESTION: What is the story on the evolution of species?
RESPONSE: First, let's look at a few facts generally accepted by most of the science community:

- The age of the universe: 14,000,000,000 years old. (14 billon)
  (plus or minus 50 million years)
- The age of the earth: 4,500,000,000 years old. (4.5 billion)
- Single life cell age: 3,800,000,000 years old. (3.8 billion)
- Human life age: 200,000 years old. (200 thousand)
  (end of internet data)
- The scientific community tells us that the earth's magnetic field is declining about 6.4% every 100 years, the moon is moving away from earth about one inch per year *"stretched them out."* (Is 42:5).

If one takes the "single life cell age" of 3,800,000,000 years old minus "human life age" of 200,000 years old, it equals 3,799,800,000 years. That's 3.799 billion years for human life to develop. The science community tells us that in order for evolution from a single cell to be true it would have taken 15 billion years. As you can see, this "15 billion years" is one billion years greater than "the age of the universe" (14 billion years), let alone the above human life development of 3.799 billion years. When you look at 15 billion years versus 3.799 billion years, there's a difference of 11.201 billion years. One could understand this being off maybe 50 million or even 100 million years, but 11.201 billion years! That just seems to indicate that there is something very wrong with the evolution theory.

The Catholic Church agrees that there can be evolution within each species. However, there has never been any proof that any species evolved (jumped) to another species. If they did, why do we still have monkeys and apes? Why do we still have single cell life on earth? In the hundreds of years that science has been studying single cells, why haven't they observed any of them evolve into a new species? Why haven't they found any species that are in between current species?

There are many fossils displayed in museums today that indicate certain ancient links between species; however, the authenticity of these fossils is highly questionable. In a few recorded cases (where scientists were allowed to investigate), the fossils were scientifically proven to be fakes.

The discovery of DNA proves that each species offspring can only be a combination of its parents and nothing else (no new species). A German biochemist, Frederich Miescher, in 1869 first observed what is now called DNA in human cells. Then in 1953, an American, James Watson, and an Englishman, Francis Crick, along with the help of Rosalin Franklin and Maurice Wilkins, discovered the double helix, a twisted ladder like structure of human DNA that is in every cell of the human body. It is difficult to imagine that this double helix structure within the nucleus of every cell of our body, when uncoiled is about two inches long and it contains all the unique information for each species to develop, survive, and reproduce. The human cells contain 23 pairs of chromosomes, 22 pairs plus one sex pair that consists of a female "XX" and a male "YY" chromosome. Any offspring is a combination of its parents' chromosomes. No species can modify or add chromosomes which proves species cannot jump (evolve) to another species. Hebrews 13:8. *"Jesus Christ is the same yesterday, today, and forever."* Genesis 1:26. [the 6th day]" ...*God said: Let us make human beings in our image, after our likeness."* Therefore, if Jesus Christ (God) is the *"same" "forever,"* and humans are created in God's *"likeness,"* [1] then one would have to conclude that humans were created not to change (evolve) or be part of any form of evolution of species but remain the same (similar to God) as when created. The human body has 206 bones. Only five of those bones provide a location in which bone marrow (stem cells) can be extracted. The five bones are the skull, sternum, vertebrae, pelvis, and the rib. Out of these five, doctors find the rib to be the easiest to extract bone marrow. Have you ever wondered why out of 206 bones the rib (side) from Adam was used to create Eve? Our all-knowing God had to have guided Moses to write about using the rib (side) in the book of Genesis because only God at that time knew it could be scientifically possible.

According to the scientific community, the measured and documented value of our earth's magnetic field over time is declining by 6.4% every 100 years. If one calculates this decline in reverse, in the year 10,000 BC, the earth's magnetic field would have been so strong that there would not be any life at all on earth. So how could 15 billion years of evolution have occurred? The scripture scholars tell us that the earth is about 6,000 years old and the great flood occurred about 4,400 BC. The oldest tree discovered in the world is a bristlecone pine that is 4,000 years old.

> (1) Theologians suggest that our "*likeness*" to God has to do more with our ability for reason and/or our capacity to love as God loves in the Trinity, making us the only creatures capable of Gods Spirit to dwell within us to receive His grace. Our "*likeness*" reflects the Trinity of God because we are Body, Soul, and Spirit (according to scripture).

SUMMARY – RESPONSE:

- Born again? If you have been baptized, you have been born again according to Scripture.
- Pray for the dead? Catholics pray for the living soul of a person whose body has died.
- Purgatory? Scripture does not use the term "Purgatory" but does support the idea of purification by telling us that nothing unclean will enter heaven.
- Baptize infants? Catholics baptize infants/children because it's a tradition that is stated in Scripture.
- Priest called "father"? Catholics call their priest "father" similar to St. Paul in Scripture using the term "father," even referring to himself as "your father."
- Confess to a priest? Catholics confess their sins to a priest because Catholic priests have been given the authority directly from Jesus Christ to lose (forgive) or bind sins.
- Sign of the cross? Catholics use the sign of the cross because it has deep roots in the Old Testament, and it was handed down as a tradition of the original Apostles.

- Seven sacraments? All of the seven sacraments can be found in Scripture as commands mostly from Jesus Christ.
- Bible and tradition? Catholics believe in the Bible and use tradition handed down to worship and praise the Lord as instructed in Scripture.
- Books of the Bible? The Catholic Bible has more books than the Protestant Bible because at some point the Protestants removed certain books.
- Rapture? The concept of "rapture" is not supported by Scripture.
- Holy Communion? Catholics believe in the real presence of the body and blood of Jesus Christ is in the Eucharist as stated in Scripture.
- Break bread? The priest physically breaks bread at Mass to follow Christ's example to remember Him and what He did.
- Random creation? Scientific evidence supports the "Big Bang" theory which had to have been designed by a high degree of intelligence.
- Evolution of species? The discovery of DNA has proven that the theory of evolution cannot have occurred, plus it would have taken more time than the calculated age of the earth.

References:
Scripture quotations are ***italicized and bold*** from The New American Bible (NAB) – revised edition, Fireside Catholic Publishing. Certain words may be <u>underlined</u> for emphasis added.
Karl Keating's book: "Catholicism and Fundamentalism", Ignatius press.
Anthony E. Gills book: "Fundamentalism – What every Catholic Needs to Know".

SCRIPTURE RESPONSE: Assembled by Paul Wilchek, edited by Kristin Trepanier–Henry.
Reviewed by Spence McSorley 12OCT20.

CHAPTER 10

SELECTED SUBJECTS

Let Scripture Speak for Itself with this alphabetical list of certain selected words. In most cases the scriptural quotation contains the actual word listed or the scriptural quote is related to that word. The selected word/words are underlined for emphasis added.

ABANDON: Hebrews 13:5–6 *₅... be content with what you have, for He has said, "I will never forsake you or <u>abandon</u> you." ₆ Thus we may say with confidence: "The Lord is my helper, and I will not be afraid ..."*

ACKNOWLEDGE: Matthew 10:32–33 *Everyone who <u>acknowledges</u> me before others I will <u>acknowledge</u> before my heavenly Father.* Also, Luke 12:8–9.

ALONE, AFFLICTED: Psalms 25:16–17 *Look upon me, have pity on me, for I am <u>alone</u> and <u>afflicted</u>. Relieve the <u>troubles</u> of my heart; bring me out of my <u>distress</u>.*

ANGER: Ephesians 4: 26–27 *₂₆ Be <u>angry</u> but do not sin; do not let the sun go down on our <u>anger</u>, ₂₇ and give no opportunity to the devil. ₃₁ Let all bitterness and wrath and <u>anger</u> and clamor and slander be* *put away from you with all malice, ₃₂ and be kind to one another, tenderhearted, forgiving one another, as God in Christ forgave you.* Psalms 37: 8 **Refrain from <u>anger</u>, and forsake wrath! Do not fret; it tends only to evil.**

ANGELS: Psalms 91:11 **For his <u>angels</u> he has given command about you, that they guard you in all your ways.**

Psalms 34:8 **The <u>angel</u> of the Lord, who encamps with them, delivers all who fear God.**

Matthew 18:10 **See that you do not despise one of these little ones; for I say to you that their <u>angels</u> in heaven always look upon the face of my heavenly Father.**

In above, an angel "**guard you in all your ways**" in which they have to be with you always and an angel "**encamps with**" us and also simultaneously "**looks upon ... my heavenly_Father.**", from this, one would have to conclude that God must always be very close to us in order for this to occur!

ANGUISH: Psalms 55:4,22 ... ₄**My heart is in <u>anguish</u> within me, the terrors of death have fallen upon me. ₂₂ Cast your burden on the Lord, and He will sustain you;** ... Romans 9:2 **I have great sorrow and constant <u>anguish</u> in my heart.**

ANXIETY: Philippians 4:6 **Have no <u>anxiety</u> about anything, but in everything by supplication with thanksgiving let your requests be made known to God.**

ARMOR: Ephesians 6:10–11 **Finally, draw your strength from the Lord and from his mighty power, put on the whole <u>armor</u> of God, that you may be able to stand against the wiles of the devil.**

ASSURANCE, BELIEVE IN HIM: John 3:16 **For God so loved the world that he gave his only Son, that whoever <u>believes in him</u> should not perish but have eternal life.**

BELIEVE, BELIEIVING: Acts 16:31 <u>*Believe*</u> *in the Lord Jesus, and you will be saved, you and your household.*

1 Corinthians 7:12–14 *₁₂... if any brother has a wife who is an unbeliever, and she consents to live with him, he should not divorce her. ₁₃If any woman has a husband who is an unbeliever, and he consents to live with her, she should not divorce him. ₁₄For the unbelieving husband is consecrated through his wife, and the unbelieving wife is consecrated through her husband.*

BROKENHEARTED: Psalms 34:19–20 *₁₉ The Lord is close to the* <u>*brokenhearted,*</u> *saves those whose spirit is crushed. ₂₀Many are the* <u>*troubles*</u> *of the righteous, but the Lord delivers him from them all.*

BREAD, COMMUNION, EUCHARIST:
- In Gn 14:18 <u>bread</u> and wine were given to Abram from Melchizedek, then Abram gave 1/10 of everything, because of the importance of <u>bread</u> and wine.
- Heb 7:1–4 tells us: *"Melchizedek.... Resembles the Son of God"*
- Malachi 1:11 tells us that: God desires a *"pure offering"*– pre-figuring Holy communion.
- Exodus 16:15 tells us that manna is the: *"<u>bread</u> which the Lord has given you to eat"*.
  The "<u>Bread</u> of the Presence" Hebrew for "<u>bread</u> of the face" is the name given to the twelve loaves of unleavened <u>bread</u> that the Jews displayed in the Temple sanctuary that symbolized the covenant between God and the twelve tribes of Israel (Lev 24:5–9). The Bread of the Presence was placed on a golden table in the Holy Place, just outside the Holy of Holies that was replaced each sabbath and the "old" loaves were eaten by the priests (Lev 24:9).
- Bethlehem, Christ's birth place means house of <u>bread</u>.
- Luke 2:7 tells us that: Mary laid the new born Christ in a manger (a feeding trough) that symbolized Christ was to become our food for salvation.
- Jesus is speaking in John 6:31 *"our fathers did eat manna in the desert, as it is written: he gave them <u>bread</u> from heaven to eat"*

- Luke 22:14–20 describes the last supper where Jesus broke the <u>bread</u> and said ₁₉*"this is my body"* then ₂₀*"and likewise the cup"* then stated: *"in memory of me"*. In Hebrew "memory" means to re–live. Similar passages can be found in: Matthew 26:26–29, Mark 14:22–24.

- 1 Cor 10:16 states: ₁₆*"the cup....is it not a participation in the blood of Christ"*, *"the <u>bread</u>...is it not a participation in the body of Christ"*

- Jesus is speaking in 1 Cor 11:23–29: ₂₄*"this [bread] is my body"*, ₂₅*"This cup is the new covenant in my blood,"* Then we are told: ₂₆*".... As you eat this <u>bread</u> and drink this cup, you proclaim the Lord's death"* *"proclaim"* is to announce officially as being true. Then scripture goes on to say: ₂₉*".... Anyone who eats and drinks without discerning the body, eats and drinks judgment on himself."* Why such a stern warning to discern prior to eating? Because at the time of the early Church (first 100 years) they believed in the real presence of Christ in the bread & wine, "Eucharist," which has been passed on through to today.

- The following is a brief overview of John, chapter 6:
  1) The multiplication of loves that fed 5000 and 4000, shows that Christ has power over man–made bread. Also described in: Mt 15:32–39, Mk 6:41. 44, 8:1–9, and Lk 9:13–17.
  2) Christ walks on the sea which shows that Christ has power over himself.
  3) The bread of life discourse: *"I am the <u>bread</u> of life"* (Jn 6:35), along with 15 other similar references, shows its importance that Jesus has the power to turn bread and wine into His body and blood.

- John 6:60–69 tells us that many disciples turned away from Christ, why? They could not accept or believe what Christ said: *"my flesh is true food, and my blood true drink"* (Jn 6:55), the Apostles accepted this but did not understand until after the Last Supper, Resurrection, Ascension, and Pentecost.

- Jesus appeared (after His resurrection) on the road to Emmaus where He blessed and broke bread with two disciples: Luke

24:30–31 *"… He was at table with them, He took <u>bread</u>, and blessed, and broke, and gave to them. And their eyes were open and they knew Him: and vanished out of their sight."*, Jesus himself performed the first mass, then Jesus' body vanished from their sight to signify that He was spiritually present in the bread, Eucharist, that He blessed, broke, and gave to them.

- Eucharist in Greek means "thanksgiving", other names are: Holly Communion, the Lord's Supper, the table of the Lord, the breaking of the bread, the most blessed sacrament, our daily bread, the unbloody sacrifice, the sacrifice of praise, and agape.

CONFESS, CONFESSION: Romans 10:9,13 *₉because, if you <u>confess</u> with your lips that Jesus is Lord and believe in your heart that God raised him from the dead, you will be saved. ₁₃For, every one who calls upon the name of the Lord will be saved.* James 5:16 *Therefore <u>confess</u> your sins to one another, and pray for one another, that you may be healed.* 1John 1:9 *If we <u>confess</u> our sins, he is faithful and just and will forgive our sins and cleanse us from unrighteousness.*

DEAD SEA SCROLLS:
The following is from "Wikipedia.org/wiki/Dead_Sea_Scrolls" as of 9/21/18.

- The" Dead_Sea Scrolls" were discovered in a series of caves near the Dead Sea in the West Bank of the Jordan river between 1946 and 1956 with additional finds up through 2017.
- Archeologists and researchers have assembled over 981 different manuscripts written in Hebrew, Aramaic, and a few in Greek including 235 Biblical Texts. Some scholars believe the scrolls were hid in the caves by Jews who were fleeing the Romans during the destruction of Jerusalem in the year A.D. 70. The scrolls are on papyrus, parchment, and some on copper and bronze, they were found in traditional Jewish pottery, some scrolls in the pottery were wrapped in linen. Some of the papyrus scrolls were as long as 35 feet that consisted of papyrus sheets glued together.
- The following is a list of the Biblical texts and (number of copies found):Psalms (39), Deuteronomy (33), Genesis (24), Isaiah (22),

Jubilees (21), Exodus (18), Leviticus (17), Numbers (11), Daniel (8), Jeremiah (6), Ezekiel (6), Job (6), Tobit (5), 1 & 2 Kings (4), 1 & 2 Samuel (4), Judges (4), Song of Songs (Canticles) (4), Ruth (4), Lamentations (4), Sirach (3), Ecclesiastes (20), and Joshua (2).

- The Isaiah Scrolls are 1000 years older than any previously known copy of Isaiah. Do you think that St. Paul may have predicted the "Dead Sea Scrolls?" In 2 Corinthians 4:4 he states: ***But we hold this treasure in earthen vessels, the surpassing power may be of God and not from us.***

DESERTED: 2 Timothy 4:16,17,22 *₁₆At my first defense no one appeared on my behalf, but everyone <u>deserted</u> me. May it not be held against them! ₁₇But the Lord stood by me and gave me strength. ₂₂The Lord be with your spirit. Grace be with all of you.*

DISMAYED, DISCOURAGED: Isaiah 41:10 *fear not, for I am with you, be not <u>dismayed</u>, for I am your God; I will strengthen you, I will help you, I will uphold you with my victorious right hand.*

EMPTIED HIMSELF: Philippians 2:6–8 *Christ Jesus, ₆who, though he was in the form of God, did not count equality with God a thing to be grasped, ₇but <u>emptied himself</u>, taking the form of a servant, being born in the likeness of men. ₈And being found in human form he humbled himself and became obedient unto death, even death on a cross.* Hebrews 2:9 *...He who "for a little while" was made "lower than the angels," that by the grace of God He might taste death for everyone.* Note: The Jews believed, rightly so, that if a human were to be face to face with God, they would become so overwhelmed by his power that they would die. Therefore, Jesus, per the above, *"emptied himself"* of certain powers so He could mingle with humans without overwhelming them with God's power. This may be why Jesus prayed to the father.

FAITH: Hebrews 11:1–40 *<u>Faith</u> is the realization of what is hoped for and evidence of things not seen. Because of it the ancients were well attested. By <u>faith</u> we understand that the universe was ordered by the word of God, so that what is visible came into being through the* *invisible.* Romans 5: 1–2 ***Therefore, since we have been justified by*** *faith*, ***we have peace with God through our Lord Jesus Christ, through whom we have gained access [by*** *faith]* ***to this grace in which we stand, and we boast in*** *hope* ***of the glory of God.*** Also see HOPE.

FEAR: 1 John 4:18 ***There is no*** *fear* ***in love, but perfect love drives out*** *fear* ***because*** *fear* ***has to do with punishment, and so one who*** *fears* ***is not yet perfect in love.*** Luke 12: 5,7 ₅***I shall show you whom to*** *fear.* ***Be*** *afraid* ***of the one who after killing has the power to cast into Gehenna; yes, I tell you be*** *afraid* ***of that one.*** ₇***Even the hairs of your head have all been counted. Do not be*** *afraid.* ***You are worth more than many sparrows.***

FORGIVE, FORGIVENESS: Matthew 18:21–22 ₂₁***Then Peter came up and said to him, "Lord, how often shall my brother sin against me, and I*** *forgive* ***him? As many as seven times?"*** ₂₂***Jesus said to him, "I do not say to you seven times, but seventy times seven."*** Colossians 3:13 ... *forgiving* ***each other as the Lord has*** *forgiven* ***you, so you also must*** *forgive.*

FRUIT OF THE HOLY SPIRIT: Galatians 5:22–23 ... ***the fruit of the Spirit is love, joy, peace, patience, kindness, generosity, faithfulness, gentleness, self–control.***

GIFTS OF THE HOLY SPIRIT: The seven gifts of the Holy Spirit are given at baptism and reminded at confirmation. Isaiah 11:2 ***The spirit of the Lord shall rest upon him: a spirit of*** *wisdom* ***and of*** *understanding*, ***a spirit of*** *counsel* ***and*** *strength [fortitude]*, ***a spirit of*** *knowledge* ***and of*** *fear of the Lord [piety]*, ***and his delight shall be*** *the fear of the Lord.***

Charisms may be given to specific individuals as the Holy Spirit chooses that are for the service of others and the building up of the Church. 1 Corinthians 12: 8–11 ***To one is given through the Spirit the expression of*** *wisdom; to another the expression of* *knowledge* ***according to the same Spirit; to another*** *faith* ***by the same Spirit; to another gifts of*** *healing* ***by the one Sprit; to another*** *mighty deeds; ***to another*** *prophecy; ***to another*** *discernment* ***of spirits; to another*** *varieties of tongues; ***to another*** *interpretation of tongues. But one and the same Spirit produces all of these, distributing them individually to each person as he wishes.*

A person full of the Spirit can be recognized: Galatians 5: 22–23 *...the fruit of the Spirit is love, joy, peace, patience, kindness, generosity, faithfulness, gentleness, self–control.*

GRACE: According to the Catholic Bible Dictionary, "grace is a supernatural gift surpassing the attributes of created nature." "The supernatural gift that God bestows entirely of his own benevolence upon men and women for their eternal salvation." Ephesians 2:8 *For by grace you have been saved through faith, and this is not from you; it is the gift of God; it is not from works, so no one may boast.* Ephesians 4:7 *But grace was given to each of us according to the measure of Christ's gift.* Also see "RIGHTEOUSNESS / JUSTIFICATION" herein.

GRIEVE: 1 Thessalonians 4:13–14 *₁₃ ... about those who are asleep, so that you may not grieve like the rest, who have no hope. ₁₄ For if we believe that Jesus died and rose, so too will God, through Jesus, bring with him those who have fallen asleep.* Psalms 55:3. *Hear me and give answer. I rock with grief...*

GUIDANCE: Psalms 73:24 *You guide me with your counsel, and afterwards you will receive me to glory.* Psalms 119:105 *Your word is a lamp to my feet and a light to my path.* Proverbs 3:6 *In all your ways acknowledge him, and he will make straight your paths.*

HOLY SPIRIT: Creation: Genesis 1:2 *... a mighty wind swept over the water.* Prophesied: Joel 3: *₁ Then afterwards I will pour out my spirit upon all mankind. ₂ Even upon the servants and the handmaids, in those days, I will pour out my spirit.* Conception: Matthew 1:20 *... For it was through the holy Spirit that this child has been conceived in her.* Resurrection: Romans 8:11 *If the Spirit of the one who raised Jesus from the dead dwells in you, the one who raised Christ from the dead will give life to your mortal bodies also, through his Spirit that dwells in you.* Ascension: Acts 1:9 *as they were looking on, he was lifted up. And a cloud took him from their sight.* End Times: Revelation 22:17 *The*

Spirit and the bride say, "Come." Let the hearer say, "Come." Let the one who thirsts come forward, and the one who wants it receive the gift of life-giving water.

HOPE: In scripture, <u>Hope</u> is tied to <u>Faith</u>, the supernatural confidence that we will attain the promises of Christ and rely on the grace of the Holy Spirit rather than our own strength. Hebrews 10:23 ***Let us hold unwaveringly to our confession that gives us <u>hope</u>, for He who made the promise is trustworthy.*** Jesus Christ fulfills the <u>hope</u> of the Old Testament: John 8:56,58 ₅₆ *"Abraham your father rejoiced to see my day; he saw it and was glad." ...* ₅₈*Jesus said to them, "Amen, amen, I say to you, before Abraham came to be, I AM."* Romans 15:13 ***May the God of <u>hope</u> fill you with all joy and peace in believing, so that you may abound in <u>hope</u> by the power of the Holy Spirit.*** 1 Peter 1:3 ***Blessed be the God and Father of our Lord Jesus Christ! By His great mercy we have been born anew to a living <u>hope</u> through the resurrection of Jesus Christ from the dead, and to an inheritance which is imperishable, undefiled and unfading, kept in heaven for you, ...***

JOY: John 16:24 [...In the name of Jesus] ***ask and you will receive, so that your <u>joy</u> may be complete.*** Romans 14:17 ***For the kingdom of God is not a matter of food and drink, but of <u>righteousness</u>, <u>peace</u>, and <u>joy</u> in the holy Spirit.*** Romans 15:13. ***May the God of <u>hope</u> fill you with all <u>joy</u> and peace in believing, so that you may abound in <u>hope</u> by the power of the holy Spirit.*** Psalms 126:5–6 ***May those who sow in tears reap with shouts of <u>joy</u>!***

JUDGMENT, JUSTICE, AND MERCY: <u>Justice</u> is to be fair, decent, right, accurate with punishment for wrongdoing. <u>Mercy</u> and <u>merciful</u> are in scripture 62 times. <u>Mercy</u>, of course, is to be kind, forgiving, and compassionate. One might think these two words should not be in the same sentence together, which may be the case in our civil society. However, they do appear together in scripture. Matthew 23:23 *"...<u>judgment</u> and <u>mercy</u> and fidelity. Those you should have done..."* James 2:13 *"For the <u>judgment</u> is <u>merciless</u> for one who has not shown <u>mercy</u>, <u>mercy</u> triumphs over <u>judgment</u>."* Zechariah 7:9 *"Thus says the Lord of host:*

Judge with true justice, and show kindness and compassion [mercy] *toward each other."* Matthew 5:7 *"Blessed are the merciful, for they will be shown mercy."* Luke 6:36 *"Be merciful, just as your father is merciful."* Also, Titus 3:5–7.

LOVE: 1 Corinthians 13:4–7,13 *₄Love is patient, love is kind. It is not jealous, [love] is not pompous, it is not inflated. ₅It is not rude, it does not seek its own interest, it is not quick–tempered, it does not brood over injury, ₆it does not rejoice over wrongdoing but rejoices with the truth. ₇It bears all things, believes all things, hopes all things, endures all things. ₁₃So faith, hope, love remain, these three; but the greatest of these is love.*

PEACE: Psalms 34:15 *seek peace and pursue it.* John 14: 27. [Jesus] *Peace I leave with you; my peace I give you.* Romans 2:10 *But there will be glory, honor, and peace for everyone who does good, ...* 2 Thessalonians 3:16 *Now may the Lord of peace himself give you peace at all times in all ways.* Philippians 4:7 *Then the peace of God, which passes all understanding, will guard your hearts and minds in Christ Jesus.*

PRAY, PRAYED, PRAYER(S), AND ASK: Pray, prayed, prayer and prayers appear in scripture 516 times.

Matthew 7:7–11 *Ask and it will be given to you; seek and you will find; knock and the door will be opened to you. For every one who asks receives; and the one who seeks, finds; and to the one who knocks, the door will be opened.*

Matthew 18:19–20 *... I say to you, if two of you agree on earth about anything for which they are to pray, it shall be granted to them by my heavenly Father. For where two or three are gathered together in my name, there am I in the midst of them.* Matthew 21:22 *Whatever you ask for in prayer with faith, you will receive.*

Mark 11:24 *Therefore I tell you, all that you ask for in prayer, believe that you will receive it and it shall be yours.*

Luke 6:28 *... bless those who curse you, <u>pray</u> for those who mistreat you.*

Romans 8:26–27 *...the Spirit too comes to the aid of our weakness; for we do not know how to <u>pray</u> as we ought, but the Spirit itself intercedes with inexpressible groanings. And the one who searches hearts knows what is the intention of the Spirit, because it intercedes for the holy ones according to God's will.*

Ephesians 6:18 *With all <u>prayer</u> and supplication, <u>pray</u> at every opportunity in the Spirit.*

James 5:16 *<u>pray</u> for one another, that you may be healed. The fervent <u>prayer</u> of a righteous person is very powerful.*

The "Our Father" can be found in Luke 11:1–4 and Matthew 6:9–13. The basis of "Hail Mary" can be found in Luke 1:28 & 42.

Some additional passages on prayer: Mt 6:5,6,7, Mt 5:44, Mt 26:44, Lk 11:9–13, Lk 22:41, Lk 18:1, Acts 2:42, Acts 4:31, Rom 12:12, 1 Cor 14:14–18, Phil 1:9, Col 1:9–12, Col 4: 12, 1 Thes 5:17, 1Tm 2:1–3, Heb 5:7–9, James 1:5–8, 1 Pt 4:7, 1John 3:22, 1 John 5:14–15.

PROMISES:
Exodus 14:14 *The Lord will fight for you; you have only to keep still.*
Exodus 20:12 *Honor your father and your mother, that you may have a long life...*
Deuteronomy 31:8 *It is the Lord who goes before you; he will be with you and will never fail you or forsake you. So do not fear or be dismayed.*
Joshua 1:9 *I command you: be strong and steadfast! Do not fear nor be dismayed, for the Lord, your God, is with you wherever you go.*
2 Chronicles 7:14 *...upon whom my name has been pronounced, humble themselves and pray, and seek my face and turn from their evil ways, I will hear them from heaven and pardon their sins and heal their land.*
Psalms 9:10 *The Lord is a stronghold for the oppressed, a stronghold in times of trouble.*

Psalms 23:4 ***Even though I walk through the valley of the shadow of death, I will fear no evil, for you are with me; your rod and your staff comfort me.***

Psalms 37:4 ***Find your delight in the Lord who will give you your heart's desire.***

Psalms 50:15 ***Then call on me on the day of distress; I will rescue you, and you shall honor me.***

Psalms 86:5 ***Lord, you are good and forgiving, most merciful to all who call on you.***

Proverbs 3:5–6 *₅ **Trust in the Lord with all your heart. On your own intelligence do not rely; ₆ In all your ways be mindful of him, and he will make straight your paths.***

Proverbs 22:6,9 *₆ **Train the young in the way they should go; even when old, they will not swerve from it. ₉ The generous will be blessed, for they share their food with the poor.***

Isaiah 40:29 ***He gives power to the faint, abundant strength to the weak.***

Isaiah 40:31 ***They that hope in the Lord will renew their strength, they will soar on eagles 'wings'; They will run and not grow weary, walk and not grow faint.***

Isaiah 41:10 ***Do not fear: I am with you; do not be anxious: I am your God. I will strengthen you; I will help you, I will uphold you with my victorious right hand.***

Isaiah 41:13 ***...It is I who say to you, do not fear, I will help you.***

Isaiah 54:10 ***My love shall never fall away from you nor my covenant of peace be shaken, says the Lord, who has mercy on you!***

Isaiah 61:1 ***The spirit of the Lord God is upon me, because the Lord has anointed me...***

Jeremiah 29:11–14 ***For I know well the plans I have in mind for you— oracle of the Lord—plans for your welfare and not for woe, so as to give you a future of hope. When you call me. And come and pray to me, I will listen to you. When you seek me with all your heart, I will let you find me—oracle of the Lord.***

Matthew 11:28–30 ***Come to me, all you who labor and are burdened, and I will give you rest. Take my yoke upon you and learn from me, for I am meek and humble of heart; and you will find rest for yourselves. For my yoke is easy and my burden light.***

Mark 11:24 *…I tell you, all that you ask for in prayer, believe that you will receive it and it shall be yours.*

John 3:16 *For God so loved the world that he gave his only Son, so that everyone who believes in him might not perish but might have eternal life.*

John 3:36 *Whoever believes in the Son has eternal life,*

John 7:38 *Whoever believes in me, as scripture says: "Rivers of living water will flow from within him."*

John 14:15–17 *If you love me, you will keep my commandments. And I will ask the Father, and he will give you another Advocate to be with you always, the Spirit of truth, …*

Romans 10:9 *for if you confess with your mouth that Jesus is Lord and believe in your heart that God raised him from the dead, you will be saved.*

Philippians 4:6–7 *₆Have no anxiety at all, but in everything, by prayer and petition, with thanksgiving, make your request known to God, ₇ Then the peace of God that surpasses all understanding will guard your hearts and minds in Christ Jesus.*

Philippians 4:19 *My God will fully supply whatever you need, in accord with his glorious riches in Christ Jesus.*

James 1:5 *But if any of you lacks wisdom, he should ask God who gives to all generously and ungrudgingly, and he will be given it.*

James 4:6–8,10 *₆…he bestows a greater grace; therefore, it says: "God resists the proud, but gives grace to the humble." ₇ So submit yourselves to God. Resist the devil, and he will flee from you. ₈ Draw near to God, and he will draw near to you. ₁₀ Humble yourselves before the Lord and he will exalt you.*

James 5: 14–16,20 *₁₄ Is any among you sick? He should summon the presbyters of the church, and they should pray over him and anoint [him] with oil in the name of the Lord, ₁₅ and the prayer of faith will save the sick person, and the Lord will raise him up. If he has committed any sins, he will be forgiven. ₁₆ Therefore, confess your sins to one another and pray for one another, that you may be healed. The fervent prayer of a righteous person is very powerful. ₂₀ …whoever brings back a sinner from the error of his way will save his soul form death and will cover a multitude of sins.*

REST FOR YOUR SOUL: Matthew 11:28–30 *28 Come to me, all who labor and are heavy laden, and I will give you <u>rest</u>. 29 Take my yoke upon you, and learn from me; for I am gentle and lowly in heart, and you will find <u>rest for your souls</u>. 30 For my yoke is easy, and my burden is light.*

RIGHTEOUSNESS / JUSTIFICATION: The dictionary tells us: "<u>righteousness</u> is the quality of being morally right," and "<u>justification</u> is the action of showing something to be right or reasonable in the sight of God." The glossary of the New American Bible states: "<u>Righteousness</u> is the justice, uprightness; conformity of life to the requirements of moral law; virtue and integrity," and "<u>justification</u> is being made right (righteous) with God by grace." Luke 1:6 ***<u>righteous</u> in the eyes of God, observing all the commandments and ordinances of the Lord blamelessly.***
Romans 5:17 ***how much more will those who receive the abundance of grace and the gift of <u>justification</u> come to reign in life through the one person Jesus Christ.***

When one looks up <u>righteousness</u> in the Catholic Bible Dictionary you will find <u>righteousness</u> refers you to see <u>justification</u>. The write up on <u>justification</u> is a bit long, however, a brief summary of the writeup would be: <u>justification</u> is a personal action (or an ongoing process) where the believer totally commits themselves to God and to the leading of the Spirit. <u>Righteousness</u> is a gift from God to a just person, and, the final paragraph, in part states: "<u>justification</u> for us is the grace by which He makes us <u>righteous</u>."

The Catechism of the Catholic Church (CCC) tells us: (CCC 1266) "The Holy Spirit gives the baptized sanctifying grace, the grace of <u>justification</u>." 1 Cor 6:11 ***you have had yourselves washed, you were sanctified, you were <u>justified</u> in the name of the Lord Jesus Christ and in the Spirit of our God.*** (CCC 1446) "The Sacrament of Penance offers a new possibility to convert and to recover the grace of <u>justification</u>." (CCC 1987) "The grace of the Holy Spirit has the power to justify us, that is, to cleanse us from our sins and give us the <u>righteousness</u> of God through faith in Jesus Christ."

Romans 3:24 & 28 ₂₄ *They Are <u>justified</u> freely by His grace through the redemption in Christ Jesus,* ²⁸ *For we consider that a person is <u>justified</u> by faith apart from works of the law.*

The Council of Trent in 1547 issued the "Decree on <u>Justification</u>" that was defined as: "the translation from that state in which a person is born a son of the first Adam into a state of grace and adoption as sons of God through the second Adam, Jesus Christ."

To summarize the above: One receives <u>justification</u> at baptism, if serious sin occurs one can recover the grace of <u>justification</u> through the Sacrament of Penance. Also, when a person commits themselves to Jesus Christ as their Lord and savior and accepts the holy Spirit within, they receive <u>justification</u>. After which, they receive the free gift of <u>righteousness</u> which assists them in observing the commandments of the Lord and the Lord's will (Lk 1:6 above). Therefore, it appears that one receives the grace gift of <u>justification</u> (Rom 3:24) after which God bestows upon us <u>righteousness</u>.

Some additional Bible passages on <u>justification</u>: Also see: Rom 4:22,23,24,25; Rom 5:1, Rom 5:9, Rom 10:10, 1 Cor 6:11, Gal 2:16,21, Gal 3:24, Titus 3:7.

SACRAMENTS (7): (**bold** passages are the words of Jesus)
ANOINTING OF SICK: Mk 6:13, Jas 5:14, Lk 13:13, Acts 9:17–18, 1 Cor 12:9,30
BAPTISM: **Jn 3:5, Mt 28:19, Mk 16:16**, Acts 2:38; 16:15, 33; 18:8;22:16
CONFIRMATION: Acts 19:5,6, Heb 6:2, 2 Cor 1:21–22, Eph 1:13.
EUCHARIST: **Mt 26:26–28, Mk 14:22–24, Lk 22:19–20**, Jn 6:47–66, 1Cor 10:16;11:23
HOLY ORDERS: **Jn 20:21–23, Lk 22:28–30.**
MATRIMONY: **Mt 19:4–6**, Eph 5:25–31, **Mk 10:7–9.**
PENANCE: **Mt 18:18/16:19**, Mk 1:4, **Jn 20:21–23**, 2 Cor 5:18–20.
Note: For more details on the sacraments see Chapter 9.

SALVATION: Mark 16:16 *Whoever believes and is baptized will be <u>saved</u>; ...* Acts 16:31 *Believe in the Lord Jesus and you and your household will be <u>saved</u>.* Matthew 10:22 *You will be hated by all* *because of my name, but whoever endures to the end will be <u>saved</u>.* John 6:53–54 *Jesus said to them, "Amen, amen, I say to you, unless you eat the flesh of the Son of Man and drink his blood, you do not have life within you. Whoever eats the flesh and drinks my blood has eternal life, and I will raise him on the last day.*

SIN: Romans 3:23,24 *₂₃ since all have <u>sinned</u> and fall short of the glory of God, ₂₄ they are <u>justified</u> by his grace as a gift, through the redemption which is in Christ Jesus, whom God put forward as an expiation by his blood, to be received by <u>faith</u>.* 1 John 1:8–9 *If we say we have no <u>sin</u>, we deceive ourselves, and the truth is not in us. If we confess our <u>sins</u>, he is faithful and just, and will forgive our <u>sins</u> and cleanse us from all unrighteousness.* 1 John 5:16,17 *₁₆... There is <u>sin</u> which is deadly; ... ₁₇ All wrongdoing is <u>sin</u>, but there is <u>sin</u> which is not deadly.*

John 20:23 *Whose <u>sins</u> you forgive are forgiven them, and whose <u>sins</u> you retain are retained.* Psalms 51:4 *Have mercy on me, God in accord with your merciful love; in your abundance compassion blot out my <u>transgressions</u>. Thoroughly wash away my guilt; and from my <u>sin</u> cleanse me.*

Are the "Seven Deadly Sins" in the bible? The more accurate description might be "Seven Capital Vices", since a vice is not the same as a sin, rather, it is a habit that may incline one or lead one to sin. Scripture has no reference to seven vices as "capital," however, we find several biblical warnings against these "seven", which are: <u>pride</u> (Sir 10:13), <u>envy</u> (Wis 2:24), <u>sloth</u> (Prv 12:24), <u>lust</u> (Prv 6:25–29), <u>greed</u> (Prv 15:27), <u>gluttony</u> (Prv 23:21), and <u>anger</u> (Ps 37:8).

SORROWFUL: Matthew 26:38–39 [Jesus said], *₃₈ "My soul is <u>sorrowful</u> even to death....", ₃₉ ..." My Father, if it is possible, let this cup pass from me; yet, not as I will, but as you will."*

SPIRIT: Joel 3:1 *Then afterword I will pour out my <u>spirit</u> upon all mankind.* Acts 2:16–17 *...this is what was spoken through the prophet Joel: 'It will come to pass in the last days, 'God says, 'that I will pour out a portion of my <u>spirit</u> upon all flesh...'* Matthew 26:41 *...the <u>spirit</u>*

is willing but the flesh is weak. John 3:34 *...He does not ration his gift of the <u>Spirit.</u>* John 4:24 *God is <u>Spirit,</u> and those who worship him must worship in the <u>Spirit</u> and truth.* Romans 8 11 *If the <u>Spirit</u> of the one who raised Jesus from the dead dwells in you, the one who raised Christ from the dead will give life to your mortal bodies also, through his <u>Spirit</u> that dwells in you.* Romans 8:26–27 *... The <u>Spirit</u> to comes to the aid of our weakness; for we do not know how to pray as we ought, but the <u>Spirit</u> itself intercedes with inexpressible groanings. And the one who searches hearts knows what is the intention of the <u>Spirit,</u> because it intercedes for the holy ones according to God's will.*

SPIRITS IN PRISION: 1 Peter 3:18–20 *18... [Jesus] being put to death in the flesh but made alive in the spirit; 19 In which he went and preached to the <u>spirits in prison</u>, ...* 1 Peter 4:6 *For this is why the gospel was preached even to the dead, that though judged in the flesh like men, they might live in the spirit like God.*

SPIRIT/SOUL/BODY: 1Thessalonians 5:23 *May the God of peace himself make you perfectly holy and may you entirely, <u>spirit, soul,</u> and <u>body,</u> be preserved blameless for the coming of our Lord Jesus Christ.*

TEMPTATION: 1 Corinthians 10:13 *14 No <u>temptation</u> has overtaken you that is not common to man. God is faithful, and he will not let you be <u>tempted</u> beyond your strength, but with the <u>temptation</u> will also provide the way of escape, that you may be able to endure it.* Hebrews 2:18 *Because he himself was <u>tested</u> trough what he suffered; he is able to help those who are being <u>tested</u>.* James 1:13 *Let no one say when he is <u>tempted,</u> "I am <u>tempted</u> by God"; for God cannot be <u>tempted</u> with evil and he himself <u>tempts</u> no one;*

TEN COMMANDMENTS: Exodus 20: *3 You shall not have other gods besides me. 4 You shall not carve idols for yourselves... 7 You shall not take the name of Lord, your God, in vain. 8 Remember to keep the sabbath day. 12 Honor your father and your mother, 13 You shall not kill. 14 You shall not commit adultery. 15 you shall not steal, 16 You shall not bear false witness against your neighbor. 17 You shall not covet* *your neighbor's house. You shall not covet your neighbor's wife.* Also see Deuteronomy 5:7–21. Matthew 19:17–19 [Jesus] *"If you wish to enter into life, keep the commandments. ... "You shall not kill; you shall not commit adultery; you shall not steal; you shall not bear false witness; honor your father and your mother; and you shall love your neighbor as yourself."*

TESTING: (Testing the spirits of a message you may receive)
1 John 4:1–3 *₁Beloved, do not trust every spirit but <u>test</u> the spirits to see whether they belong to God, because many false prophets have gone out into the world. ₂This is how you can know the Spirit of God: every spirit that acknowledges Jesus Christ come in the flesh belongs to God, ₃ and every spirit that does not acknowledge Jesus Christ does not belong to God.*
1 Thessalonians 5:20–21 *₂₀Do not despise prophetic utterances. ₂₁<u>Test everything</u>; retain what is good. Refrain from every kind of evil.*
Deuteronomy 18: 22 *When a prophet speaks in the name of the Lord, if the word does not come to pass or come true, that is a word which the Lord has not spoken; ..."*
The above scripture readings tell us to *"<u>Test everything</u>"* and you will: *"<u>know the Spirit of God:</u>",* because, *"every spirit that acknowledges Jesus Christ... belongs to God,"*
Another test is to observe if a person, giving a message, has the characteristics of the *"<u>Spirit of God</u>"* within them, as in the following:
Galatians 4:22–23 *₂₂... the fruit of the <u>Spirit</u> is love, joy, peace, patience, kindness, generosity, faithfulness, ₂₃gentleness, self–control."*
Usually, logic will tell you if any message is in keeping with what Jesus Christ might say, and in accordance with His teachings.

THANKS, THANKSGIVING: Psalms 107:8 *Let them <u>thank</u> the Lord for his mercy.* Psalms 100:4 *Enter his gates with <u>thanksgiving</u>, his courts with praise.* 2 Corinthians 9:11 *You are being enriched in every way for all generosity, which through us produces <u>thanksgiving</u> to God.* Philippians 4:6 *by prayer and petition, with <u>thanksgiving</u>, make your requests known to God.*
See <u>BREAD/COMMUNION/EUHARIST</u> herein, EUCHARIST means <u>thanksgiving</u>.

TRADITIONS: 2 Thessalonians 2:17 *Therefore, brothers, stand firm and hold fast to the <u>traditions</u> that you were taught, either by an oral statement or by a letter of ours.*

TRIALS: 1 Peter 1:6 *although now for a little while you may have to suffer through various <u>trials</u>, so that the genuineness of your faith, more precious than gold that is perishable even through tested by fire, may prove to be for praise, glory, and honor at the revelation of Jesus Christ.*

TRIBULATION: Matthew 24:29 *Immediately after the <u>tribulation</u> of those days, the sun will be darkened, the moon will not give its light, and the stars will fall from the sky, and the powers of the heaven will be shaken.*

TROUBLE: Psalms 9:10–11 ₁₀ *The Lord is a stronghold for the oppressed, a stronghold in times of <u>trouble</u>. ₁₁ And those who know your name put their trust in you, for you, O Lord have not forsaken those who seek you.* John 14:1 *Do not let hearts be <u>troubled</u>. You have faith in God; have faith also in me.* Psalms 27:5 *For God will hide me in his shelter in time of <u>trouble</u>.* Psalms 25:17 *Relieve the <u>troubles</u> of my heart; bring me out of my <u>distress</u>.*

TRUST: Psalms 32:10 *… Love surrounds those who <u>trust</u> in the Lord.* Psalms 62: 9 *<u>Trust</u> God at all times, my people! Pour out your hearts to God our refuge!* Hebrews 2:13 *I Will put my <u>trust</u> in Him.*

WITTNESS – END TIMES: Revelation 11: ₃*I will commission my two <u>witnesses</u> to prophesy… ₇When they have finished their testimony, the beast that comes up from the abyss will wage war against them and conquer them and kill them. ₈Their corpses will lie in the main street of the great city, which has the symbolic names "Sodom" and "Egypt," where indeed the Lord was crucified. ₉Those from every people, tribe, tongue, and nation will gaze on their corpses for three and a half days, and they will not allow their corpses to be buried. ₁₁But after the three and half days, the breath of life from God entered them. When they stood on their feet, great fear fell on those who saw them.* Notice verse 9, how else can all people and nations gaze on their corpses other than national television!

WORRY: 1 Peter 5:7 *₇ Cast all your <u>worries</u> upon Him because He cares for you.*

Matthew 6: 25, 27 *₂₅ Therefore I tell you, do not <u>worry</u> about your life, ₇ Can any of you by <u>worrying</u> add a single moment to your life–span?*

References:

The ***bold and italicized*** Bible quotation are from the New American Bible (NBA), World Press, Translated from the Original Languages.

Certain words may be <u>underlined</u> for emphasis added.

The New American Bible Revised Edition, Fireside Catholic Publishing.

Catholic Bible Dictionary, Doubleday, general editor Scott Hahn.

Catechism of the Catholic Church, Doubleday.

The New American Bible Concordance. Oxford University Press.

SELECTED SUBJECTS: Assembled by Paul Wilchek, 17OCT20.

CHAPTER 11

THE APOSTLES, DISCIPLES, CHURCH FATHERS

Apostles:

Luke 6:13–16 ... *He called his disciples to himself, and from them He chose twelve, whom He also named apostles: Simon, whom He named Peter, and his brother Andrew, James, John, Philip, Bartholomew, Matthew, Thomas, James the son of Alphaeus, Simon who was called a Zealot, and Judas the son of James, and Judas Iscariot, who became a tritor.*

The title Apostle(s) used in the New Testament primarily denotes the Twelve closet disciples of Christ. The title is also used for Christ himself as the one sent by the Father (Heb 3:1), also the title is used for those sent by Churches (Acts 1:21–22; 2 Cor 12:12). The use of the Apostle title for those other than the Twelve, in no way compromises the unique position of the Twelve Christ chose to be witnesses of His Resurrection and commissioned by Christ to proclaim the Gospel and to organize the Kingdom of God (the Church) on earth.

The title Disciple, meaning a follower of Jesus Christ, is occasionally used in the New Testament in reference to the Apostles, but generally means other than the twelve Apostles. The following is a brief description of the Twelve Apostles in order of their selection:

Andrew:

Andrew meaning "many" was the first apostle selected, then he brought Simon, his brother, to Jesus. Andrew was a Galilean fisherman by trade (Mt 4:18). According to apocryphal books, Andrew conducted missions in: Cappadocia, Galatia, Bithynia (in modern Turkey), Scythia, Byzantium (Istanbul), Thrace, Macedonia, Thessaly, and Achaea (in modern Greece). Andrew is the patron Saint of: butchers, fisherman, miners, rope–makers, spinsters, water carriers, and weddings.

Andrew died a martyr's death, approximately A.D. 60, by crucifixion on a X shaped cross in Patras, in Achaea. He is buried at St. Andrew's Cathedral, Patras, Greece. Andrew's feast day in November 30.

Peter, Simon–Peter, Simon Bar Jonah (Johanna), Son of John:

Simon meaning "listen", "the best", Peter (in Greek–Petros) (in Aramaic–Cephas) meaning "rock", was a fisherman of Galilee (Lk 5:1–5), brother to Andrew. Simon was ranked "first" among the Twelve (Mt 10:2). Simon–Peter the Apostle was identified in scripture as having a wife. Simon–Peter's mother–in law was healed by Jesus (Mt 8: 14–18; Mk 1:29–34; Lk 4:38–41). Scripture does not identify his wife by name; therefore, it is not known for sure if Peter's wife was alive during his apostleship.

Peter was given great responsibilities from Jesus, as the "rock" and foundation of the Church, he was entrusted with the "keys of the Kingdom" and given authority of heaven to "bind' and "loose" as chief steward of disciples on earth (Mt 16:19). Simon–Peter was the first Apostle to inspect the empty tomb (Lk 24:12; Jn 20: 3–7) and the first of the Twelve to see Jesus risen again (Lk 24:34; 1 Cor 15:5).

Peter, the most lightly author of two of the seven letters "Catholic Epistles" are: 1 Peter and 2 Peter. They were written and sent from "Babylon" (1 Pet 5:13) which may be a symbolic name for Rome. His letters are intended to: encourage young Christians to preserve when facing hostility, remind them of the reward that awaits them, and suffering persecution for Christ is a blessing.

Peter was martyred, crucified upside down at his own request in Rome, during the reign of Neo around A.D. 67. St. Peter is buried in St. Peter's Basilica – Vatican City, Rome, Italy. The feast day of St. Peter and Paul is June 29.

James, Son of Zebedee:

James meaning "one who follows", Jesus nicknamed James and his elder brother John, "Sons of Thunder" (Mt 10:2; Mk 3:417; Lk 6:14), he was a Galilean fisherman by trade and also a business owner. James witnessed the transfiguration of Jesus and was in the garden of Gethsemane with Jesus. The Letter of James, the first of seven "Catholic Epistles" of the New Testament, which appears to be addressed to the entire Church. The author identified as "James a servant of God and the Lord Jesus Christ" (James 1:1). James preached in Spain before his death.

James is the first Apostle to be martyred as described in scripture (Acts 12: 1–3), he was beheaded by the command of King Agrippa I of Judea in A.D. 62.

James is buried in Santiago de Compostela Cathedral in Galicia, Spain. His feast day is July 25.

John, Son of Zebedee: *

The name John means "God is gracious". The younger brother of James (Mt 4:21), also called "Sons of Thunder". John was a fisherman and also a business owner. Scripture referrers to John as "the disciple Jesus loved". John alone among the Twelve stood at the foot of the Cross at Calvary with Mary and other pious women, and received Mary into his care at the request of Jesus on the Cross (Jn 19: 25–27). Some say that John was a "brother" to Jesus, however he cannot be a blood brother, because by Jewish tradition he would have automatically taken care of Mary and there would have been no need for Jesus on the cross to ask John the take in Mary. John wrote a large portion of the New Testament: the book of John, 1,2, & 3 John and Revelation. He wrote more about love than any other New Testament author. By order of Emperor Domitian, he was cast into boiling oil but came out unhurt, then he was banished to the island of Patmos for one year. John founded many churches in Asia Minor and he governed Churches in Asia. John died of old age, about the age of 97, in the year A.D. 103.

He is buried in the Basilica of St. John in Ephesus, Turkey. His fest day is December 27.

Philip:

Philip's name means "Lover of Horses". Philip is from Bethsaida of Galilee (Jn 1: 43–44), may have been a fisherman. At the Last Supper, Philip asked Jesus to show them the Father. Philip's activities in later years are uncertain, because there are six Phillips in the Bible, these doubts are compounded by the confusion in tradition of Philip with Philip the Evangelist, one of the seven deacons appointed in Acts 6. Philip was stoned and crucified in Hierapolis, Phrygia (AD 80). Philip is buried in The Church of the Holy Apostles in Rome, Italy (or possibly Hierapolis, Turkey, with his two daughters). Philip's feast day is May 3, with St. James the Less.

Bartholomew, Nathaniel:

Bartholomew (son of Talmai) was a friend of Philip (Jn 1:45), and may have been a fisherman. He was selected in Galilee (Jn 1:47), and was from Cana in Galilee (Jn 21:2), believed to have preached in India. He translated the book of John to India's language. Bartholomew was beaten, crucified and beheaded as a martyr in Albanopolis in Armenia.

He is buried in the Basilica of Benevento, Italy (or Basilica of St. Bartholomew, on the Island in the Tiber River near Rome, Italy). His feast day is August 24.

Matthew, Levi Son of Alphaeus: *

Matthew means "gift of Yahweh" (gift of the Lord). He was a tax collector (Mt 9:9). Matthew's wealth may have helped fund Jesus' ministry. Author of the Book of Matthew, suggested to have been written A.D. 80–90. Matthew preached to his fellow Jews and brought the gospel to Ethiopia and Egypt. King Hircanus had Matthew killed (martyred) with a spear.

He is buried at Salerno Cathedral, Salerno, Italy. Matthew's feast day is September 21.

Thomas Called Didymus the Twin:

Thomas may have been a fisherman. Remembered for his doubts. Early Christian stories say he started the Christian Church in India. Believed to died (martyred) by being run through with a spear.

Thomas is buried in the Basilica of St. Thomas Apostle in Orton, Abruzzo, Italy (or San Thomas Basilica in Madras, India). His feast day is July 3.

James, Thaddaeus, Son of Alphaeus: *
James "one who follows", the brother of Joseph, called "Brother of the Lord" (Mt 13:55; Mk 6:3; Gal 1:19), also called "James the Lesser", apparently to distinguish him from "James the Greater", who was possibly older or taller. Mark 15:10 describes "James the younger" as the son of Mary, a woman who, with May Magdalene, stood and witnessed the Crucifixion and calls this Mary "the mother of James", in Mark 16:1. This Mary, "the mother of James" cannot be Mary, the mother of Jesus, because this James is also called "Son of Alphaeus". The author of The Book of James is simply identified as "James a servant of God and of the Lord Jesus Christ" (Jas 1:1). The authorship is technically uncertain of which James, but many scholars agree that this James was called "brother of the Lord" (Gal 1:19) who governed the Jerusalem community of Christians after Peter (Acts 12:17; 15:13–21), making this James the most lightly author.
According to a second century historian Hegesippus, James was put to death by the Sanhedrin in A.D. 62 by being thrown off a tower in the Temple of Jerusalem, then stoned and clubbed to death.
He is buried in the Cathedral of St. James in Jerusalem (or Church of the Holy Apostles in Rome). His feast day is May 3.

Judas (Not Iscariot), Thaddaeus, Son of James (Lebbaeus): *
Judas "the praised one", is believed to be the brother of St. James the Lesser. After the Pentecost, he took the gospel north to Edessa, healed the King of Edessa, Abgar. A publication declares that Jude went to Persia with Simon. Believed to be the author of the Letter of Jude (the 26th book of the New Testament) because in the letter he calls himself: "Judas, a servant of Jesus Christ and brother of James", His book may have been written between A.D. 50 and 70.
It is believed he was cubed to death for his faith. He is buried in St. Peter's Basilica under the St. Joseph altar with St. Simon. Two bones (relics) are located at the National Shrine of St. Jude in Chicago, Ill. His feast day is October 28.

Simon, the Zealot, a Canaanite:
Simon was a political activist and Jewish freedom fighter who wanted to liberate Palestine from Roman rule. According to tradition, he preached

in Egypt and Mesopotamia, going to Persia with St. Jude. He may have preached the west coast of Africa and went to England where he was crucified in A.D. 74. He is buried at St. Peter's Basilica in Rome under the St. Joseph altar with St. Jude. His feast day is October 28.

Judas Iscariot:

Judas's name means a man from Kerioth, may have been from Judea, the only Apostle not from Galilee. He served as treasurer of the group; the Gospels tell that he embezzled money from the common funds (Jn 12:6). According to scriptures, Judas never seemed to have a strong belief in Jesus by referring to Jesus only as "Rabbi" (Mt 26:25). After his betrayal of Jesus, he hanged himself (Mt 27:5), (AD 33). His remains are in Akeldama, near the Valley of Hinnom, in Jerusalem, Israel.

Matthias (replaced Judas Iscariot):

Matthias "a variation of Matthew", the disciple chosen by lot to fill the vacancy of the Twelve left by the death of Judas Iscariot (Acts 1:26). There is very little in scripture about him. According to ancient tradition by St. Clement of Alexandria and confirmed by St. Jerome, Matthias was one of the seventy–two sent out by Jesus and was with the Apostles at Pentecost. May have been martyred in Asia Minor (modern–day Turkey). He is buried at St. Matthias Benedictine Abby in Trier, Rhineland–Palatinate, Germany. His feast day is February 24.

Regarding the Twelve Apostles:
- It is important to note that ten of the Apostles died a martyr's death, John died of old age and Judas Iscariot by suicide. A martyr (from the Greek word for "witness") was one who gave testimony (witness) to Christ, to the point of death (Acts 22:20). If a person is seeking proof of the resurrection of Jesus, this is perhaps one of the best examples where ten men, the Apostles of Jesus, independently were willing to accept death rather than lie or deny the resurrection of Jesus Christ that they personally witnessed. Most of the Apostles

were put on trial and point blank told to refute the resurrection of Jesus and every one of them refused, which lead to their death.

- Also note that there are public records of where each one of the Apostles are buried (even Judas Iscariot). This signifies that it is very important for the Church to keep records of the remains of certain people, there are no known records or relics of Mary, Mother of Jesus. This fact must have been very significant in making the decision, after over 1900 years of debate, where on November 1, 1950, Pope Pius XII declared that the Virgin Mary, Mother of Jesus, "having completed the course of her earthly life, was assumed body and soul into heavenly glory". In scripture, Enoch (Gn 5: 22–24) and Elijah (1 Kings 2:11) were assumed into heaven. It is believed that Mary experienced earthly death, then was assumed into heaven.

- Scripture identifies Peter as being married by referring to his mother–in–law. Public records seem to indicate that Philip was married because he may have been buried over his daughters. However, the following scripture passage seems to indicate that other Apostles may have been married: 1 Cor 9: 5 [St. Paul talking] ***"Do we not have the right to take along a Christian wife, as do the rest of the Apostles, …"***. Jewish tradition was that women about the age of 12 to 14 were betrothed and men about the age 16 to 18 were married, or usually for sure by the age of 21. The Apostles ranged in age of 24 to 30 when they were selected by Jesus, so by Jewish tradition, some of them may have been married.

Authors of the New Testament:

The Gospel books of Matthew, Mark and Luke are called "Synoptic Gospels". Synoptic is from a Greek word meaning "view together", therefore these three Gospels are considered similar in content.

Matthew (See Matthew under The Twelve Apostles) *

Mark (also called John Mark):

Mark means "hand–held hammer", the son of Mary of Jerusalem (Acts 12:12), and a cousin of Barnabas (Col 4:10), he companied Paul and Barnabas on Paul's first missionary trip. According to a second century bishop, Mark was an interpreter for Peter that led him to The Gospel of Mark, which he wrote after the martyrdom of Peter between A.D. 65 and 67. Mark was known to be a disciple of Peter (not one of the Apostles). Mark preached and became the first bishop of the Alexandrian Church (Egypt). It is not known for sure but Mark may have been martyred in Alexandria. Mark is also connected with Venice, where his relics were taken in A.D. 829 and put into the original church of St. Mark's (San Marco). His feast day is April 25.

Luke:

Luke meaning "a man from Lucania", or "Light", may have been born in Antioch and was a Gentile Christian (Col 4:11) and a companion of Paul (2 Tm 4:11; Phlm 24). In Col 4:14, Paul speaks of him as "Luke the beloved physician". Luke authored the Gospel of Luke as well as the Acts of the Apostles, he is considered the most literary of the four Evangelists. Luke was unmarried and it is said he died at the age of eighty–four and "full of the Holy Spirit". Luke is the patron saint of doctors and also of painters. In medieval times it was stated that Luke painted a picture of the Virgin Mary that was preserved in the Sant Maria Maggiore, Rome. His feast day is October 18.

John (See John under The Twelve Apostles). *

Paul, Saul of Tarsus:

Saul meaning "inquired of God", "ask for". Paul meaning "humble", a Jewish Pharisee, of the tribe of Benjamin (Rom 11:1; Phlm 3:5) may have taught religion, and was a tent maker (Acts 18:1–3). Paul was highly educated where he studied "at the feet of Gamaliel," a very famous rabbi (Acts 22:3). Paul's conversion occurred on his trip to Damascus where he encountered the glorified Christ. After his conversion he spent about three years in Arabia in prayer and meditation.

Paul is known for his three missionary journeys, taking the Gospel message to both Jews and Gentiles. His first missionary journey was to Cypress and southern Asia Minor (Acts 13:4; 14:28) sometime prior to A.D. 49. Paul brought the matter of circumcision to the Church's first council in Jerusalem about A.D. 49. His second missionary journey (about A.D. 50) lasted two years traveling to Tarsus, revisited Asia Minor, Macedonia (Europe), Thessalonica, Berea (Beroea), Athens, Greece, and Corinth.

His third missionary journey started about A.D. 53 (Acts 19:1 – 21:16) traveling to Asia Minor, Ephesus, Macedonia, Corinth. Paul is known as the Apostle to the Gentiles (Rom 11:13).

Paul authored most of the New Testament Letters, the following list indicates the approximate year written, or noted if authorship is questionable: Romans (57–58), 1 & 2 Corinthians (53–58), Galatians (49–50), Ephesians (if by Paul 60, if not 90), Philippians (62), Colossians (if by Paul 50–51), 1 & 2 Thessalonians (50–51), 1 & 2 Timothy (if by Paul 67, if not 80–110), Titus (if by Paul 63–66, if not 80–110), Philemon (60–62), and Hebrews (if by Paul 60).

He was martyred A.D. 67, his relics are in the Basilica of St. Paul outside the walls in Rome, Italy. The feast day of St. Peter and Paul is June 29.

James (see James under The Twelve Apostles). *
Peter (see Peter under The Twelve Apostles). *
Jude (see Judas under The Twelve Apostles). *

The 27 Books of the New Testament:

Book of:	YEAR WRITTEN	AUTHOR	PURPOSE/ THEME	NOTES
Matthew Gospel	50 to 70	Matthew	The divinity and trinity of Christ	Written in Hebrew (Aramaic). Alone uses "Church". Shows promises of O.T. fulfilled in N.T.
Mark Gospel	Prior to 70, (41 to 54 or 65 to 67)	Mark	Reveals the identity of Jesus as Messiah and son of God.	Written in koine Greek. For gentile Christians. Mark was an interpreter for Peter.

Book of:	YEAR WRITTEN	AUTHOR	PURPOSE/ THEME	NOTES
Luke Gospel	About 60	Luke	Mercy of God & merciful acts of Christ. Good news.	Written in Greece. Luke, a Greek scholar & physician, the only gentile–Christian of all gospels.
John Gospel	Prior to 70	John	Mystical & theological depth. The divinity & humanity of Christ	John uses miracles to serve as "signs" who Christ is.
Acts of the Apostles	62 or 63	Luke	Continuation of Luke's Gospel with focus on Peter and Paul	Covers some thirty years as the Church spread from Palestine to Italy.
Romans Epistle	57 or 58	Paul	Covers the mysteries of sin and salvation.	He explains that both the Jews and Gentiles are part of God's plan for salvation.
1Corinthians Epistle	56	Paul	Covers early Christian community and local church organization.	Paul started the Church in Corinth about the year 51.
2Corinthians Epistle	57	Paul	Paul tried to resolve a troubling situation in Corinth.	Paul stresses his preaching comes from God.

Book of:	YEAR WRITTEN	AUTHOR	PURPOSE/ THEME	NOTES
Galatians Epistle	52–56	Paul	Man is saved by faith in Jesus not the Jewish Law.	Paul is strong in his defense of the Gospel and of himself.
Ephesians Epistle	60 to 62	Paul	Concerned with the doctrine of the Church & mystical body of Christ.	Paul writes as the body of Christ, with Christ as the head. Asks faithful to pray to comprehend the mystery.
Philippians Epistle	61 to 62	Paul	Greetings and encouragement due to persecutions they faced.	Paul encouraged unity among the faithful with humility and charity.
Colossians Epistle	60 to 61	Paul	A warning against false teachings.	Paul stresses compassion, kindness, humility, meekness, and patience.
1Thessalonians Epistle	50 to 51	Paul	Expresses his joy in their growth and encouragement in time of troubles.	Paul answered certain questions about the resurrection.
2Thessalonians Epistle	50 to 51	Paul	A follow–up to previous letter to clarify the second coming.	Paul explains a series of signs/ events to take place prior to second coming.

Book of:	YEAR WRITTEN	AUTHOR	PURPOSE/ THEME	NOTES
1 Timothy Epistle	60 to 61	Paul	Emphasizes pastoral responsibility to preserve unity of the doctrine.	Addressed to Timothy in Ephesus forming the Christian community.
2 Timothy Epistle	60 to 62 or 64 to 67	Paul	Continues focus on Pastoral ministry.	Paul's final testament during imprisonment in Rome.
Titus Epistle	63 to 66	Paul	Concerned with the pastoral care of early Christian community.	Appoint leaders with strength, leadership, and teaching ability.
Philemon Epistle	60 to 62	Paul	Letter to a Christian slave owner to forgive a runaway slave.	The shortest of Paul's letters gives us a glimpse of Roman slavery.
Hebrews Epistle	About mid 60's	Paul	The high priesthood of Christ and superiority of the New Covenant over the Old.	A lesion in the covenant oath where Jesus' sacrifice is superior because He sacrificed Himself.
James Epistle	62	James the Just	Teachings on: joy in suffering, place of the Father, the poor, the kingdom, neighbor love, humility and confidence in prayer.	The first of seven Catholic Epistles that all appear to be written to the whole Church.

Book of:	YEAR WRITTEN	AUTHOR	PURPOSE/ THEME	NOTES
1 Peter Catholic Epistle	64 to 67	Peter	Encourage Christians to preserve in the hostility from the world.	Readers are reminded the reward that awaits them. Peter sees it is a blessing to suffer persecution for the name of Christ.
2 Peter Catholic Epistle	60 to 90	Peter	Encourages Christians to grow in the knowledge of God and of Jesus.	The text is like a homily. Be watchful of false teachers: full of deceit, errors, appose authority, & angel slander.
1 John Catholic Epistle	95 to 100	John	Written to confront false teachers.	The only way to overcome sin is to admit it and seek forgiveness through Christ.
2 John Catholic Epistle	95 to 96	John	Encourages the faithful to practice perseverance in the face of false teachers.	Refers to himself as "the elder" and offers fraternal love, devotion and rejection of false doctrines.
3 John Catholic Epistle	95 to 96	John	Covers important information about certain features of the early Church.	The letter is the shortest in the New Testament. Addresses questions of jurisdiction & rivalry among leaders.,

Book of:	YEAR WRITTEN	AUTHOR	PURPOSE/ THEME	NOTES
Jude Catholic Epistle	50 to 70	Jude	Addresses the community in a crisis of false teaching.	Judas Thaddaeus or Judas Barsabbas. Author uses biblical history to show the ultimate inevitable destruction of the wicked.
Revelation Catholic Epistle	95 to 96 John's exile AD 94–95	John	The purpose and theme are difficult to interpret, could be: (1) prophecy of the end of the world, (2) past history having taken place, (3) Churches' history – first century to the end of time, (4) signs and symbols to give encouragement to Christians.	John wrote this during his exile. The purpose (on the left) is in order of popularity, or a combination 1 thru 4. Revelation is highly symbolic imagery and mysterious content about history's final days, sets it apart due to its use of liturgical hymns and clear focus on Jesus Christ as the Lamb of God.

Note: The above chart was developed using material from the "Catholic Bible Dictionary" Doubleday Publishing, general editor Scott Hahn. Some of the "Authors" and "Year Written" above are questioned by some theologians, however, the "Authors" and "Year Written" above are the ones most commonly accepted. The seven letters: James, 1&2 Peter, 1,2, & 3 John and Jude are "Catholic Epistle" books that are so named because they appear to be written to the entire (universal, Catholic) Church.

Disciples, Sometimes Called Apostles, (Not of the twelve Apostles): Luke 10: ₁*After this the Lord appointed seventy [–two] others whom He sent ahead of Him in pairs to every town and place He intended to visit.* Then later in Luke 10, it tells us: ₁₇*The seventy [–two] returned and said, "Lord, even the demons are subject to us because of your name."* The following disciples may or may not be part of the seventy [–two]:

Andronicus:
The Greek meaning of this name is "victorious over men". Andronicus was a Jewish Christian who received greetings from Paul (Rom 16:7), and Paul described him as "prominent among the Apostles."

Apollos:
A Jewish Christian from Alexandria (Acts 18:24–28), described as being eloquent, well versed in Scripture, and had considerable oral talent. He preached in the synagogue of Ephesus and it is said that he attracted Priscilla and her husband Aquila (followers of Christ) to a fuller understanding of the Gospel. It was noted by Paul (1 Cor 3:6) that Apollos had watered what Paul planted.

Barnabas:
His name in Aramaic means "son of the Sabbath", considered one of the Apostles (not the twelve) by the Fathers of the Church, He was a Jewish Christian from the tribe of Levi. Joseph Barnabas called Justin, was a disciple of Christ who was also one of the two candidates, with Matthias, proposed to take the place of Judas Iscariot among the Apostles (Acts 1:23). He went to Antioch to assist the Church there. Tradition relates that he died at Salamis in Cyprus, after being stoned. His feast day is June 11.

Silas (also known as Silvanus):
A Jewish Christian and a leading member of the community in Jerusalem who was blessed with prophetic gifts (Acts 15: 22,32). He became a companion of Paul on Paul's second journey (Acts 15:36–41). Silas was one of the first Christians to proclaim the Gospel in Europe (Acts 16:10). May have been martyred A.D. 65–100 in Macedonia. His feast day is July 13.

Stephen:
Stephen in Greek means "crown," "that which surrounds," was a Hellenist Jew and one of the seven chosen by the Apostles to care for the needs of the widows in the Jerusalem Christian community (Acts 6:1–6). He was a remarkable preacher that performed miracles and was described as being full of grace and power (Acts 6:8). He was falsely accused of blasphemy by the Sanhedrin and stoned to death. The Aramaic name of "Kelil" was inscribed on a stone slab found in his tomb that was discovered in A.D. 415. A church was built in his honor just beyond the Damascus Gate that was dedicated in 460. His feast day is December 26.

Timothy:
Timothy meaning "honoring God", born in Asia Minor, the son of a Jewish woman and Greek father (Acts 16:1;2 Tm 1:5). He was educated in reading of the Scriptures and a companion of Paul, who called him "fellow Worker" (Rom 16:2), "Our brother" (2 Cor 1:1), and "my beloved and faithful child in the Lord" (1 Cor 4:17). Timothy was circumcised (directed by the Apostle Paul) so he could perform the rite to preach among the Jewish regions of Phrygia and other Jewish areas. According to tradition, Timothy spent his later years at Ephesus as its Bishop. He was martyred, in his old age, during the winter of the year 97. His feast day is January 24.

Women Disciples who Followed Jesus

Mary Mother of Jesus:
There is very little in scripture about Mary's family background. One tradition, that dates back to the second century A.D., describes Mary as the daughter of a Jewish father Joachim and Jewish mother Anna. The story tells us that Joachim and Anna were childless for a long time, but after much prayer and a promise to devote any future child to the Temple, Mary was born. At the age of three, Mary was taken to Jerusalem to live with the sorority of Temple virgins until she was twelve years old. After that time, she was given to the care of Joseph, a building contractor and widower, who had fathered several children by a previous marriage (end of second century tradition).

The names of Joseph's children are not known; however, it is possible that they may have been called "brothers" to Jesus (just speculation, since there is no Jewish term for step–brother).

The Gospels of Matthew and Luke introduce Mary as a virgin betrothed to Joseph, whose family descended from the royal line of David (Mt 1:18–21; Lk 1:26–27). Mary conceived a child by a miracle of the Holy Spirit (Mt 1:18) and then Joseph finally accepted this after an angel, in a dream, assured him that God wanted him to be the legal father and caretaker of Jesus (Mt 1:19–25).

Mary's life was not easy, her and Joseph had to travel to Bethlehem (meaning house of bread) due to a census requirement, where Jesus was born (Lk 2:6–7). Even though Mary and Joseph were very poor, at some point in time, they somehow were able to live in a house (Mt 2:11). Herod the Great, king of Juda, sent the military to kill the infant Jesus in Bethlehem (Mt 2:16–18).

Joseph had an angelic intervention so, with their child Jesus, they fled to Egypt, where they remained until Herod's death (Mt 2:13–15), after which they returned to Nazareth of Galilee (Mt 2:19–23).

At the wedding of Cana, with Mary's influence, Jesus performed his first miracle of turning water into wine (John 2:3). At the crucifixion, Jesus entrusted the care of his mother to the beloved disciple John (John 19:25–27). Mary is last heard of in the New Testament in the upper room, where she along with the other disciples devoted themselves to prayer to prepare for Pentecost (Acts 1:14).

One tradition states that Mary died a natural death, while another just states her "falling asleep." However, both agree that Mary was assumed bodily into heaven. There are no known bones or relics of Mary which may have influenced Pope Pius XII in 1950 to define a Catholic dogma on the Assumption of Mary.

Scripture references of Mary, Mother of Jesus: Mt 1: 16–25, Lk 1: 27–56, Lk 2: 1–40, Lk 2 41–52, Jn 2: 1–5, Mk 3:21, and at the cross Jn 19:25–27.

The name Mary (Greek is Maria, Hebrew is Miriam) meaning "beloved", "wished–for child", appears many times in scripture as important women. Not all scholars agree on the identity of each Mary, therefore, the Mary's presented here (except the mother of Jesus above) are the most widely accepted identifications. Matthew 27:55–56 *There were many women there, looking on from a distance, who had followed Jesus from Galilee, ministering to him, among them were Mary Magdalene and Mary the mother of James and Joseph, and the mother of the sons of Zebedee.*

Mary Magdalene:

Scripture scholars have had controversy over the identity of Mary Magdalene since early Church times because of the many Marys in scripture. Father William Saunders, professor of catechetics and theology at Notre Dame Graduate School in Alexandria, agrees with Pope St. Gregory (A.D. 509–604) as being the most plausible after researching scripture. They profess that Mary Magdalene, a follower of our Lord (John 20:11–18); "from whom seven devils had gone out" (Luke 9:1–13); the anonymous penitent woman, who washed Jesus' feet (Luke 7:36–50); and Mary of Bethany, the sister of Martha and Lazarus (Luke 10:38–42), are all the same person, though compelling, this still remains uncertain. Pope St. Gregory realized that Mary Magdalene is a beautiful example of a woman who found new life in Christ.

She was present at the foot of the Christ's cross (Mt 27:56; Mk 15:40; Jn 19:25) and witnessed the placing of Christ in the tomb (Mt 27:61; Mk 15:47), and notably, she was the first recorded eyewitness of His Resurrection (Mt 28: 1–10; Mk 16: 1–8; Lk 24:10). John 29:1–18, describes Mary's remarkable experience at Christ's tomb where she met the risen Lord and took that message to the other disciples. The feast of St. Mary Magdalen is celebrated by the Greeks as well as the Latins on July 22.

Mary Salome Mother of James and Joses:

St. Mary Salome was the wife of Zebedee and the mother of the apostles John and James the Greater (Mk 15:40; Mt 27:56) that were called "Sons of Thunder" by Jesus. It is believed that Mary Salome was one of the three Mary's to follow Jesus and thought to be one of the several financial sources for the Apostle's travels. In the Gospel, Mary Salome asked Jesus what place her sons would have in the Kingdom (Mt 20:20–28). She was a witness to the crucifixion, entombment and was mentioned by St. Mark as one of the women who went to anoint Jesus' body. Legend states that after the Pentecost, Mary Salome traveled to Veroli, Italy where she preached the Gospel for rest of her life. She is the patron saint of Veroli, Italy.

Mary of Clopas:
The Greek text describes her only as "Mary of Clopas" which most lightly means wife of Clopas, but could also mean daughter or mother of Clopas. She stood at the foot of the Cross of Jesus (John 19:25). Some scholars think that Colpas might be the same person as Cleopas, one of the two disciples who met Jesus on the road to Emmaus (Luke 24:18).

Mary Sister of Martha and Lazarus:
It is not clear; this Mary may be the same as the above. In Luke 10: 38–42, Mary sat at the feet of Jesus while her sister, Martha was busy being a hostess. Mary anointed Jesus with expensive ointment in Jn 12: 1–3, Mt 26: 6–13, and Mk 14: 3–9.

Maratha:
Martha In Aramaic means "lady" or "mistress", the elder sister of Mary Magdalene (Luke 10:38–42) and the sister of Lazarus (John 11:1–12:11). The family lived in Bethany, which is about two mile east of Jerusalem (John 11:18). Martha welcomed Jesus into her house (Luke 10:38). The personalities of Martha and Mary show up in the Gospel of Luke and John where Martha hurries out to meet Jesus, while Mary sits and waits for the Lord. In the Gospel of John 11:20–27, Martha declares her trust that God will do whatever Jesus asks, and she confesses faith in Jesus as the Messiah and Son of God.

Joanna:
The Joanna name was originally Hebrew but is also Greek meaning "God is gracious", The wife of Herod's Stewart Chuza and follower of Jesus, was one of the women healed by Jesus. Her wealth helped support the Apostles (Lk 8:3). Joanna along with Mary Magdalene and Mary mother of James, returned from the tomb and announced all that they had seen to the Apostles (Lk 24:9,10). An interesting note here, Jewish tradition required three witnesses and there were three women here that testified to the resurrection.

Susanna:
Susanna originally derived from Hebrew, adapted by Greek, meaning "Lilly", "True Beauty", was another woman that provided for the Apostles out of her wealth. She traveled with Jesus and the Apostles and is only mentioned in Luke 8:3.

This is not, by far, a complete list of all the Disciples, during the time of Jesus and in scripture. Many are just called disciple, and not identified by name. The twelve Apostles were sent out by Jesus to preach repentance and were given authority to drive out demon and anoint may who were sick, curing them (Matthew 10:1–15; Mark 6:7–13; Luke 9: 1–6). Jesus also sent out Seventy[–two] disciples (un–named) to preach the Kingdom of God and cure the sick (Luke 10:1–12; 10:17–20). In the "Acts of the Apostles" the Church also sent out an un–known number of disciples who spread the "Good News" across the known world.

Apostolic Fathers and Doctors of the Early Church
To put the time frame into perspective, the last Apostle to die was St. John in the year 103 at the age of 97. Therefore, some of the early Fathers of the Church were disciples of John the Apostle. There are 76 early Church Fathers/Doctors documented from the year AD80 to AD500. The Apostolic Fathers are so named because they personally knew some of the twelve apostles. The following are some of the "key" Fathers/Doctors of the Early Church and their remarkable contribution to our Church today:

Pope St. Clement I of Rome (Rein 88AD – 99AD):
Clement I is considered to be the first Apostolic Father of the Church. It's believed that Clement was consecrated by Peter the Apostle. Some of his writings became part of the Church canon. his feast day is November 23.

St. Ignatius of Antioch (AD110):
Apostolic Father of the Church St. Ignatius, also called Theophorous, was born in Syria and the legend is that he was the child whom Jesus took up in His arms as described in Mark 9: 36. Ignatius was instructed by the Apostle

St. John. The approximate year of 67, St. Peter appointed Ignatius as Bishop of Antioch where he governed for forty years. Ignatius was a disciple of St. John the Apostle and a close friend with St. Polycarp the bishop of Smyrna. Ignatius is best known for his seven letters to various faith communities outlining many important points about the faith of the early Church that are still prevalent today, such as: the belief in the real presence of Christ in the Eucharist, the divinity of Christ, the hierarchical structure of bishops, priests, deacons, and laity, the importance of the Bishop of Rome, and the understanding of Mary as Mother of God. His letters contained the first recorded use of the term "Catholic." In his letter to the Romans, he stated *"I have no taste for the food that perishes…I want the Bread of God which is the Flesh of Christ…and for drink I desire His Blood, which is love that cannot be destroyed."* He referred to the Holy Eucharist as *"medicine of immortality."* In the year 110, St. Ignatius was taken from Antioch to Rome by Roman solders and in the amphitheater two lions devoured him. His approximate age was 75, his bones are buried in St. Peter's Basilica. His feast day is February 1.

Papies of Hierapolis (AD60–AD130):
A Greek Apostolic Father, Bishop of Hierapolis that wrote the Exposition of the Sayings of the Lord in five books, however the full text is lost but his writings are noted by other authors from which theologians are attempting to re-construct his writings.

St. Polycarp Bishop of Smyrna (AD69 – AD166):
Apostolic Father of the Church St. Polycarp, born in the year AD69 was a disciple of St. John the Apostle and friends with St. Ignatius. St. John the Apostle appointed Polycarp Bishop of Smyrna (now part of Turkey) where he governed for seventy years. A few of his disciples are St. Irenaeus and Papias, a writer. During the reign of Emperors Lucius Verus and Marcus Aurelius, Polycarp was told to deny Christ, which he refused to do. He was then condemned to be burned. Witnesses stated that the flames did not touch him, but formed an arch over his head. Then he was pierced with a sword and such a great amount of blood came forth that it extinguished the fire. This occurred about the year 166. His bones are still preserved in the church of San Ambrogio in Massine, Rome. His feast day is January 26.

Epistle of Barnabas (AD70–AD132):
The complete Greek epistle text is preserved in the fourth century as one of the writings that some Christians looked on as sacred scripture, while others excluded them. It was written after the destruction of the Temple in AD 70. It is attributed to Barnabas; the companion of St. Paul the Apostle and it is somewhat like the Epistle to the Hebrews. The first part of the Epistle gives a Christ–centered interpretation of the Old Testament. Possibly the reason it did not make it into Scripture is that it is a bit anti–Jewish.

St. Justin Martyr (AD100 – AD165):
Father of the Church St. Justin, born in the year 100, the son of a pagan in Flavia Neapolis, Palestine was a Greek philosopher–apologist who converted to Christianity after which he devoted his life to the defense of the Church (Apology). Justin wrote his "First Apology" about the year AD155, that was directed to the Emperor Antoninus Pius (132–191), followed by his "Second Apology" addressed to Caesar. Both of which explain and justify Christian doctrine, worship and demands justice for Christians.

Justin writes about how impressed he is with the struggle of Christians:
"For I myself, I discovered the wicked disguise which the evil spirits had thrown around the divine doctrines of the Christians, to turn aside others from joining them, laughed both at those who framed these falsehoods, and at the disguise itself, and at popular opinion; and I confess that I both boast and with all my strength strive to be found a Christian."

Justin also writes about the angels who watch over and protect mankind and describes in detail the rites of Baptism and the Eucharist. When describing the Eucharist he refers to "bread and wine and water" and emphasizes that when blessed, it becomes the body and blood of Christ:
"For not as common bread and common drink do we receive these; but in like manner as Jesus Christ our Savior, having been made flesh by the Word of God, had both flesh and blood for our salvation, so likewise have we been taught that the food which is blessed by the prayer of His word, and from which our blood and flesh by transmutation are nourished, is the flesh and blood of that Jesus who was made flesh."

Justin died in the year AD 165, his fest day is April 14.

St. Irenaeus of Lyons (AD130 – AD202):
Father of the Church St. Irenaeus, Greek, was born in Smyrna in Asia Minor (Turkey) which was St. Polycarp's home town and was under the care and study of St. Polycarp who was a model of perfection. St. Polycarp sent him to Lyons in AD177 (age 47) where he was ordained a priest and later to become a Bishop, then a deputy to Pope #13 Eleutherius. Irenaeus was the first to draw the comparison between Eve and Mary and also the first to use the principle of apostolic procedures against Gnostics. He also pointed out that all of the Apostolic Churches preserved all the same traditions, teachings, succession of elders, as well as the central point of teachings and professing unity. Irenaeus authored many books that were mostly against the harasses of the time. In one of his writings, he stated: *"One should not seek among others the truth that can be easily gotten from the Church. For in her, as in a rich treasury, the apostles have placed all that pertains to truth, so that everyone can drink this beverage of life. She is the door of life."*
Irenaeus died in AD220 at the age of 90 and was buried under the Church of St. John in Lyon that was later renamed to St. Irenaeus which was desecrated in 1562 by the Calvinists. His feast day is June 28.

Shepherd of Hermas (AD170–):
This is a Christian literary work of the late first half of the second century considered by some Christians a valuable book. It pays special attention to the Church calling the faithful to repent of the sins that have harmed it.

St. Athanasius (AD296–AD373):
Father and Doctor of the Church, the 20th Bishop of Alexandria during the Council of Nicaea.

St. Jerome (AD347 – AD420):
Doctor of the Church, St. Jerome was born in the year AD347, he was baptized in Rome as an adult, then spent four years in Chalcis of Syria in the desert in prayer and study with the holy Abbot Theodosius. About 377 he received his Holy Orders and for some time served as secretary to Pope #37 St. Damascus. Jerome in addition to being a priest is called: confessor, translator. theologian, Bible scholar, writer, and historian. During the years 382 to 405 he translated most of the Old and New Testaments to Latin from

their original source. Jerome's commentaries on Scripture (Vulgate) are still reorganized and used today as well as his teachings on moral life. Jerome retired in Bethlehem where he continued to study and write. He is the second most voluminous writer after Augustine of Hippo. Jerome died in Bethlehem in the year AD420 at the age of 73. His feast day is September 30.

St. John Chrysostom (AD347–407):
Father and Doctor of the Church, Archbishop of Constantinople, noted for preaching, and public speaking. He was born in Antioch then in the year 375 he became a hermit where he started memorizing the bible. In 381 he was ordained a deacon, then in 357 became Archbishop of Constantinople. He is noted for his hundreds of homilies as well as works such as: "On the Priesthood", "On the incomprehensibility of the Divine Nature." His works had a strong influence on the Catholic Liturgy.

St. Augustine of Hippo (AD354–AD430):
Doctor of the church, theologian, philosopher, and bishop. Contributed many writings such as "The City of God" on Christian Doctrine and confessions.

St. Cyril of Alexandria (AD378 – AD444):
Doctor and Father of the Church, St. Cyril was born in Tuscany, Western Rome Empire in the year 378. He is referred to as: philosopher, teacher, scholar, confessor, pillar of faith, seal of all the Fathers, and missionary – primarily to the Slavs. St. Cyril, Bishop, was a strong defender of the faith and condemned the Nestorianism heresy. Nestorianism claimed two persons in Christ, dividing the human person from the divine person and advocated that Mary was the mother only of the human person of Christ. St. Cyril wrote several letters to the emperor and Pope #43 St. Celestine I, defending the faith, emphasizing that the Church believed in unity, all priests and leaders were unified in their belief. The pope condemned Nestorius' teachings and called the Council of Ephesus in AD431 where St. Cyril led the proceedings that condemned and disposed of Nestorius' heresy – wrong teachings on Christ and His Blessed Mother. St. Cyril died in AD444 and his feast day is February 9.

Pope #45 St. Leo the Great (AD 400 – AD461):
Only three popes in Church history to date have been granted the title "The Great" with St. Leo I being the first, followed by pope #64 St,

Gregory I (AD590–604), and pope #105 St. Nicholas I (AD858–867). During the reign of Pope St. Leo was a time of great political turmoil in the Roman Empire with weak leaders. The pope was a very strong leader, he defended papal primacy, enforced discipline, fought heresies, and defended the people of Rome. He condemned and defeated current heresies at the Council of Chalcedon (AD451) with the writing of his "tome" that explains the mystery of the incarnation and the mystery that Jesus is both "true God and true man". The Decree of the Council of Chalcedon (AD451): *"We all with one voice confess our Lord Jesus Christ one and the same Son, the same perfect in Godhead, the same perfect in manhood, truly God and truly man... to be acknowledged in two natures, without confusion, without change, without division, without separation; the distinction of nature's being in no way abolished because of the union, but rather the characteristic property of each nature being preserved, and concurring into one person."*

Perhaps the most lightly accomplishment that may account for St. Leo's "the Great" title is his defense of the city of Rome against Attila the Hun. Pope St. Leo using his diplomatic skills and mostly trusting in the Lord, in AD452, personally engaged in dialogue at the gates of Rome with Attila the Hun after which Atilla's army turned away from the threatened total destruction of Rome. Some theologians state that if Attila had destroyed Rome, it could have been destructive to the Church. Pope St. Leo died in the year 461, leaving many epistles and writings of great historical value. His feast day is April 11.

The term "book" used in the time of Jesus was commonly a scroll of papyrus about 9 to 12 inches high and some were up to 35 feet long. They were made by gluing sheets of papyrus together, also, other material such as leather or parchment were used. John 21:24 tells us: ***There are also many other things that Jesus did, but if these were to be described individually, I do not think the whole world would contain the books that would be written.*** We certainly need to be very thankful for all of those that preserved, and passed on the "Good News "of Jesus Christ for all of us today.

See the APPENDIX for a list of Doctors and Fathers of the Church.

Paul Wilchek

SUMMARY – APOSTLES, DICIPLES:

- The Twelve Apostles willingly followed Jesus and after the resurrection of Jesus, all of them, except for two, were martyred defending the true resurrection of Jesus that they personally witnessed.
- Seven of the Twelve Apostles, Matthew, Mark, Luke, John, James, Peter, and Jude went on to became some of the authors in the New Testament.
- The disciples of Jesus were faithful to His orders in caring out the announcement of the "Good News" of Jesus Christ throughout the then known world.
- Mary Mother of Jesus, the key woman disciple, along with many other women disciples were critical in assisting Jesus throughout His ministry here on earth.
- In addition to the writings in the New Testament, the Church Fathers and Church Doctors continued to document the traditions and teachings that Jesus gave to the Twelve Apostles and us.

References:
Scripture quotations are ***italicized and bold*** from The New American Bible (NAB).
Catholic Bible Dictionary, General Editor – Scott Hahn, Published by Doubleday.
Lives of the Saints, Catholic Book Publishing Co., NY.
Catholicexchange.com, jesus.com/bible–list–disciples–htm/, simple.wikipedia.org/wiki/twelve_ apostles, Wikipedia.org/wiki/apostles.
Bible Study Workbook: Epic – A journey through Church History, The early church by Steve Weidenkopf.

THE APOSTLES, DICIPLES, CHURCH FATHERS: Assembled by Paul Wilchek, Bradenton, FL, 7FEB20

## CHAPTER 12

THE THEMES THROUGH SCRIPTURE

The Theme of Bread Through Scripture

The following *scripture quotations* are in the order as they appear in the Bible. Take particular notice of the progression, or development that <u>bread</u> takes as the "Theme of Bread" passes through the Bible. In addition to <u>bread</u> (loaves), in order to make this more inclusive, words like <u>flesh</u>, <u>wine</u>, and <u>blood</u> need to be included as they are associated with <u>bread</u>. Let Scripture Speak for Itself on <u>bread:</u>

The Theme of Bread Through the Old Testament:

The first two books of the bible, Genesis and Exodus, were written about 1,400 BC. The very first occurrence of "<u>bread</u>" in scripture is in Genesis 3:19 where God said to Adam, after the fall: 19 ***By the sweat of your face shall you get <u>bread</u> to eat,*** ... Scripture uses "<u>bread</u>" here rather than any number of things that could have been used like: grains, vegetables, or even fruit. However, <u>bread</u> is used to show its importance. Later on, in Genesis 14:18,20 we are told: 18 ***Melchizedek, king of Salem, brought out <u>bread</u> and wine, and being a priest of God Most High, he blessed Abram...*** 20 ***Then Abram gave him a tenth of everything.*** Notice the importance of <u>bread</u> and the associated blessing here by the fact that Abram gifted a tenth of everything for receiving the ***bread and wine*** and the blessing.

The tenth plague of Moses was the death of the firstborn in Egypt. To protect the firstborn of the Israelite people, they were instructed by God to slaughter a year–old male lamb that did not have a blemish (symbolizing without sin). Exodus 12:7 instructed the Israelites: ***They shall take some of its <u>blood</u> and apply it to the two doorposts and the lintel of every house in which they partake of the lamb.*** Notice the physical action to put the blood on the lintel (door top) and two doorposts (door sides) that generates the sign of the cross. Then in Exodus 12:8,10 They are told: ₈ ***That same night they shall eat its roasted <u>flesh</u> with unleavened <u>bread</u> and bitter herbs.*** ₁₀ ***None of it must be kept beyond the next morning; whatever is left over in the morning shall be burned up.*** It is interesting to notice the use of the word <u>flesh</u> here; we will see that word used much later by Christ. The consumption of the <u>flesh of the lamb</u> has to be very important, otherwise why are they instructed by God to burn all leftovers? Also notice, that now the feast of unleavened <u>bread</u> has become part of a sacred Israelite ritual later on called Passover. Exodus 12:14,15 ₁₄ ***This day shall be a memorial feast for you, which all your generations shall celebrate with pilgrimage to the Lord, as a <u>perpetual institution</u>.*** ₁₅ ***For seven days you must eat unleavened <u>bread</u>.*** Exodus 12:17 ***Keep, then, this custom of unleavened <u>bread</u>.***

After the Israelites departed from Egypt, Exodus 16:2–3 tells us: ₂ ***Here in the desert the whole Israelite community grumbled against Moses and Aron.*** ₃ ***The Israelites said to them, "Would that we had died at the Lord's hand in the land of Egypt, as we sat by our fleshpots and ate our fill of <u>bread</u>! But you had led us into this desert to make the whole community die of famine!*** Then Moses responded in Exodus 16:4,15,31 ₄ ***Then the Lord said to Moses, "I will now rain down <u>bread from heaven</u> for you."*** ₁₅ ***On seeing it, the Israelites asked one another, "What is this?" for they did not know what it was. But Moses told them. "This is the <u>bread</u> which the Lord has given you to eat."*** ₃₁ ***The Israelites called this food <u>manna</u>. It was like coriander seed, but white, and it tasted like <u>wafers</u> made with honey.*** Notice here that the <u>manna</u> is described as ___bread from heaven,___ a term we will see later on where Christ describes himself as ___bread from heaven.___ Also, it is interesting that the manna is described ___like wafers,___ which also describes Holy Communion. Later in Exodus 16:35 it tells us: ***The Israelites ate ___manna___ for forty years, … they ate ___manna___ until they reached the borders of Canaan.***

Exodus 23:15 ***You shall keep the feast of Unleavened ___Bread.___ As I have commanded you, you must eat unleavened ___bread___ for seven days at the prescribed time in the month of Abib, for it was then that you came out of Egypt.*** Notice that Scripture continues to emphasize the sacred nature of bread, ***you shall keep the feast of Unleavened ___Bread.___***

Leviticus and Deuteronomy were written between the years 538 BC and 332 BC, through the direction of Moses from God, the Israelites had many ritual customs such as: The Daily Holocaust, Daily offering, Sin Offerings, Guilt Offerings, and the following Peace Offerings:

Leviticus 7:11,13 ₁₁ ***This is the ritual for the ___Peace Offering___ that are presented to the Lord… he shall offer unleavened ___cakes___ mixed with oil, …*** ₁₃ ***His offering shall also include ___loaves___ of leavened ___bread___ along with the victim of peace offering for ___thanksgiving.___*** Bread continues to be part of most Israelite ritual customs. Notice the use of ***"___thanksgiving.___"*** The Greek word for "thanksgiving" is eucherestein (euxapiotia), where the word Eucharist name derived.

Leviticus 7:15,17 ₁₅ ***The ___flesh___ of the ___thanksgiving___ sacrifice shall be eaten on the day it is offered; none of it may be kept till the next day.*** ₁₇ ***Should any ___flesh___ from the sacrifice be left over on the third day, it must be burned up in the fire.*** As pointed out previously this sacrifice must be considered very important and sacred because if it is not all eaten then left overs, ***must be burned up.*** Also note the continued use of the word flesh.

Deuteronomy 8:3 ***He therefore let you be afflicted with hunger, and then fed you with ___manna___ a food unknown to you and your fathers, in order to show you that ___not by bread___ alone does man live, but by every word that comes forth from the mouth of the Lord.*** Later in Matthew 4:4, Jesus Christ quotes part of the above starting with ***___not by bread.___***

Deuteronomy 16:2–3 *2 You shall offer the Passover sacrifice from your flock or your herd to the Lord, your God… 3 You shall not eat leavened* **bread** *with it. For seven days you shall eat with it only unleavened* **bread**, *the bread of affliction, …* The Israelites believe the symbolism of yeast in <u>bread</u> represents sin, ***the* bread** *of affliction.*

Deuteronomy 29:4 *4 I led you for forty years in the desert. Your <u>clothes</u> did not fall from you in tatters nor your <u>sandals</u> from your feet;* Notice the miracle of **<u>clothes</u>** and **<u>sandals</u>** for 40 years.

1 Samuel 21:5 (about 550 BC) **But the priest replied to David, "I have no ordinary <u>bread</u> on hand only holy <u>bread</u>;**

The Lord instructed Elijah to go and hide east of the Jordan. 1 Kings 17:4,6 *4 "…You shall drink of the stream, and I have commanded ravens to feed you there." 6Ravens brought him <u>bread</u> and meat in the morning, and <u>bread</u> and meat in the evening, and he drank from the stream.* This is another case where God provides <u>bread</u> from heaven.

Several scripture passages started using use the word "<u>bread</u>" as a metaphor to describe a particular situation. The readers at that time knew that <u>bread</u> was considered very sacred because of its use in many of Israelites ritual customs.

Proverbs 20:17 **The <u>bread</u> of deceit is sweet to a man, but afterword his mouth will be filled with gravel.**

Ecclesiastes 9:7 **Go, eat your <u>bread</u> with joy and drink your wine with a merry heart, because it is now that God favors your works.**

Sirach 15:3 (about 180 to 175 BC) **Nourish him with the <u>bread</u> of understanding.**

In the book of Isaiah is a chapter called, "An Invitation to Grace" where <u>bread</u> is used, knowing that <u>bread</u> is considered sacred in Israelite's ritual customs: Isaiah 55:2 **Why spend your money for what is not <u>bread</u>; your wages for what fails to satisfy?** This instruction tells us to concentrate on what is sacred (as <u>bread</u> is sacred) and not on worldly things that do not satisfy.

Amos 8:11 ***Yes, days are coming, says the Lord God, when I will send famine upon the land! Not famine of <u>bread</u>, or thirst for water, but for hearing the word of the Lord.***

Malachi 1:11 *... **everywhere they bring sacrifice in my name; and a <u>pure offering</u>; For great is my name among nations, says the Lord of hosts.***

In the verse just prior to the above passage, the Jewish people were offering imperfect sacrifices (animals with blemishes) that was displeasing to the Lord. The above verse 11 anticipates that someday a ***pure offering*** to be sacrificed in messianic times, which is the universal Sacrifice of the Mass (the Eucharist) as we are told by the Council of Trent.

The Theme of Bread Through the New Testament:
Matthew 4:3–4 (written about 85 AD) ₃ ***The tempter approached and said to Him [Jesus], "If you are the Son of God, command that these stones become <u>loaves of bread</u>."*** ₄ ***He said in reply, "it is written: 'one does not live by <u>bread</u> alone, but by every word that comes forth from the mouth of God."*** Jesus is quoting Deuteronomy 8:3. Luke 4:4 is similar to Matthew 4:3–4.

Matthew 6:11 ***Give us today our daily <u>bread</u>;*** ... Also, in Luke 11:3, which is part of the "Our Father" prayer that Jesus taught us. ***daily <u>bread</u>*** may have a double meaning, <u>bread</u> for substance, and/or to receive the Eucharist daily.

The Feeding of the Five Thousand:
In Matthew 14:17 the disciples said to Jesus: ₁₇ ***"Five <u>loaves</u> and two fish are all we have here."*** ₁₉ ... *[Jesus]* ***Taking the five <u>loaves</u> and the two fish, and looking up to heaven, He said the <u>blessing</u>, <u>broke</u> the loaves, and <u>gave</u> them to the disciples, who in turn gave them to the crowds.*** ₂₀ ***They all ate and were satisfied, and they picked up the fragments left over – twelve wicker baskets full.***

Mark chapter 6 starting with verse 34 and John 6: 8–14, both also describe The Feeding of the Five Thousand similar to Matthew. Notice the actions of Jesus where He ***blessed***, ***broke***, and ***gave*** the bread.

The Feeding of the Four Thousand:

Matthew 15: tells us: ₃₃ ***The disciples said to Him*** [Jesus], ***"Where could we ever get enough bread in this deserted place to satisfy such a crowd? ₃₄ Jesus said to them, "How many loaves do you have?" "Seven," they replied, "and a few fish." ₃₆ Then He took the seven loaves and the fish, gave thanks, broke the loaves, and gave them to the disciples, who in turn gave them to the crowds. ₃₇ They all ate and were satisfied. They picked up the fragments left over – seven baskets full.***

Mark chapter 8 also tells us the same story about The Feeding of the Four thousand.

The Lord's Supper:

Matthew 26:26–28 ₂₆ ***While they were eating, Jesus took bread, said the blessing, broke it, and giving it to his disciples said, "take and eat; this is my body." ₂₇ Then He took a cup, gave thanks, and gave it to them, saying, "Drink from it, all of you, ₂₈ for this is my blood of the covenant, which will be shed on behalf of many for the forgiveness of sins."*** Notice the wording here: ***this is my body, this is my blood***, it does not say represents or symbolizes but says, ***"is my body", "is my blood."*** Mark chapter 14 starting with verse 22 and Luke 22:19–20 also tell us about The Lord's Supper. Jesus has now established the highlight (Eucharist) portion of the Catholic mass where, ***Jesus took bread, said the blessing, broke it, and giving it*** as a ***"perpetual institution"*** (Ex 12:14). Also notice that at the end of Matthew 26:28 above, Jesus Himself stated "***for the forgiveness of sins.***" Consider this, how could just symbolic bread and wine forgive sins? The only way the host can forgive sins is if the bread and wine (Eucharist) actually contain Jesus Himself in order to forgive one's sins by its consumption by a worthy participant. Jesus is the only one that can forgive sin.

After the resurrection of Jesus, Luke tells us about the events on the Road to Emmaus, where Jesus met up with two disciples, one named Cleopas, and Jesus prevented them from recognizing him as they walked along. Then near evening the disciples urged Jesus to stay with them. Luke 24:30–31 tells us: *₃₀ And it happened that, while He was with them at table, He took __bread__, said the __blessing__, __broke it__, and __gave it__ to them. ₃₁ With that their eyes were opened and they recognized Him, but He vanished from their sight.* Notice the same words as the Last Supper where *Jesus took __bread__, said the __blessing__, __broke it__, and __gave it__ to them.* Therefore, Jesus performed the very first mass where He explained scripture (the word) as they walked along then concentrating the __bread__, now called Eucharist. One might question why did Jesus vanish as soon as He gave them the Eucharist? That action demonstrates, symbolizes, and proves that Jesus' living spiritual body, blood, and divinity are present in the Eucharist.

The __Bread__ of Life Discourse:

The Book of John (written about 90 to 100 AD) chapter 6 starting at verse 22 is titled: "The __Bread__ of Life Discourse" contains many references to __bread__, __loves__, __flesh__, __blood__, and __manna__. It is important to mention that just prior to "The Bread of Life Discourse," John also describes the Multiplication of the Loves and Jesus Walking on Water, which show the reader that Jesus has the power over earthly __bread__ and power over himself by walking on water, Thus, of course, the power to be in the Eucharist. John chapter 6: *₃₂ So Jesus said to them, "Amen, amen, I say to you, it was not Moses who gave the __bread from heaven__; my Father gives you the true __bread__ from heaven. ₃₃ For the __bread__ of God is that which comes from heaven and gives life to the world."*

₃₅ Jesus said to them, "I am the __bread__ of life; whoever comes to me will never thirst...." ₄₁" I am the __bread__ that came down from heaven.

₄₈ I am the __bread__ of life ₄₉ your ancestors ate the __manna__ in the desert, but they died; ₅₀ this is the __bread__ that comes down from heaven so that one may eat it and not die. ₅₁ I am the living __bread__ that came down from heaven; whoever eats this __bread__ will live forever; and the __bread__ that I will give is my __flesh__ for the life of the world.

₅₃ Jesus said to them, "Amen, amen I say to you, unless you eat the __flesh__ of the Son of Man and drink his __blood__, you do not have life within you. ₅₄ Whoever eats my __flesh__ and drinks my __blood__ has eternal life, and I will raise him on the last day. ₅₅ For my __flesh__ is true food, and my __blood__ is true drink, ₅₆ Whoever eats my __flesh__ and drinks my __blood__ remains *in me and I in him. ₅₇ Just as the living Father sent me and I have life because of the Father, so also the one <u>who feeds on me</u> will have life because of the Father, so also the one who feeds on me will have life because of me. ₅₈ This is the <u>bread</u> that came down from heaven. Unlike your ancestors who ate and still died, whoever eats this <u>bread</u> will live forever."* What more can be said about the above, it cannot be any clearer, so just Let Scripture Speak for Itself. Most theologians tell us that an important issue is very often repeated more than once in scripture. <u>Bread</u> is considered extremely important here because in the above "<u>Bread</u> of Life Discourse," <u>bread</u> is mentioned eleven times, flesh four times, and blood four times.

Following the above, Jesus said in John 6: 62–63 *It is the spirit that gives life, while the flesh is of no avail. The words I have spoken to you are <u>spirit and life</u>, ...* The footnotes of the (NAB) bible state: "Spirit and life: all Jesus said about the bread of life is the revelation of the Spirit."

After Pentecost in Jerusalem:
After the Apostles received the Holy Spirit at Pentecost: Acts 2:41 *They devoted themselves to teaching of the apostles and to the communal life, to the <u>breaking of the bread</u> and to prayers.* Notice that <u>bread</u> is now referred to as ***the bread***, giving it the sacred importance, it deserves. Acts 2:46 *Every day they devoted themselves to meeting together in the temple area and to <u>breaking bread</u> in their homes.* (As a *"perpetual institution"*)

In 1 Corinthians (about 53 to 57 AD) chapter 5, St. Paul gives us a little more information about the Israelite thinking or symbolism of yeast and unleavened <u>bread</u> that we saw earlier in the Old Testament. ₆ *... Do you not know that a little yeast leavens all the dough? ₇ Clear out the old yeast, so that you may become a fresh batch of dough, inasmuch as <u>you are unleavened</u>. For our paschal lamb, Christ, has been sacrificed. ₈ Therefore let us celebrate the feast, not with the old yeast, the yeast of malice and wickedness, but with the unleavened <u>bread</u> of sincerity and truth.*

St. Paul relates yeast (as a metaphor) to *malice* and *wickedness* and unleavened <u>bread</u> as *sincerity and truth*, then he compares unleavened to those that accepted Christ, ***<u>you are unleavened</u>***.

1 Corinthians 10:16–17 ₁₆ *This cup of blessing that we bless, is it not a __participation__ in the __blood__ of Christ? The __bread__ that we break, is it not a __participation__ in the body of Christ?* ₁₇ *Because the __loaf__ of __bread__ is one, we, though many, are one body, for we all __partake__ of the one __loaf__.* The __loaf of bread__ *is one* has the same meaning as, John 6:56 telling us, *whoever eats my __flesh__ and drinks my __blood__ __remains in me and I in him__.* `What a wonderful gift and promise Jesus has given for us when we participate in the Eucharist, we become one with Jesus and He *__remains in me and I in him__*.

1 Corinthians 11: ₂₃ *For I received from the Lord what I also handed on to you, that the Lord Jesus, on the night he was handed over, took __bread__,* ₂₄ *and after he had __given thanks__, __broke it__ and said, "this is my body that is __for you__. Do this in __remembrance of me__."* ₂₅ *In the same way also the cup, after supper, saying, "This cup is the __new covenant__ in my blood. Do this, as often as you drink it, __in remembrance of me__."* ₂₆ *For as often as you eat this __bread__ and drink the cup, you __proclaim__ the death of the Lord until he comes.* ₂₇ *Therefore whoever eats the __bread__ or drinks the cup of the Lord unworthily will have to answer for the body and __blood__ of the Lord.* ₂₈ *A person should examine himself, and so eat the __bread__ and drink the cup.* ₂₉ *For anyone who eats and drinks without discerning the body, eat and drinks judgment on himself.* To assist us with this, at every mass we prey the "Act of Contrition."

From the footnotes of The Didache Bible for 1 Corinthians 11:23: "The Eucharist is the source and summit of the Christian life. Paul recounts the history of the institution of the Holy Eucharist to emphasize to the Corinthians that they received the true Body and Blood of Christ. Christ left us the Eucharist as a visible, unbloody, sacrament sign by which his one, bloody Sacrifice on the Cross would be re–presented and remembered until he comes again. For so great a privilege, the faithful must be properly prepared…" The footnote continues regarding 11:23–26, "The celebration of the Eucharist has not changed in its essence from the practice of the early Church, for it is by Christ's own instruction that we continue to gather together to celebrate and receive this great Sacrament. The word eucharist is derived from the Greek eucharistia, meaning thanksgiving." (End of footnote)

1 Corinthians 11 (above) verse 23 through 27 covers a number of important areas:

+ St. Paul first establishes his authority as ***received from the Lord***.
+ He confirms the Eucharist procedure to ***give thanks***, ***break it***, and distribute it ***for you*** as instructed by our Lord Jesus Christ.
+ St. Paul then tells us to ***do this often, in remembrance of*** [Christ].
+ St. Paul wrote to the Corinthians during the time period of 53 to 57 AD. Verse 27 through 29 is the best scripture proof that the early Christians believed in the real presence. St. Paul tells us to examine oneself prior to receiving, because if you do not, you bring judgement on yourself. This stern warning by Paul confirms early belief in the real presence in the Eucharist, why else would there be such a stern warning?

The Didache – Year 80AD:

In 1983 an original copy of a document called "The Didache", also known as "The Teaching of the Twelve Apostles" was discovered in an accent Constantinople Monastery of which scholars verified its organ to be the year 80AD. In the year 80AD, St. John the Apostle was still alive, he died in 103AD at the age of 97. "The Didache" instructs early converts on the ethics and practices on how to be a Christian. "The Didache" includes descriptions of the rituals of Baptism (including using the Sign of The Cross on a candidate's forehead), fasting, and description of the Eucharist Ritual (being the very first known text using the term Eucharist), thus, verifying (in writing) that the early Christians believed in the real presence, which was during the time when the Apostle John was still live.

The Bread of God – Year 110AD:

One of the early Fathers of the Church, St. Ignatius of Antioch (at the age of 75, died 110AD) was a disciple of St. John the Apostle. In St. Ignatius' writings he wrote about Mary as the mother of God and is the first recorded use of the term "Catholic." In his letter to the Romans he stated, "*I have no taste for the food that parishes…I want the Bread of God which is the flesh of Christ…and for drink I desire His blood, which is love that cannot be destroyed.*" He also referred to the Holy Eucharist as "*medicine of immortality.*"

SUMMARY – THEME OF BREAD:

What does the theme of bread through scripture tell us?

From the year 1400 BC where *"By the sweat of your face shall you get bread to eat"* (Gen 3:19) to *"You shall keep the feast of Unleavened Bread"* (Ex 23:15) as a sacred ritual, and to keep this as a *"perpetual Institution"* (Ex 12:14) to the prophesy of a *"pure offering"* (Mal 1:11) all the way through to Jesus Christ Himself in 33 AD telling us: *"I am the bread of life"* (Jn 6:35), *"whoever eats this bread will live forever"* (Jn 6:58), *"take and eat; this is my body"* (Mt 26:26) and do this *"in remembrance of me"* (1 Cor 11:24) *"for the forgiveness of sin"* (Mt 26:28) which tells us this all led to the New Eternal *"Covenant"* (Mt 26:27) and our *"thanksgiving"* (Lev 7:13) of the real presence in the Eucharist since the start of the Church through to today.

Throughout scripture bread is mentioned: as a means of substance, a gift of God, used in sacred rituals, a sign of sharing, a perpetual institution, it symbolizes the word of God which nourishes, and it becomes the body and blood of our Lord Jesus Christ.

- Genesis is the first mention of bread to show its importance then bread and wine is part of a blessing to Abram. Bread is mentioned 18 times in Genesis.
- Exodus tells us about the bread from heaven (manna) that God provided for forty years, and establishes the feast of unleavened bread. Bread is mentioned 23 times in Exodus,
- Leviticus establishes the requirements for the sacred ritual of the Peace Offering using bread. Bread is mentioned 12 times in Leviticus.
- Deuteronomy tells us of the miracle of clothes and sandals for 40 years. Bread is mentioned 8 times in Deuteronomy.
- 1 Samuel distinguishes between ordinary and holy bread. Bread is mentioned 19 times in 1 Samuel
- Proverbs, Ecclesiastes, and Sirach use bread as a metaphor because of its sacred reference in scripture.
- In Matthew, the tempter suggests that stones be turned into bread to tempt Jesus.
- Matthew and Luke mention bread as part of the "Our Father" prayer.

- Matthew, Mark and John tell us the multiplication of <u>bread (loves)</u> performed by Jesus to feed the five thousand which pre–figures the distribution of the Eucharist

- Matthew and Mark tell us the multiplication of <u>bread (loves)</u> performed by Jesus to feed four thousand which also pre–figures the distribution of the Eucharist.

- Matthew, Mark, Luke and John tell us about "The Last Supper" (Lord's Supper) where Jesus establishes and verifies His real presence in the Eucharist as the New Covenant and the Eucharist forgives sins which can only be done by Jesus, so, the host has to contain Jesus in order to forgive sins.

- Luke tells us about the Road to Emmaus, where Jesus performed the first mass after the Last Supper and after His resurrection, then Jesus vanishes to show us that He is present within the Eucharist.

- The "Bread of Life Discourse" In the book of John mentions <u>bread</u> eleven times.

- In chapter 6 of John, Jesus himself is quoted multiple times that he is $_{48}$ ***the <u>bread</u> of life*** and that $_{55}$ ***my <u>flesh</u> is true food, and my <u>blood</u> is true drink***, of which it cannot be any clearer that He is present in the Eucharist.

- Toward the end of chapter 6 Jesus explains: $_{63}$ ***The words I have spoken to you are spirit and life*** to clarify that He was not talking about his earthly physical body, but about His living spiritual body after His resurrection.

- After the Pentecost in Jerusalem, the apostles "***devoted themselves…to the breaking of <u>the bread</u> and to prayers***" (Acts 2:42), following Jesus' recommendations.

- ST. Paul wrote a letter to the Corinthians to clarify the proper Eucharist procedure, "***For anyone who eats and drinks without <u>discerning</u> the body, eats and drinks judgement on himself***" (1Cor 11:29), <u>discerning</u> prior to receiving verifies His real presence in the Eucharist.

- In all of the Bible, the word <u>bread</u> is used 492 times.

The Theme of Redemption and the Time–Line Through Scripture
This is intended to Let Scripture Speak for Itself on the major events in scripture using as many actual quotations as possible and placing them in chronological order along with the year reference, where available. The year references are the most acceptable time periods agreed upon by most theologians. Take notice of the "Theme of Redemption" throughout scripture and the unbelievable patience and love of our God as he guided the many generations of people to the salvation available to everyone.

The Beginning of Time.
+ Genesis 1:1 *In the beginning, ... God created the heavens and the earth.* The creation of the heavens included the creation of the multitude of angels. The earth was perfect and pure. God then created all living things including Adam and Eve who were perfect and pure with the gift of free–will. Genesis 2:3 *So God blessed the seventh day and made it holy, because on it he rested from all the work he had done in creation.* Isaiah 42:5. *"Thus says God, the Lord, who created the heavens and <u>stretched them out</u>,"* The Hubble telescope has confirmed that the universe is expanding (stretching out) as the result of the "big bang" that had to have been generated by intelligence in order to form everything so perfect!

Covenant with Adam.
+ Genesis 1:28 *God blessed them, saying: "Be fertile and multiply; fill the earth and subdue it. Have dominion over the fish of the sea, the birds of the air, and all the living things that move on the earth.*

The Fall of Mankind.
+ Genesis 3:11 *Then God asked, "who told you that you were naked? You have eaten, then, from the tree of which I had forbidden you to eat!" The man replied, "The woman whom you put here with me – she gave me fruit from the tree, so I ate it." The Lord God then asked the woman, "why did you do such a thing?" The woman answered, "The serpent tricked me into it, so I ate it."* Adam and Eve were deceived by the evil

one and with their free–will chose to defy God which made them ashamed of their guilt and they tried to hide it with fig leaves.

+ Genesis 3: *14Then the Lord God said...15 I will put enmity between you and the woman, and between your offspring and hers.* To Adam God said: *19 by the sweat of your face shall you get bread to eat.*

The Early World.

+ Genesis 3:21 *For the man and his wife the Lord God made leather garments, with which he clothed them.* In front of Adan and Eve, God slew an innocent animal and used animal skin to cover their shame, this is the first biblical sacrifice. Adam and Eve had their first experience of what it ment to see death because of sin.

+ Adam and Eve now had to toil for their existence outside of the Garden of Eden where they had two sons, Cain and Abel. In a fury of jealousy, Cane killed Able then Cane went on and intermarried that resulted in disobedient people that became very violent.

+ Genesis 5:3 *Adam was one hundred and thirty years old when he begot a son...named Seth.* Seth became a man of faith.

TIME LINE – Adam to Noah's Children Including Shem

Genesis Chapter 5 gives us the nine generations from Adam to Noah: Adam > Seth > Enosh > Kenan (Cainan) > Mahalalel > Jared > Enoch > Methuselah > Lamech > Noah > Shem. Genesis 5:32 *When Noah was five hundred years old, he became the father of Shem, Ham and Japheth.*

The Flood – 4,400 BC.

+ Genesis 6: 13–14 *[God] said to Noah: "I have decided to put an end to all mortals on earth; the earth is full of lawlessness because of them. So I will destroy them and all life on earth. Make yourself an ark of gopherwood."* Genesis 7:6 *Noah was six hundred years old when the flood waters came upon the earth.*

Covenant with Noah and all Humanity.

+ After the flood: Genesis 9:13 *I set my bow in the clouds to serve as a sign of the covenant between me and the earth.*

People Scattered at Babel – 3500 TO 3000 BC.

+ Genesis 11:4 ***"Come, let us build ourselves a city and a tower with its top in the sky, and so make a name for ourselves; otherwise, we shall be scattered all over the earth."*** The descendants of Noah did not follow God's commission to inhabit the whole earth. They started to build a tower to center their communal unity. God had to intervene by confusing their speech while they were working on the Tower of Babel so that they would have to scatter to form different nations on earth.

TIME LINE – Shem to Abram (Abraham)

Genesis 11:10 thru 26 provides the nine generations from Shem to Abram: <u>Shem ></u> Arpacjsjad (Arphaxad) > Shelah > Eber > Peleg > Reu > Serug > Nahor > Terah > <u>Abram.</u> Later on, God renamed Abram to be Abraham.

Abraham Called Out of Ur – 2220 BC.

+ Genesis 12:1 ***The Lord said to Abram: "Go forth from the land of your kinsfolk and from your father's house to the land that I will show you."*** By faith, Abram (age 70) his wife Sarah (Sarai) and all his possessions along with his brother's son Lot and his possessions departed from Ur, the Mesopotamian valley, as directed by God, they traveled to the land of Canaan where: Genesis 12:7 ***The Lord appeared to Abram and said, "To your descendants I will give this land."***

Abraham Blessed by Melchizedek.

+ Abram's nephew. Lot was captured. Abram assembled a force where: Genesis 15: ₁₆***He recovered all the possessions, besides bringing back his kinsman Lot and his possessions, ...*** ₁₇***When Abram returned from his victory...*** ₁₈***Melchizedek, King of Salem, brought out <u>bread and wine</u>, and being a priest of God Most High, he blessed Abram...*** ₂₀ ***Then Abram gave him a tenth of everything.***

Covenant with Abraham.

+ God spoke to Abram, Genesis 17:4–5 *"My <u>covenant</u> with you is this: you are to become the father of a host of nations. No longer shall you be called Abram; your name shall be Abraham, for I am making you the father of a host of nations.*

Destruction of Sodom and Gomorrah – 1900 BC.

+ Lot, the son of Abraham's brother was living in Sodom where angels from the Lord could not find even ten innocent people in the city. Genesis 19:29 ***Thus it came to pass: when God destroyed the Cities of the Plain, he was mindful of Abraham by sending Lot away from the upheaval by which God overthrew the cities where Lot had been living.***

Abraham put to the Test.

+ Genesis 22:1–2 *… God put Abraham to the test, He called him, "Abraham!" "Ready!" he replied. Then God said: "Take your son Isaac, your only one, whom you love, and go to the land of Moriah. There you shall offer him up as a holocaust on a height that I will point out to you."*

Abraham Died – 1975 BC (age 175).

TIME LINE – Abraham to Jacob and His 12 Sons Including Judah

<u>Abraham</u> > Isaac > Jacob (Israel) who has 12 sons: Ruben, Simeon, Levi, <u>Judah</u>, Dan, Naphtali, Gad, Asher, Issachar, Zebulun, <u>Joseph</u>, Benjamin. Genesis 25:7 ***The whole span of Abraham's life was one hundred and seventy–five years.*** Abraham died in 1975 BC. Archaeological evidence has been found to verify the patriarch, Abraham.

Joseph Sold to Slavey – 1882 BC.

+ Genesis 37:28 ***They sold Joseph to the Ishmaelites for twenty pieces of silver.*** Joseph was 17 years old when he was sold to slavery. Genesis 41:46 ***Joseph was thirty years old when he entered the service of Pharaoh, king of Egypt.*** The Pharaoh at the time was Ramses II. Archeologist discovered ancient Egyptian coins bearing the name and image of the biblical Joseph which are now on display at the Museum of Egypt.

Jacob's Family Moves to Egypt – 1860 BC.
+ Because of a severe famine in Canaan and because Jacob's son Joseph was in Egypt: Genesis 46:8 *Jacob and his descendants, ...migrated to Egypt.* Later on, there arose a Pharaoh who did not know Joseph resulting in the Israelites becoming slaves of the new ruler of Egypt. Genesis 50:26 *Joseph died at the age of a hundred and ten. He was embalmed and laid to rest in a coffin in Egypt.*

TIME LINE – Jacob to Nahshon

Jacob > Judah > Perez > Hezron > Ram > Amminadab > Nahshon.

Moses, the Exodus and First Passover – 1280 BC.
+ During the time of Nahshon, the Lord raised up Moses to deliver his people from the bondage and slavery of the Egyptians. Exodus 3:10, 14 ₁₀*...I will send you to Pharaoh to led my people, the Israelites, out of Egypt.* ₁₄ *I am who am, "This is what you shall tell the Israelites; I AM sent me to you."* Exodus 7:7 *Moses was eighty years old and Aaron eighty–three when they spoke to Pharaoh.*
+ The Ten Plagues: water turned into blood (Ex 7:14–24), the frogs (Ex 8:25–29, the gnats (Ex 8:12–15), the flies (Ex 8:16–28), the pestilence (Ex 9:1–12), the hail (Ex 9:13–35), the locust (Ex 10:1–20), the darkness (Ex 10:21–29), the death of the first born (Ex 11:1–10).
+ PASSOVER: Exodus 12:5,7,14 ₅*The lamb must be a year–old male and without blemish.* ₇*They shall take some of its blood and apply it to the two doorpost and the lintel of every house in which they partake of the lamb.* ₁₄*This day shall be a memorial feast for you, which all your generations shall celebrate ... as a perpetual institution.* Exodus 12:23 *For the Lord will go by,*

striking down the Egyptians. Seeing the blood on the lintel end the two doorposts, the Lord will pass over that door… Applying the blood on the lintel and two doorposts they formed the sign of the cross. Exodus 12:40 *The time the Israelites had stayed in Egypt was four hundred and thirty years.*

Covenant with Moses (Mount Sinai).

+ Exodus 20: 1*Then God delivered all these commandments…:* 3*You shall not have other gods besides me..* 7*You shall not take the name of the Lord your God in vain…* 8*Remember to keep holy the sabbath day…* 12*Honor your father and your mother…* 13 *You shall not kill.* 14*You shall not commit adultery.* 15*You shall not steal.* 16*You shall not bear false witness against your neighbor.* 17*You shall not covet your neighbor's house. You shall not covet your neighbor's wife…*

TIME LINE – Nahshon to David and His Son Solomon

Nahshon > Salmon > Boaz > Obed > Jesse > David > Solomon.

David King of Israel – 1010 TO 970 BC.

Covenant with David.

+ 2 Samuel 7:16 *Your house and your kingdom shall endure forever before me; your throne will stand firm forever.*

Solomon King of Israel – 970 TO 931 BC.

First Temple Built – 964 to 957 BC.

+ 2 Chronicles 3:1 *Then Solomon began to build the house of the Lord in Jerusalem on Mount Moriah, which had been pointed out to his father David, on the spot which David had selected…*

TIME LINE – Solomon to Rehoboam

Solomon's son Rehoboam takes over the kingdom after Solomons death.

Jewish Kingdom Divides – 930 BC.

+ The people revolt against heavy taxes imposed by Solomon and his son Rehoboam which resulted in the house of Israel dividing into two kingdoms, the Northern Kingdom of Israel with 10 tribes, and the Southern Kingdom of Juda with 2 tribes.

TIME LINE – Rehoboam to Manasseh

Rehoboam > Abijah > Jehoshaphat > Joash > Uzziah > Jotham > Ahaz > Hezekiah > Manasseh.

Israel Falls to Assyria – 722 BC.

+ The Northern Kingdom of Israel and its 10 tribes were overtaken by the Assyrians putting them into exile.

TIME LINE – Manasseh to Zerubbabel

Manasseh > Amon > Josiah > Jechonikim (Babylonian exile) > Shealtiel > Zerubbabel.

The Prophet Isaiah – 740 TO 701 BC.

+ Part of the prophet Isaiah's writings are written as though he was present at the crucifixion of Christ: Isaiah 53: 4*Yet it was our infirmities that he bore...,* 5*...he was pierced for our offenses, ...* 6*We had all gone away like sheep...*7*Though he was harshly treated, he submitted and opened not his mouth; like a lamb led to the slaughter...and opened not his mouth...,* 9*A grave was assigned him among the wicked...,* 10 *he gives his life as an offering for sin...*

The Prophet Jeremiah – 626 TO 587 BC.

+ Jeremiah was the last prophet of the Kingdom of Judah; he predicted the fall of Judah to the king of Babylon as well as the Israelites to be in exile for 70 years. 2 Maccabees 2:4–5 *[Jeremiah] ordered that the tent and the ark should accompany him and how he went off to the mountain which Moses climbed to see*

> *God's inheritance. When Jeremiah arrived there, he found a room in a cave in which he put the tent, the ark, and the altar of incense; then he blocked up the entrance.* This is the last mention in scripture (the cave in Mt. Nebo) as to where the ark was placed. Jeremiah predicted the New Covenant: Jeremiah 31:31 *The days are coming, says the Lord, when I will make a <u>new covenant</u> with the house of Israel and the house of Judah.*

The Prophet Daniel – 620 TO 538 BC.
+ Daniel, from David's royal family, is noted for his righteousness and wisdom along with his many apocalyptic visions and dreams. Daniel was the first in scripture to introduce us to the two angels of both the Old and New Testaments, Gabriel and Michael.

The Southern Kingdom, Judah, Falls to Babylon – 587 BC.
+ The Southern Kingdom, Juda, goes into exile under Babylonian captivity for 70 years.

First Temple Destroyed – 587 BC.
+ Nebuchadnezzar, the Babylonian king's forces destroyed the first Temple.

Temple Rebuilt Under Zerubbabel – 537 BC.
+ Cyrus the Persian gave the Israelites permission to return to Jerusalem and build their holy Temple. The Babylonian captivity resulted in three establishments which God has blessed. First, the Jews never were idolatrous again. Second, the synagogue was borne which modeled the Church. The services of the synagogue are similar to the services of the Church today. Third, from the captivity came the canon of the Holy Scripture.

The Prophet Malachi – 450 TO ABOUT 425 BC.
+ Malachi 1:11 *For from the rising of the sun, even to its setting, my name is great among nations; And everywhere they bring*

sacrifice to my name; and a <u>pure offering</u>. The "<u>*pure offering*</u>" represents the universal Sacrifice of the Mass, as we are told by the Council of Trent.

Alexander the Great – 356 TO 323 BC.

+ Alexander the Great, through the Roman Republic, spread one language and one culture throughout the civilized world making one language the basis to quickly spread the news of Jesus Christ later on.

Temple is Desecrated – 167 BC.

+ 2 Maccabees 5:17 *... **Antiochus did not realize that it was because of the sins of the city's inhabitants that the Lord was angry for a little while and hence disregarded the holy Place.*** 2 Maccabees 6:2 ***also to profane the temple in Jerusalem and dedicate it to Olympian Zeus.*** ... Antiochus, king of Syria, captured Jerusalem. According to Jewish tradition, King of Syria sacrificed a pig on the temple alter to his false god Zeus.

Maccabean Revolt – (167 to 160 BC).

Purification of the Temple – 164 BC.

+ 2 Maccabees 10:3 ***After purifying the temple, they made a new altar. Then, with fire struck from flint, they offered sacrifice for the first time in two years.***

TIME LINE – Zerubbabel to Jesus Christ

<u>Zerubbabel</u> > Abihud > Eliakim > Azor > Zadok > Achim > Eliud > Eleazar > Matthan* > Jacob > Joseph, the husband of Mary, Mary's father was Joachim (son of Matthan*), and Mary's mother was Anne > **<u>Jesus Christ</u>**.

Birth of Jesus – about 4 BC.

+ Jesus was born during the Roman Empire rein of Caesar Augustus (27 BC to 4 BC). The birth of Jesus is estimated to be 4 BC, the changes and corrections to the calendar during that time period is part of the reason for the estimated date. King Herod ordered the death of all male children up to two years old and he died in 4 BC. It is not clear the exact age of Jesus at that time, Jesus could have been under a year or about two years old making the birth year of Jesus 6 BC to about 4 BC. 4 BC seems the most lightly because most scholars agree that Jesus was about 33 years old at his crucifixion.

Baptism of Jesus – about 27AD.
+ Luke 3:23 *When Jesus began his ministry, he was about thirty years of age.*

Crucifixion, Resurrection and Appearance of Jesus – 33AD.

Commissioning of the Apostles – 33AD.
+ Mark 16:15 *He [Jesus] said to them [the Apostles], "Go into the whole world and proclaim the gospel to every creature. Whoever believes and is baptized will be saved..."* Jesus' commissioning of the Apostles was the start of the Apostolic Succession by continuous succession within the Catholic Church. St. Peter became the first pope in the year 33 and the Apostolic Succession has continued for 1,989 years to the present (2022) with 266 popes along with bishops and many priests. Apostolic Succession is a foundational doctrine in the Catholic Church, the bishops form an unbroken line of bishops stemming from the original apostles commissioned by Jesus Christ. The Apostolic Succession guarantees the truth of what is preached can be traced back to the Apostles and Jesus himself. The Apostolic Succession is proven by written records, see the list of popes.

Spread of the Church Throughout the Known World – 47 TO 58 AD.
+ St. Paul (formally Saul) went on three missionary journeys into the then known world. The first missionary is described in Acts 13 and 14, The second in Acts 15:36 to 18:22, and Paul's third missionary journey is described in Acts 18:23 to 21:16, where he primarily evangelized the Gentiles.
+ St. Paul's final voyage was from Jerusalem to Rome where his life ended the year of 67 AD.

The 27 Books of the New Testament – Written 50 to 100AD.

+ The four Gospels, seven Catholic Epistles, Acts of the Apostles, 14 Epistles, and Revelation (Apocalyptic book) were written at various times between the year 50 and 100 AD. The last Apostle, St. John died in the year 103. The seven Catholic Epistles were written to the entire Church as compared to the 14 Epistles that were written to specific churches.

Apostolic Fathers of the Early Church – 88 to about 170AD.

+ The Apostolic Fathers lived in the first and second centuries AD who personally knew some of the Twelve Apostles and were significantly influenced by the Apostles. The Apostolic Fathers' writings were widely circulated in the early Church and originally written in Greek. Some of the Apostolic Fathers' writing are: Epistle to Diognetus, Clement of Rome, The Didache (The Teaching of the Twelve Apostles), Epistle of Barnabas, Ignatius of Antioch, Martyrdom of Ignatius, Epistle of Polycarp, Martyrdom of Polycarp, Shepherd of Hermas, Papias of Hierapolis, and St. Quadratus of Athens.

Summary – Time–Line – Adam to Jesus:

Adam to Noah's Children Including Shem – Beginning to 4400 BC

Genesis Chapter 5 gives us the nine generations from Adam to Noah: **Adam** > Seth > Enoch > Kenan (Cainan) > Mahalalel > Jared > Enoch > Methuselah > Lamech > Noah > Shem. Genesis 5:32 *When Noah was five hundred years old, he became the father of Shem, Ham and Japheth.*

Shem to Abram (Abraham) – 4400 to 1975 BC

Genesis 11:10 THRU 26 provides the nine generations from Shem to Abram: Shem > Arpacjsjad (Arphaxad) > Shelah > Eber > Peleg > Reu > Serug > Nahor > Terah > Abram. Later on, God renamed Abram to be Abraham.

Abraham to Jacob and His 12 Sons Including Judah – 1975 to 1800 BC

Abraham > Isaac > Jacob (Israel) who has 12 sons: Ruben, Simeon, Levi, Judah, Dan, Naphtali, Gad, Asher, Issachar, Zebulun, Joseph, Benjamin. Genesis 25:7 *The whole span of Abraham's life was one hundred and seventy-five years.* Abraham died in 1975 BC. Archaeological evidence has been found to verify the patriarch, Abraham.

Jacob to Nahshon – 1800 to 1400 BC

Jacob > Judah > Perez > Hezron > Ram > Amminadab > Nahshon.

Nahshon to David and His Son Solomon – 1400 to 931 BC

Nahshon > Salmon > Boaz > Obed > Jesse > David > Solomon.

Solomon to Rehoboam – 931 to 930 BC

Solomon's son Rehoboam takes over the kingdom after Solomons death.

Rehoboam to Manasseh – 930 to 600 BC

Rehoboam > Abijah > Jehoshaphat > Joram > Uzziah > Jotham > Ahaz > Hezekiah > Manasseh.

Manasseh to Zerubbabel – 600 to 537 BC

Manasseh > Amon > Josiah > Jechoniah (Babylonian exile) > Shealtiel > Zerubbabel.

Zerubbabel to Jesus Christ – 537 to 4 BC

Zerubbabel > Abiud > Eliakim > Azor > Zadok > Achim > Eliud > Eleazar > Matthan* > Jacob > Joseph, the husband of Mary, Mary's father was Joachim (son of Matthan*), and Mary's mother was Anne > **Jesus Christ**.

References:
The **bold and italicized** bible quotations are from The New American Bible, Revised Edition, Fireside Catholic Publishing. Certain words may be underlined for emphasis added.
Time Line names from: Matthew 1:1-16, Luke 3:23-38.
The New American Bible Concordance-John R. Kohlenberger III, Editor
Time Line date verification: The Bible Timeline, Jeff Cavins & Sarah Christmyer, Ascension
THE THEMES THROUGH SCRIPTURE: Assembled by Paul Wilchek 10JUN20.

CHAPTER 13

THE BRIEF HISTORY OF
THE CATHOLIC CHURCH

It is important that Catholics are familiar with the History of the Catholic Church, which is our Catholic family history. This is an important building block in the foundation of our identity as Catholics, and it serves as a valuable aid and support on our faith journey. There are a lot of misconceptions out there, and one needs to know the facts. This brief history is based on written historical facts that clearly show that the early Christians were indeed Catholic. The very early documents reveal that the Church was called Catholic and the early Christians attended mass, believed in the sacraments, celebrated the liturgy, and most of all, they believed in the real presence of Jesus in the Eucharist.

It is extraordinary that within the first five hundred years, all of the basic foundation beliefs of the Catholic Church were established and have remained the same to this day. Oh yes, we have had changes, but not to any of the basic beliefs. The early Church and the Church today are essentially the same! The four marks of the Church can be traced to the earliest teachings of Christ and the apostles: The Church is **one** through its one source of unity with the Trinity. The Church is **holy**, because Christ is holy. The Church is **catholic** as mandated by Jesus as universal (worldwide). The Church is **apostolic** because Jesus taught the apostles how to form the Church with an unbroken line of succession to the present day. Proper names are **bold** for reference purposes.

Back Ground:
509BC–27BC The Roman Republic.

Roman Empire:
27BC–14AD The <u>Roman Republic</u> became the <u>Roman Empire</u> under Caesar Augustus.

The year that Jesus Christ was born was calculated based on Jewish records, counting back from the recorded Passover in the year of 33AD.

4AD Birth of Jesus Christ:
Luke 2:4–6 ***And Joseph too went up from Galilee from the town of Nazareth to Judea, to the city of David that is called <u>Bethlehem</u>, because he was of the house and family of David, to be enrolled with Mary, his betrothed, who was with child. While they were there the time came for her to have her child, and <u>she gave birth</u> to her firstborn son.***

30AD Forty Days in the Desert:
Luke 4:1 [Jesus]*... **was led by the Spirit into the <u>desert for forty days</u>, ...***

33AD Crucifixion of Jesus:
Luke 23:33 ***When they came to the place called the Skull, they <u>crucified him</u>...***

> Burial of Jesus:
> Luke 23: 53 ***After he had taken the body down, he wrapped it in linen cloth and laid him in a rock–hewn tomb in which no one had yet been <u>buried.</u>***
>
> Resurrection of Jesus:
> Luke 24:12 ...***Peter got up and ran to the tomb, bent down, and saw the burial cloths alone; then he went home amazed at what had happened.*** Why was Peter "***amazed?***" Jewish tradition was that at dinner when a

guest departed from the table, if they planned to return, they folded up their napkin (cloth) and set it alone, if they were not returning, they crumpled their napkin on their seat, therefore, Peter was amazed because Jesus left a sign *"the burial cloth alone"* that ment he was returning.

Appearance of Jesus:
1 Corinthians 15:5–8 *…He appeared to Cephas [Kephas], then to the Twelve. After that, He appeared to more than five hundred brothers at once, most of whom are still living, though some have fallen asleep. After that He appeared to James, then to all the apostles.*

Commissioning of the Apostles and the Church:
Mark 16:15 *He said to them, "Go into the whole world and proclaim the gospel to every creature. Whoever believes and is baptized will be saved; …"*

Ascension of Jesus:
Mark 16:19 *So then the Lord Jesus, after He spoke to them, was taken up into heaven and took His seat at the right hand of God.*

Pentecost (Ten days after the Ascension of Jesus):
Acts 2: 1–4 *When the time for Pentecost was fulfilled, they were all in one place together. And suddenly there came from the sky a noise like a strong driving wind, and it filled the entire house in which they were. Then there appeared to them tongues as of fire, which parted and came to rest on each one of them. And they were all filled with the holy Spirit and began to speak in different tongues, as the Spirit enabled them to proclaim.*
This event marks the beginning of the Catholic Church along with the apostles being commissioned by Christ to:
"Go into the whole world and proclaim the gospel…"

33AD: The keys of the Church were given to **St. Peter**: Matthew 16: 18–19 [Jesus talking to Peter] **"I say to you, you are Peter, and upon this rock I will build my church, and the gates of the netherworld shall not prevail against it. I will give you the keys to the kingdom of heaven. Whatever you bind on earth shall be bound in heaven; and whatever you loose on earth shall be loosed in heaven."** The Catholic Church refers to **St. Peter** (the first "Bishop of Rome") as the first Pope.

36AD First Martyr:

Acts 7:59–60 *As they were stoning <u>Stephen</u>, he called out, "Lord Jesus receive my spirit," Then he fell on his knees and cried out in a loud voice, "Lord, do not hold this sin against them"; and when he said this, he fell asleep.*

Saul of Tarsus (St. Paul) in the year 33AD was converted on his way to Damascus, then spends three years in Arabia before returning to Damascus (36AD) to preach the gospel of Jesus.

47AD – 48AD **St. Paul's** first missionary trip to Cyprus and Galatia and continued to other areas up through to 58AD.

49AD All the apostles, including **St. Paul**, gathered in Jerusalem for the <u>Council of Jerusalem</u> where after much discussion, **St Peter** declared the first definitive statement of the Church, that non–Jewish converts were not required to be circumcised.

AD 33 to AD 100: The Passion, Resurrection, Ascension, and Pentecost occurred in AD 33. Saul's conversion was about AD 33/34, and **St. Paul's** 3 missionary journeys were AD 45 to 58. The <u>Council of Jerusalem</u> (AD 49) was attended by the elders of the Church in Jerusalem and Antioch, and the Apostles, including **St. Paul** and **Barnabas**. The Council announced that Gentiles were not to be asked to undergo circumcision to be saved, which led to a strong push of the Church's Gentile mission. The Gospel of Luke was written prior to the Roman conquest (AD 64 to 70). Acts of the Apostles, also written by Luke, was written in AD 63. The great fire in Rome (AD 64), that Nero may have started, was politically blamed on the Christians. This led to Christian persecution by Roman emperors **Nero** and **Domitian. St. Paul** was believed to have been martyred in AD 67. Pope **St. Peter** was martyred in AD 67.

The 2nd pope (Bishop of Rome), **St. Linus** (AD 67–76), ordered women to cover their heads in church. He was martyred in AD 79. The Gospel of Mark was written prior to the destruction of the Jerusalem Temple, destroyed by emperor **Vespasian** (AD 60–70). The Gospel of Matthew was written about AD 50–70. The Gospel of John was written prior to AD 100; however, this date is questionable. This was a time of initial growth within the Christian Church. The early Christians were an offshoot of Judaism. They attended Jewish services to hear scripture read and explained, then they went to various homes to proclaim the gospels (by word of mouth) followed by breaking bread (Eucharist) together. The Christian and the Jewish community combined services separated sometime after AD 70 but prior to AD 110.

In 1983, the original text of the *Didache* (teaching of the 12 apostles) was discovered in an ancient Constantinople monastery. Scholars traced its origin to AD 80. The *Didache* lists the rite of baptism, the Liturgy, and the selection of clergy. It also exhorts the faithful to prayer, and contains the doctrine of the early Church.

Roman Persecution of Christians:
64AD: Emperor of Rome, **Nero**, may have started the fire that burned much of Rome, then blamed it on the Christians which was the start of Christian persecution that lasted until 306AD.
66AD: This was the start of the Jewish revolt.
67AD: **St. Peter** and **St. Paul** were martyred.
70AD: The Jerusalem Temple was destroyed.
88AD–97AD: Pope #4 **St. Clement** in the year 96AD wrote a letter expressing the primacy of the Roman pontiff, he was martyred.
97AD–105AD: Pope #5 **St. Evaristus** continued under Christian persecution by Roman Emperor **Nerva**.
100: All 27 books of the New Testament were written by the year 100.
105–115: Pope #6 **St. Alexander I.**
107: **St. Ignatius of Antioch** first (in written form) used the term "Catholic Church." He also testified that the Church is not some loose association

but is a highly organized and disciplined body with its own officers and doctrine. He was martyred in 115.

Martyred Popes (year reign, pope #, name of pope martyred to date):
115–125: Pope #7 **St. Sorer**, 125–166 Pope #8 **St. Telesphorus**, 155–166 Pope #11 **St. Anicetus**,
166–175: Pope #12 **St. Sorer**, 199–217 Pope #15 **St. Zephyrinus**, 217–222 Pope #16 **St. Callistus.**

AD 100 to AD 200 recap: By the year 100, all 27 books of our New Testament were written. Under the 6th pope, **Alexander I** (105–115), Christians grew in numbers and influence in spite of persecutions. In the year AD 107, **St. Ignatius of Antioch** wrote a letter to six different faith communities that first used the term "Catholic Church." The letter discussed the belief in the real presence of Christ in the Eucharist, the divinity of Christ, and the Church's structure of bishops, priests, deacons, and laity. **St. Ignatius** was converted by the disciple **St. John. St. Ignatius** was martyred by two lions in the amphitheater. The bishops of the Church had to confront improper teachings by the Gnostics, Maricon, and similar heretic groups. One of the Churches' first apologists, **Justin Martyr** (100–165), wrote a letter to emperor **Antoninus** in AD 155 concerning the doctrine of the real presence of Christ in the Eucharist and used the term "Catholic Mass." The 14th pope, **Victor I** (189–199), was the first African pope.

AD 200 to AD 300 recap: Christianity was expanding and developing theologically until the persecutions by Roman Emperor Decius (reign: 249–251) which then raised questions about how to deal with those who denied the faith. They concluded that the Church was not just for the perfect but for repentant sinners. Many schools of Christian teaching were developed in major cities, with such great teachers as **St. Clement** (150–215) and **Origen of Alexandria** (184–253).

220–230: Pope #17 **St. Urban I**. The Roman Emperor **Severus** forbade new converts to the Church. **St. Urban** was martyred.
230–235: Pope #18 **St. Pontian**. The Roman Emperor **Maximinus Thrax** ordered church leaders to be put to death. **St. Pontian** was martyred.

The 19th Pope **St. Anterus**, the 20th Pope **St. Fabian**, and the 21st Pope **St. Cornelius** were all martyred by the Roman Empire.

In the year 257 Roman Emperor **Valerin** issued an edict ordering all bishops, priest, and deacons to sacrifice to pagan gods and forbade visits to cemeteries and any Christian assemblies.

Roman Emperor **Diocletian** (284–305) had an understudy named **Galerius** that enforced an empire–wide campaign to eradicate the Church, thousands upon thousands were tortured and killed.

286–304: Pope #29 **St. Marcellinus.** The Roman Emperor **Diocletian** executed Christians that refused to worship pagan gods, he destroyed churches, and burned sacred books. **St. Marcellinus** was martyred along with the martyring of the largest number of church leaders and fathers of any other time period.

The 30th Pope **St. Marcellus**, and the 31st Pope **St. Eusebius** (309–311) were martyred.

312 **Constantine** became emperor and in 313 legalized Christianity that started to end the Roman percussions. In 324 **Constantine** became the sole Roman Emperor and in 330 he split the empire into the East and West.

End of Roman Persecution of Christians:
Through the guidance of the Holy Spirit, the One, Holy, Catholic and Apostolic Church survived its first major test.

314–335: Pope #33 **St. Sylvester**.

325: The Council of Nicaea finalized the Nicaea Creed, declared Christ as true God and true man, and used the term "Consubstantial" (of the same substance) with God the Father.

336: Pope # 34 **St. Marcus** recorded the first Christmas Mass.

337: **Constantine** was baptized on his death bed.

337–352: Pope #35 **St. Julius I** declared Christmas to be celebrated on December 25th.

366–384: Pope #37 **St. Damascus I**.

367: **St. Athanasius** was the first to list the 27 books that became the New Testament.

381: The Council of Constantinople reaffirmed the Nicaea Creed and declared the Holy Spirit a divine person.

This period of time brought out several famous theologians, fathers and doctors of the Church such as: **St. Gregory Nazianzen** (b.329–d.390), **St. Basil the Great** (b.330–d.379), **St. Ambrose** (b.340–d.397), **St. John Chrysostom** (b.347–d.407), **St. Jerome** (b.347–d.420) who in the year 400 published Jerome's Vulgate Latin Bible, **St. Augustine of Hippo** (b.354–d.430), **St. Cyril of Alexandria** (b.376–d.444).

AD 300 to AD 400 recap: The severe persecution ended as the result of the first Christian Roman emperor, **Constantine** (emperor 306–337). **Constantine** legalized Christianity for the first time and passed laws favoring Christians. The down side was that **Constantine** started to intervene in Church affairs through the first ecumenical council of Catholic bishops, the Council of Nicaea (AD 325), where he attempted to control certain aspects of the Church. This started the government (emperor) involvement in the Catholic Church along with certain heresies. The council also developed the Nicene Creed, several disciplinary cannons, and the celebration of Easter to be on the first Sunday after the first full moon of the vernal equinox. In 382, the 37th pope, **Damascus** (366–384), and his bishops established the canon of the Bible and translated it to Latin. This era saw the emergence of some great scholar–saints such as: **St Ambrose** (340–397), **St Martin of Tours** (316–397), **St. Jerome** (342–420), **St. John Chrysostom** (347–407), and **St. Augustine of Hippo** (354–430). Most of the people within the Roman Empire became Catholic Christians, at least in name. The First Council of Constantinople (381) defined four canons, developed teachings on the divinity of the Holy Spirit as well as the Son, and added to the Nicene Creed: "we believe in the Holy Spirit, the Lord and Life–giver, who proceeds from the Father, who with the Father and Son is worshiped and glorified." In 367, **St. Athanasius** (296–373), in his *"Festal Letter,"* was the first to list the 27 books that would become the New Testament. The first recorded Catholic celebration of Christmas was in the year 336. A few years later the 35th pope, **St. Julius** I (337–352), declared December 25th as the Christmas day celebration.

422–432: Pope #43 **St. Celestine I.**
431: The Council of Ephesus declared Mary is the Mother of Christ, who is one person, the Son of God. Therefore, Mary is the Mother of God.

440–461: Pope #45 **St. Leo I (the Great)** met with **Attila the Hun** and convinced him not to sack the city of Rome.

451: The Council of Chalcedon declared Christ is one divine person with two natures, human and divine.

481–509: King **Clovis I**, king of the Franks (what is now France, Belgium, and Germany) was the first Catholic King.

476: Due to Roman changes, reduction in the military, political corruption, divisions, and Barbarian invasion, the roman Empire fell.

492–496: Pope #49 **St. Gelasius I. St. Patrick** took the gospel to Ireland.

AD 400 to AD 500 recap: Jerome's Vulgate–Latin Bible was published in the year 400.

The Roman Empire fell in AD 476, however, in the East, the Byzantine Empire continued for another 1000 years. The pagans blamed Christians for the fall, however, historians tell us it was the governments internal changes, political corruption, and the division between Greek–speaking East and the Latin–speaking West that started its decline and eventual fall. The Romans were very proud and excited to be citizens of the Roman Empire, and the military was considered an elite privilege. The military, which made and unmade emperors, was reduced from 500,000 to 200,000, forcing them to depend on Roman auxiliary forces.

The Roman government allowed the massive migration of Germanic Tribes with the understanding that they would serve as soldiers. This eventually led to the majority of the auxiliary forces to be made up of non–Roman, ethnically Germanic soldiers. The reduction of elite forces, and the take–over by Germanic Tribes, started the rapid decline of Roman pride and enthusiasm that had kept the Roman Empire great for 450 years (27–476).

The final blow to Rome took place in AD 476 when the barbarian chieftain, Odoacer, demanded to rule over one–third of the Italian mainland. His demand was rejected, so he overthrew the "boy emperor" of Rome, **Romulus Augustulus**, the very last emperor of the Western Roman Empire.

The 45th pope, **Leo I** (440–461), had to protect God's people both spiritually and physically from the barbarian invaders. Heresy occurred outside the Church, and the West began denying the full effect of original sin. The

East struggled with clarifying how Christ's divine and human natures are joined. At the <u>Council of Ephesus</u> (AD 431), Mary was proclaimed "Mother of God." The <u>Council of Chalcedon</u> (AD 451) agreed with **Pope Leo** I that Christ was both God and man.

The Start of Islam (Muslims):
553: The <u>Second Council of Constantinople</u> reaffirmed the teachings of Ephesus and Chalcedon.
Muhammed (b.570–d.632), born as an Arab was active in political/religious life (609–632). He had 14 wives, claimed to have receive Islam words (610–632) for the Koran (Quran). He ordered assassination of non–believers in Islam. Muslims use the Koran to follow and practice the Islam thinking.
590–604: Pope #64 **St. Gregory I the Great**. During a society in conflict, the pope not only governed the Church, but also the City of Rome after the collapse of the central government. The pope established hospitals, schools & universities, and fed the hungry. The pope sent **St. Augustine of Canterbury** to led a missionary expedition to convert the British which brought the whole country into the Church.

AD 500 TO AD 600 recap: The East and the West struggled with survival in a new political order, and they tried to convert the barbarian conquerors of the Roman Empire. In AD 529, the order of **St. Benedict** (480–543), a missionary outreach, preserved the Christian culture. The gospel was planted in Ireland by **St. Patrick** (387–493) and in Scotland by Celtic (Irish) monks. The <u>Second Council of Constantinople</u> (553) dealt with the two natures of Christ.

622–750: The rapid spread of Islam and the start of the Islamic Empire. In less than 100 years one–half of Christian land and wealth was under Islam control: Egypt, Antioch, Jerusalem, and Iberian Peninsula. The battle of 732 in France put a halt to Muslim advances in that area. In 647 the Muslims captured Alexandria.
678–681: Pope #79 **St. Agatho.**

680–681: The <u>Third Council of Constantinople</u> established that Christ has two wills: human and divine.

700: The Muslims conquered all of North Africa. The Chinese invented gun powder that initially was used for fireworks.

711: The Muslims invaded Spain. The creation of the Holy Roman Empire by **Charlemagne,** crowned emperor in 962 by **Pope John XII** Western Europe. **Charlemagne** operated very similar to **Constantine**; except he did not interfere with church affairs.

AD 600 to AD 700 recap: The Catholic Church expanded as a result of the 64th pope, **Gregory I** (590–604). His missionary work led to the conversion of England by **St. Augustine of Canterbury** and the Benedictine monks. The <u>Third Council of Constantinople</u> (680–681) reaffirmed Christ as being human and divine. Islam began to take over the Eastern (Byzantine) Empire.

757–767: Pope #93 **St. Paul I.**
768: The creation of The Holy Roman Empire, **Charlemagne** king of the Franks.
787: The <u>Second Council of Nicaea</u>, defended Church's understanding of Sacred Images, art and images help everyone contemplate divine mystery.
795–816: Pope #96 **Leo III** crowned **Charlemagne** Holy Roman Emperor who was a patron of education and the arts, and he directed **Alcuin** to focus on grammar, logic, rhetoric, arithmetic, geometry, astronomy, and music.
867–872: Pope #106 **Adrian II.**
869–870: The <u>Fourth Council of Constantinople</u> temporarily ended the East and West schism.

AD 700 to AD 900 recap: St. Boniface (680–755), a Benedictine missionary, was instrumental in the conversion of Germany and helped set up an alliance between the pope and the king. This was the start of Christendom, an alliance of the Church and the state of the West. The <u>Second Council of Nicaea</u> (787) was the last council to be accepted by both the Eastern and Western Churches. **Charles the Great (Charlemagne)** became king in AD 768. **Charles** took authority from the pope and alienated the Byzantine Church. The breakdown of **Charles's** empire caused the decline of the Western Church and increased Islamic presence in the Eastern Church. Missionaries were sent to Sweden in 829. Relations between the East and the West became broken from AD 858–887. The Fourth Council of Constantinople (869–870) had 10 sessions and issued 27 cannons. **St. Cyril** and **St. Methodius** evangelized the Slavic peoples, and in 863, scripture was translated into the Slavonic language.

900 The first recorded use of a hand–pumped pipe organ was in the Winchester Cathedral. The pipe organ was invented by a Greek engineer **Ctesibius of Alexandria** in the 3rd century BC.

East/ West Great Schism:

1049–1054: Pope #152 **St. Leo IX**. In 1054 **Michael Cerularius** of Constantinople was excommunicated from the Church which was the start of the great schism splitting the Church into the Roman Catholic and Eastern Orthodox Churches. Also, there was a difference of opinion regarding the use of unleavened bread for communion, supported by the west. In addition, there was a dispute of the exact wording of the Nicene Creed as well as the west believed the clerics should remain celibate.

1073–1085: Pope #157 **St. Gregory VII** defends the papal primacy and settles the controversy of who appoints the bishops – the pope or the ruler? The agreement was that the pope gave the bishops spiritual guidance and the king provided civil guidance.

AD 900 to AD 1100 recap: Poland accepted Catholicism in 966. In the year 1012, **Burchard of Worms** completed the Catholic Cannon Law. The Western Church started a renewal as the result of new monastic orders by **St. Romuald** (986–1027) and **St. Bruno** (1030–1101). **Otto I**, the new emperor from Germany, started to reform the Western Church by appointing so called "worthy" popes and bishops. This action caused controversy between popes and emperors all throughout the Middle Ages. The 145th pope, **Benedict IX** (1032–1045), was the youngest pope politically installed. After a period of time, he sold his position, then a few months later he forcibly took it back from Pope **Sylvester III** (1045) and became the 147th pope (2nd time in office). It is not clear what occurred at this time, but in 1045 the 148th pope, **Gregory VI,** was in office (1045–1046), and then the 149th pope, **Clement II,** was in office immediately after (1046–1047). For the 3rd time, **Benedict IX** was installed in office as the 150th pope (1047–1048). The 157th pope, **Gregory VII** (1073–1085), tried to end the corruption in the Catholic Church by attempting to free the Church from the control of emperors and secular rulers. However, Pope **Gregory VII** was only successful in enforcing spiritual authority.

AD 1054 began another disagreement between the Eastern and Western Churches that has lasted to the present time. The Muslims were severely persecuting the Christians. In response, the 159th pope, **Urban II** (1088–1099), launched the First Crusade in 1095 in an attempt to free the Holy Land from Muslim control. In 1099, Jerusalem was re–taken (1st Crusade by Christian Knights).

The Era of the Crusades:
1088–1099: Pope #159 **Urban II** raised an army of 60,000 men to defend Jerusalem that was occupied and controlled by the Muslims. The crusades were not a religious conflict it was primarily to free the Holy Land so pilgrims could travel and visit Jerusalem without being harassed and killed. The shock that launched the crusades was when **Bishop Bamberg** and 12,000 pilgrims were massacred by the Muslims near Jerusalem. The Christian Byzantine Emperor wrote **Pope Urban II** a letter requesting his assistance because the Muslims were persecuting the Jews and Christians. The crusaders allowed the Muslims to keep their faith and practice openly upon surrender, this shows that the conflict was not to force any religion on anyone.

1096–1102: The First Crusade was the only successful crusade by Christian Nights to free the Holy Land so pilgrims could visit. However, it did not remain open for pilgrims for very long.

1119–1124: Pope #162 **Callistus II.** In 1123 The First Council of Lateran was called.

1139: The Second Council of Lateran reaffirmed baptism of infants, sacraments of holy orders, marriage, and the Eucharist.

1145–1153: Pope #167 **Eugene III** calls the second crusade which included the king of France **Louis VII.**

1147–1149: The Second Crusade. St. Bernard and his brothers traveled through Europe exhorting warriors to aid their fellow Christians being harassed and killed by the Muslims. The Christian crusaders and **Louis VII** forces cannot seem to get coordinated and their efforts fail to push the Muslims out of Jerusalem. Many Jewish people were harmed and some killed during the crusading conflict, the Church did not sanction this and worked to try to stop this.

1179: The Third Council of Lateran condemned heresy at that time, matter is good (created by God), papal elections require two–thirds vote of cardinals.

1187–1191: Pope #174 **Clement II** calls for another crusade (#3) and the three major monarchs of Europe respond, the Holy Roman Emperor **Frederick Barbarossa**, **Richard I** of England, and **Philip II** of France

1189–1192: The Third Crusade. Unfortunately, **Fredrick** drowns crossing a river, **Richard I** and **Philip II** cannot seem to get long, leaving **Richard's** forces alone who were not able to recapture the Holy City. **Richard I,** enters into a peace treaty that protects the pilgrims for three years. This is considered a partial success.

1198–1216: Pope #176 **Innocent III** called The Fourth Council of the Lateran in 1215 that instituted the Easter Duty, where the minimum annual Eucharist and Confession were established. It also first used the term "Transubstantiation", and the pope calls for the Fourth Crusade.

1201–1205: The Fourth Crusade. The leaders decide to go by the sea to the Holy Land and entered into a contract with the Venetians for boats, unfortunately fewer than one half of the crusaders arrived in Venice and could not pay the debt owed. The Venetian leader, **Enrico Dandolo**, proposed a plan that if the crusaders would help Venice to capture the Christian city of Zara it would be considered payment for the debt. Even though **Pope Innocent III** told them not to attack Zara, the crusaders went on and captured the city. After the capture, an exiled Byzantine prince, **Alexius Angelus**, offered the crusaders gold and assistance in the crusade in exchange for their help to capture Constantinople, which they did in the year 1204. This severely damaged the relationship between the East and the West even though **Pope Innocent III** did not agree with the attack on Constantinople.

1216–1227: Pope #177 **Honorius III** organized crusading armies led by **King Andrew II** of Hungary and **Leopold VI**, Duke of Austria against Jerusalem.

1218–1221: The Fifth Crusade was called for by the pope to recapture the Muslim controlled city of Jerusalem, ultimately, they left the city with the Muslims in control, this was considered a failure.

1228–1229: The Sixth Crusade, seven years after the fifth crusade, led by **Frederick II** to try and recapture Jerusalem involved very little actual fighting. In 1229 a treaty restored Jerusalem to the Christians, then in the year 1244 the city was lost to the Muslims.

AD 1100 to A.D.1200 recap: All of the popes during this time period continued to try to eliminate the secular rulers that were corrupting the Church. The crusades in the East continued with only mixed results. The monastic orders also attempted to free the Church of outside heresy and corruption problems that were due to secular appointed rulers. A new approach by **St. Anselm** (1033–1109) of Canterbury and **Peter Lombard** was introduced by founding universities which taught philosophy and reason to enhance the truths of faith. The First Council of the Lateran (1123) ratified agreements for the pope alone to appoint bishops as spiritual leaders, and the emperor had the right to direct secular offices. At this time, many new Gothic churches were being built to enhance worship and prayer.

The Second Council of the Lateran (1139) defined and declared the celibacy of Catholic priests. In 1164, Russia accepted Catholic missionaries, however, they favored the Russian Orthodox Church. Roman Catholics in Russia make up less than 0.5% even through to modern times. The Third Council of the Lateran (1179) established the new 2/3rd majority requirement to elect a pope. This remained in effect until Pope Benedict

XVI (2005–2013) reverted back to the old 2/3rd majority system. The Ayyubid forces captured Jerusalem in 1187 (3rd Crusade).

1243–1254: Pope #180 **Innocent IV** called <u>The First Council of Lyons</u> in 1245. The pope was threatened by Holy Roman Emperor **Fredrick II,** who was excommunicated.

1248–1254: The First Crusade of King **St. Louis IX**. His troops were surrounded and were forced to surrender, **St. Louis IX** was in captivity for ransom by the Muslims, he was released after paying the ransom.

1269–1272: The Second Crusade of King **St. Louis IX**. Fifteen years later **St. Louis IX** attempted another crusade that was ill–fated by a disease that broke out in camp and he died. **St. Louis IX** was labeled the "perfect crusader" because he crusaded for pure motives; love of Christ, the Church, and the Holy Land.

The Inquisition:
The background of the "Inquisition" was the spread of the Albigensian heretics who were essentially Gnostics. They held that a god of light created all good things which are spiritual, and the god of darkness created all evil things which are material, like a person's body. They rejected the Incarnation, the Eucharist, and marriage.

1227–1241: Pope #178 **Gregory IX**. The heretics were doing a lot of harm to the Church due to their non–biblical beliefs. In 1231 the pope established the Inquisition to restore peace and unity to the faith. There are many myths about the Inquisition so here are the facts: (1) Usually conducted by the Dominican order, they traveled to a town or area and conducted sermons about the truth of the Catholic faith. (2) They then encouraged people to volunteer if they believed in this heresy. (3) The Dominicans then provided confession, pennants, and guidance to those volunteers that leaned toward this heresy. (4) An Inquisition was held to identify those that did not volunteer. Detailed records were kept of each Inquisition. (5) The accused were interviewed; witnesses were called and the accused was given many chances to repent. The detailed records of the guilty were turned over to secular courts.

The secular court did have the option of using torture only for the purpose to obtain information, not punishment. Heresy was considered a secular crime. Therefore, it was the state, not the Church, that condemned the guilty to punishment or in some cases to death.

1274: The <u>Second council of Lyons</u> established a temporary union of the East and West, established regulations for papacy; conclaves.

The Papacy in Rome: (Secular Influence).
1292: the 191st **Pope Nicholas IV** died (1288–1291).
No successor was elected for two years.
1293: **King Charles II** (Naples) and **St. Louis IX** went to Rome to urge the cardinals to end their bickering, with no success.
1294: **King Charles II** met with **Peter Morrone. Peter Morrone** wrote a letter to **Cardinal bishop of Ostia** encouraging the cardinals to elect a pope.
Cardinal bishop of Ostia read **Peter's** letter to all the cardinals at the conclave and then nominated **Peter Morrone** for pope, and he was elected.
1294: **Peter** became the 192nd Pope **Celestine V**. Being a man in his eighties, he discovered that he could not handle the temporal skills and after five months resigned.
1294: Pope **Boniface VIII** became the 193rd pope (1294–1303). **Boniface** could not get along with **King Philip IV** (the Fair, France) or **King Edward I** (the Longshanks, England). The main conflict was that the church was being taxed and they were using that money to finance their wars (considered an unjust tax).
1296_**King Philip IV** arrested Pope **Boniface VIII** and accuse him of insurrection. Pope **Boniface** threatened to excommunicate **King Phillip IV.**
Pope Boniface VIII stated: There are two powers, spiritual and temporal – the spiritual can judge the temporal, only God can judge the spiritual (pope).
King Philip IV captured Pope **Boniface** and was physically assaulted, a month later (1303) the pope died.
The End of an Era.

AD 1200 to AD 1300 recap: The 176th pope, **Innocent III** (1198–1216), as well as other popes attempted to gain full authority of both spiritual and government control of the Church. Also, they continued the crusades and established the Inquisition (1229) to root out heresy outside the Church during this Middle Age time period. To enhance the renewal and attempt to solve the heresy and secular rule problems, three important reform councils were called: the <u>Fourth Council of the Lateran</u> (1215) mandated that Christians are to attend mass, go to confession, and receive the Eucharist once a year. In the <u>First Council of Lyons</u> in (1245), and the <u>Second Council of Lyons</u> in (1274), the cardinals established the conclave (meaning locked in with a key). The cardinals took 2 years (1241–1243) to select the 180th pope, **Innocent IV** (1243–1254).

However, the best renewal of the Catholic Church for this time frame came through the rise of Mendicant orders that focused on living in the poverty and humility of Christ. They were founded by **St. Francis of Assisi** (1182–1226), **St. Clare** (1193–1253), and **St. Dominic** (D.1221). These new orders were the source of such great theologians as the Franciscan, **St. Bonaventure** (1221–1274) and Dominicans, **St. Albert the Great** (1206–1288) and **St. Thomas Aquinas** (1226–1274). The first official papal election held by the Catholic Church was in the year 1276 for the 187th pope, **John XXI** (1276–1277), however, the in–house Church selection of popes did not last.

1305–1314: Pope #195 **Clement V** (a Frenchman).
King Philip IV imposed three demands on Pope **Clement V**: (1) Put Pope **Boniface VIII** (now dead) on trial, (2) Condemn the Templar order, (3) move the papacy from Rome to Avignon, France. Pope **Clement V** yielded to all three demands. He attempted to have a trial, and he broke up the power of the Templars.

Papacy Moved to France:
1309: Pope **Clement V** moved the papacy to Avignon, France, (for about 68 years).

1311–1312: The <u>Council of Vienne</u> suppressed the Knights.

1316–1334: Pope #196 **John XXII** in France, 1334–1342 Pope #197 **Benedict XII** in France, 1342–1352 Pope #198 **Clement VI** in France.

1347–1351: The Bubonic Plague arrived from China, its estimated that 23.8 million people died.

1352–1362: Pope #199 **Innocent VI** in France, 1362–1370 Pope #200 **Urban V** in France.

1370: Pope **Gregory XI** became the 201st pope (the 7th pope in France).

Catherine of Siena wrote several letters to various popes encouraging them to move back to Rome.

1377: Pope **Gregory XI** was influenced by **Catherine's** letters.

Papacy Moved Back to Rome:

1377: January 17th Pope **Gregory XI** moved the papacy back to Rome.

1377: **John Wyclif** was excommunicated and dismissed from Oxford University, England, for his preaching that rejected the sacraments, denied the church's authority to teach in universities, denied pope's authority, and declared scripture the only source of God's revelation.

1378: Pope **Gregory XI** died.

The Start of the Great Western Schism:

1378: Pope #202 **Urban VI** (born 1318, Naples, Italy). This is the start of the Great Western Schism. **Pope Urban VI**, even though in Rome, was elected by mostly French cardinals. Afterwards, the French cardinals claimed they were influenced by a Roman mob that surrounded the conclave demanding a Roman pope. The French cardinals escaped the mob and returned to France where they then elected their own pope **Clement VII** (antipope). The French cardinals tried to end the schism they created by attempting to dispose of the legitimate Pope **Urban VI** and antipope **Clement VII,** replacing them with another antipope **Alexander V.** Basically, causing two men (antipopes) to claim being pope with only one legitimate pope, **Urban VI.**

Pope Urban VI replaced all the cardinals, he died in 1389 after 11 years in office.

1389–1404: Pope #203 **Boniface IX**, 1404–1406 Pope #204 **Innocent VII**.

1406–1415: Pope #205 **Gregory XII**.

1414–1418: The <u>Council of Constance</u> (1414–1418) was called by **Sigismund** the King of Germany and confirmed by the legitimate Pope **Gregory XII**. The council lasted 5 years and had 45 sessions and was the longest council to date. The council consisted of 29 cardinals, 100 doctors of law/divinity, 134 abbots and 183 bishops/archbishops and represented England, France, and Germany with Poles, Hungarians, Danes and Scandinavians. The council disposed of antipope **Clement VII** and antipope **Alexander V**, as well as condemning **Jan (John) Haus (Hauss)** as a heretic. **Jan Haus'** writings were very influential on **Martin Luther**. 1415: Pope **Gregory XII**, after 9 years in office, in a very humble act, he resigned to assure the end of the schism and so a new pope could be elected. End of the Great Western Schism.

Pre–Reformation:

1415: Jan Hus, a priest, was excommunicated then turned over to civil authorities and executed for being a heretic. He followed **John Wyclef's** teachings of: rejection of the sacraments, denial of church's authority to teach in universities, denied pope's authority, and declared scripture the only source of God's revelation.

1417–1431: Pope #206 **Martin V** was elected by the cardinals.

1429: Joan of Arc, as a teenager, lead the French troops to victory against the English.

1431: Joan of Arc was burned at the steak. Twenty years after her death, **Charles VII** ordered an inquiry into **Joan's** charges and her charges were overturned. She was declared a saint in 1920.

1431–1445: The <u>Council of Florence</u> reaffirmed papal primacy, temporarily established union of East and West.

1434–1447: Pope #207 **Eugene IV**, 1447–1455 Pope #208 **Nicholas V.**

1453: Constantinople falls in battle to the Ottoman army, which is the end of the Byzantine Empire effectively the end of the Roman Empire.

1454: Gutenberg invented the first wood/movable metal type printing press that generated the first printing of the Bible.

1455–1458: Pope #209 **Callistus III.**

1448: Queen Isabel and **Ferdinand II** establish the Spanish Inquisition.

1458–1464: Pope #210 **Pius II**, 1461–1471 Pope #211 **Pius II,**

1471–1484: Pope #212 **Sixtus IV**, 1484–1492 Pope #213 **Innocent VIII.**

1492: Spanish **Queen Isabel** commissions Christopher Columbus.

1492–1503: Pope #214 **Alexander VI** the first conclave election in the Sistine Chapel.

1503–1503: Pope # 215 **Pius III.**

1503–1513: Pope #216 **Julius II** called the "warrior pope," was one of the most powerful and influential popes, He raised an army campaign to protect the papal states, established the Swiss Guard in Rome, and started construction of St. Peters Basilica.

1508–1512: **Michelangelo** painted the Sistine Chapel under Pope **Julius II.**

1512–1517: The Fifth Council of the Lateran (1512–1517) was attended by 100 bishops with little accomplished except for addressing Church discipline and requiring permission to print books.

1513–1521: Pope #217 **Leo X.**

A.D. 1300 to A.D. 1513 recap: The 195th pope, **Clement V** (1305–1314), dissolved the Knights Templar (1308) and opened the Council of Vienne (1311–1312) with 4 topics: the Order of Knights Templar (which became an obstacle to the bishops), the Holy Land controlled by Muslims, reforming public morality, and freedom for the Church. The late Middle Ages was a difficult period for the Roman Catholic Church. **Pope Clement V** was a pawn under **King Phillip IV**, and he moved the headquarters of the church to Avignon, France. Successive popes lived in Avignon, France from 1305 to 1357, and due to the political situation, they were under French control. It has been recorded that the popes that lived in France expressed their concern of being away from the tomb of **St. Peter** in Rome. In approximately 1347, the plague wiped out almost 90% of the population, adding to the political situation. Much worse is that between 1378 and 1417, two, then later three men, claimed to be the legitimate pope, which severely damaged the image of the papacy. After the 201st pope, **Gregory XI**, died in 1378, the 202nd pope, **Urban VI** (1378–1389), moved back to Rome. About one half of the cardinals refused to move to Rome, and then they selected their own pope, causing the multiple pope situation. The 205th pope, **Gregory XII** (1406–1415), resigned from office to allow proper selection of a successor.

An Englishman, **John Wycliff**, and **John Hus**, a Czech, were challenging the Church's authority to teach. Even though these problems were going on, there was a spiritual awakening. Classic spiritual publications were abounding, such as **Thomas a Kempis',** "The Imitation of Christ." The vision of **St. Joan of Arc** (1412–1431, burned at the stake) brought victory to France, and in the East, there was a new spiritual life in the Church.

The Council of Constance (1414–1418), with 45 sessions, was the longest council to date.

The Councils of Basel, Ferrara and Florence (1431–1442) started in Basel, Germany (did not close), then moved to Ferrara and Florence, Italy, and finally ended up in Rome in 1442. In 1443, construction of the Sistine Chapel (originally called Cappella Magna) started and was completed in 1488. The first conclave in the chapel was for the 214th pope, **Alexander VI** (1492–1503).

The second voyage to America by **Christopher Columbus** in 1492 carried some Spanish Catholic missionaries that were some of the first recorded in the U.S.A. The 215th pope, **Pius III** (1503), was in office less than a year. Under the direction of the 216th pope, **Julius II** (1503–1513), **Michelangelo** painted the Sistine Chapel ceiling (1508 to 1512). **Michelangelo** died in 1564 at the age of 88.

The first wood (with metal type) printing press by **Johannes Gutenberg** printed the first Bible in 1454 or 1455. On the negative side, the Church was suffering from severe financial difficulties. To gain revenues for the Church, the popes started selling high offices to the wealthy or secular rulers who had very little concern for the spiritually of God's people. Also, the clergy were often uneducated and unfaithful to their vow of celibacy.

The 216th pope, **Julius II** (1503–1513), called the Fifth Council of the Lateran in 1512 to attempt Church reform, but many of the decrees were not implemented. The selling of offices resulted in the return of secular, non-in-house selected, rulers who often became bishops and popes that did not bother to implement the decrees for Church reform. This action, of course, caused the Church to lose control of in-house selections of popes since 1276.

Protestant Reformation:
Some theologians classify the Reformation (a change for the better) was maybe more like a revolution (a radical break, destruction, or replacement) because it dealt with: political, economic, social, and religious ideas.

1517: **Martin Luther** posted his ninety–five Theses on Wittenberg's Castle Church, Germany. His intention was to reform the church due to secular appointed church leaders (bishops, cardinals and even popes) where some of them were accused of selling indulgences.

1520: **Martin Luther** published three additional writings where he attacked the Church, professing: destruction of the hierarchical structure of the Church, for individual interpretation of Scripture, for the elimination of the mass and holy days, eliminate pilgrimages, elimination of clerical celibacy, eliminate the sacraments except for Baptism and the Eucharist, and for the establishment of a national German Church separate from Rome. With the new printing press, his words spread quickly through Germany and Europe.

1524–1525: German Revolt: **Martin Luther's** revolutionary writings produce a wave of violence throughout Germany leading nobility to use force of arms where more than 130,000 German peasants were slaughtered.

1523–1534: Pope #219 **Clement VII** became politically involved that led to France and the Holy Roman Empire at war over Milan. The Imperial Army (1527), mostly Lutheran Germans, sacked the Eternal City forcing **Clement VII** to take refuge, where he finally surrendered. This came at a difficult time, not allowing the pope the time to deal with the **Luther** situation.

1531: December 12th the blessed Mother of God appeared to **St. Juan Diego** in Mexico, she asked him to go to the bishop and request a shrine be built in her name. The miracle of the roses and the image of Mary on his clothing convinced the bishop. This resulted in over a 4–year period (1532–1536) for 1.3 million people to be baptized.

1533: The first Protestant Archbishop **Cranmer** of Canterbury England abolished the Catholic Mass. The Catholic Mass, which is in accordance with scripture, had been in practice for over 1500 years. **Cranmer** and **John Calvin** developed their own liturgy in substitution for the Mass.

1534: **Martin Luther** translated the New Testament to the German language and one of the key changes he made was to add the word "**only**" so his translated bible stated: "by faith **only**," to support his thinking.

1534: **King Henry VIII** pressured Pope #219 **Clement VII** for an annulment from **Catherine Aragon** that was refused, leading **Henry VIII** to separate from Rome.

1534–1549: Pope #220 **Paul III.**

1535: **St. John Fischer** bishop of Rochester, England was put into prison by **King Henry VIII** for not supporting his annulment request. Pope #220 **Paul III** made **Fisher** a cardinal thinking that would protect him, which it did not, he was beheaded. **St. Thomas More**, Lord High Chancellor of England apposed **Martin Luther/John Calvin**, and did not support any separation from Rome, he was convicted of treason and beheaded.

1536: **John Calvin** published his very influential Protestant writings, "Institutes of the Christian Religion" that was widely circulated containing his heretical beliefs. **Calvin** moved to Geneva and established a "government" where the civil, church, and government were all one. **Calvin** outlawed: dancing, singing, jewelry, makeup, theatrical plays, and children were to be named after biblical figures. He established that capital crimes were: adultery, pregnancy out of wedlock, blasphemy, heresy, idolatry, and striking a parent. All Christians were required to confess their sins to a magistrate in a court of law. **Calvin** wrote many letters throughout Europe encouraging people to rebel against the Catholic Church.

1542–1546: as a result of **Calvin's** "government" there were 58 executions, 23 exiles, and 900 imprisonments.

1545: **Martin Luther's** last writings were very critical of the pope and **Luther** stated his disappointment for not converting the Jews to become Lutheran so he denounced the Jews and urged their persecution. Germany was mostly Lutheran and the Lutheran leaders followed **Luther's** thinking and wanted all Jewish businesses and places of worship closed as well as the Jews removed from Germany. In later years, this idea was picked up by **Adolph Hitler** and put into effect. **Luther** died in 1546.

1545–1549, 1551–1552, 1562–1563: The Council of Trent had 25 sessions over 18 years lasting through 5 popes. Session 1 thru 10 under Pope #220 **Paul III** established: The Nicene Creed, Vulgate (Latin version of the Bible), Defined the nature of original sin and justification, began doctrinal review of the sacraments, and defined baptism and confirmation. The council abolished abuses and reaffirmed Catholic doctrine.

1547: **Henry VIII** died making 6-year-old **Edward VI** the king who in 1558 died of consumption and appoints **Lady Jane Grey** his successor, then in office for only nine days the crown is given to **Mary Tudor** (1553 to 1558) who attempted to restore the Catholic faith to England.

1558–1603: **Queen Elizabeth** (b.1533–d.1603) was motivated to eradicate the Catholic Church from England, which she accomplished by declaring those of Catholic Faith a treasonous act punishable by death. Catholics are persecuted in great numbers by the state.

1546: The Catholic–Protestant conflict (war) in Germany lasted 9 years 1546 to 1555.

1551–1552: The Council of Trent sessions 11 thru 16 under Pope #221 **Julius III** established: A definition of the Eucharist (doctrine of the real presence), penance, extreme unction (anointing of the sick).

1552: the German Protestant Prince, lead a revolt against The Hoy Roman Emperor, **Charles V** that caused a suspension of The Council of Trent.

1555: The "Peace of Augsburg" agreement was established, ending 9 years of Catholic–Protestant conflicts. The terms were most favorable to the

Lutherans. Lutheran territories were given legal recognition equal with Catholic states. Lutherans were allowed to keep any property seized from the Catholics. If the ruler of a state was Lutheran, then all the realm was Lutheran, the same was granted to Catholic sates. If any person apposed the faith of the state, they were allowed to sell everything and leave the state. Most people were not happy with the terms, after which 63 years later, lead to a 30–year war (1618 to 1648).

1562–1563: The Council of Trent sessions 17 thru 25 under **Pope #223 Paul IV** defined: Additional teachings on the Eucharist, the holy orders, matrimony, purgatory, veneration of saints, relics, sacred art, and indulgences. Called for: revision and publication of a Roman Missal, divine office, authored universal catechism, creation of seminaries, and priests to reside within parishes.

As a result of **Martin Luther** and **John Calvin's** profession of individual interpretation of Scripture, it led to many religious divisions.

1590: the Presbyterian Church was founded by **John Knox** in Scotland.

1583: the Congregationalist Church was founded by **Robert Brown** in Holland.

The problem with individual interpretation of Scripture is that most people do not have a complete full knowledge of the Old as well as the New Testaments in order to make a proper interpretation. One may interpret a passage "out of context," where the Church interpretants according to the entire Bible, which in some cases have taken several years to complete. Also, the individual interpretation has led to many religious divisions, today there are more than 33,000 religious divisions.

Reformation of the Catholic Church:
The Council of Trent (1545–1563) established the foundation for the Reformation of The Catholic Church with its many decrees, however, there was the need to implement these reforms. A prominent pope and several holy men and women arose to do just that.

1566–1572: Pope #225 **Pius V** restored discipline, morality, standardized the Holy Mass with his introduction of a Roman Missal (1570), and introduced a Universal Catechism.

St. Teresa of Avila (b.1515–d.1582), a mystic, along with **St. John of the Cross** (1542–1591) wrote many classics still used today and they both reformed the Carmelite order that greatly contributed to the Catholic Reformation.

1564–1584: **St. Charles Borromeo** Archbishop of Milan was instrumental in executing the decrees of the Council of Trent, including the Roman Catechism (1566). **St. Charles** was the leading person along with a Spanish Catholic priest **St. Ignatius of Loyola** (1491–1556) and an Italian Priest **St. Philip Neri** (1515–1595) in combating the Protestant Reformation through missions and implementing the decrees of the council.

1565: The Ottoman Empire (Muslims) overtake the Island of Malta and use the Christians as slaves. The Muslims prepare to attack Rome.

1566–1572: Pope #228 **Pius V** formed the Holy League and put **Don Juan** of Austria in charge.

1571: **Don Juan** by direction of the pope, assembled a Christian fleet, even though outnumbered, defeated the Muslims from their attack on Rome. The "Battle of Lepanto", a sea battle, was the last historical water battle using rowing vessels.

1590: Pope #228 **Urban VII** had a conflict with **Galileo** (b.1564–d.1642) Italian astronomer, mathematician, and professor of physics at the Catholic University of Pisa. **Galileo** was teaching the theory as a fact that the earth rotated around the sun which was not proven at that time. He was told to teach it as a theory only, which he did not do, that led to his chastisement.

1620: The Mayflower departed from England with 102 people abord. 40 of the passengers were Protestant–Pilgrims that called themselves saints. The Mayflower was 100 feet long by 25 feet wide and it took 66 days to make the voyage to America.

AD 1513 to AD 1650 recap: The <u>Fifth Council of the Lateran</u> (1512–1517) issued dogmas to combat heresies at the time and decreed that the souls of humans live forever. The secular rulers of the Church started selling indulgences to boost the financial situation. In the year 1517, Martin Luther, an Augustinian monk and professor of Scripture in Wittenberg, Germany, posted his Ninety–Five Theses on Indulgences. Initially, **Luther** had no intention of leaving the Catholic Church. He only wanted the reforms to be put into practice. However, the German nobility and people responded by forming the "Lutheran" Church. The followers of **Luther** retained many Catholic traditions, but later reforming groups, such as those led by **Jean Calvin** in Geneva, Switzerland, and **Huldreich Zwingli** in Zurich, rejected many of the Catholic traditions. This was called "The Protestant Reformation." In many European states, the Protestants forcibly took over some Catholic churches, removing the priests to occupy the church. Some churches were later returned to the Catholic Church.

In the early 1500s, Jesuit missionary, **Francis Xavier** (1506–1552), introduced Catholicism to Japan. It flourished until 1597 when **Shogun Hideyoshi** instituted severe persecution on Catholics, after which very few Catholics survived.

The Roman Catholic Church in Mexico dates from the period of the Spanish conquest of 1519 to 1521 and remains the largest religious group in Mexico. In 1521, the Philippines became the first Southeast–Asia Catholic nation. Our Lady of Guadalupe appeared in Mexico to **Juan Diego** (1531). The 219th pope, **Clement VII** (1523–1534), excommunicated England's King **Henry VIII** for his persistent pressure for an annulment from **Catherine of Aragon** to marry **Anne Boleyn**. England's break from Rome occurred in 1534 when Parliament passed the "Act of Supremacy." **Henry VIII** declared himself "Supreme Head on Earth of the Church of England." Starting in 1536, over 825 Catholic monasteries in England, Wales, and Ireland were dissolved, and Catholic churches were confiscated. The Irish Catholics prevented some church eliminations.

The first edition of the Tyndale Bible (1526) was a translation from Greek and Hebrew into the English language. Catholic scholars led by **Erasmus of**

Rotterdam appealed for reform. As a result, the Catholic Reformation became the Society of Jesus (Jesuits) founded by Spaniard, **St. Ignatius of Loyola** (1491–1556). Also, other new Catholic orders of men and women emerged and old orders were reformed. The 220th pope, **Paul III** (1534–1549), called the Council of Trent (1545–1565), which continued under the 221st pope, **Julius III** (1550–1555), as well as the 224th pope **Pius IV** (1559–1565). This council made some very significant changes. It defined Catholic doctrine, tightened discipline, established the seminary system to provide holy educated priests, reformed the popes and bishops, and reaffirmed the Bible canon of A.D. 382.

As a result of this reform, many great saints emerged: Jesuit missionaries **St. Francis Xavier** (Far East); **St. Jean de Brebeuf** and **Isaac Jogues** (North America, both were martyred by the Iroquois Indians 1642 & 1648); Spanish mystics **St. Teresa of Avila** and **St. John of the Cross** (both of the Carmelite Order); Jesuit theologians **St. Peter Canisius** and **St. Robert Bellarmine**; bishops **St. Charles Borromeo** and **St. Francis de Sales**; religious foundress **St. Jeanne de Chantal**; and **St. Vincent de Paul**. By the grace of God, the Catholic Church returned to strength and virtue with discipline, devotion, and a clear doctrine.

In 1604, the Church of England authorized the translation of the Christian Bible that was completed in 1611. It was known as the King James Version, and certain passages on divorce and Mary (mother of Jesus) were minimized (the 20th century revisions corrected these errors). In 1565, St. Augustine, Florida, established the oldest continuous Catholic parish in the United States.

Modernism:
A new kind of heresy developed that was an attack on the fundamentals of faith: it rejected the existence of the supernatural, and rejected a God centered society in favor of a man centered society. Modernism originated in Europe and it swept to the United States and impacted literature, art, music, science and The Church.

King Louis XIV of France, reigned 1774 to 1792, embraced civil authority over the Catholic Church as well as embracing modernism. Modernism along with the quest for liberty and a democratic government led to the French Revolution 1789–1799. Wide persecution occurred of the Catholic bishops, priests, and lay people for not swearing an oath to the government. Over 20,000 citizens were beheaded.

1799: **General Napoleon** overthrew the government that ended the French Revolution.

1846–1878: Pope #255 **Pius IX** called the First Vatican Council (1868–1870) that defined the popes roll on infallibility to be successor of Peter, to be on faith and morals, to be for all faithful, and to be definitive. Also, Catholics allowed to receive the Eucharist once a day, and declared the doctrine on the Immaculate Conception of Mary.

1905: The Church and the State separated.

AD 1650 to AD 1800 recap: This era of the Catholic Church is at times referred to as the "modern era" when the emergence of science, technology, and philosophy based on reason, strongly influenced the Church. Religion was thought to divide mankind, whereas reason was thought to bring unity. The Catholic Church's condemnation of **Galileo** for his teaching as facts things that had not been proven yet, led to the appearance that the Church was against modern science. However, the Church was not against science, and in many ways, the Catholic Faith gave rise to science. In the time frame of 1650 to 1800, France contributed to the crisis of the Church. Absolutist ruler, **King Louis XIV**, called for a decreased influence of the Church in public affairs, and even for a national church free from Rome's control. **King Louis XIV** threatened the 240th pope, **Innocent XI** (1676–1689) with military take–over. The strongest opponents to such movements were the controversial Jesuits. Due to pressure from secular rulers, the popes were pressured to suppress the Society of Jesus (Jesuits). This 1773 suppression first occurred in France then worldwide (except Russia). In the 1700s, the Catholic Church had to work with the Spanish Crown and their military to put missions in what is now the Western United States. About 1781, routes were established from Mexico City for missions in Texas and New Mexico. In 1820, Mexico shut down the missions and sold the lands. Baltimore, Maryland was the first Catholic Archdiocese in America, established in 1789, under Bishop **John Carrol**. Georgetown University, founded as Georgetown College in 1789, became the first Catholic university in the United States. The French Revolution (1789) severely weakened the Church when France went so far as to abolish Christianity altogether and set up a religion of reason.

The 250th Pope **Pius VI** (1775–1799), was against the revolution. Consequently, **Napoleon Bonaparte** put the 82–year–old pope in a French prison, where he died soon after. The Western civilization was shocked by France's reaction. During this same period, the movement for representative types of government which incorporated freedom of speech, press, conscience, and religion steadily grew. This new movement led intellectuals to apply this freedom to the Bible. The Catholic Church generally was against this, fearing the erosion of the Bible. In the late 1800s, Catholic missionaries were in Africa building schools, hospitals, monasteries, and churches. In 1802, the Catholic Church was re-established in France.

AD 1800 to AD 1900: During the reign of the 254th pope, **Gregory XVI** (1831–1846), the Jesuits were in South America protecting the native people from enslavement. The Sisters of Mercy, founded by Catherine McAuley (Ireland 1831) and her nuns, established hospitals and schools across the world. The Little Sisters of the Poor was founded by **Saint Jeanne Juan** in France to care for the impoverished elderly. The 255th pope, **Pius IX** (1846–1878), in 1846, granted the unanimous wish of the United States bishops to name the Immaculata as the patron of the United States. Pope **Pius IX** called the First Vatican Council (1868–1870) where they affirmed the primacy of faith over reason and defined the teaching infallibility of the pope in certain clearly defined instances.

In 1854, people were allowed to receive Holy Communion once a day. In 1870, the doctrine of the Immaculate Conception of Mary was established. Also, in 1870, Rome was forcefully taken over by the Italian Army, and Pope **Pius IX** became a prisoner in the Vatican. The Pope's civil authority was taken away which in turn greatly enhanced the pope's spiritual authority.

The 256th pope, **Leo XIII** (1878–1903), continued the strong spiritual leadership of the Church and enhanced the dialog with the modern world.

Pope **Leo XIII** published his encyclical which set the terms for Catholic social teaching, rejected socialism, and advocated the regulation of working conditions. In 1879, numerous civil laws were passed to weaken the Catholic Church. One such example was that priests were excluded from administrative positions in hospitals (even from hospitals that the Catholic Church started). Then in 1890, lay women were substituted for many nuns in hospitals.

In 1882, for a brief period of time, privately funded Catholic schools were tolerated, then the laws were changed to set up a national system of public schools that taught strict morality but no specific religion. In the late 1800s, **Saint Marianne Cope** (1838–1918) of the sisters of St. Francis of Syracuse, NY, opened and operated some of the first general hospitals in the United States, instituting cleanliness standards which influenced the development of America's modern hospital system.

Also, in the United States, **Saint Katharine Drexel** (Philadelphia, PA 1858–1955) and the sisters of the Blessed Sacrament founded Xavier University of Louisiana to provide education to African and Native Americans.

World War I 1914 to 1918:
1914–1922: Pope #258 **Benedict XV**. The pope called for peace and to stop bombing civilians.
1914, July 28 was the start of World War I primarily due to the assassination of **Archduke Franz Ferdinand** of the Austro–Hungry Empire. War was originally declared against Serbia for the assassination, however, due to international agreements, Russia became involved leading to Germany and France then Belgium which then involved England. The war ended November 11, 1918.

Bolshevik Revolution:
1917: the Bolshevik Revolution led to the Communist (socialist) party ruling Russia. In the 3rd of October, 1917 the Blessed Virgin Mary appeared

in Fatima, Portugal where 70,000 people witnessed the miracle dancing of the sun. Holy Virgin Mary, appearing at Fatima, predicted the end of World War I as well as the coming World War II during the reign of Pope **Pius XII.**

Mexico Turns Socialist:
In 1917 **Lenin** and **Stalin,** inspired anti–religious socialists, took over the Mexican government that closed Catholic Churches, schools, hospitals, orphanages, and confiscated Catholic Church property. In 1927 the Jesuit Priest Blessed **Miguel Pro** was executed by firing squad for his faith and about 300,000 people were executed by the socialist Mexican government under the regime of **Calles.**

World War II 1939 to 1945:
The people of Germany endorsed **Adolf Hitler** of the National Socialist Workers Party on the promise of a better economy and to restore German pride. 1939–1958 Pope #260 **Pius XII** led the efforts in speaking out against anti–Semitism that **Hitler** was professing in Germany. In 1939 **Hitler's** forces invaded Poland, starting World War II. Pope **Pius XII** was instrumental in hiding and saving over 860,000 Jews. The extermination of the Catholic Church was another of **Hitler's** goals. In addition to the Jews, over three million Catholics died in Auschwitz alone. World War II ended in 1945 after the United States dropped atomic bombs on Japan, one of which was above St. Mary Catholic Church in Nagasaki, Japan.

Modern Times:
1958–1963: Pope #261 **John XXIII** called the <u>Second Vatican Council</u> (1962–1965) which was the first council called not to address a heresy or an attack on the Church but to address the roll of the Church in a rapid changing modern world. The main points of the council were: The reform and promotion of the Liturgy, Emphasis on the importance of the Eucharist, proper liturgical worship and sacraments, renewal of the Roman Missal, greater acceptance of the use of the vernacular, universal mission and call to holiness, Scripture divinely inspired, the roll of the Magisterium, the situation of modern humankind, special problems including marriage, family, culture, economic and social life.

1962 the US Supreme Court outlawed the Bible in public schools.

1963–1978 Pope #262 **Paul VI** continued the <u>Second Vatican Council</u>, which he closed in 1965. He fostered improved relations with the Eastern Orthodox and Protestant churches.

1900 to 1958: Advances were continuing in science and technology; however, mankind was not growing in wisdom and morality. More people were killed in warfare in this century than ever before. Ideologies competed for people's allegiance and divided the world. Fascism and Nazism were against democracies, communism was against capitalism, and poor nations were against rich nations. Communism suppressed the faith in much of the East. From 1902 to 1905, ministries outside the Catholic Church fought with the Vatican over the appointment of bishops. The French Prime Minister was determined to defeat Catholicism. He closed down all Catholic schools, removed Catholic chaplains from naval and military hospitals (1904–1905), and soldiers were ordered not to frequent Catholic clubs.

In 1905, the Church and the State finally separated. The 257th pope, **St. Pius X** (1903–1914), worked vigorously to strengthen Catholic worship and teaching to protect the Church against modern errors. He called for the codification (arranging laws/rules into a system or plan) of the canon law which was completed in 1917. He also condemned the use of modern historical and biblical scholarship that led to a denial of certain truths of faith, which probably saved the Catholic Church from the division that split Protestantism into two camps: liberal and fundamentalist. The 258th pope, **Benedict XV** (1914–1922) spent most of his time trying to maintain neutrality of the Church prior to and during World War I (July 28, 1914 to Nov. 11, 1918).

In 1917, the Communist Party started ruling Russia, the same year as the appearance of Mary in Fatima, Portugal, in which Mary called all Christians to repent and pray for the conversion of Russia. The 259th pope, **Pius XI** (1922–1939), strongly condemned communism and had to contend with the growing threat of **Mussolini** in Italy and **Adolph Hitler** in Germany. The pope signed agreements with Mussolini, Hitler, and other nations to preserve the freedom of Catholics. He continued to condemn Fascism and Nazism. Pope **Pius XI** established the "Feast of Christ the King" in 1925 to proclaim Christ's kingship over the world. The persecution of Mexico's Catholics started in 1926 and lasted until 1940.

In 1929, the Vatican signed the Lateran Treaties Agreement where Vatican City was given sovereignty as an independent nation. In return, the Vatican had to relinquish its claim to all former territories of the Papal States and remove religious instruction from public schools. Italy paid the Vatican for the seizure of church property. **Pius XI** then became head of a tiny state with its own territory, army, radio station, and diplomatic representation. It is not clear the exact date, but it appears that between 1929 and the mid–1900s, the Catholic Church finally regained in–house control of papal selection. The 260th pope, **Pius XII** (1939–1958), prior to and during World War II, worked behind the scenes to save the lives of hundreds of thousands of Jews. World War II started with Germany's invasion of Poland on Sept. 1, 1939, and Japan's attack on the U.S.A. on Dec. 7, 1941. It ended Sep. 2, 1945. In 1944, Germany violated its agreement with Pope **Pius XII** and invaded Rome. However, it was only occupied for a short period of time prior to the U.S.A. forces liberating Rome on June 4–5, 1944. It appears that Vatican City was not occupied. **Pius XII** began to open the Catholic Church to new methods of scholarship and Bible criticism with his encyclical of 1943, which also included new ways of looking at the Church. He called it the "Mystical Body of Christ," and it began to break down the image of the Catholic Church as an unchanging fortress opposed to the modern world. He increased the number of non–Italian cardinals to show the universality of the Church. In 1950, he defined the doctrine of Mary's bodily assumption into heaven.

1958 to 1978 recap: The 261st pope, **John XXIII** (1958–1963) called the Second Vatican Council (1962–1965) a "new Pentecost" which was a landmark event for the Church, defining itself and its relationship to the modern world. The purpose was to renew the Church and to bring it up to date while still maintaining its eternal truth and continuity with the past. Pope **John XXIII** was a seventy–six–year–old cardinal who attributed his calling of the council to the Holy Spirit. He did not allow the council to repeat old formulations of Catholic doctrine but insisted on a fresh restatement of Catholic tradition that would speak to the modern world. In 1963, Pope **John XXIII** died suddenly after the first session of his council.

In 1960, the 35th president of the United States, **John F. Kennedy**, became the first Catholic president. Prior to Kennedy, Catholics were not very socially accepted in America, and there were many Anti–Catholic organizations including the KKK. In fact, before **Kennedy's** presidency, all U.S.A. government policies were anti–Catholic, including a movement to restrict Catholic immigrants. **John F. Kennedy** was assassinated November 22, 1963.

On June 25, 1962, the U.S. Supreme Court decided in the **Engel** v. **Vitale** case that prayer and Bible readings were not allowed in public schools. The 262nd pope, **Paul VI** (1963–1978), took on the task of completing and guiding the work of the <u>Second Vatican Council</u> as well as implementing its results. He guided the work of the council and saw the importance of implementing it gradually. In spite of his efforts, the Catholic Church underwent a very unsettled period of time. Some Catholics interpreted the council in distorted ways, causing some priests and religious to abandoned their vocations. However, this did not outweigh the positive accomplishments of <u>Vatican II.</u> It is thought that the Church would have been in serious trouble if <u>Vatican II</u> had not opened the Church to the modern world.

During the 1960's, Pope **Paul VI** was challenged by the so–called sexual revolution. His 1968 encyclical reaffirmed the traditional view of marriage, reaffirmed the sanctity of life from conception to natural death, and condemned abortion and euthanasia. Pope **Paul VI** announced officially that the tomb of the 1st pope had been archeologically found and identified conclusively, including inscriptions of **St. Peter's** burial site. For more information see **John Evangelist Walsh's**, "The Bones of St. Peter." On January 22, 1972, the U.S. Supreme Court legalized abortion in the case of **Roe** v. **Wade**. The 263rd pope, **John Paul I** (1978), died only thirty–three days after his election.

1969: The 20th of July, US Apollo Module Eagle and astronauts landed on the moon.

1972: The 22nd of January, the US Supreme Court legalized abortion.

1978–2005: Pope #264 **St. John Paul II** was the first Polish pope and he had firsthand experience of the Nazi and communist regimes which lead him in peaceful protest of the communist. He also strongly supported the teachings of the <u>Second Vatican Council</u>, and had strong devotions to the Blessed Virgin Mary. The pope also wrote 14 encyclicals, 45 apostolic letters, and published 5 books.

1978 to 2005 recap: The 264th pope, **John Paul II** (1978–2005), was the first Polish pope and the first non–Italian pope since the 17th century. Pope John Paul II was totally dedicated to advancing the principles of Vatican II, while cautioning against possible abuses. His encyclicals stressed primacy of Christ, the mercy of God, the rights and dignity of workers, the dignity of the human person, and the defense of orthodox Catholic teaching as the key themes of his papacy.

He traveled worldwide more extensively than any previous pope, in spite of an assassination attempt (May 13, 1981) that nearly took his life. The Soviet Union dissolved on December 31, 1991, after which the persecuted Catholics re–emerged from hiding, especially in the Ukraine and Baltic states. **Mother St. Teresa** of Calcutta was born in Skopje, Macedonia, August 26, 1910. She was of Albanian–Indian descent, and was known for caring for the poor. She received over 120 awards, including the Nobel Peace Prize in 1997 and the highest U.S. Presidential Medal of Freedom in 1985. She died September 5, 1997 at the age of 87.

2005 to 2013: The 265th pope, **Benedict XVI,** was in office from 2005–2013. Generally, to this point in the Church's history, there was a continuation of the policies from pope to pope. However, Pope **Benedict XVI** decentralized beatifications and reverted the decision of his predecessors regarding papal elections, returning to the old 2/3rd majority that was in existence prior to the year 1179. Pope **Benedict XVI** also eased permission for the optional Latin Mass to be celebrated upon request of the faithful. In 2007, he set a church record by approving the beatification of the 498 Spanish Martyrs. His first encyclical discussed love and sex in opposition to several views on sexuality. Pope **Benedict XVI** resigned in 2013 at the age of 85 due to declining health. He was a humble, holy and courageous man who loved Christ and the Church.

2013: The 266th pope, **Francis** (2013–_____), was the first Jesuit pope, the first pope from the Americas, the first pope from the Southern Hemisphere, the first to take the name from Assisi, and the first pope outside of Europe since the 90th Pope **St. Gregory III** from Syria. Pope **Francis** started several dramatic changes in policy, such as removing conservatives from high Vatican positions, calling on bishops to lead a simpler life, and taking a more pastoral attitude toward homosexuality.

The preceding "Brief History of the Catholic Church" is continually marked by renewal brought about by the power of God's Holy Spirit. In addition to the many spiritual accomplishments, the Catholic Church established many benefits to society. For example, the Catholic Church established the first school system, the first university system, the first hospitals, and the first orphanages. It is important to note that during the periods of early corruption, the Church was under the control of politically (king) appointed (secular) popes. It is hard to believe, but it appears that the Catholic Church did not gain complete control of in–house papal selection until the mid–1900s. It is so impressive and comforting that our Catholic unity of belief and organization has not changed since early times. Also, our Catholic bishops can trace their lineage of office back through the Apostles to Jesus Christ. No other group, except Eastern Orthodox, can make this claim. The Catholic Church is not part of any denomination, it is "The Church." All religious denominations have branched from the Catholic Church. Even though there have been periods of struggle within the Church, Jesus' promise has been kept to always remain with the Church, which has been very evident. Matthew 28:20 [Jesus talking] *"...And behold, I am with you always, until the end of the age."*

The 16 documents approved by the Second Vatican Council:
Constitution on the Sacred Liturgy
Decree on the Instruments of Social Communication
Dogmatic Constitution on the Church
Decree on Ecumenism
Decree on Eastern Catholic Churches
Decree on the Bishops' Pastoral Office in the Church
Decree on Priestly Formation
Decree on the Appropriate Renewal of the Religious Life

Declaration on the Relationship of the Church to Non–Christian Religious

Declaration on Christian Education

Dogmatic Constitution on Divine Revelation

Decree on the Apostolate of the Laity

Declaration on Religious Freedom

Decree on the Ministry and Life of Priests

Decree on the Churches' Missionary Activity

Pastoral Constitution on the Church in the Modern World

> The 16-documents are from: "Quick Summaries of Vatican II's Documents" [the catholicspirit.com].

SUMMARY – CHURCH HISTORY:

+ 509 BC – 27BC – The Roman Republic
+ 27 BC–14AD – The Roman Republic to the Roman Empire
+ 4 BC – Birth of Jesus
+ 30 AD – Jesus' forty days in the Desert
+ 33 AD – Crucifixion of Jesus
+ 33 AD – Resurrection of Jesus
+ 33 AD – Appearance of Jesus
+ 33 AD – Commissioning of the Apostles and the Church
+ 33 AD – Ascension of Jesus
+ 33 AD – Pentecost
+ 33 AD – St. Peter became the first pope
+ 36 AD – First martyr, Stephen
+ 64 AD – Roman persecution of Christians
+ 115 AD – Martyred popes
+ 314 AD – End of roman persecution
+ 367 AD – St. Athanasius listed 27 books of the New Testament
+ 400 AD – Jerome's Vulgate–Latin Bible published
+ 553 AD – Start of Islam
+ 1049 – East/West Great Schism
+ 1088 – Era of the Crusades
+ 1227 – Inquisition
+ 1292 – Papacy in Rome

+ 1309 – Papacy moved to France
+ 1377 – Papacy moved back to Rome
+ 1375 – Start of the Great Western Schism
+ 1414 – Pre–Reformation
+ 1454 – First printed Bible by Gutenberg
+ 1517 – Protestant Reformation
+ 1545 – Reformation of the Catholic Church
+ 1774 – Modernism
+ 1905 – The Church and the state separated
+ 1917 – World War I
+ 1917 – Bolshevik revolution
+ 1917 – Mexico turns socialist
+ 1939 – World War II
+ 1958 – Modern times
+ 2013 – Pope Benedict resigned
+ 2013 – Pope Francis became the 266th pope

References:
The Brief History of the Catholic Church through to 2005: is referenced from Alan Schreck's book, "The Compact History of the Catholic Church," with some inserts from Wikipedia. Information after 2005: Wikipedia's, "History of the Catholic Church."

The dates of the Saints: "Lives of the Saints," Catholic Book Publishing Co. The dates of popes (in parenthesis) represent the years of their term in office, the (parentheses) dates after other names represent birth "b" and death "d" years, or other criteria as noted herein. All of the councils of the Catholic Church herein are <u>underlined</u> for emphasis added and for reference purposes.
EPIC–A Journey Through Church History" by Steve Weidenkopf, Ascension Press, Chester. PA.

THE BRIEF HISTORY OF THE CATHOLIC CHURCH: Assembled by Paul Wilchek 17–May–2018, edited by Kristin Trepanier–Henry, 2019, Up dated 10JAN21, added inserts from EPIC reference above.

SUMMARY – LET SCRIPRURE SPEAK FOR ITSELF:

+ ANGELS, the first of God's creation are the purely spiritual creatures created by God to be messengers, guardians, ministers, and worshipers of God. The countless number of angels are immortal and can appear and disappear, can be in the wind and fire, have emotions, appear in dreams, and do things to help people. Angels are obedient to God, assigned to stations, and minister to humans. Angels announced the birth of Jesus, ministered to and strengthened Jesus. Rolled back His grave stone, and clarified the ascension of Jesus. Angels are structured in hierarchical order of Counselors, Governors, and Messengers and Soldiers with assigned stations.

+ COVENANTS all through scripture were to establish a relationship between God and humans and gradually develop humankind to a better understanding of God showing that a violation of God's law can result in separation from God. The final New Covenant of Eternal Salvation established by Jesus provides a perpetual institution for humans to receive grace from God after confessing their sins.

+ EUCHARIST AND THE MASS are gradually developed all through scripture from the first prefigured mass by Melchizedek and then later the manna including the mysteries of the Tabernacle and then the miracles of Jesus' feeding thousands through the multiplication of the loves.

+ HOLY DAYS AND FEAST DAYS within the Catholic Church honor significant religious events through Holy Days of Obligation and Feast Days.

+ THE HOLY SPIRIT and Spirit are in scripture from Genesis through Revelation. God the father, God the Son, and God the Holy Spirit are uniquely unified as one Triune God. The Holy Spirit has many titles and symbol in Scripture. The Holy Spirit can drive out demons, baptize, give gifts, has given the Church leaders the power to forgive/retain sins, and the Holy Spirit resides within those who have accepted Jesus as the Temple of the Holy Spirit. At Mass it is the Holy Spirit that comes down like the due fall within the bread and wine that becomes the body and blood of Jesus.

+ THE HUMAN SPIRIT is the inter most part of humans that communicates with God and aids one in worship. Upon death the human spirit returns to God.

Paul Wilchek

+ THE SOUL gives life and is what makes each person unique, only humans have both spirit and soul. After death the soul goes to heaven (may be in Purgatory temporally), or to hell.

+ THE BODY created by God in His image and through baptism we are restored to communicating with God after the fall of Adam. After death the body returns to dust, however, at the final resurrection, the body and soul re–unite.

+ PROPHECIES, PARALLELS, SYMBOLISM, MIRACLES are all in Scripture and used by God to verify his love for humans.

+ PROPHETS are listed in Scripture by name and spoke to bring people back to God.

+ PURGATORY is a place of purification where the soul is purified through fire so that nothing unclean will enter heaven.

+ SCRIPTURE RESPONSE has many earthly questions that are responded to through the use of Scripture.

+ SELECTED SUBJECTS, herein, lists many important words and where in Scripture they can be found.

+ THE APOSTLES, DISCIPLES, CHURCH FATHERS is a list of the twelve Apostles and their contribution to Church history. This includes a partial list of the many disciples that helped to spread the Good News of Jesus Christ, including the many women disciples. The early Apostolic Fathers and Doctors of the Church continued to spread the apostolic truth and understanding of Jesus Christ.

+ THE BRIEF HISTORY OF THE CATHOLIC CHURCH provides some of the important facts on the 2000 years of development of the Catholic Church.

+ THE THEMES THROUGH SCRIPTURE provides the scripture readings that contain the theme of bread and the theme of redemption through scripture.

+ THE POPES from 33AD (1st pope) through to 2021, the 266th pope (2013), are listed along with the major civil leaders at that time and notes showing the major events that occurred during the reign of some popes.

References:

The **bold and italicized** Bible quotations are from The New American Bible (NAB), World press. Certain words may be <u>underlined</u> for emphasis added.

Footnotes from The Didache Bible with commentaries that are based on the Catechism of the Catholic Church, Ignatius Bible Edition.

## CHAPTER 14

THE POPES

This chart of the popes is arranged by the number "#" they reigned in office and the year they reigned. Also included is the name of some "Major civil leader(s)" and the "Dominate Power" of the state at that time. The "*" under the "Pope Name" column represents martyred popes. The "Martyr(s)" column lists the most known, readily available and is not a complete list of martyrs.

#	Pope Name	Year Reign of pope	Major civil leader(s) [Dominate Power]	Martyr(s)	Notes
			[Roman Empire]		
	Papal Martyrs of the Early Church *				The Roman Republic (509 BC to about 27 AD).
			Augustus		(27 BC – 14 AD) The Roman Empire. **Christs was born during this reign (4 AD).**
			Tiberius	•	(14–37)
			Caligula		(37–41)
			Claudius		(41–54)

#	Pope Name	Year Reign of pope	Major civil leader(s) [**Dominate Power**]	Martyr(s)	Notes
					NEW COVENANT & CHURCH. ROMAN PERSECUTION.
1	St. Peter* In Antioch prior to Rome.	33–67	Nero (54–68), Vespasian (69–79)	St. Peter & St. Paul	The Council of Jerusalem met in year 49, Gentiles not required to be circumcised. Year 64, Rome destroyed by fire. Nero put to death large numbers of Christians.
2	St. Linus	67–76	Otho		**Christian persecution. Year 70, Jerusalem Temple destroyed.**
3	St. Anacletus I*	76–88	Titus (79–81)		Empire wide Christian persecution.
4	St. Clement*	88–97	Domitian (81–96)		Empire wide Christian persecution.
5	St. Evaristus	97–105	Nerva		Continued Christian persecution. All 27 books of the New Testament written by year 100.
6	St. Alexander I*	105–115	Trajan (98–117)	St. Ignatius of Antioch	Only Christians who refuted Roman false gods were executed. St. Ignatius first used "Catholic Church" term in 107.
		107			"Catholic Church", first written record of its name.
7	St. Sixtus I*	115–125	Hadrian (117–138)		Continued Trajan's execution policy.
8	St. Telesphorus*	125–136	Hadrian		Hadrian executed Pope Telesphorus.

#	Pope Name	Year Reign of pope	Major civil leader(s) [**Dominate Power**]	Martyr(s)	Notes
9	St. Hyginus	136–140	Antonius Pius (138–161)	St. Polycarp	
10	St. Pius I	140–155	Antonius Pius	St. Polycarp	
11	St. Anicetus*	155–166	Marcus Aurelius (161–180)	St. Justin Martyr	St. Justin wrote about the "Catholic Mass" & the real presence in communion.
12	St. Soter*	166–175	Marcus Aurelius	Martyrs of Lyons	Great teachers: St. Clement, Origen of Alexandria.
13	St. Eleuterius	175–189	Commodus (180–192)		
14	St. Victor I	189–199	Pertinaz, Sepimus Sevenrus (193–211)		The first African Pope.
15	St. Zephyrinus*	199–217	Antoninus		
16	St. Callistus I*	217–222	S. Severus	St. Felicity, St Perpatua	Severus forbade new converts to the Faith.
17	St. Urban I*	222–230	A.Severus (222–235)	St. Crcilia, St.Callistu I	Severus Persecuted only local (Romans).
18	St. Pontian*	230–235	Maximinus Thrax (255–238)	St. Pontian	Thrax Ordered Church leaders to be put to death.
19	St. Anterus*	235–236	Maximinus Thrax	St.Hippolytus	
20	St. Fabian*	236–250	Decius (249–251)	St. Fabian, St. Agatha, St. Denis.	All of the empire was required to perform an act of worship to pagan gods. Those who refused were executed.
21	St. Cornelius*	251–253	Gallus	St. Cornelius	Continued Decius' persecution.
22	St. Lucius I	253–254	Gallus		Continued Decius' persecution.

#	Pope Name	Year Reign of pope	Major civil leader(s) [**Dominate Power**]	Martyr(s)	Notes
23	St. Stephen I	254–257	Valerin (253–260)	St. Cyprian, St.Lawrence, St. Sixtus II St. Tarcisus	Valerin's edict of 257 ordered all bishops, priests, and deacons to sacrifice to pagan gods; forbade visits to cemeteries and Christian assemblies.
24	St. Sextus II*	257–258	Valerin		
25	St. Dionysius	259–268	Gallienus		
26	St. Felix I	269–274	Claudius II		
27	St. Eutychian	275–283	Tacitus		
28	St. Caius	283–296	Carinus		
			[**Roman Empire**] (E)=East, (W)=West		
29	St. Marcellinus*	296–304	Diocletian (284–305)	St. Sebstian, St.Marcellinus, St. Peter, St. Lucy, St. Cosmas, St. Damken, St. George, St. Pancras	Diocletian executed Christians who refused to worship pagan gods, destroyed churches, burned sacred books, and forbade Christian assemblies.
30	St. Marcellus I*	304–309	Galerius, Licinius (308–32)	St. Agnes, St. Catherine of Alexandria	Continued emperor Diocletian persecutions.
31	St. Eusebius*	309–311	Galerius/ Maximin		
32	St. Melchiades	311–314	Maxentius (306–312)		
					ROMAN PERSECUTION ENDED

#	Pope Name	Year Reign of pope	Major civil leader(s) [**Dominate Power**]	Martyr(s)	Notes
33	St. Sylvester I	314–335	(W) Constantine I (306–337) Legalized Christianity and persecution ended		COUNCIL #1, Year 325, Council of Nicaea, in addition to the Nicaea Creed, declared Christ is true God and true man, He is "consubstantial" with God the Father.
34	St. Marcus	336	(W) Constantine I		336 first recorded Christmas Mass Celebration. Constantine baptized on his death bed in 337AD
35	St. Julius I	337–352	Constantine II (337–340)		Year 337 Pope declared December 25 as Christmas.
36	Liberus	352–366	(W) Constans (337–350)		
37	St. Damasus I	366–384	Valentinian I (E) Valens (364–378)		St. Athanasius in 367 was the first to list the 27 books for our New Testament. COUNCIL #2, Year 381, Council of Constantinople reaffirmed Council of Nicaea; the Holy Spirit is a divine Person.
38	St. Siricius	384–399	(W) Theodosius I (378–395)		Theodosius, the last ruler of United Roman Empire.
39	St. Anastasius I	399–401	(E) Arcadius (W) Honorius		Year 400 Jerome's Vulgate–Latin Bible published.
40	St. Innocent I	401–417	(E) Arcadius (E) Theodosius II (408–450) (W) Honorius		

#	Pope Name	Year Reign of pope	Major civil leader(s) [**Dominate Power**]	Martyr(s)	Notes
41	St. Zosimus	417–418	(E) Theodosius II (W) Honorius		
42	St. Boniface I	418–422	(E) Theoeosius II (W) Honorius		
43	St. Celestine I	422–432	(E) Theodosius II (W) Constantius III		COUNCIL #3, Year 431, Council of Ephesus declared Mary is the Mother of Christ, who is one Person, the Son of God. Therefore, Mary is the Mother of God.
44	St. Sixtus III	432–440	(E) Theodosius II (W) Valentinian III		
45	St. Leo I The Great 1st official use of "Pope"	440–461	(E) Theodosius II (E) Marcian (W) Valentinian III		COUNCIL #4, Year 451, Council of Chalcedon declared Christ is one divine Person with two natures, human and divine.
46	St. Hilarius	461–468	(E) Marcian (E) Leo I		
47	St. Simplicius	468–483	(E) Leo I, (E) Leo II, (E) Zeno, (E) Basilicus (476) (W) Olybrius), (W) Glycerius, (W) Julius Ndpos, (W) Romulus Augustulus (475–476)		Due to Roman changes, political corruption, divisions and barbarian invasion the Roman Empire fell in 476.
			[**Byzantine Empire**] [**(KF)=Kingdom of France**]		

#	Pope Name	Year Reign of pope	Major civil leader(s) [**Dominate Power**]	Martyr(s)	Notes
48	St. Felix II	483–492	(KF) Clovis (481–511) 1st Catholic King		The Julian calendar became effective.
49	St. Gelasius I	492–496	(E) Anastasius (491–518)		St. Patrick took the gospel to Ireland. 1st record of Advent.
50	Anastasius II	496–498			
51	St. Symmachus	498–514			500, Start of the "Middle Ages" sometimes called the "Dark Ages."
52	St. Hormisdas	514–523	(E) Justin I (518–527)		
53	St. John I	523–526			
54	St. Felix III	526–530	(E) Justinian I (527–565)		
55	Boniface II	530–532			
56	John II	533–535			
57	St. Agapitus I	535–536			
58	St. Silverius	536–537			
59	Vigilius	537–555			COUNCIL #5, Year 553, Second Council of Constantinople dealt with the two natures of Christ.
60	Pelagius I	556–561			**START OF ISLSM (MUSLIMS)**
61	John III	561–574			
62	Benedict I	575–579			
63	Pelagius II	579–590			
64	St. Gregory I The Great	590–604			St. Augustine of Canterbury missionary work converted England.
65	Sabinianus	604–606			
66	Boniface III	607			
67	St. Boniface IV	608–615			
68	St, Deusdedit	615–618			

#	Pope Name	Year Reign of pope	Major civil leader(s) [Dominate Power]	Martyr(s)	Notes
69	Boniface V	619–625			
70	Honorius I	625–638			
71	Severinus	638–640			
72	John IV	640–642			
73	Theodore I	642–649			
74	St. Martin I	649–655			
75	St. Eugene I	655–657			
76	St, Vitalian	657–672			
77	Adeodatus	672–676			
78	Donus	676–678			
79	St. Agatho	678–681			COUNCIL #6, Year 680–681, Third Council of Constantinople reaffirmed Christ as being human and divine.
80	St, Leo II	682–683			Islam started takeover of Eastern Empire.
81	St. Benedict II	684–685			
82	John V	685–686			
83	Conon	686–687			
84	St. Sergius I	687–701			
85	John VI	701–705			Year 700, China invented gun powder.
86	John VII	705–707			
87	Sisinnius	708			
88	Constantine	708–715		Valentine Engatia	
89	St. Gregory II	715–731	(E) Leo III (717–741)		1st non–European pope, Syria
90	St, Gregory III	731–741			
91	St. Zacharias	741–752			
92	Stephen II	752–757	(KF) Pepin the Short (751–768)		

#	Pope Name	Year Reign of pope	Major civil leader(s) [**Dominate Power**]	Martyr(s)	Notes
93	St. Paul I	757–767			COUNCIL #7, The Second Council of Nicaea (757) was last council of both Eastern and Western churches.
94	Stephen III	768–772	(KF) Charlemagne (768–814)		
			[**(HRE)=Holy Roman Empire**] [**(KE)=Kingdom of England**]		
95	Adrian I	772–795	(E) Constantine VI (780–797)		
96	St. Leo III	795–816	(E) Irene 797–802) (HRE) Charlemagne (800–814)		
97	Stephen IV	816–817	(HRE) Louis the Pious (814–840)		
98	St. Paschal	817–824			
99	Eugene II	824–827			
100	Valentine	827			
101	Gregory IV	827–844			
102	Sergius II	844–847			
103	St. Leo IV	847–855			
104	Benedict III	855–858			
105	St. Nicholas I The Great	858–867			
106	Adrian II	867–872	(KE) Alfred the Great (871–899)		COUNCIL #8, 869 to 870 was the Fourth Council of Constantinople.
107	John VIII	872–882	(HRE) Charles the Fat (881–887)		
108	Marinus I	882–884			
109	St. Adrian III	884–885			
110	Stephen V	885–891			

#	Pope Name	Year Reign of pope	Major civil leader(s) [**Dominate Power**]	Martyr(s)	Notes
111	Formosus	891–896	(HRE) Guy of Spoleto (891–894)		
112	Boniface VI	896	(HRE) Lambert of Spoleto (894–896)		
113	Stephen VI	896–897			
114	Romanus	897			
115	Theodore II	897			
116	John IX	898–900			Year 900, 1st recorded use of pipe organ in churches.
117	Benedict IV	900–903			
118	Leo V	903			
119	Sergius III	904–911			
120	Anastasius III	911–913			
121	Lando	913–914			
122	John X	914–928			
123	Leo VI	928			
124	Stephen VII	928–931		Ludmila of Bohemia	
125	John XI	931–936			
126	Leo VII	936–939			
127	Stephen VIII	939–942			
128	Marinus II	942–946			
129	Agaptus II	946–955			
130	John XII	955–964	HRE) Otto the Great (962–973)		
131	Leo VIII	964–965			
132	Benedict V	965			
133	John XIII	965–972			In 966 Poland accepted Catholicism.
134	Benedict VI	973–974			
135	Benedict VII	974–983			
136	John XIV	983–984			
137	John XV	985–996			
138	Gregory V	996–999			

#	Pope Name	Year Reign of pope	Major civil leader(s) [**Dominate Power**]	Martyr(s)	Notes
139	Sylvester II	999–1003	(HRE) St. Henry II (1002–1024)		
140	John XVII	1003			
141	John XVIII	1003–1009			
142	Sergius IV	1009–1012			
143	Benedict VIII	1012–1024			
144	John XIX	1024–1032			
145	Benedict IX	1032–1045	(KE) St. Edward the Confessor (1042–1066)		Benedict's 1st term
146	Sylvester III	1045			
147	Benedict IX	1045			Benedict's 2nd term
148	Gregory VI	1045–1046			
149	Clement II	1046–1047			
150	Benedict IX	1047–1048			Benedict's 3rd term
151	Damasus II	1048			**EAST/WEST GREAT SCHISM**
152	St. Leo IX	1049–1054			In 1054 started the separation of the Eastern and Western Churches.
153	Victor II	1055–1057	(HRE) Henry IV (1056–1105)		Muslims were persecuting Christians.
		1058	[**Turkish Empire**]		
154	Stephen IX	1057–1058			1058 Byzantine Empire invade by Turkish Empire.
155	Nicholas II	1059–1061	(KF) Philip (1060–1108)		
156	Alexander II	1061–1073	(KF) Harold Godwinson (1066)		
157	St. Gregory VII	1073–1085	(KF) William I (1066–1087)		Pope tried to end secular rulers' control of Churches' leaders.

#	Pope Name	Year Reign of pope	Major civil leader(s) [**Dominate Power**]	Martyr(s)	Notes
158	Bl. Victor III	1087			**ERA OF THE CRUSADES**
159	Bl. Urban II	1088–1099	(E) Alexois I (1081–1118)		Muslim control of Jerusalem started 1st crusade 1096 to 1102 – Christians liberated Jerusalem.
160	Paschal II	1099–1118			St. Anselm of Canterbury and Peter Lombard founded universities of faith.
161	Gelasius II	1118–1119			
162	Callistus II	1119–1124			COUNCIL #9, The First Council of Lateran in 1123. Many new Gothic churches being built.
163	Honorius II	1124–1130			
164	Innocent II	1130–1143	(HRE) Conrad III (1138–1152)		COUNCIL #10, The second council of the Lateran in 1139.
165	Celestine II	1143–1144			
166	Lucius	1144–1145			
167	Bl. Eugene III	1145–1153			
168	Anastasius IV	1153–1154			
169	Adrian IV	1154–1159	(KF) Henry II (1154–1189)		
170	Alexander III	1159–1181			COUNCIL #11, The Third Council of the Lateran in 1179.
171	Lucius III	1181–1185			
172	Urban III	1185–1187			
173	Gregory VIII	1187			
174	Clement III	1187–1191	(KF) Richard I (1189–1199)		
175	Celestine III	1191–1198	(E) Alexlus III (1195–1203)		

#	Pope Name	Year Reign of pope	Major civil leader(s) [**Dominate Power**]	Martyr(s)	Notes
			[**Mongol Empire – Genghis Khan**]		
176	Innocent III	1198–1216	(KF) John (1199–1216) (E) Alexius IX (1203=1244)		COUNCIL #12, The <u>Fourth Council of the Lateran</u> in 1215.
177	Honorius III	1216–1227	(HRE) Frederick II (1212–1250) (KF) St. Louis IX (1226–1270)		New orders of poverty and humility founded by: St. Francis of Assisi, St. Clare, and St. Dominic started the Dominicans in 1216.
178	Gregory IX	1227–1241			
179	Celestine IV	1241			
180	Innocent IV	1243–1254			It took 2 years to select a pope. COUNCIL #13, The <u>First Council of Lyons</u> in 1245.
		1258	[**Byzantine**] [**Mongols**]		Byzantine Empire re–established. Mongols becoming a strong force.
181	Alexander IV	1254–1261			
182	Urban IV	1261–1264			
183	Cement IV	1265–1268			
184	Bl. Gregory X	1271–1276	(KF) Edward I (1272–1307)		Great theologians at this time: St. Bonaventure, St. Albert the Great, St. Thomas Aquinas. COUNCIL #14, The <u>Second Council of Lyons</u> 1274.
185	Bl. Innocent V	1276			
186	Adrian V	1276			
187	John XXI	1276–1277			The first in–house papal election in 1276, which did not last.

#	Pope Name	Year Reign of pope	Major civil leader(s) [**Dominate Power**]	Martyr(s)	Notes
188	Nicholas III	1277–1280			
189	Martin IV	1281–1285			
190	Honorius IV	1285–1287			
191	Nicholas IV	1288–1291			No pope elected for 2 years.
192	St. Celestine V	1294			In office 5 months.
193	Boniface VIII	1294–1303	[**Ottoman Empire**]		
194	Benedict XI	1303–1304			
					PAPACY MOVED TO FRANCE
195	Clement V	1305–1314	France: King Phillip IV		COUNCIL #15, The Council of Vienne (1311–1312). 1309 Clement V moved Church headquarters to France (under French control).
196	John XXII	1316–1334	[**England**]		The Holy Land controlled by Muslims.
197	Benedict XII	1334–1342			
198	Clement VI	1342–1352			The plague of 1347 to 1375 about 200 million died.
199	Innocent Vi	1352–1362			
200	Bl. Urban V	1362–1370	[**Fall of the Mongol Empire 1368**]		
					PAPACY RETURNED TO ROME
201	Gregory XI	1370–1378			1377 Gregory moved to Rome
202	Urban VI	1378–1389			**The Great Western Schism** due to French Cardinals.
203	Boniface IX	1389–1404			
			[**Ming Dynasty**]		
204	Innocent VII	1404–1406			

#	Pope Name	Year Reign of pope	Major civil leader(s) [**Dominate Power**]	Martyr(s)	Notes
205	Gregory XII	1406–1415			COUNCIL #16, 1414–1418 Council of Constance. 1415 Gregory XII resigned, ending the schism and to permit election of a successor.
206	Martin V	1417–1431			In 1431 Joan of Arc burned at the stake.
207	Eugene IV	1431–1447	[**Fall of Byzantine Empire 1453**]		COUNCIL #17, The Councils of Basel, Ferrara and Florence (1431–1445)
			[**Ming Dynasty**] [**Ottoman Empire**]		
208	Nicholas V	1447–1455			1453 fall of Constantinople.
209	Callistus III	1455–1458			
210	Pius II	1458–1464			
211	Paul II	1464–1471			
			[**France**] [**Holy Roman Empire**] [**England**]		
212	Sixtus IV	1471–1484			
213	Innocent VIII	1484–1492			In 1492 Christopher Columbus carried some Spanish Catholics to America.
214	Alexander VI	1492–1503			First Conclave in Sistine Chapel
215	Pius III	1503			
216	Julius II	1503–1513			COUNCIL #18, The Fifth Council of the Lateran (1512–1517). 1508 to 1512 Michelangelo painted the Sistine Chapel.

#	Pope Name	Year Reign of pope	Major civil leader(s) [Dominate Power]	Martyr(s)	Notes
217	Leo X	1513–1521			In 1517 Martin Luther posted his Ninety–Five Theses.
		1517			Lutheran church, founded by Martin Luther in Germany.
218	Adrian VI	1522–1523			**PROTESTANT REFORMATION**
219	Clement VII	1523–1534			In 1531 Our Lady of Guadalupe appeared in Mexico. In 1534 England's' King Henry VIII separated from Rome; same year St. Ignatius started the Jesuits.
		1525			Mennonite, founded by Grebel, Mantz, and Blaurock.in Switzerland.
		1534			Church of England, Anglican, began with King Henry VIII in England.
220	Paul III	1534–1549			COUNCIL #19, The Council of Trent (1545–1563).
221	Julius III	1550–1555			First Bible printed on Johannes Gutenberg's printing press.
222	Marcellus II	1555			**CATHOLIC CHURCH REFORMATION**
223	Paul IV	1555–1559			
224	Pius IV	1559–1565			Continued Council of Trent, end 1563
		1560			Presbyterian church, founded by John Knox in Scotland.
225	St. Pius V	1566–1572			**MODERNISM**

#	Pope Name	Year Reign of pope	Major civil leader(s) [**Dominate Power**]	Martyr(s)	Notes
226	Gregory XIII	1572–1585			
		1583			Congregationalist, founded by Robert Brown in Holland.
227	Sixtus V	1585–1590			1789–1792 French Revolution.
228	Urban VII	1590			
229	Gregory XIV	1590–1591			
230	Innocent IX	1591			
231	Clement VIII	1592–1605			
			[**Ottoman Empire**] [**Kingdom of France**]		
232	Leo XI	1605			
233	Paul V	1605–1621		Francis Taylor	Religious foundress: St. Jeanne de Chantal, and St. Vincent de Paul.
		1606			Baptist church, founded by John Smith in Amsterdam.
234	Gregory XV	1621–1623			
235	Urban VIII	1623–1644		Magdalene of Nagasaki Lorenzo Ruiz	Mystics: St. Teresa of Avila and St John of the Cross. 1630 Puritans to the New World.
236	Innocent X	1644–1655		Arthur Bell OFM John deBrilto	Missionaries: St. Francis Xavier, St. Jean de Brebeuf, and Isaac Jogues.
		1645			Unitarian church, founded by John Biddle in London.
		1647			Quakers, founded by George Fox in England. Episcopalian church, founded by Samuel Seabury in America (not sure of the date)

#	Pope Name	Year Reign of pope	Major civil leader(s) [Dominate Power]	Martyr(s)	Notes
237	Alexander VII	1655–1667			Theologians: St. Peter Canisius. St. Robert Bellarmine, St. Charles Borromeo. And St. Francis de Sales.
238	Clement IX	1667–1669			
239	Clement X	1670–1676			
240	Bl. Innocent XI	1676–1689			King Louis XIV threatened pope with military take–over.
241	Alexander VIII	1689–1691	[Russian Empire] [Spain] [France] [England]		
242	Innocent XII	1691–1700			
243	Clement XI	1700–1721			
		1770			Universalists, founded by John Murray in New Jersey.
244	Innocent XIII	1721–1724			
245	Benedict XIII	1724–1730			
246	Clement XII	1730–1740			
		1739			Methodists, founded by John & Charles Wesley in England.
			[France] [Britain]		
247	Benedict XIV	1740–1758			
248	Clement XIII	1758–1769			
249	Clement XIV	1769–1774			
250	Pius VI	1775–1799	[United States independence from Britain 7/4/1776]		First Catholic Archdiocese in America, 1789 and first Catholic University, Georgetown. France put pope in prison.

#	Pope Name	Year Reign of pope	Major civil leader(s) [Dominate Power]	Martyr(s)	Notes
			[France] [Britain] [Prussia] [Russia]		Start of the Industrial Revolution.
251	Pius VII	1800–1823			
		1803			Evangelicals, founded by Jacob Albright in Pennsylvania.
252	Leo XII	1823–1829			
253	Pius VIII	1829–1830			
		1829			Mormon (Later Day Saint) founded by Joseph Smith in New York.
254	Gregory XVI	1831–1846			Catherine McAuley founded The Sisters of Mercy in 1831, her nuns set up hospitals and schools worldwide.
		1831			Seven Day Adventist, founded by William Miller in New York.
			[British Empire] [Russian Empire] [France]		
255	Pius IX	1846–1878	[United States civil war 1861–1865]		COUNCIL #20, The First Vatican Council (1868–1870). Catholics allowed to receive Eucharist once a day (1854). In 1870, established doctrine of the Immaculate Conception of Mary.

#	Pope Name	Year Reign of pope	Major civil leader(s) [**Dominate Power**]	Martyr(s)	Notes
		1872			Jehovah Witness, founded by Charles Taze Russell then renamed in 1932 by Judge Rutherford.
			[**British Empire**] [**German Empire**] [**USA**]		
256	Leo XIII	1878–1903			1879 civil laws passed to weaken the Catholic Church.
		1879			Christian Scientist, founded by Mary Baker Eddy in Massachusetts.
257	St. Pius X	1903–1914			In 1905 the Church and State separated. **World War I**, 7/28/1914 to 11/11/1918.
258	Benedict XV	1914–1922	**1918 the fall of the Ottoman Empire**		The Sisters of St. Francis opened first general hospitals in the USA. In 1917 the Communist Party ruling Russia, and Mary appearance in Fatima Portugal.
		1914			Assembly of God, then a General Assembly in Arkansas.
		1919			Church of the Nazarene, then Union at General Assembly.

#	Pope Name	Year Reign of pope	Major civil leader(s) **[Dominate Power]**	Martyr(s)	Notes
			[British Empire] [USA] [Soviet Socialist] [French]		
259	Pius XI	1922–1939			After the death of all civil appointed Church leaders, the Church finally had control of pope and bishop appointments. In 1929 the Vatican City became an independent nation.
		1934			Evangelical Reformed, created by Union at General Assembly.
			[Nazi Germany] [USA] [British Empire] [Soviet Union]		
260	Pius XII	1939–1958	**[USA] [Soviet Union] [Great Britain]**		Fascism, Nazism, and Communism on the rise. 9/1/1939 Germany invaded Poland, 12/7/1941 Japan attacked the USA. **World War II** ended 9/2/1945.
261	John XXIII	1958–1963			COUNCIL #21, The Second Vatican Council (1962–1965). In 1960 the First Catholic US President, J. F. Kennedy. 6/25/1962 the US Supreme Court outlawed the Bible in public schools.

#	Pope Name	Year Reign of pope	Major civil leader(s) [**Dominate Power**]	Martyr(s)	Notes
262	Paul VI	1963–1978			7/20/69 USA's Apollo Module Eagle landed on the moon. 1/22/1972 the US Supreme Court legalized abortion.
263	John Paul I	1978			Pope died after 33 days in office.
264	John Paul II	1978–2005			The first Polish pope. St. Teresa of Calcutta died 9/5/1997.
			[**USA**] [**Soviet Union**] [**China**]		
265	Benedict XVI	2005–2013			Pope Benedict XVI (age 85) resigned 2013.
266	Francis	2013–		Frans Vander Lugt SJ	The first Jesuit pope and first from the Americas.

Reference:

The Pope Name and Year Reign are from the "List of Popes" through to #264 from The New American Bible, World Press.

The remaining material is from the internet search by year for Major civil leaders, and Martyrs for that time frame.

POPES: Assembled by Paul Wilchek, 5JAN22

ABOUT THE AUTHOR

Paul Wilchek was born and raised in Brookpark, Ohio, a community just southwest of Cleveland. He played the trumpet in the high school band and orchestra, then attended Cleveland Engineering Institute for a two–year degree in Architectural, Engineering Drafting. After a few local drafting jobs, he ended up as a design draftsman at Carrier Air Conditioning Company, Cleveland, Ohio. In 1954 he was drafted into the U.S. Army and attended cartographic (map drafting) school at Fort Belvoir Virginia, Corps of Engineers. He ended up teaching cartographic drafting as well as construction drafting. While stationed in Virginia, Paul attended night college at George Washington University.

In 1956 Paul returned back to Carrier Air Conditioning Company and continued night college at Baldwin Wallace College in Berea, Ohio. In 1959 he was transferred to Detroit, Michigan as a branch engineer technician and continued his night college at the University of Detroit, specializing in mechanical engineering. Being a Jesuit college, they required some theology classes to be taken, which gave Paul some of his religious foundation.

In 1961 Paul married Lois Jean Baumgardner, a lifelong Catholic. Their first son was born in Dearborn, Michigan. About three months after his birth, they were transferred to Columbus, Ohio as the Branch Service Manager. Paul and Lois had three more sons in Ohio then in 1972 they were transferred to Chicago, Illinois as the Regional Service Sales Manager, then after a short time the job became the Zone Service Marketing Manager.

An executive of Carrier worked on Paul and Lois for over three months trying to convince them to transfer to Syracuse, New York, Carrier's home office. Finally, in 1979 they accepted the transfer as the National Service Marketing Manager. Paul and Lois never liked the climate conditions in Syracuse and were looking forward to maybe another transfer at some point, which never came about. They attended St. Ann's Church in Manlius, NY, where Paul was asked to attend a "Life in the Spirit Seminar" (in 1982). He experienced his first religious experience after being introduced to the Holy Spirit within. For several years, Paul assisted in putting on "Life in the Spirit Seminars" at various churches within the Syracuse diocese under the direction of Father Regis. Also, with Father Regis, Paul was very involved in the charismatic movement which mainly consisted of weekly prayer group meetings and attending monthly first Friday charismatic masses at various churches within the diocese. Paul has quite a story to tell of another religious experience in 1988 while attending a first Friday charismatic mass.

Paul's religious experiences may have been what were needed to prepare him for what was about to happen. Lois his wife of 37 years, had a stroke while going down the stairs at home and her fall caused serious brain damage. She was in a non–responsive coma for one and a half years then passed away in 1997. About a year later, after 45 years with Carrier Corporation, he retired. About two years later, Paul married Shirley Marie Holmes, a religious Baptist. She attended a non–denominational church, Eastern Hills Bible Church in Manlius, NY.

At that point in time, the Catholic Church in Manlius, NY was not offering bible study classes. Shirley invited Paul to attend bible study classes with her and he accepted. After about a year Paul was asked to lead the bible class, which was a surprise to Paul being Catholic at a non–Catholic church. The classes were strictly according to the bible and they went very well.

Shirley and Paul purchased an RV motor home and through the course of over six years they traveled to almost every state including Alaska. They spent most winters in Florida and ended up liking the Bradenton area. They sold their RV motor home and purchased a small Florida villa house there. For the next five years or so they were "snow birds."

Shirley and Paul were married eleven years when in December of 2010 Shirley passed away from a somewhat rare bile duct cancer. About one year after Shirley passed, Paul attended a hospice memorial service where doves were released to signify the rising of the spirit. A photograph of the doves reviled seven significant facts about Shirley and Paul which was a remarkable religious experience.

At Our Lady of the Angels Church in Lakewood Ranch, Florida, Paul attended a week–end retreat called "Christ Renews His Parish" which greatly helped the depression thing. After which he assisted in putting on three similar retreats. After several years, Paul was asked to attend training and become a member of the bereavement committee. Paul has served as an usher at Our Lady of the Angels since 2004.

June of 2017 Paul self–printed his book called "Holland Road" which was the result of 28 years of part–time family–tree research. It summarizes the Wilchek family going back to the oldest available record of his fourth great–grandfather, Joannes Vilcek, who was married in 1755. In addition to family tree research, Holland Road, has many stories of Paul's experiences growing up. The final chapter of Holland Road describes Paul's October 2016 visit to Nova Lubovna and Stara Lubovna, Slovakia. His research traced the Wilchek family to the Vilcek ancestors in Nova Lubovna, where Paul met up with his third cousin once removed, Milan Vilcek. Milan's great grandfather, Stephanus, and Paul's great grandfather, Gasparus, were brothers.

RELIGIOUS EXPERIENCES

In 1982 I (Paul Wilchek) was asked to attend a "Life in the Spirit Seminar" at St. Ann's Church in Manlius, NY by a very spiritual lady, Freda Hagerty. I was involved as an usher at St. Ann's and met Freda through ushering. The seminar was about receiving the Holy Spirit and it was six weeks long where the fifth week they prayed over each person to receive the Holy Spirit. Receiving the Holy Spirit is not very descriptive; it means to make one more aware of the Holy Spirit already present in a baptized person. After I was prayed over during the fifth week, I felt a nice sense of joy that evening. However, when I got up the next morning and I looked at myself in the mirror and I spontaneously lifted my arms in the air and I shouted "God loves me!" This was followed by such a wonderful overwhelming feeling of joy and love that is difficult to explain! The only way I can explain it was that I felt filled with the Holy Spirit throughout my entire body. After I got ready for work, I found myself sitting at the bottom of the stairs looking up the stairs and mentally sensed a voice saying to me, "You have taken the first step and have a long way to go." At that point I just sat there for several minutes in tears of joy.

Although I did not feel like eating breakfast or going to work, but I got in my van and started driving thinking that I just had to share this feeling and hug someone. As I drove, I just turned into St. Ann's Church parking lot without thinking. I walked into the chapel and I felt that I needed to talk to Father Paul (the assistant pastor) and that I needed a hug! There was no one in the chapel so I knocked on the door to the rectory and sat down to wait for Father Paul. Father Paul was involved in the "Life in the Spirit Seminar" sessions so I felt he would understand what happened to me. This is difficult to explain but all of the sudden I saw Jesus kind of floating toward me in a dazzling white robe, as he approached me, I stood up and Jesus gave me the hug I was looking for. I really felt the hug along with hearing the rustling of his clothing as he put his arms around me; then he was gone! I stood there for several minutes with tears just pouring down my cheeks. I thought, "did this really just happen to me?" My analytical mind wanted proof. Who will believe me? Logically I just could not discount the facts that I really saw Jesus, felt his arms around me, and heard the movement of his clothing. Then I went back to my van and remembered that I had commitments that morning and had to go to work. I just could not help sharing this experience with anyone that would listen. This wonderful joyful feeling lasted over two weeks and I had a few more spiritual experiences during that time.

In April of 1988 Lois and I received a call from Lois' first cousin David Brick telling us that his wife Mikel had a re–lapse of the cancer that she had been fighting for several years. At that time, I was very heavily involved in the charismatic movement in the Catholic Church. I typically attended the charismatic mass every first Friday evening of each month. At a point during the mass with my arms up high while singing the "Our Father" a part of my mind started traveling through space above the clouds; it was like I was flying through the air and clouds; then I came down toward the back of David and Mikel's house in Swanton, Ohio. As I came down, I noticed that something there was bright red and then I approached the large glass picture window, facing the rear of their farm house, and I could see inside.

I could see the living room couch at a right angle to the picture window with Mikel lying there in a night gown with family and friends standing in a large semi–circle facing the couch. Mikel's night gown was white with light blue print and had ruffles around the sleeves. Then I saw a transparent image of Mikel rise up from her body that was still on the couch and the image smiled and her mouth appeared to say "thank you" and then the image departed. After getting home from this mass, I just could not forget the experience I had and was trying to figure out what it meant. The next morning, I was sitting in the living room pondering this experience when Lois walked in and asked what was wrong. I then told her of my experience and was wondering if I should share it with David and

Mikel. We discussed it and then Lois said maybe you should call David and see what he thinks.

I called David Brick and told him of my experience. He immediately felt that I should share it with Mikel so he got his wife on the phone. After telling them of my experience I said that there are a few things I question. I don't think you have a bright red door and the last time we visited you your couch backed up to the picture window and not at a right angle to the window. There was a bit of silence on the phone then David said that they very recently rearranged their living room where the couch is now at a right angle to the picture window as a separator from the dining room. Mikel also said that she has a night gown that is white with light blue print and ruffles on the sleeves, and their back door or anything else is not bright red. Mikel was very pleased with what I told her and thanked me for sharing.

In about two weeks, David took his wife Mikel to their doctor and the doctor said that there was nothing that could be done to help her and he suggested she go home and advise her relatives and friends that she did not have very long to live. As it turned out, she died at the age of 56 on the couch at home with her relatives and friends there with her, the 3rd of March, 1988. As I understand visions or prophesies that are from God, they have to be 100% accurate and happen exactly as visioned. The thing I did not understand yet was my vision of something bright red, the only part not fulfilled.

Lois and I were on an airplane traveling from Syracuse, NY to Swanton, Ohio, actually the Toledo airport, for Mikel's funeral. On the airplane I had another vision of me doing a reading at the wake. I thought that this did not make sense since I was not a blood relative and why should they ask me. At the funeral parlor, the evening before the funeral I was asked to read Mikel's favorite bible passage which fulfilled 100% of that vision. The next morning as Lois and I walked into the Catholic Church there was a very bright red covering on the alter that hung down to the floor. Chills ran up my back and I said to myself and then to Lois "there is the bright red that I saw in my vision;" the bright red alter cloth that to me represented the door to heaven. So, my vision did come 100% true and to this day I do not know why it was given to me and totally what it all meant. The only explanation I have is that after the funeral, David asked me to tell of my vision to his children, Dean, Dianna, and LeeAnn. They seemed to get comfort from hearing about the vision, especially the part where Mikel's image said "thank you" – that may have had them feel that their mother was OK.

In March of 1996 Lois and I went to Hawaii to use our timeshare at the Sands of Kahana, Maui. Lois and I had a really great time together on this

 vacation. After 36 years of marriage, we were getting kind of complacent, and during this time together we re–connected and re–established our relationship with each other. One afternoon in the timeshare while we were getting ready to go out to eat, I noticed a beautiful stark white dove

sitting just outside of our sliding door. I opened the door and the dove just sat there looking at me. I had an unusual feeling that this dove has some meaning. I took a photo of it and it just stayed there looking at me following my movements. I called Lois to look and when she entered the room the dove flew away – making me feel that this may have something to do with Lois.

Our really good relationship continued after our return to Manlius, NY. It was about a month after our Hawaii trip and I was scheduled to go out of town the 18th of April, 1996. The evening prior to this I felt like I was getting the flu, so I called and cancelled my trip. Then 3:30am on the 18th I woke up hearing a loud bump sound. Lois was not in bed and I checked the bathroom and then walked out of our bedroom to the top of the stairway and Lois was at the bottom of the stairs. I ran to her and she was breathing kind of strange and did not respond, I called 911. Lois had been on a new medication for over five years to prevent lumps from forming after her cancer surgery. She was clear of cancer for five years but this new medication had a side effect of blood clots or stroke. Apparently, a stroke occurred while she was going down the stairs, the fall caused serious brain damage. She spent one month in the hospital, three months in a special coma–recovery unit, then in a nursing home where she remained in a non–responsive coma, where I visited her every day.

At the nursing home Lois frequently got pneumonia. They would take a chest x–ray and draw blood. The results were back in a few days then they would start her on an antibiotic. Even though they got Lois in a wheel chair each day and a few times a week did range–of–motion therapy, she spent a lot of time in bed which made her very prone for pneumonia (or lung infections). When Lois was first in the nursing home the resident Dr. Stringer explained to me that it was not required to medicate Lois. If I gave them permission, they would stop all medication except for only what was required to keep her comfortable. I told the doctor that I could not make that decision, and he understood.

One day early in October, 1997, Lois got her usual pneumonia and they did the usual routine tests. A few days later the nurse at Hill Haven told me that they found a spot on Lois' lungs and did not know what that meant and they were waiting for the results of the blood test. I started thinking about this and thought that maybe her cancer may have returned like her mother's did after five years. I started praying what is called a "fleece prayer." In the Bible (Old Testament) there is a story about a profit that prayed to God to help him make a decision. He prayed and told God he would place a lamb's wool (fleece) on the desert floor and if in the morning there was moisture under the fleece then he would take that as a sign from God to decide one way and if there was no moisture under the fleece then he would decide the other way. The term "fleece prayer" came from Judges 6:37–40 *Gideon said:"…I am putting a woolen fleece on the threshing floor, and if dew is on the fleece alone, while all the ground is dry, I shall know that you will save Israel through me, as you promised. That is what took place. Early the next morning he wrung the due from the fleece, squeezing out of it a bowlful of water."*

My "fleece" prayer was, "if the blood test results came with something more serious than pneumonia, I would take that as a sign from God to stop medication," a decision I could not previously make. On the other hand, if the blood test was her usual pneumonia, I would have them continue medication. It took over two weeks for the results of the blood test to return. Upon my visit to Lois the doctor explained that the reason it took so long to get the blood results was that Lois has been on so many different antibiotics the past year and a half and has become immune to them. The results showed that there were only three antibiotics left in the world that could be used. Two of them can only be used one time and the other had very serious side effects. I asked the doctor what Lois had and his very words to me were, "what she has is much <u>more serious than pneumonia</u> – what do you want me to do?" I looked at the doctor for a few seconds (recalling that those were the exact word of my fleece prayer) and then said to him I want to stop medication. The doctor said to me if that was my mother there, I would make the same decision, we will only give her medications necessary to keep her comfortable. I asked the doctor how long she had and he said about three to five days.

I returned to Lois' side and told her my decision and also told her that it was okay to let go. The lady that invited me to the "life in the spirit seminar", Freda Hagerty, had a son that was in a coma and she told me she had to tell him that it was okay to let go, so I felt it was time to tell Lois the same thing – she had been suffering too long now.

I continued to visit Lois each day and after about a week I noticed that she appeared to be getting better. I went to the doctor's office to inquire and he looked at me and said in all my many years of practice I have never seen anyone come out of that type of lung infection without medication. Do you believe what an understanding God we have! If she died, I most likely would have felt guilty for making the decision to stop medication and God spared me from that!

I had to travel out of town for a funeral of a relative. I arrived back in the Syracuse, NY area about eleven in the evening and considered stopping in Hill Haven Nursing Home to see Lois, since I had not seen her in a few days, but I was tired and then decided to go right home. Approximately 3:40am, October 29, 1997 I got a call from Hill Haven Nursing Home that Lois was having a seizure and they were having trouble controlling her temperature and I better get there soon. I drove to Hill Haven Nursing Home and when I arrived, the nurse met me as I approached Lois' room and informed me that Lois had died. Apparently, she had another blood clot or stroke that was in the area of her brain that controlled her temperature that caused the seizure.

After her funeral and all the company went back home things got really quiet around the house. I decided to keep on working as long as I could to keep occupied. In about a month or so after Lois died, I was attending a first Friday mass at a church in Syracuse where Father Regis was the resident priest. Just before mass started, I was praying and looking up at the beautiful ornate ceiling when it seemed like the ceiling opened up to a large patch of clear blue sky surrounded by white clouds and I saw a long white table with many people sitting there in white garments. Then Lois appeared in a white gown like she was serving the people at the table and she looked at me and smiled. I shared this with Father Regis and he thought it was just a sign to help comfort me while grieving and to let me know that Lois was okay.

Lois Jean Witchel's grave site at Holy Cross Cemetery, Cleveland, Ohio. Section 46, number 3023 P2.

Photo taken May 7, 1998 above Lois' grave site.

Since she died at the start of winter I had to wait until spring to inter her ashes. On May 6, 1998 I drove to Ohio and interred her ashes at the Holy Cross Cemetery on Brookpark Road, Cleveland, Ohio. After her ashes were in the ground, I placed some flowers on her grave and with my finger I put a cross in the loose dirt. After doing this I looked up in the sky and there was a large cross in the sky and I heard a voice: "you can't out do me." Then I took a photo of the grave and the cross in the sky. I consider all of this as a sign from God.

The lower photo is a bit faded and you have to look close to see the cross.

My second wife Shirley Marie Holmes passed the 16th of December, 2010 after we had been married for 11 years. About a year after she passed, I received a letter from Tidewell Hospice inviting me to an annual memorial service for all the hospice patients who had passed away the previous year. The service was at the United Methodist Church which is one of the oldest churches in Manatee County, Florida – it is a beautiful building. I estimate that there were more than 250 people who attended. Tidewell had asked every family to bring a photograph of their departed loved one, and they displayed the photos on the railing around the altar. During the service, they recognized each family by having them stand up as they read off their loved one's name. It was a beautiful service with lots of tears! When the service ended, I departed through the side door into a court yard. As I walked out of the church, a person handed me a live stark white dove and instructed me how to hold it and wait to release it all together. I was told that doves were handed to the first 20 people departing the church. I was not aware of this ahead of time. All of us holding the doves formed a circle and were instructed to release the doves all at once. The white doves flew up high, gathered together for a moment then flew away. The symbolism of all the departed souls ascending and then departing was so beautiful and also very sad. Everyone there was in tears, but they were kind of joyful tears!

I attempted to take a photo of the doves overhead with my cell phone but I was not quick enough. I looked around and a lady from my past bereavement group, Carol Tebo, had just taken a photo. I asked her to email me a copy. After receiving the photo, I printed out a copy and as I looked at it, I noticed that the doves formed an "S" (for Shirley). Looking further, I counted the doves in the "S" and there were 16 (Shirley died on the 16th) and then off to the side there were two more doves making a total of 18 (Shirley's birthday is the 18th).

At a later time, I printed a very large copy of the photo and noticed in the bottom portion of the "S" that there was the formation of the letter "P" (for Paul) with 11 doves in the "P" (we were married 11 years). Remember there were

20 doves released and they are not all in the photo which is also amazing in order for the group of 16 and group of 2 to make this apply to Shirley and Paul.

To summarize this amazing occurrence:

1. The doves formed the letter "S" for Shirley.
2. There are 16 doves in the "S" and Shirley passed away on the 16th of December.
3. Two additional doves making 18 representing Shirley birthday, November 18th.
4. In the lower portion of the "S" is the formation of the letter "P" for Paul.
5. The letter "P" has 11 doves; Shirley and I were married 11 years.
6. There were 20 doves released and only 18 appear in the photo to make this work.
7. With 250 people attending, what are the odds that I was one of the 20 to receive a dove?

What are the chances of all these things occurring in a single instant of time this photo was taken? I consider this a beautiful sign from our God! Finally, as an analytical type, I have physical proof (a photo) to prove my religious experience. Paul Wilchek 5–Mar–2021.

On the 5th of February, 2022 I was not feeling well and was very dizzy, as a result I had a fall at home. I had a friend drive me to the ER where I tested positive for covid–19. I was admitted and put in a covid isolation room. I was very sick and weak, had difficulty breathing and an occasional feeling of drowning, with "brain fog," as well as no energy, very little taste or smell and a dry mouth. I knew I had to keep up my strength so I forced myself to eat a small amount of food.

I was so weak that I started thinking maybe I should just give up. To add to this, the attending doctor visited me and said, "your breathing is deteriorating and you will have to be put on a ventilator, then you will die." I could not believe a doctor would tell a patient that, but that is exactly what he said. I told the doctor, "I refuse the ventilator."

The hospital room was very dim due a negative pressure unit blocking the window. At one point, I noticed on the far right of the blank wall at the foot of my bed, there appeared a very large swarm of distant birds gathering. The birds then turned into rows of hand writing on the wall. The hand writing appeared to be brown or gold in color. The hand writing slowly flowed from right to left and was on a slight angle. I could not read the hand writing and there were gaps in the writing where there appeared single line sketches of Jesus and Mary as well as sketches of beautiful churches and of the altars inside of churches. Rows and rows of hand writing slowly moved across the wall for at least three minutes. When it stopped, I just started to think "What does this mean?" Then after a few minutes it started all over again, also lasting several minutes. However, the second time as the hand writing was flowing across the wall, I mentally heard a voice that said, "These are all the prayers being said for you that are written in heaven for a special blessing to each person praying." Then again after a few minutes the same vision occurred for a third time.

When I mentally heard my response to "What does this mean," I knew it was from God and it just overwhelmed me, giving me hope of recovering and it took away that negative feeling of giving up. I felt that I had to recover to tell those people praying for me of this profound message that their prayers were heard as well as being written in heaven and that they would receive a blessing because of them.

After 13 days in the hospital, it took over 3 months to recover at home.

TOPICS BY CHAPTER

Holy Spirit Prophesied
Holy Spirit Christians to faith
Holy Spirit Drive out demons
Holy Spirit Baptizes and gifts
Holy Spirit, per Saint Paul
Holy Spirit, never misrepresent
Holy Spirit and Jesus
Holy Spirit Taches us
Holy Spirit, Power to forgive/retain
Holy Spirit, Prophets
Holy Spirit, Temple of
Holy Spirit Raised Christ
Summary – Holy Spirit
Spirit
Soul
Body
Summary – Spirit, Soul, Body

6 PROPHECIES, PARALLELS, SYMBOLISM, MIRACLES:

Prophecies fulfilled in Jesus
Prophecies Jesus made
Parallels Jewish and Christ
Parallels Jewish/Christian days
Old Covenant feasts fulfilled
Old Covenant to be fulfilled
Parallel between God and Jesus
Parallel–5 thousand and Last supper
Parallels of Trinity/Humans
Hidden prophecy
Hidden message
Hidden symbolism
Hidden numbers
Seven in Scripture
Seven Sacraments
Miracles at the Temple
Miracle of the Eucharist
Summary – miracles
Mary's Miraculous Conception
Mary Full of Grace
Mary ark of covenant

Old Testament confirmed in New
Mary's Assumption
Miracles of the word of Jesus
Miracles of Jesus in order
Summary – Prophecies

7 PROPHETS:

Prophets in Old Testament
Prophets in New Testament
Prophets, false
Summary – Prophets

8 PURGATORY:

Purgatory Purification
Purgatory Cleansing by fire
Purgatory, age to come
Purgatory, pray for the dead
Purgatory, spirits in prison
Purgatory, atonement
Purgatory, sin
Purgatory, tradition
Summary – Purgatory

9 SCRIPTURE RESPONSE:

Response – Born again
Response – Pray for the dead
Response – Purgatory belief
Response – Baptize infants
Response – Call a priest Father
Response – Confess to a priest
Response – Sign of the cross
Response – Sacraments in scripture
Response – Traditions
Response – Books in the Bible
Response – Rapture
Response – Holy Communion
Response – Break the host
Response – Creation of the universe
Response – Evolution
Summary – Response

10 SELECTED SUBJECTS:

Abandon
Acknowledge
Alone, afflicted
Anger
Angels
Anguish
Anxiety
Armor
Assurance, believe
Believe, believing
Brokenhearted
Bread, communion, Eucharist
Confess, confession
Dead sea scrolls
Deserted
Dismayed, discouraged
Empty himself
Faith
Fear
Fruit of the Spirit
Forgive, forgiveness
Gifts of the Holy Spirit
Grace
Grieve
Guidance
Holy Spirit
Hope
Joy
Judgement, Justice, Mercy
Love
      Peace
Pray, prayed, prayers, ask
Promises
Rest for the soul
Righteousness, justification
Sacraments
Salvation
Sin
Sorrowful
Spirits in prison

Spirit/Soul/Body
Temptation
Ten Commandments
Testing
Thanks, Thanksgiving
Traditions
Trials
Tribulation
Trouble
Trust
Witness – End Times
Worry

11 THE APOSTLES, DICIPLES, CHURCH FATHERS:

Twelve apostles
Authors of the New Testament
Books of the New Testament
Disciples
Women Disciples
Fathers & Doctors
Summary – Apostles, Disciples

12 THEMES THROUGH SCRIPTURE:

THEME OF BREAD:
Bread, Old Testament
Bread, New Testament
Bread, Feeding the five thousand
Bread, Feeding the four thousand
Bread, Lord's Supper
Bread of Life Discourse
Bread, after Pentecost
Bread, Didache
Bread of God
Summary – Theme of Bread
THEME OF REDEMPTION:
Redemption, beginning
Redemption, Adam Covenant
Redemption, the fall
Redemption, early world

13 THE BRIEF HISTORY OF THE CATHOLIC CHURCH:

14 THE POPES:

TOPICS ALPHABETICALLY
With Chapter Numbers (CH-#)

APPENDIX

BRIEF SUMMARY OF CHURCH HISTORY:
(Councils are underlined, ~ = approximate)

+ 722 BC ~ The nation of Israel was recognized until exiled by Assyrians
+ 509 BC – 27BC – The Roman Republic
+ 444 BC ~ (Some claim 425 or 458) – Ezra set the canon of the Old Covenant for the Scripture books at that time. Maccabees and other books were added later.
+ 250 BC – The Hebrew written Scripture collection was translated to Greek, called the Septuagint. The 46 books of the Old Testament (Covenant) later became the official Old Testament Bible of the Catholic Church
+ 200 BC ~ Independent State of Juda (remnant of Israel) briefly under Maccabees
+ 63 BC ~ Roman domination of Israel
+ 27 BC–14AD – The Roman Republic became the Roman Empire
+ 3/4 BC ~ Birth of Jesus (Matthew 2:1)
+ 30 AD – Jesus' forty days in the Desert (Matthew 4:1)
+ 33 AD – Crucifixion of Jesus (Matthew 27:33)
+ 33 AD – Resurrection of Jesus (Matthew 28:1–9)
+ 33 AD – Ten Appearances of Jesus (Mark 16: 4–13) (Luke 24:13–49) (John 20:11–30, 21:1–19)
+ 33 AD – Commissioning of the Apostles and the Church (Mark 16:14–18)
+ 33 AD – St. Peter – appointed head of the Church by Jesus Christ (Matthew 16:19)

- + 33 AD – Ascension of Jesus (Mark 16:19–20)
- + 33 AD – Pentecost (Acts 2:1–1–13)
- + 36 AD – First Martyr, Stephen (Acts 7:54–60)
- + 49 AD – Council of Jerusalem – Circumcision not required for Christians (Acts 15:1–21)
- + 64 AD – Roman Persecution of Christians
- + 70 AD – Roman Emperor Nerva destroyed Jerusalem Temple (Israel scattered)
- + 80 AD – "The Didache"– "The Teaching of the Twelve Apostles" – first written record of the "Eucharist" other than "Breaking of the Bread" in Scripture
- + 80/100 – All 27 books of the New Testament were written
- + 103 – The last Apostle, John, died at the age of 97
- + 107 – St. Ignatius first used the term "Catholic"
- + 313 – Constantine legalized Christianity
- + 314 – End of Roman Persecution, 18 of previous 31 popes were martyred
- + 325 – The Council of Nicaea – Nicaea Creed, Christ is consubstantial with the Father
- + 367 – St. Athanasius listed 27 books of the New Testament
- + 381 – The First Council of Constantinople – Reaffirmed Nicaea Creed, Holy Spirit is a divine Person
- + 400 – Jerome's Vulgate–Latin Bible published
- + 419 – Christian scholars from over the world gathered and confirmed the 46 Old Testament and 27 New Testament books, then approved by Pope Boniface (422)
- + 431 – The Council of Ephesus – Christ Divine Person; Mary Mother of God
- + 451 – The Council of Chalcedon – Christ is divine one person two natures
- + 440 – First official use of "Pope" as head of the Church, St. Leo I (440–461)
- + 553 – Start of Islam, Muslims
- + 553 – The Second Council of Constantinople – Delt with heresies, reaffirm previous teachings

+ 622–750 – Islamic Empire, Muslims, occupied/controlled Jerusalem
+ 680–681 – <u>The Third Council of Constantinople</u> – Christ has two wills: human and divine
+ 787 – <u>The Second Council of Nicaea</u> – Images/art help contemplate divine mystery
+ 869–870 – <u>The Fourth Council of Constantinople</u> – delt with East and West schism
+ 1049 – East/West Great Schism
+ 1088–1099 – Era of the Crusades, to try and free Holy Land so Christians could visit
+ 1096–1102 – The first crusade, to keep Christians safe in Jerusalem from Muslims
+ 1119–1124 – <u>The First Council of Lateran</u> – confirmed agreement with Holy Roman Empire, regarding appointment of Bishops/Abbots
+ 1139 – <u>The Second Council of Lateran</u> – Confirmed baptism of infants, Holy Orders, Marriage, and Eucharist
+ 1147–1149 – The second crusade, Christians were being harassed/killed by Muslins
+ 1179 – <u>The Third Council of Lateran</u> – Papal elections require 2/3 vote of Cardinals
+ 1189–1192 – The third crusade, Pease treaty established to protect Christians
+ 1198–1216 – <u>The Fourth Council of Lateran</u> – instituted Easter Duty, annual Eucharist, and confession minimum requirements
+ 1201–1205 – The fourth crusade, Muslins did not honor Peace Treaty
+ 1218–1221 – The fifth crusade, failed to halt Muslin control of Jerusalem
+ 1228–1229 – The sixth crusade, Year 1229, second Pease Treaty to protect Christians
+ 1227 – Inquisition
+ 1243–1254 – <u>The First Council of Lyons</u> – Excommunicated Fredric II, Holy Roman Emperor

+ 1244 – Muslins resume control, continue Pilgrim harassment/ killing in Jerusalem
+ 1274 – <u>The Second Council of Lyons</u> – Regulations for papal conclave elections
+ 1276 – First official papal election, after, State continued to influence selections
+ 1292 – To this point Papacy is in Rome
+ 1309 – Papacy moved to France (a political move)
+ 1311–1312 – <u>The Council of Vienne</u> – Suppressed the Knights
+ 1377 – Papacy moved back to Rome
+ 1378 – Start of the Great Western Schism
+ 1414 – Pre–Reformation
+ 1414–1418 – <u>The Council of Constance</u> – Ended Great Western Schism
+ 1415 – End of the Great Western Schism
+ 1431–1445 – <u>The Council of Basel, Ferrara and Florence</u> – Reaffirm papal primacy
+ 1448 – The Spanish Inquisition
+ 1454 – First printed Bible by Gutenberg
+ 1492–1503 – The first conclave in the Sistine Chapel
+ 1512–1517 – <u>The Fifth Council of Lateran</u> – Prohibit heresies
+ 1517 – Protestant Reformation
+ 1534 – By decree – England separated from the Catholic Church in Rome
+ 1536 – England dissolved Catholic monasteries and Churches
+ 1545 – Reformation of the Catholic Church
+ 1551–1563 – <u>The Council of Trent</u> – Reaffirm Catholic doctrine on: Scripture, Tradition, Grace, Sin, Justification, The Mass, Sacrifice, Purgatory. Reformed: Clergy, Seminaries, and the Liturgy
+ 1558–1603 – Queen Elizabeth issued decrees to eradicate Catholics in England
+ 1562–1563 – Completion of The Council of Trent
+ 1570 – The first Universal Catechism introduced
+ 1774 – The start of Modernism
+ 1789 – The first Catholic Archdiocese established in USA

+ 1869–1870 – <u>The First Vatican Council</u> – justified: Faith and reason, papal infallibility
+ 1890 – Catholics established first hospitals in USA
+ 1905 – The Church and the State (Europe) separated
+ 1914–1918 – World War I
+ 1917 – Bolshevik Revolution, Communism rules Russia, Mary appeared at Fatima
+ 1917 – Mexico turns Socialist – confiscated all Catholic Church property
+ 1927 – Mexico executed over 300,000 Catholics including priests and bishops
+ 1929 – Vatican City becomes an independent nation
+ 1939–1945 – World War II
+ 1945 – (prior to) Over 3 million Catholics died at Auschwitz
+ 1947 – United Nations decree for Israel to be independent (not a state since 722 BC)
+ 1948 – May 14, granted State of Israel an independent nation. This fulfilled the passage of, Isaiah 66:8 *"...Can a land be brought forth in one day or a nation be born in a single moment?"*
+ 1950 – Catholic Church now has full control of papal selection, free from the State
+ 1950 – Pope #260, Pius XII, declared Mary's assumption to heaven
+ 1958 – Modern Times
+ 1962–1965 – <u>The Second Vatican Council</u> – Reaffirm Catholic teaching on divine revelation and mystery of the Church. 16 decrees, including to reform the Liturgy
+ 1962 – US Supreme Court outlawed the Bible and prayer in public schools
+ 1972 – US Supreme Court legalized abortion
+ 2013 – Pope Benedict resigned
+ 2013 – Pope Francis became the 266th pope
+ 2022 – US Supreme Court removed abortion legalization

DOCTORS OF THE CATHOLIC CHURCH are saints that are recognized as having made a significant contribution to theology or doctrine through their research, study or writing. As of 2022 there are 37 Doctors of the Catholic Church.

Doctors of the Church	Born	Died	Title – Accomplishment(s)
Irenaeus of Lyon	130	202	Bishop – Theologian, teacher
Athanasius	298	373	Bishop – Father of orthodoxy
Hilary of Poitiers	300	367	Bishop – Vestments, writer
Ephrem the Syrian	306	373	Deacon – Pomes, hymns, writings
Cyril of Jerusalem	315	386	Archbishop – Doctrinal writer, speaker
Gregory of Nazianzus	329	389	Archbishop – Theologian
Basil the Great	330	379	Bishop – Homilies & rules
Ambrose	340	397	Bishop – Theologian, statesman
John Chrysostom	347	407	Archbishop – Homilist, commentaries
Jerome	347	420	Priest/Monk – Translate bible to Latin
Augustine	354	430	Bishop – Theological systems, teaching
Cyril of Alexandria	376	444	Archbishop – Doctrinal treaties
Peter Chrysologus	406	450	Bishop – Homilist, writer
Leo the Great	440	461	Pope #45 – Christological writer
Isidore of Seville	560	636	Archbishop – Scholar
Gregory the Great	590	604	Pope #64 – Strengthened the Papacy

Bede the Venerable	672	735	Priest – Historian, writer
John Damascene	676	749	Priest – Apologist, Writer
Gregory of Nerek	951	1003	Monk – Poet
Peter Damian	1007	1072	Bishop – Reformer
Anselm of Canterbury	1034	1109	Archbishop – Father of Scholasticism
Bernard of Clirvaux	1090	1153	Priest – Writer
Albertus Magrius	1193	1280	Bishop – Dominican, writer
Anthony of Lisbon & Padua	1195	1231	Priest – Theologian, preacher
Hildegard of Bingen	1098	1179	Visionary/Theologian – Writer, prophecy
Bonaventure	1221	1274	Bishop – Franciscan
Thomas Aquinas	1225	1274	Priest – Theologian, Catholic doctrine
Catherine of Siena	1347	1380	Mystic – Author, papal politics
John of Avila	1500	1569	Priest/Mystic – Reformer
Teresa of Avila	1515	1582	Mystic – Writer, 1st woman Dr. of Church
Peter Canisius	1521	1597	Priest – Catechist
John of the Cross	1542	1591	Priest – Catechisms, doctrinal defenses
Robert Bellarmine	1542	1621	Archbishop – Theology professor
Lawrence of Brindisi	1559	1619	Priest – Diplomat, Franciscan, preacher
Francis de Sales	1567	1622	Archbishop – Spiritual direction writings
Alphonsus Liguori	1696	1787	Bishop – Theologian, apologist
Therese of Lisieux	1873	1897	Nun – Spiritual autobiography

FATHERS OF THE EARLY CATHOLIC CHURCH are mostly saints and the intelligent Christian Fathers that were theologians, philosophers, apologist, and writers that influenced the doctrines and the very foundation of the Catholic Church. Apostolic Fathers are the same except are the core Christian theologians who are believed to personally have known some of the 12 Apostles, indicated (A) below. Some Fathers are also Doctors of the Church, indicated (D) below.

Fathers of the Church	Born	Died	Title – Accomplishment(s) ~ means approx. early/mid/late century
Pope St. Clement I (A)(D)	88	99	< (yr. reign) Pope # 4 – papal vestments
St, Ignatius of Antioch (A)	35	110	Bishop – Apostolic Father
Papias of Hierapolis (A)	60	130	Apostolic Father
St. Polycarp (A)	69	155	Bishop – Theological literature
St. Justin Martyr	100	165	Apologist, Philosopher
St. Irenaeus of Lyon (D)	130	202	Bishop – Theologian, teacher
The Shepherd of Hermas		~175	Author – on morals and works
St. Melito of Sardus		180	Bishop – Old Testament Canon
St. Theophilus of Antioch		~185	Patriarch – against heresy
St. Clement of Alexandria	150	215	Theologian, Philosopher
Tertullian	155	222	Author – Church doctrine, Trinity
St. Hippolytus	170	236	Christian Theologian
Marcus Minucius Felix		250	Latin Apologist for Christianity
Origen	185	254	Christian Theology, Apologetics
Novatian	200	258	Priest – Scholar, Theologian
St. Cyprian of Carthage	210	258	Bishop – Christian writer
Gregory of Thaumaturgus	213	270	Bishop – Miracle–Worker
Lactantius	250	325	Author – advisor to Constantine I
Pope St. Cornelius	251	253	< (yr. reign) Pope # 21– fight persecution

Fathers of the Church	Born	Died	Title – Accomplishment(s) ~ means approx. early/mid/late century
Pope St. Dionysius	259	268	< (yr. reign) Pope # 25 – reorganize
St. Firmilian		269	Bishop –
St. Archelaus		278	A foe of heresies
St. Pamphilus of Caesarea		309	Presbyter –
St. Methodius of Olympus		311	Bishop – Author
Arnobius		330	
Eusebius of Caesarea	265	339	Bishop – Scholar of Biblical canon
St. Aphrahat	280	345	Author – Doctrine and practice, homilies
St. Eustathius of Antioch		360	Archbishop – Christian manuscripts
Marius Victorinus		355	Writer, Translator
St. Eusebius of Vercelli	283	371	Bishop – Affirmed the divinity of Jesus
Athanasius (D)	298	373	Bishop – Father of orthodoxy
St. Hilary of Poitiers (D)	300	367	Bishop – Vestments, writer
St. Macarus	300	391	Monk – hermit – founded a monastery
St. Ephrem the Syrian (D)	306	373	Deacon – Pomes, hymns, writings
St. Pacian	310	391	Bishop – writer
St. Epiphanius	310	403	Bishop – Defender of orthodoxy
Cyril of Jerusalem (D)	315	386	Archbishop – Doctrinal writer, speaker
St.Gregory of Nazianzus (D)	329	389	Archbishop – Theologian
St. Basil the Great (D)	330	379	Bishop – Homilies & rules
St. Caesarius of Nazianzus	331	368	Physician/Politician –
St. Gregory of Nyssa	335	395	Bishop – Theologian, trinity, creed
Pope St. Julius I	337	252	< (yr. reign) Pope # 35 – strong leader

Fathers of the Church	Born	Died	Title – Accomplishment(s) ~ means approx. early/mid/late century
St. Ambrose of Milan (D)	340	397	Bishop – Theologian, statesman
Rufinus of Aquileia	344	411	Monk –historian, theologian, translator
St. John Chrysostom (D)	347	407	Archbishop – Homilist, commentaries
St. Jerome (D)	347	420	Priest/Monk – Translate bible to Latin
Theodore of Mopsuestia	350	428	Bishop – school of hermeneutics
St. Dionysius the Great	259	268	< (yr. reign) Pope #25 – rebuild Church
St. Nilus the Elder		430	Theologian, Bible scholar, writer
St. Augustine (D)	354	430	Bishop – Theological systems, teaching
St. Paulinus of Nola	354	431	Writer, senator, started bells in worship
St. John Cassian	360	435	Monk – theologian, mystical writings
St. Serapion		370	Bishop – Created Eucharist verses
St. Athanasius of Alexandria		373	Priest – defender Church orthodoxy
St. Optatus		~375	Bishop – Author of about 7 books
Pope St. Damasus I	366	384	< (yr. reign) Pope # 37 – scripture canon
Diodore of Tarsus		390	Bishop – Theologian, monastic reformer
St. Phoebadius of Agen		392	Bishop – Author of several works
St. Gregory of Elvira		392	Bishop – writer
Didymus the Blind		398	Theologian – commentaries, teacher

Fathers of the Church	Born	Died	Title – Accomplishment(s) ~ means approx. early/mid/late century
St. Cyril of Alexandria (D)	376	444	Archbishop – Doctrinal treaties
St. Eucherius of Lyons	380	449	Writings and homilies
St. Maximus of Turin	380	465	Bishop – theological writer, expand Christ
Pope St. Siricius	384	399	< (yr. reign) Pope # 38– Church discipline
St. Chromatius of Aquileia		407	Bishop – theologian
St. Proclus	390	446	Archbishop –
St. Isidore of Pelusium		450	Writings on the Greek bible
Salvina		~450	
Gennadius I		471	Patriarch – Historian
Theodoret of Cyrrhus	393	458	Theologian – Church controversies
Pope St. Innocent I	401	417	< (yr. reign) Pope # 40 – arbitrator
St. Vincent of Lerins		445	Monk – theologian
St.Peter Chrysologus (D)	406	450	Bishop – Homilist, writer
Pope St. Celestine I	422	432	< (yr. reign) Pope # 43 – Mary's title
Marius Mercator		451	
Pope St. Leo the Great	440	461	< (yr. reign) Pope # 45 – Christ divinity

BREAD AND EUCHARIST
THROUGH SCRIPTURE

The Eucharist name does not appear in scripture; however, "Thanksgiving" does appear in reference to the Last Supper. The Greek word for thanksgiving is eucharisteo, where the Eucharist name derived from. Eucharist is the sacrament of Holy Communion; the sacrifice of the Mass; the Lord's Supper; the consecrated elements of Holy Communion; the giving of thanks; thanksgiving.

A few of the names for the Eucharist that appear in Scripture:
Luke 22: 19 ***the bread. This is my body.*** Luke 22: 20 ***the cup This cup my blood***
1 Cor 11:*20* ***Lord's Supper.*** Acts 2:42 ***breaking of the bread.***
1 Cor 10:16 ***The cup*** *of blessing that we bless, is it not a participation in* ***the blood*** *of Christ?* ***The bread*** *that we break, is it not a participation in* ***the body*** *of Christ?*

Scripture passages here are from the New American Bible and are ***bold and italicized*** for convince. Certain words may be underlined for emphasis added. Take particular notice of the progression and development that bread takes through scripture.

The first two books of the bible, Genesis and Exodus, were written about 1,400 BC. The very first occurrence of "bread" in scripture is in Genesis 3:19 where God said to Adam, after the fall: [19] ***By the sweat of your face shall you get bread to eat,*** ... Scripture uses "bread" here rather than any number of things that could have been used like: grains, vegetables, or even fruit. However, bread is used to show its importance in scripture.

Genesis 4:4 ...*Abel, for his part, brought one of the best firstlings of his flock. The Lord looked with favor on Abel and his <u>offering</u>,* ... Hebrews 11:4 **by faith Abel offered to God a <u>sacrifice</u>...** Genesis is the first mention of a <u>sacrifice</u> <u>offering</u> in scripture.

Gn14:18 *Melchizedek, king of Salem, brought out bread and wine, and being a priest of God Most High, he blessed Abram with these words: "Blessed be Abram by God Most High, the creator of heaven and earth; and blessed be God Most High, who delivered your foes into your hands." Then Abram gave him a tenth of everything.*
The blessing given to Abram (later called Abraham) with the bread and wine must have been highly valued for Abram to give Melchizedek one tenth of everything. King of Salem is interpreted as King of Peace (shalom) in the following:

Hebrews 7:1–3 *This Melchizedek, king of Salem and priest of God Most High, "met Abraham as he returned from his defeat of the kings" and "blessed him." And Abraham apportioned to him a tenth of everything." His name first means righteous king, and he was also "King of Salem," that is, king of peace. Without father, mother, or ancestry, without beginning of days or end of life, thus made to resemble the Son of God, he remains a priest forever.*

Melchizedek, king of rightness, foreshadows Jesus, the eternal high priest's offering of bread and wine in thanksgiving to the Father. Melchizedek's offering of bread and wine looks forward to both the Last Supper and the Mass, where not only bread and wine are offered, but they are now changed into the Body and Blood of Jesus. In the New Testament where Jesus is talking about the law: Matthew 5:17: *I have come not to abolish but to fulfill.* The New Testament tells us that Jesus is: *...a great high priest...* Thus, Jesus fulfilled the prefigured Old Testament statement of:
"Priest of God Most High" (Heb 7:1) as well as fulfilling the "blessing" and distribution of bread performed at the Last Supper.

The tenth plague of Moses was the death of the firstborn in Egypt. To protect the firstborn of the Israelite people, they were instructed by God to slaughter a year–old male lamb that did not have a blemish (symbolizing without sin). Exodus 12:7 instructed the Israelites: *They shall take some of its __blood__ and apply it to the two doorposts and the lintel of every house in which they partake of the lamb.* Notice the physical action to put the blood on the lintel (door top) and two doorposts (door sides) that generates the sign of the cross. Then in Exodus 12:8,10 They are told: ₈ *That same night they shall eat its roasted __flesh__ with unleavened __bread__ and bitter herbs.* ₁₀ *None of it must be kept beyond the next morning; whatever is left over in the morning shall be burned up.* It is interesting to notice the use of the word __flesh__ here; we will see that word used much later by Christ. The consumption of the __flesh of the lamb__ has to be very important, otherwise why are they instructed by God to burn all leftovers? Also notice, that now the feast of unleavened __bread__ has become part of a sacred Israelite ritual later on called Passover. Exodus 12:14,15 ₁₄ *This day shall be a memorial feast for you, which all your generations shall celebrate with pilgrimage to the Lord, as a __perpetual institution__.* ₁₅ *For seven days you must eat unleavened __bread__.* Exodus 12:17 *Keep, then, this custom of unleavened __bread__.*

After the Israelites departed from Egypt, Exodus 16:2–3 tells us: ₂ *Here in the desert the whole Israelite community grumbled against Moses and Aron.* ₃ *The Israelites said to them, "Would that we had died at the Lord's hand in the land of Egypt, as we sat by our fleshpots and ate our fill of __bread__! But you had led us into this desert to make the whole community die of famine!* Then Moses responded in Exodus 16:4, 8,15,31 ₄ *Then the Lord said to Moses, "I will now rain down __bread from heaven__ for you."* ₈ *...the Lord gives you __flesh__ to eat in the evening... and in the morning your fill of __bread__...* John 6:51 *...the __bread__ that I will give is my __flesh__ for the life of the world,* a parallel of the Old and New Testament.

₁₅ *On seeing it, the Israelites asked one another, "What is this?" for they did not know what it was. But Moses told them. "This is the __bread__ which the Lord has given you to eat."* ₃₁ *The Israelites called this food __manna__. It was like coriander seed, but white, and it tasted __like wafers__ made with honey.* Notice here that the __manna__ is described as __bread from__ *heaven,* a term we will see later on where Christ describes himself as ***bread*** ***from heaven****.* Also, it is interesting that the manna is described as ***white*** and ***like wafers,*** which also describes Holy Communion. Later in Exodus 16:35 it tells us: ***The Israelites ate*** *manna* ***for forty years, … they ate*** *manna* ***until they reached the borders of Canaan.***

Exodus 23:15 ***You shall keep the feast of Unleavened*** <u>***Bread.***</u> ***As I have*** ***commanded you, you must eat unleavened*** <u>***bread***</u> ***for seven days at the*** ***prescribed time in the month of Abib, for it was then that you came out*** ***of Egypt.*** Notice that Scripture continues to emphasize the sacred nature of <u>bread</u>, ***you shall keep the feast of Unleavened*** <u>***Bread.***</u>

Exodus 24:8 [Moses said] ***This is the*** <u>***blood of the covenant***</u> ***which the*** ***Lord has made with you in accordance with all these words of his.*** Matthew 26:28 [Jesus said] ***For this is my*** <u>***blood of the covenant,***</u> ***which*** ***will be shed on behalf of many for the forgiveness of sins.*** Old and New Testament parallel.

Exodus 25:30 ***On the table you shall always keep*** <u>***showbread***</u> ***set before*** ***me.*** The <u>showbread</u> (also called Bread of the Presence or Bread of the Face) was always present on a gold table in the tabernacle then later the Temple. The bread was replaced each sabbath. The table of the "***Bread*** ***of the Presence***" (Ex 26:30) with <u>bread and wine</u> recalls the heavenly banquet that Moses and the others had with God. This prefigures the Real Presence in the Eucharist and the Mass resembles the sacrifice on Mount Sinai with God.

The first–century Jewish priests had a custom during the Passover of taking the ***"Bread of the Presence"*** out of the Holy Place and lifting it up to the pilgrims saying "<u>Behold</u> God's love for you". The priest today holds up the Eucharist saying "<u>Behold</u> the lamb of God". The Eucharist is the fulfillment of the Old Testament "<u>Bread of the Presence.</u>"

The "burnt offering" of the Jews was a total sacrifice in which the sacrifice was entirely consumed by fire. However, at the Passover they were instructed to eat the lamb's flesh with unleavened bread, then anything leftover was to be burnt. The eating of the <u>flesh</u> during Passover was considered sacred and <u>bread</u> pre–figures the Mass.

Leviticus and Deuteronomy were written between the years 538 BC and 332 BC, through the direction of Moses from God, the Israelites had many ritual customs such as: The Daily Holocaust, Daily offering, Sin Offerings, Guilt Offerings, and the following Peace Offerings:

Leviticus 7:11,13 $_{11}$ *This is the ritual for the <u>Peace Offering</u> that are presented to the Lord... he shall offer unleavened <u>cakes</u> mixed with oil, ...* $_{13}$ *His offering shall also include <u>loaves</u> of leavened <u>bread</u> along with the victim of peace offering for <u>thanksgiving</u>.* <u>Bread</u> continues to be part of most Israelite ritual customs. Notice the use of *"<u>thanksgiving</u>."* The Greek word for "<u>thanksgiving</u>" is eucherestein (euxapiotia), where the word Eucharist name derived.

Leviticus 7:15,17 $_{15}$ *The <u>flesh</u> of the <u>thanksgiving</u> sacrifice shall be eaten on the day it is offered; none of it may be kept till the next day.* $_{17}$ *Should any <u>flesh</u> from the sacrifice be left over on the third day, it must be burned up in the fire.* As pointed out previously this sacrifice must be considered very important and sacred because if it is not all eaten then left overs, *must be burned up.* Also note the continued use of the word <u>flesh</u>.

Deuteronomy 8:3 *He therefore let you be afflicted with hunger, and then fed you with <u>manna</u> a food unknown to you and your fathers, in order to show you that <u>not by bread</u> alone does man live, but by every word that comes forth from the mouth of the Lord.* Later in Matthew 4:4, Jesus Christ quotes part of the above starting with *<u>not by bread</u>.*

Deuteronomy 16:2–3 $_2$ *You shall offer the Passover sacrifice from your flock or your herd to the Lord, your God...* $_3$ *You shall not eat leavened <u>bread</u> with it. For seven days you shall eat with it only unleavened <u>bread</u>, the bread of affliction, ...* The Israelites believe the symbolism of yeast in <u>bread</u> represents sin, *the <u>bread</u> of affliction.*

Deuteronomy 29:4 $_4$ *I led you for forty years in the desert. Your <u>clothes</u> did not fall from you in tatters nor your <u>sandals</u> from your feet;* Notice the miracle of *<u>clothes</u>* and *<u>sandals</u>* for 40 years.

1 Samuel 21:5 (about 550 BC) *But the priest replied to David, "I have no ordinary bread on hand only holy bread;*

The Lord instructed Elijah to go and hide east of the Jordan. 1 Kings 17:4,6 ₄ *...You shall drink of the stream, and I have commanded ravens to feed you there.* ₆ *Ravens brought him bread and meat in the morning, and bread and meat in the evening, and he drank from the stream.* This is another case where God provides bread from heaven.

Several scripture passages started using use the word "bread" as a metaphor to describe a particular situation. The readers at that time knew that bread was considered very sacred because of its use in many of Israelites ritual customs.

Proverbs 20:17 *The bread of deceit is sweet to a man, but afterword his mouth will be filled with gravel.*

Ecclesiastes 9:7 *Go, eat your bread with joy and drink your wine with a merry heart, because it is now that God favors your works.*

Sirach 15:3 (about 180 to 175 BC) *Nourish him with the bread of understanding.*

In the book of Isaiah is a chapter called, "An Invitation to Grace" where bread is used, knowing that bread is considered sacred in Israelite's ritual customs: Isaiah 55:2 *Why spend your money for what is not bread; your wages for what fails to satisfy?* This instruction tells us to concentrate on what is sacred (as bread is sacred) and not on worldly things that do not satisfy.

Amos 8:11 *Yes, days are coming, says the Lord God, when I will send famine upon the land! Not famine of bread, or thirst for water, but for hearing the word of the Lord.*

Malachi 1:11 *... everywhere they bring sacrifice in my name; and a pure offering; For great is my name among nations, says the Lord of hosts.*

In the verse just prior to the above passage, the Jewish people were offering imperfect sacrifices (animals with blemishes) that was displeasing to the Lord. The above verse 11 anticipates that someday a *pure offering* to be sacrificed in messianic times, which is the universal Sacrifice of the Mass (the Eucharist) as we are told by the Council of Trent.

The New Testament: Bethlehem, Christ's birth place means house of bread.
Luke 2:7 tells us that: Mary laid the new born Christ in a manger (a feeding trough) that symbolized Christ was to become our food for salvation.

Mark 8:6 *...Then, taking the seven loaves He [Jesus] gave thanks, broke them, and gave them to His disciples to distribute.*
Mark 8:18–21 [Jesus speaking] *Do you have eyes and not see, ears and not hear? And do you not remember, when I broke five loaves for the five thousand, how many wicker baskets full of fragments you picked up? They answered him, "Twelve." When I broke the seven loaves for the four thousand, how many full baskets of fragments did you pick up? They answered him, "Seven." He said to them, Do you still not understand?*
In the above, Jesus is pointing out to His disciples (and to us) that scripture is full of signs and prefigured messages that we need to understand. The feeding of the five thousand was in Israel territory, and the twelve baskets represents the twelve tribes of Israel. The feeding of the four thousand was in Gentile territory, and the seven baskets represents the seven Gentile nations in that area. Acts 13:19 *When he* [Moses] *had destroyed seven nations in the land of Canaan, ...*
The act of: blessing, breaking, and distribution of bread prefigures Holy Communion by using similar terminology:
Luke 22: ₁₉ *Then He took the bread, said the blessing, broke it, and gave it to them, saying, "This is my body, which will be given for you; do this in memory of me."*
₂₀ *And likewise the cup after they had eaten, saying, "This cup is the new covenant in my blood, which will be shed for you."*
Notice in the above, at the Last Supper, that there is no mention of lamb or flesh. Lamb is not mentioned because the true Lamb, Jesus, sat at the

head of the table, the ultimate fulfillment in the sacrifice of the spotless (un–blemished) Lamb of God.

The emphasis in this "Last Supper" discourse is on bread and wine as being: *"This is my body"* (Lk 22:19) and we are to eat and drink it in *"memory"* (Lk 22:19) of Him. The *"memory"* (or memorial) is the fulfilment of Ex 12:14 *"...a memorial feast for you..."*, *"as a perpetual institution."* The act of taking the <u>bread</u>, <u>blessing it</u>, and <u>distributing it</u>, is performed by a priest at every Catholic Mass in the world to fulfill the command of Jesus to: *"do this in memory of me"* (Lk 22:19) and *"as a perpetual institution."* (Ex 12:14)

The New Testament account of the Road to Emmaus is a very interesting account. On the first Easter Sunday two of Jesus' disciples (one named Cleopas) were walking to Emmaus and Jesus joined them. Scripture tells us that they were prevented from recognizing Him. When the disciples arrived at Emmaus, Luke 24 tells us what happened:

30 *And it happened that, while He* [Jesus] *was with them at table, He* [Jesus] *<u>took bread</u>, said the <u>blessing</u>, <u>broke it</u>, and <u>gave it</u> to them.* 31 *With that their eyes were opened and they recognized Him, but He vanished from their sight.*

Notice the same words as the Last Supper of taking <u>the bread</u>, <u>blessing it</u>, <u>breaking it,</u> and <u>giving it</u>. This was the very first Mass performed by Jesus Himself (after His Resurrection). One might question; why did Jesus vanish after giving them the bread? The only logical answer is that Jesus was showing us that His glorified, resurrected body is <u>in the bread</u>. Therefore, His real presence in the Eucharist.

Luke 24: 35 *Then the two recounted what had taken place on the way and He was made known to them in the <u>breaking of the bread</u>.*

In the sixth chapter of John titled, "<u>The Bread of Life Discourse</u>" can be divided into two main parts. Ironically both parts, (1) John 6:35 and (2) John 6:48, each start with the exact same statement: *"I am the bread."*

<u>Part (1)</u> John 6: 35 – 42. In this first part, Jesus compares Himself to the Old Testament manna (which the Jews listening understood) that came down from heaven.

John 6: 41 *I am the bread that came down from heaven.*
Therefore, Jesus wants us to believe and have faith in His divinity that He is the Holy One of God. So, in part one, we need to believe and have faith that Jesus came down from heaven in order to understand part (2).

Part (2) John 6: 48 – 58. The second part of this discourse is about <u>eating</u> and the <u>spiritually</u> of Jesus.
John 6: 51. *I am the living <u>bread</u> that came down from heaven; whoever <u>eats</u> this bread will live forever; and the <u>bread</u> that I will give is my <u>flesh</u> for the life of the world.*
John 6: 55 – 56. *For my <u>flesh</u> is true food, and my <u>blood</u> is true <u>drink</u>, whoever <u>eats</u> my <u>flesh</u> and drinks my <u>blood</u> remains in me and I in him.*
Some of Jesus' disciples did not have the faith (that Jesus explained in part 1), because they misunderstood eating His flesh: John 6:52 *"How can this man give us [His] flesh to eat?"* Jesus does not change but strongly re–affirms what he has been telling them: John 6:54 *Whoever eats my <u>flesh</u> and drinks my <u>blood</u> has eternal life, and I will raise him on the last day.*
John 6: 60. *Then many of His disciples who were listening said, "This saying is hard; who can accept it?"* By this statement, they had to have been thinking of cannibalism, which verifies that they understood that Jesus was talking about <u>real flesh and real blood</u>.

John chapter 6: ₆₁ *Since Jesus knew that His disciples were murmuring about this, He said to them, "Does this shock you?* ₆₂*What if you were to see the Son of Man <u>ascending</u> to where He was before?* ₆₃*It is the <u>spirit</u> that gives life, while <u>the flesh</u> is of no avail. The words I have spoken to you are <u>spirit and life</u>. But there are some of you who do not believe."*
Jesus' statement of: *"Does this shock you?"* further proves that Jesus is talking about His flesh and blood. Notice in the above that Jesus states, *"<u>the flesh</u>"* He does not state "his flesh", this most lightly refers to John 8: 15 *You judge by appearances, ...* Of which, the literal translation of *"by appearances"* is "according to the flesh". In other words, they see and judge His earthly body (flesh) and do not see or understand His spirit.
It is important to put the above scripture statement: *"it is the spirit that gives life, while the flesh is of no avail"* (Jn 6:63) into its proper context within this entire discourse:

John 6:41 ...*I am the bread that came down from heaven.* Note here that only the spirit can come down from heaven.

John 6:51 ...*the bread that I will give*... Notice here that Jesus states *"that I will give"* (future tense), not his current earthly body, which was misunderstood by the disciples at that time.

In John 6:62 ...*see the Son of Man ascending...*, this sets the spiritual framework for "*the flesh is of no avail*" (judging by appearance).

Therefore, the bread and wine of the Eucharist is the resurrected, glorified living body and blood, as well as the divinity of Jesus Christ: John 6: 51 *I am the living bead that came down from heaven; ...*, John 6:48 *I am the bread of life.* John 6: 63 *It is the spirit that gives life.* When one combines the meaning of the two parts of this "Bread of Life Discourse:" (1) faith and believing in the divinity of Christ, (2) the eating of bread and the spirituality of Jesus, one can now conclude: Faith in Christ's divinity is foundational to the faith in believing His real presence in the Eucharist.

John 6: ₆₈ *Simon Peter answered Him, "Master, to whom shall we go? You have the words of eternal life.* ₆₉ *We have come to believe and are convinced that you are the Holy One of God."* This occurred in scripture right after Jesus stated: "*my flesh is true food and my blood is true drink*" (Jn 6:55).

By saying "*we*", Simon Peter must be talking for all the apostles, they may not have understood, but they did believe Jesus is "*the living bread that came down from heaven*" of which they are to eat so that they "*may have eternal life,*" (Jn 6:64) and where Jesus "*remains in me and I in him*" (Jn 6:56) – the real presence of Jesus in the Eucharist.

St. Paul established a Christian community in Corinth about the year 51AD, where they continued the "*perpetual institution*" (Ex 12:14) of bread and wine, "*breaking of the bread.*" (Acts 2:42) There apparently was some misunderstanding in Corinth regarding the Lords Supper for St. Paul to write the following:

1 Corinthians 11: ₂₃ *For I* [St. Paul] *received from the Lord what I also handed on to you, that the Lord Jesus, on the night he was handed over, took bread,* ₂₄ *and, after he had given thanks, broke it and said, "This is my body that is for you. Do this in remembrance of me."* ₂₅ *In the same way also the cup, after supper, saying, "This cup*

*is the new covenant in my **blood**. Do this, as **often** as you drink it, in remembrance of me." ₂₆ For as **often** as you eat this **bread** and drink the cup, you **proclaim** the death of the Lord until he comes.*

"For I received from the Lord what I handed on to you, …" establishes St. Paul as having the authority and also pointing out the proper way to celebrate the Eucharist according to the instructions from Jesus.

The Hebrew definition of **"_remembrance_"** or **"_memory_"** is to re–live. We may interpret memory to just recall to mind, but the meaning here is to re–live. We are told here to do (re–live) this **often,** just as in the prayer Jesus gave us: **"give us this day our daily bread"** (Mt 6:11). To "proclaim" is to announce officially as being true. Therefore, at every Catholic Mass when we eat His Bread and/or drink the **"Cup of the Lord"** we publicly announce (proclaim) that Christ is really present.

1 Corinthians 11: ₂₇ *Therefore whoever eats the bread or drinks **the cup of the Lord unworthily** will have to answer for the body and **blood** of the Lord. ₂₈ A person should **examine himself,** and so eat the **bread** and drink the cup. ₂₉ For anyone who eats and drinks **without discerning** the body, eats and drinks **judgement** on himself.*
Two important elements in the above: (1) **"the bread or drinks the cup of the Lord** "tells us that the Lord is present in the bread and wine. (2) It is very clear here that these early Christians believed in the Real Presence in the bread and wine, otherwise, why such a stern warning of **judgment** if eaten "**without discerning?**"

Acts 2:46 **"They devoted themselves… to breaking of the bread."** Considering the 31,426 words Jesus spoke in the New Testament, Jesus always spoke, performed, and acted with a definite purpose. There are no accounts in Scripture where Jesus spoke, performed or acted frivolously, without a definite reason or lesson. Therefore, how can some people possibly say that it was "symbolic" when at the Last Supper Jesus stated: **"This is my body, which will be given for you; do this in memory of me"** (Luke 22:19). This cannot be any clearer that the Eucharist is His body, of which in Scripture, Jesus himself declared it so.

The command of Jesus to, "*do this in memory of me*" is one of 48 commands by Jesus in the New Testament. However, this command is in the same sentence as, "*This is my body,*" which means that if a person does not believe that Jesus is in the Eucharist, they are not following that command of Jesus. John 14:15 "*If you love me, you will keep my commandments.*"

Jesus himself in Matthew 10:33, stated, "*But whoever denies me before others, I will deny before my heavenly father.*" Then in Mark 8:38, Jesus stated, "*Whoever is ashamed of me and of my words ... the Son of Man will be ashamed of when he comes in his Father's glory...*" It can be understandable that a person may struggle with believing in His real presence in the Eucharist, that person needs to work on their faith. On the other hand, any person that *denies* or is *ashamed* of His *words* and denies His actual living presence in the Eucharist has a problem because scripture states: "*But whoever denies me before others, I will deny before my heavenly father.*" Scripture confirms His real presence in John 6:51, "*I am the living bread... the bread that I will give is my flesh...*" and in John 6:55, "*For my flesh is true food, and my blood is true drink.*" Therefore, the Eucharist truly is the resurrected, spiritual, glorified living body, blood, and divinity of Jesus Christ. Of which we cannot earthly see, in the same way we cannot see Christ or the Holy Spirit even though Christ himself told us: Matthew 28:20 "*I am with you always...*"

God created everything by His spoken word – not by the written word: Genesis 1:3 "*Then God said: Let there be light, and there was light.*" During Jesus time on earth, he never told his disciples to write anything. He instructed them to: "*follow after me*" (Mt 10:38), "*whoever loves me will keep my word.*" (Jn 14:23), and, "*do this in memory of me.*" (Lk 22:19). The development of Christianity was accomplished in scripture by the spoken word, actions, way of thinking, which is the tradition handed down generation to generation before the written word was ever was fully established (*). God reveals Himself through tradition.

(*) The hand written words of scripture were assembled by St. Athanasius in 367 to become the 27 books of the New Testament. In the year 400, St. Jerome's Vulgate (Latin) Bible was published. In 1455 Johann Gutenberg printed the first Bible. The first USA published Catholic Bible was in 1790.

John 1: ₁*"... the <u>word</u> was with God, and the <u>word</u> was God."* ₁₄ *"And the <u>word</u> became flesh..."*

Matthew 8:23–27: The <u>word</u> of Jesus calmed the sea.

John 9:1–7: The <u>word</u> of Jesus healed a blind man from birth.

Luke 17:11–19: The <u>word</u> of Jesus healed 10 lepers.

John 11:1–45: The <u>word</u> of Jesus raised Lazarus from the dead.

Therefore, since the <u>word</u> of Jesus can: Calm the sea, heal the blind, cure lepers, raise Lazarus from the dead, then surely the <u>word</u> of Jesus actually changes bread and wine into His Body and Blood as: Matthew 26:26, *"...Jesus took bread, said the blessing, broke it, and giving it to His disciples said, 'take and eat; this is my body.'"*

The Catechism of the Catholic Church (CCC 1548) tells us that by virtue of our priest's sacrament of Holy Orders, the priest's role at Mass is to act in the person of Jesus Christ himself, who is present to his Church "In the person of Christ the Head" *(in persona Christi Capitis).*

At Mass, when the priest recites the Scriptural <u>words</u> of Jesus, *"this is my body," "this is my blood,"* (Lk 22:19) it is the same as Jesus himself being present and speaking. Therefore, at every Mass, Jesus <u>is</u> re–living His miraculous <u>words</u> that transforms bread and wine into the living Body and Blood of Jesus Christ, transubstantiation.

Here is something puzzling. Worldwide, Christians believe and accept the miracles of Jesus. Turning water into wine, the multiplication of loves that feed the 4000 and the 5000, healing the sick, and raising Lazarus from the dead are all examples of accepted miracles. Some of these miracles are only mentioned <u>one time</u> in Scripture. Also, Christians have no idea how the miracles and the supernatural mystery of the incarnation of Jesus actually occurred, or how the Trinity is possible, or how the supernatural mystery of the Resurrection and Ascension occurred, but by faith they believe in them. What's puzzling is the greatest miracle of all that is prefigured and predicted in the Old Testament and mentioned all through the New Testament, including all the gospels and even mentioned 15 times alone by Jesus himself, speaking in the Gospel of John chapter 6:

41 *"I am the bread that came down from heaven."* 48 *"I am the bread of life."* 51 *"I am the living bread…, the bread that I will give is my flesh for the life of the world."* 53 *"…unless you eat the flesh of the son of man and drink His blood, you do not have life within you."* 54 *"Whoever eats my flesh and drinks my blood has eternal life."* The Eucharist is the most mentioned supernatural mystery and the longest lasting miracle in all of Scripture, so it's very puzzling why some Christians have difficulty accepting it? Maybe Scripture can answer part of this. In Scripture, right after the above passage from John, many disciples responded:

John 6:60. *"Then many of His disciples who were listening said, "this saying is hard, who can accept it?"* The disciples at that time did not know about Holy Communion (Eucharist), therefore they understandably and mistakenly thought Jesus was talking about His human physical flesh and human physical blood. After the Resurrection, the early Christians knew that Jesus was referring to the Eucharist that actually is the resurrected, glorified, living body, blood, soul, and divinity of Jesus Christ under the signs of bread and wine. Catholics believe in the real presence in the Eucharist because Christ Himself told us so in Scripture.

The Jewish tradition is to fast prior to the Passover, just as Catholics fast (one hour) prior to Mass. Also, similar to above, the people at Mass are led by the priest to a prayer of forgiveness (discerning) prior to the Eucharist.

St. John the Apostle writes about his *"Vision of Heavenly worship,"* the actual title of Revelation chapter 4. In addition to many of the words in the Catholic Mass prayers being directly from scripture, the Mass structure and form itself is modeled according to Revelation 4 & 5. However, the most important point is that our earthly Mass follows the command of Jesus, as Scripture states, *"do this in memory of me"* (Luke 22:19). Also, one can conclude that attending a Catholic Mass is as close to *"Heavenly Worship"* here on earth that one can possible experience based on the following passages in Revelation chapter 4 and 5 of St. John's *"Vision of Heavenly worship"* and how they relate to the Catholic Mass in following from the book of Revelation:

4:2 *"A throne was there in heaven"* {1} – just as there is a special chair for the priest at Mass to represent the throne.

4:4 *"twenty–four elders"* {2} – meaning the 12 tribes of Israel and the 12 Apostles (as described in Rev 21:12–14) represents the priest(s) at Mass.

4:4 *"white garments"* – the vestments similar to those used by a priest at Mass.

4:5 *"Seven flaming torches"* {3} – means the Menorah's 7 candles which are represented by the candles at every Catholic Mass.

4:8 *" four living creatures"* {4} *"exclaiming: Holy, holy, holy is the Lord God almighty"* {5} – similar to Holy, holy, holy sung at Mass (the Sanctus).

4:10 *"elders fall down before the one who sits on the throne and <u>worship him</u>, who lives forever and ever."* {6} – just as the people kneel, stand and sit to honor certain parts of the Mass and the intention of Mass is to *"<u>worship him</u>"*.

4:11 *"Glory and honor and power"* {7} – Said at Mass following the "Our Father".

5:1 *"I saw a scroll in the right hand of the one who sat on the throne"* {8} – just as there are scripture readings at Mass from the sacred book representing the scroll.

5:3 *"open the scroll with its seven seals"* {9} – representing the New Covenant of the Lamb who is honored at every Mass.

5:6 *"a Lamb that seemed to have been slain"* {10} – representing the risen Christ and the display of the Cross with Christ's body in every Catholic Church. (*)

5:8 *"a harp"* {11} – representing the music at most Masses.

5:9 *"they sang a new hymn"* {12} – at every Mass, psalms of praise are usually sung.

5:11 *"I looked again and heard the voices of angels who surrounded the throne and the living creatures and the elders. They were countless in number, and they cried out in a loud voice: "Worthy is the Lamb that was slain..."* Tradition tells us that there are many angels present at every mass. *"Worthy is the Lamb..."* is paralleled in the prayers at the Communion Rite.

5:14 *"The four living creatures answered, "Amen"* – just as at Mass the people respond "Amen."

(*) Note: A lamb slain is recognized by the Jews because the slain lamb is fastened to a spit that is in the shape of a cross, one of the reasons the Catholic Church displays the body of Christ on the crucifix.

The bracketed numbers {} noted in the above are further explained with the following excerpt quotes from the footnotes of the "Didache Bible":

{1} The vision of the <u>throne</u> recalls the prophecies of Isaiah (chapter 6) and (Ez 1:26–28)

{2} The <u>twenty–four elders</u> probably represent the Twelve Tribes of Israel and the Twelve Apostles, the Israel of old and the New Israel.

{3} <u>seven torches</u>: these symbolize the Holy Spirit and his seven gifts; it also recalls the Spirit who maintained the seven flames of a lampstand (Zec 4:1–6, CCC 1831)

{4} The early Church Fathers associated the <u>four living creatures</u> with the four Gospel writers. The singing of the <u>living creatures</u> represents the worship of the Pilgrim Church on earth, which is united to the worship of the <u>elders</u>, representing the just souls in the Church in Heaven. The celebration of the Eucharist, though celebrated here on earth, includes the saints in Heaven where Christ reigns with the Father (CCC 293, 662, 2642)

{5} <u>Holy, holy, holy</u>: The threefold repetition indicates unsurpassed holiness. This phrase, derived from Isaiah 6:3, is repeated at every Mass in the Sanctus at the beginning of the Eucharist Prayer. The triple repetition of the word "Holy" also points to the Trinity: one God in three persons. (CCC 559)

{6} Regarding the <u>elders,</u> see {4} above.

{7} <u>Glory and honor and power</u>: This recalls the doxology following the Lord's prayer at Mass.

{8} and {9} The sacred <u>scroll</u> contains the details of God's plan. Only Christ – described here as the Lion of Judah and the Root of David – is worthy to open and reveal its contents. For this reason, the <u>scroll</u> may be a type, or figure, of Scripture. (CCC 663)

{10} Christ is the <u>Lamb</u> of the New Passover who has been sacrificed but is alive again, risen from the dead to ransom all people through his Blood.

{11} The <u>harp</u> represents liturgical song, and the bowls of incense represent the prayers of the saints and martyrs, who intercede for the faithful on earth (Ps 142:2; Rev 8:3–4)

{12} The <u>hymn</u> of all creatures that follows praises both Christ and God the Father ("him who sits upon the throne") in similar terms that affirm the co–equality of the First and Second Persons of the Trinity (CCC 328–336, 449,2642,2855). (End of the "Didache Bible" footnote quotations)

The 2nd century (AD101–200), the Apostle St. John was still alive, he died in the year 103 at the age of 97. "The Didache" (AD80) is a document written by the early Christians known as, "The Teaching of the Twelve Apostles." All the books of the New Testament were written by the year AD80 except for 1,2,3 John and Revelation. In 1983 an original copy of "The Didache" was discovered in an accent Constantinople Monastery that scholars verified its organ to the year AD80. The document instructs early converts on the ethics and practices on how to be Christians and it includes descriptions of the rituals of Baptism, fasting, and the Eucharist Ritual (being the first known text using the term "Eucharist"). Along with other early documents such as the writings of the Fathers of the Church such as: St. Ignatius of Antioch and St. Justin Martyr, that verify the Apostles and early Christians believed in Christ's Real Presence in the Eucharist, which has been handed down to the present day. "The Didache" includes a description of using the sign of the cross on a candidate's forehead for Baptism, which was then adopted for applying ashes on Ash Wednesday. Luke 11:1–4 Gives us the short version of the "Our Father." Matthew 6:9–13 Gives us a longer version to the "Our Father." However, "The Didache" document added a doxology at the end of the "Our Father" prayer of which Catholics and Protestants adopted until today, *"For Thine is the power and the glory for evermore."*

Saint Ignatius of Antioch (35 or 50 to 98 or 117) Apostolic Father of the Church wrote: *"I have no taste for the food that perishes…I want the Bread of God which is the Flesh of Christ…and for drink I desire His Blood, which is love that cannot be destroyed."* He referred to the Holy Eucharist as *"medicine of immortality."*

St. Ignatius of Antioch's birth and death years have not been firmly agreed upon. However, the date of 110AD is firm when he was forcibility taken from Antioch to Rome. A Catholic legend is that St. Ignatius was the child whom Jesus took up in His arms as described in Mark 9:36. Ignatius was instructed by and was a disciple of the Apostle St. John. In about 67AD St. Peter appointed Ignatius as Bishop of Antioch.

Saint Justin Martyr (100–165) Apostolic Father of the Church wrote: *"We call this food Eucharist…For not as common bread nor common drink do we receive these…The food which has been made into the Eucharist by the*

Eucharistic prayer set down by Him...is both the flesh and the blood of that incarnate Jesus."

St. Justin Martyr devoted himself to the defense (apology) of the Church. The above quotation is a small excerpt from Roman records where Justin wrote to Caesar demanding justice for Christians, about 155AD.

Considering all the foreshadowing, parallels, and prophecies in Scripture that have been fulfilled, certainly could not have been random or by accident but only the design of God Himself. Therefore, one has to conclude that Jesus Christ's institution of the Eucharist is where He offered His Body and His Blood as food for our salvation which is under the appearance of bread and wine.

Scripture quotes Jesus as saying: John 6:35 *I am **the bread** of life,* John 6:41 *I am **the bread** that came down from heaven.*
John 6:48 *I am **the bread** of life,* John 6:51 *I am **the living bread...**, **the bread** that I will give is **my flesh** for the life of the world,* John 6:54 ***Whoever eats my flesh** and drinks **my blood** has eternal life,* John 6:55 *For **my flesh** is true food, and **my blood** is true drink.* In John chapter 6 verses 22 through 71, Jesus references 15 times that He is the Bread.

SUMMARY – BREAD AND EUCHARIST:
Throughout scripture <u>bread</u> is mentioned: as a means of substance, a gift of God, used in sacred rituals, a sign of sharing, a perpetual institution, it symbolizes the word of God which nourishes, and it becomes the body and blood of our Lord Jesus Christ.

- Genesis is the first mention of <u>bread</u> to show its importance then <u>bread and wine</u> is part of a blessing to Abram. <u>Bread</u> is mentioned 18 times in Genesis.
- Melchizedek *"**priest of God Most High**"* (Heb 7:1–3) foreshadowed Jesus by offering bread and wine to prefigure the Sacrifice of the Mass. (Gn 14:18)
- Exodus tells us about the <u>bread</u> from heaven (manna) that God provided for forty years, and establishes the feast of unleavened <u>bread</u>. <u>Bread</u> is mentioned 23 times in Exodus,

- Leviticus establishes the requirements for the sacred ritual of the Peace Offering using <u>bread</u>. <u>Bread</u> is mentioned 12 times in Leviticus.
- Deuteronomy tells us of the miracle of clothes and sandals for 40 years. <u>Bread</u> is mentioned 8 times in Deuteronomy.
- 1 Samuel distinguishes between ordinary and holy <u>bread</u>. <u>Bread</u> is mentioned 19 times in 1 Samuel
- Proverbs, Ecclesiastes, and Sirach use <u>bread</u> as a metaphor because of its sacred reference in scripture.
- Christ is born in Bethlehem which means house of <u>bread.</u>
- In Matthew, the tempter suggests that stones be turned into <u>bread</u> to tempt Jesus.
- Matthew and Luke mention <u>bread</u> as part of the "Our Father" prayer.
- Matthew, Mark and John tell us the multiplication of <u>bread (loves)</u> performed by Jesus to feed thousands of people which pre–figures the distribution of the Eucharist.
- Matthew, Mark, Luke and John tell us about "The Last Supper" (Lord's Supper) where Jesus establishes and verifies His real presence in the Eucharist as the New Covenant and the Eucharist forgives sins which can only be done by Jesus, so, the host has to contain Jesus in order to forgive sins.
- Luke tells us about the Road to Emmaus, where Jesus performed the first mass after the Last Supper and after His resurrection, then Jesus vanishes to show us that He is present within the Eucharist.
- The "Bread of Life Discourse" In the book of John mentions <u>bread</u> eleven times.
- In chapter 6 of John, Jesus himself is quoted multiple times that he is $_{48}$ ***the <u>bread</u> of life*** and that $_{55}$ ***my <u>flesh</u> is true food, and my <u>blood</u> is true drink***, of which it cannot be any clearer that He is present in the Eucharist.
- Toward the end of chapter 6 Jesus explains: $_{63}$ ***The words I have spoken to you are spirit and life*** to clarify that He was not talking about his earthly physical body, but about His living spiritual body after His resurrection.

- The Last Supper: That was performed by Jesus fulfills the Jewish Passover: blood of the Lamb, the bread, in memory, and perpetual institution. Also, the statements in scripture prove the early Christians believed in Christ's Real Presence in the Breaking of the Bread (Eucharist). (Lk 22:7–8,19–20)
- After the Pentecost in Jerusalem, the apostles "*devoted themselves…to the breaking of the bread and to prayers*" (Acts 2:42), following Jesus' recommendations.
- ST. Paul wrote a letter to the Corinthians to clarify the proper Eucharist procedure, "*For anyone who eats and drinks without discerning the body, eats and drinks judgement on himself*" (1Cor 11:29), discerning prior to receiving verifies His real presence in the Eucharist.
- The word of Jesus performed miracles in Scripture as well as His words that actually change bread and wine into His body and blood "*this is my body…this is my blood*" (Lk 22:19)
- In all of the Bible, the word bread is used 492 times, the word thanksgiving (Greek eucharisteo) occurs in the Old Testament 6 times and 38 times in the New Testament.

THE EUCHARIST IN SCRIPTURE.docx. Assembled by Paul Wilchek 17DEC22 re-arranging various sections from Paul's book Let Scripture Speak for Itself.

Printed in the United States
by Baker & Taylor Publisher Services